WINTER KINGS

Great Steeplechasers Lottery to Desert Orchid

Ivor Herbert and Patricia Smyly

Pelham Books
Stephen Greene Press

For all brave horsemen on the turf and under it.

PELHAM BOOKS/Stephen Greene Press

Published by the Penguin Group
27 Wrights Lane, London W8 5TZ, England
Viking Penguin Inc., 40 West 23rd Street, New York, New York 10010, USA
The Stephen Greene Press Inc., 15, Muzzey Street, Lexington, Massachusetts 02173, USA.

Penguin Books Australia Ltd, Ringwood, Victoria, Australia
Penguin Books Canada Ltd, 2801 John Street, Markham, Ontario, Canada L3R 1B4
Penguin Books (NZ) Ltd, 182–190 Wairau Road, Auckland 10, New Zealand

Penguin Books Ltd, Registered Offices: Harmondsworth, Middlesex, England

First published 1989

Printed and bound in Great Britain by The Bath Press, Bath, Avon.
Typeset by Cambridge Photosetting Services

A CIP catalogue record for this book is available from the British Library.

ISBN 0 7207 1842 2

Contents

Acknowledgement

So many people have helped us with this book that lack of space prevents us mentioning them all as we would have wished. Nor have we been able invidiously to pick out a few special helpers. So, to all those who gave us their time and memories and their help in so many ways: Thank you.

Ivor Herbert
Patricia Smyly

Photo credits

The authors and publishers are grateful to the following for permission to reproduce photographs in this book:
Arthur Ackermann & Son Ltd pages 5, 6, 9, 17; Cheltenham Newspaper Co. 82; *Country Life* page 37; Gerry Cranham pages 60, 99, 127, 130, 135, 146 (left & centre), 147 (right), 148, 158, 162, 163, 166, 167, 191, 193, 202, 211, 212, 227, 229, 244, 248, 249, 264; Michael Dickinson pages 231, 232; Mrs. C. Hill pages 240, 246; Miss M. Hilton page 172; Hulton Picture Co. pages 26 (top), 38, 41, 43; *Illustrated London News* pages 49, 54; *Mail on Sunday* and Lynn Hilton page 274; Bernard Parkin page 115; W. W. Rouch & Co. pages 26 (bottom), 70, 83, 107; Sport and General pages 52, 55, 68, 94, 96, 100, 101, 110, 114, 129, 132, 147 (left), 185, 192, 207, 225, 252, 261; Sporting Pictures page 146 (right); Pat Taaffe page 141; *The Times* page 86; Anne, Duchess of Westminster page 133. The colour photographs are credited individually.

The jacket photograph is reproduced by permission of Mr K. Edwards and The Tryon Gallery Ltd.

ONE

Lottery

THE 1830S; VICTORIA BECOMES QUEEN OF GREAT BRITAIN; THE MANCHESTER-LIVERPOOL RAILWAY OPENS; SLAVERY ABOLISHED THROUGHOUT THE BRITISH EMPIRE; POLAND REBELS AGAINST HUNGARY AND COCKNEYS ROLL A HUNGARIAN GENERAL IN A BARREL AROUND THE DOCKLANDS, PROTESTING AGAINST ATROCITIES IN POLAND; PEEL PROPOUNDS THE CONSERVATIVE MANIFESTO; FIRST TRADES UNIONS FORM AND RUMBLE.

In the spring of 1840, in the small Lincolnshire town of Horncastle (the Roman *Banovallum*) between the Fens and Thunker Hollow, a Clerk of the Course sat devising a programme for the forthcoming races. It was to be a gala week with a meet of the local hounds and possibly a ball. The show-piece would be a Grand Steeplechase, a sweepstake of 25 sovereigns with 100 added. To be sure, 100 sovereigns was a lot of money to put up, but it would be worth it; such a prize would attract the best horses in the country and that meant a good crowd, a boom for the local inns and shops and a strong market. The pleasurable daydream abruptly splintered. Such a prize would also attract Lottery – and in his present invincible form John Elmore's brown gelding would scare away all opposition: no market, very little interest, no crowd. Wretchedly the Clerk sought for a way out of his dilemma. Suddenly he seized upon simplicity and his quill and drafted *'a sweepstake of 25 sovereigns open to all horses – except Mr Elmore's Lottery'.*

More recently, handicappers who had to compress Arkle and ordinary horses 4 st. below him into a range of 35 lb. would have sympathized – one whale leaves no room for the minnows. But, though the Irish Stewards made a special law for Arkle a century and a quarter later, no one banned him like Lottery, even from being entered.

What then was this horse Lottery, who was all things to the sporting population of the late 1830s and who 20 years after his last race, was still reckoned 'the best horse that ever looked through a bridle, combining as he did speed, stoutness, ability to go through the dirt and to carry weight, extraordinary power of jumping and quickness over his fences'? Argus, the writer who delivered this effusion, ended predictably with the much misquoted line from Hamlet, 'We shall never look upon his like again'.

Lottery was bred near Thirsk in Yorkshire by a gentleman farmer named Jackson. He was a brown horse out of a half-bred mare called Parthenia and sired by another Lottery. Before the Weatherby family got a grip on the sport and finally installed a computer to dictate what you might call your horse (and certainly, where *doubles entendres* abound, what you might not) many breeders did not bother to name their young stock. They merely called them after their sire to the confusion of later researchers. In fact Lottery was originally christened Chance and it was as Chance that he first ran on the flat at the Holderness Hunt Meeting of 1834. He managed to win but, as his performance held out no promise of brilliance and he was narrow and unfurnished, he was allowed to mature before being sent up to Horncastle Fair.

This was one of the year's biggest markets for the hunter-dealers, who were then the only real props of the rickety world of steeplechasing. The few noblemen, like Earl Poulett (of whom more later) and Irish peers like the Marquis of Waterford (whose brother was a Rural Dean) and Lord Clanricarde, who rode their own horses were the exception: steeplechasing then was a coarse sport. A leading dealer and one of the first to sniff the budding market for a likely young 'chaser was John Elmore, who had a large farm at Uxenden near Harrow. He took a fancy to Lottery and as was the carefree custom dully not continued by Messrs Tattersalls and Goffs, or at Ascot or Doncaster Sales put up his nagsman, Newcomb Mason, to see how Lottery shaped over some rails. Mason returned safely from this wild assignment and reported that although desperately green, 'the 'orse can jump from 'ell to 'ackney'. This was enough for John Elmore and after prolonged haggling, Lottery changed hands for 120 sovereigns, or a round £6,500 in the perfidious paper of today.

Back at Uxenden he started his cross-country education and at this stage Newcomb's brother, Jem, enters the story. The Mason brothers came from Stilton, the Midlands cheese village on the Ermine Street, where their father ran a coaching business, but in spite of being well placed on the Great North Road, business did not prosper and the family moved down to Pinner in Middlesex. Jem, a resourceful, energetic lad, declined to travel in the stuffy coach and rode down on his pony, covering the 80 miles in a single day. The Mason family established themselves near the Old Dove House racecourse and young Jem became rough-rider to a neighbouring dealer, Mr Tilbury, who had about 200 horses on his fine stud. The boy's way with young horses earned him the plum job of showing them off with hounds and it was in the hunting field that he attracted the attention of Lord Frederick Beauclerk, the hunting parson of St Albans.

Lord Frederick, brother of the Duke of St Albans, descended from Charles Beauclerk, Knight of the Garter, the bastard son of King Charles II and Miss Eleanor Gwynn. Hunting and all sport coursed in the family's blood: the second Duke was Lord Warden of the Forests, Master Falconer of England, and a Lord of the Bedchamber. At George II's coronation he even held the Queen's crown.

The reverend nobleman put young Jem Mason up on a rogue of a horse called The Poet, a Flat reject who had a number of unpleasant habits and was to boot (or rather not to) a notoriously hard puller. So amazed was Lord Fred at the change Mason wrought in this brute, that he gave Jem the ride for the 1834 running of the St Albans Steeplechase. This was the most important cross-country race in Britain, and the course was particularly testing for deluge had turned the plough into a quagmire. The Poet, carrying 4 st. of lead to make his diminutive pilot up to 12 st., started sourly and refused the first fence. The blueblooded parson wrung his hands and uttered prayers and imprecations. But Mason had magic in his hands and quicksilver in his heels and few horses would not run sweetly for him. The Poet was no exception. Once over the first, he sped across the squelching land and romped home by 20 lengths.

This happy start made Mason widely known. Offers to ride came winging in and he shot to the top of his tree. He won every important race in the English calendar and then went to France and won the first big steeplechase in Paris on St Leger. When he became famous, he affected such dandyism that he was often mistaken for one of the gentry. He patronized one of London's most fashionable tailors, and it took the combined efforts of Messrs Wren of Knightsbridge who constructed the feet, and Messrs Bartley of Oxford Street who built the legs to achieve the perfection he demanded in his boots. (We cannot discover to which of these antique firms was entrusted the delicate assembly.) His concern for his appearance in no way muffled his horsemanship and when he died in 1866 (in agonies from cancer of the throat) his obituary described him as the finest natural horseman in England. 'It was at putting a horse at a fence that he chiefly excelled, always bringing him to the jump at the right place and in his right stride.' What more can be said of the skill of a jump jockey?*

When Lottery arrived at Uxenden, Mason was living at the Tilbury's stud about 4 miles away, and John Elmore was searching for a lad to replace his stable-jockey, Dan Seffert, whose nerve was failing. Mr Elmore accordingly encouraged young Jem to come over whenever he could. As the ride between the two farms spanned a particularly inviting stretch of country, including the rails fencing in the new London and North Western Railway, and as John Elmore had the additional bait of a pretty daughter, Mason found his way there fairly often. He soon struck up an understanding with the clumsy, headstrong Lottery, throwing out – as wise men with good hands will always do – the severe curb bit in favour of a moderate

*These words could have been applied, with equal grace and accuracy, 120 years later to that paragon of horsemanship, John Francome.

double-reined snaffle. In very little time Jem succeeded in converting an uncouth brute into a balanced, cracking hunter, and shortly afterwards became permanently attached to the Uxenden establishment – and married Miss Elmore.

During 1836 and 1837, as young Queen Victoria came to the throne, Lottery was running round the scruffy little tracks which littered the mothy fringe of London: Finchley, Barnet, the Notting Hill Hippodrome and Kensal Green were his unsalubrious haunts, and he contrived to earn his oats without distinguishing himself. At the end of 1837 he had his first big race in the St Albans Steeplechase and here he gave the nod of greatness. In abominable ground, he took up the running at half-way and was still in front two obstacles from home, but at the last he was joined by two others and run out of it on the flat. Afterwards it became known that he had been seriously amiss the weekend before and had in fact been bled, the period's standard remedy for most human and equine ailments. In the circumstances he had run a heroic race and Mason's verdict that he 'could beat any of that lot if all were well' was vindicated two months later when the pair won the big steeplechase at Barnet in a common canter. By way of a finale, he caused a minor sensation at Daventry by beating Captain Becher on his celebrated Vivian.

Next season the big new steeplechase at Liverpool was earmarked as his principal objective, and to this end he joined the Epsom yard of George Dockeray. Dockeray, who had won the 1826 Derby on Lord Egremont's Lapdog, was delighted with his new charge and soon conveyed to Uxenden the gratifying intelligence that none of his flat-horses could get away on the downs from the half-bred 'chaser.

The Grand National at Liverpool was the brainchild of Mr William Lynn, who had organized regular meetings there for three years. By 1839 he felt himself too ill to carry on and turned the meeting into a company of 1,000 proprietorships of £25 each. The course was vested in five trustees headed by Lord Stanley and its racing affairs were cared for by a committee which included the Earls of Derby and Sefton, Lord George Bentinck and Mr Lloyd Mostyn. The general management of the course was the charge of another committee chosen from the £25 subscribers.

The first great steeplechase put on by the new management was scheduled for 26 February. Entitled the Grand National Steeplechase, it was 'a sweepstake of 20 sovereigns each, 5 sovereigns forfeit, with 100 sovs added. 12 Stone, Gentlemen riders, 4 miles across country. The second to save his stake, the winner to pay 100 sovs towards expenses. No rider to open a gate or ride through a gateway or more than 100 yards down the road.' If describing an amateur still makes a nonsense of much of British sport, defining a gentleman – a title still grimly sought by self-made men – has no straight answer. No one in 1839 was at all sure what constituted a gentleman rider and certainly most of the riders in the early Nationals demonstrably rode for hire. Adam Lindsay Gordon, describing the Cheltenham Grand Annual of 1847 in *'How we Beat the Favourite'*, exploded:

A gentleman rider? Well I'm an outsider
But if he's a gent, who the mischief's a jock?

There were 29 fences in all, 15 on the first circuit and 14 on the second: these

were mostly banks about 2 ft. high, gorsed on the top and faced with small ditches – the last two (jumped only once) were ordinary flights of sheep hurdles not unlike the present ones, but stuck in upright, not sloped. There were in addition three really formidable obstacles. The first, known as Brook No. 1, was a natural stream, dammed up to a width of 8 ft. and faced with a 3 ft. 6 in. timber paling; this was approached out of a ploughed field. The second brook, which had also to be jumped out of plough, comprised a small bank guarding a deep, wide ditch and a stout post and rails. This fence had a total spread of 9 ft. and a considerable drop. The last *bête-noire* was a stone wall, nearly 5 ft. high. When news of this horror first filtered through, the more responsible sectors of the Press discounted it as mere rumour, but it proved all too true and caused much teeth-sucking to the jockeys walking the course.

The race attracted advance publicity on a scale unprecedented for a steeplechase. All the best 'chasers in Britain were entered and public interest and the volume of betting were enormous. Visitors flocked to Liverpool and lodgings were at a premium. The Waterloo (where the Elmores stayed) and the Adelphi each let out 100 beds, while the Talbot, where the eve-of-race Call-over was held, was virtually taken over by those bold Greek-quoting bucks from the golden days of fox-hunting, the Melton Corinthians.

Feature of the market was a run on Lottery and during the final fortnight he was backed from 100–6 to 5–1 favouritism. The previous ante-post favourite and his constant rival, The Nun, started at sixes and there was also money for the Irish horse Rust. Sir Edward Mostyn's classy thoroughbred from Wales, Seventy-Four, was also supported by experts who believed that his lack of cross-country

Lottery wins the 1839 Grand National from his punished pursuers. Note the last 'fence', then only upright sheep hurdles, which seem to be causing undue grief.

experience would be offset by the priceless assistance of 'Black Tom' Olliver.

The weather which had been as capricious as a spoilt girl for months, chose to relent, and Tuesday morning broke 'calm, bright and beautiful'. By 9 a.m. the road to Aintree was jammed with pie-men, chimney sweeps, cigar sellers, thimble-riggers and the small fry of the gaming table keepers. In the town not a coach nor cab was to be had for money and there was too great a rush for love. Half-a-guinea was heard being vainly offered for the two-and-sixpenny places in the omnibus. Most of the crowd had no option but to walk. The grandstand had room for only three-quarters of those who applied, and those inside were so tightly wedged as to defy motion. A precedent was set for racecourses to follow deep into the 20th century: the executive had not anticipated the demand, and the catering arrangements fell lamentably short. Most of the famished thousands had to assuage their hunger on oranges and hot gingerbread, much to their indignation. Modern racegoers who sullenly champ their way through the slab of plastic touched with a smear of butter and a flake of improbable, pink ham, and sold for the price of a pub meal, may feel our sporting predecessors were not so unlucky.

The eighteen runners appeared shortly before 3 p.m. and gathered round Lord Sefton, the umpire, who explained to the jockeys that all flags were to be left on the left except the second flag at Brook No. 1, which had been erected to prevent anyone sneaking away round the horrid obstacle.

The Irish Daxen and Captain Becher on Conrad made the early running and no trouble was encountered before the first brook. Here Captain Becher had his celebrated soaking and Cannon Ball also fell. The gallant Captain recaptured Conrad and set off damply in pursuit, but at the second brook his hydrophobic animal crashed again. This time Captain Becher called it a day. Daxen also fell

In 1840 Lottery was not so lucky – the wholesale slaughter of the three leading fancies caused the monstrous wall to be removed.

here but the pace was not such as to discourage pursuit: he was soon remounted and back with the leaders. Meanwhile the Gloucestershire mare, Charity, had gone on but she confounded her supporters by refusing to have anything to do with the dreadful wall, a type of obstacle she knew well – but perhaps too painfully – from her native Cotswolds. Lottery, who had been jumping superbly throughout, slipped over the looming stones like a cat. On the second circuit Daxen again fell at Brook No. 2 and at this vital juncture The Nun could no longer hold her place and began to drop out. Coming on to the racecourse, Lottery struck the front and although Paulina, True Blue and Seventy-Four were harrying him, it was plain he had the race sewn up. Still unbelievably fresh, his leap at the last hurdle is reputed to have spanned 33 ft. and he went on to win by 3 lengths. The handsome Welshman Seventy-Four was second, and Paulina third.

Doubt disguises the colours Mason wore. Mr Elmore's colours, straight from the hunting field, are registered as scarlet, black cap, and in the old County Stand at Liverpool used to hang a faded set answering this description, allegedly carried by Lottery in the 1839 National. But the newspapers of the day, unless all were cribbing one colour-blind writer's copy, describe them as blue, black cap, and this is how they appear in Thomas Maclean's print of the finish.

Seventy-Four was ridden by Jem Mason's great friend and rival Tom Olliver – 'Black Tom' of Adam Lindsay Gordon's 'Ye Wearie Wayfarer'. Olliver was the first of a distinguished line of Cheltenham-based jockeys which included George Stevens and Tommy Pickernell (both of whom he coached), William Archer and William Holman. Incorrigibly cheerful, disreputable and far from sartorial, he was an unlikely friend for 'Dandy Jem', the foppishly elegant Mason, but the bonds between the contrasting pair were very close. Once when Olliver was down to his last farthing – a misfortune which overtook him fairly frequently – he asked Mason to buy his beloved Trust-Me-Not. Mason refused but said he would ride the horse in his next race and sent 5 sovereigns for the horse's travelling expenses to the meeting. Trust-Me-Not, happily belying his cruel name, won his race and temporarily restored his feckless owner's fortunes.

Reports of litigation in which Olliver became involved reveal that top-flight jockeys over a century ago reckoned to get 5 sovereigns a ride and 10 sovereigns a winner, sums which must be multiplied 60-fold to relate to today's money. For an important race when a big gamble had been landed, £50 was considered reasonable. These rewards are the more staggering against the background of stable-boys earning about 4 shillings (20p) a week.

The two odd friends rode in very different styles. Mason was first and foremost a horseman with beautiful hands and a knack of getting a horse right for a fence, the precursor of John Francome, or in the 1950s of Aubrey Brabazon. Olliver, a Fred Winter *sans finesse* or a later Steve Smith Eccles, was much the stronger, especially in a finish. 'I can say without fear of contradiction,' Olliver said generously of his friend and in the pleasant cadences of the time, 'that he was the finest horseman in England. I have never ridden with him without envying the perfection of his style.'

The first National at Liverpool had been an unqualified success and everyone, bar the belligerent Irish contingent who noisily asserted the course was unfair and their horse had been stopped, went home satisfied. Plans were immediately set in train for a renewal the following year.

For the winner, this victory was the beginning of two seasons of total ascendency over his contemporaries. On 15 March he won the Grand Steeplechase at Maidstone and only a week later was saddled again for the Royal Leamington Grand Steeplechase. This was a tremendous Midland occasion and the big race, which had £200 added, was the shining climax of a splendid week which included Hunt racing at Warwick, a Stag Hunt and a glittering ball in the Assembly Rooms. Lottery was winning his race very easily when Mason realized, perhaps with a twinge of conscience, that he had gone the wrong side of a flag. He swung round, galloped back, turned the flag, thundered off in pursuit and in a pounding finish still only got beaten half a length by The Nun.

At the beginning of April that blend of outside and indoor activities so much a feature of those energetic times moved for a gala week to Cheltenham. Here festivities ranged from a meet of the Cotswold Hounds and the annual dinner of the Berkeley Hunt, to a special performance at the theatre followed by Supper and a Ball. The meeting was dominated by the Grand Cheltenham Steeplechase, and although Lottery's presence had sent a lot of rabbits scuttling, there was still a fair field to oppose him. But after biding his time in the early stages, the champion suddenly slipped from a seeming canter into full gallop and arrowed ahead for an effortless victory. Considering the distances covered and the transport at his disposal, Lottery had lived an astonishing six weeks.

Later that season he won a race at Stratford. Jem Mason and the other jockeys walking the course before the race were brought up short by a new and uncompromisingly solid five-barred gate. The only alternative was its neighbouring fence, a huge, horrible and hairy bullfinch. As the jockeys stood contemplating these two repellent obstructions, one of the younger ones piped up to ask which the great man would go for himself. Mason replied instantly that as he was going to the Opera that night and was damned if he'd go with a scratched face, he would jump the gate. He added defiantly that he dared anyone else to follow him over. He did jump the gate, alone, and having won his race, departed post-haste for London to grace the Opera House unsullied.

At the end of the season, Lottery went home to Uxenden, had a reception thrown in his honour, and lest he be spoilt or thought idle, entertained the Elmores' guests by leaping over the dining-room table set out in the garden and fully laid.

Next season he won six of his eight races including the Royal Leamington and Cheltenham Steeplechases which, now that the St Albans fixture was discontinued, followed only Liverpool in importance. He also won at Dunchurch, a sporting little country meeting near Rugby. Here he was so superior that Mason was able to let him trot across a ploughed field and then skirt some typical pounding Midlands ridge-and-furrow, and still score a comfortable victory over Alan McDonough on his old rival The Nun.

But at Liverpool that season on 5 March his gods deserted him. The Grand National was run at a furious pace set by a wild Irishman named Power who, having laid a hefty bet that he would reach the big wall first, wasn't at all concerned

J. F. Herring's study of Lottery and Jem Mason (back to us); Brunette and (centre) Tom Olliver on Discount.

with what happened thereafter. He certainly reached the monstrous thing in front, pursued by Lottery, who failed to rise at all and took a crunching fall, bringing down Columbine, The Nun and Seventy-Four in a kicking, grunting heap on top of him. Thus four of the leading fancies were removed at one fell swoop. Their débâcle did however secure the later removal of the wall itself, or what was left of its spread of stones, and it was replaced by the present water jump. Mr Power's Valentine survived and continued to lead to the second last, where he not surprisingly tired. He finally finished third. The winner was greeted with suspicion and something worse, for it was John Elmore's other runner Jerry. A spate of sinister rumours hissed like serpents through the stands. It is true that Lottery (who carried a special 7-lb. penalty above the others' 12 st.) had drifted suspiciously in the market. At one stage he had gone out to tens from twos although he hardened in the last few minutes to start second favourite. Jerry, on the other hand, had advanced steadily to 12–1. It is most unlikely that Mason was party to any chicanery and he certainly neither would nor could have engineered the crashing fall he took.

Lottery was reported to be badly shaken, but if this was so, he must have had a constitution of iron for at the end of the month he won three races in a week across the Midlands at Northampton, Leamington and at Cheltenham. This last victory

brought in its wake the contrived end of his domination. Other racecourse executives now joined Horncastle's decision to fend off the plundering hands of Lottery's entourage. Even within there were doubts; poor Mrs Elmore, who was shy and retiring, was acutely embarrassed at the regular collection of so many stakes. Accordingly, for the next two years the conditions for the Grand National contained with perfect English hypocrisy the extra proviso (not naming Lottery) that the winner of the Cheltenham Steeplechase of 1840 was to carry an extra 18 lb., thus raising his weight to a preposterous 13 st. 4 lb. Such was his fame that he still started favourite on both occasions but each time the burden crushed him in the closing stages and the thoughtful Mason pulled him up. In 1843 the condition was dropped and shortly afterwards the race became a handicap. With every racecourse's hand set against him poor Lottery only managed to win two races in his last three seasons, but Elmore contrived to make his final appearance a winning one at Windsor in the spring of 1844.

For a while George Dockeray used him as a hack but later he was passed on to the Halls, a Neasden family who ran their own pack of harriers. Lottery, though he was no longer strong enough for such work and the horse who had been the glory of all England, was condemned to spend his ailing twilight years pulling a squalid cart. The thought revolts us, but in that brutal age children were still toiling in the mines and up chimneys, were dying of starvation in Britain's dirty slums, and men could be hanged for poaching, and boys transported to Australia for stealing a loaf of bread.

Lottery's life marks the dawn of organized steeplechasing and he was the first star to shine in its new and still tarnished sky. From Lottery on, the firmament starts to open, and his name – of all the great 'chasers – will always be remembered because it is so appropriate for the first winner of a race that has become part of our strange heritage.

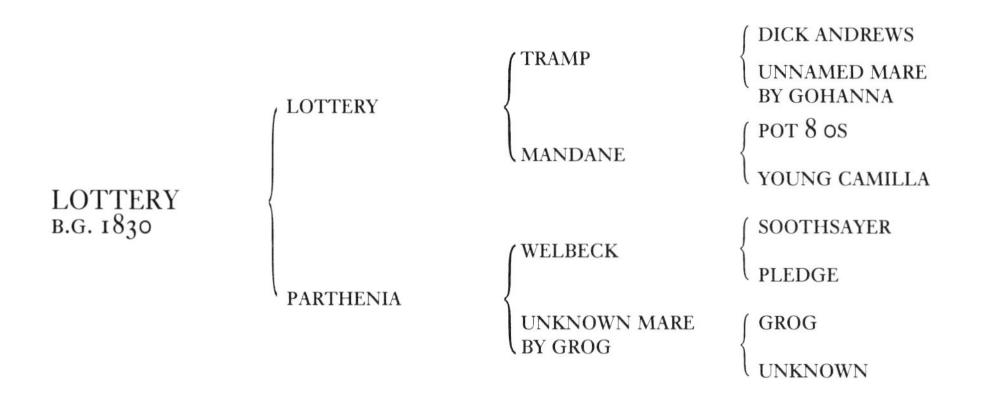

DATE	COURSE	RACE	DISTANCE	VALUE	WEIGHT	JOCKEY	PRICE	PLACE
Season 1837–38								
Dec	St Albans	Grand Steeplechase	3m	Sweepstakes	12.0	J. Mason		2nd
Feb 24	Metropolitan	Gold Cup	4m	Sweepstakes	12.0	J. Mason		won
Mar 23	Leamington	Grand Annual	4m	£150 added	12.0	Barker		unpl
Apr 3	Daventry	Grand Steeplechase	4m	£150 added	12.0	J. Mason		won
Season 1838-39								
Feb 26	Liverpool	Grand National	5m	£100 added	12.0	J. Mason	5/1f	won
Mar 15	Maidstone	Grand Steeplechase	4m	£100 added	12.0	J. Mason		won
Mar 22	Leamington	Grand Annual	4m	£200 added	12.0	J. Mason		3rd
Apr 4	Cheltenham	Grand Steeplechase	4m	£60 added	12.0	J. Mason		won
Apr 17	Stratford	Grand Steeplechase	4m	£60 added	12.7	J. Mason	1/2f	won
Season 1839–40								
Dec 17	Metropolitan	Grand Steeple	4m	Purse added	12.0	J. Mason		won
Feb 11	Dunchurch	Grand Steeple	4m	£100 added	12.7	J. Mason	4/6f	won
Mar 5	Liverpool	Grand National	4m	£150 added	12.7	J. Mason	4/1f	fell
Mar 11	Fakenham	Cup	4m	£50 added	12.0	J. Mason		unpl
Mar 20	Leamington	Grand Annual	4m	£50 added	12.0	J. Mason		won
Mar 26	Northampton	Grand Steeplechase	4m	£100 added	12.0	J. Mason		won
Apr 3	Cheltenham	Cup	4m	£100 added	13.3	J. Mason		won
Apr 8	Stratford	Grand Steeplechase	4m	£60 added	12.0	J. Mason		won
Season 1840–41								
Mar 3	Liverpool	Grand National	4m	£100 added	13.4	J. Mason		p.u.
Mar 18	Boston	Sweepstakes	4m	£100 added	12.7	J. Mason		3rd
Apr 1	Monmouth	Sweepstakes	3m	£20 added	12.0	Powell		won
Apr 6	Chelmsford							
Apr 20	Newport Pagnell	Sweepstakes	4m	£50 added	12.8	J. Mason		won

DATE	COURSE	RACE	DISTANCE	VALUE	WEIGHT	JOCKEY	PRICE	PLACE
Season 1841–42								
Nov 3	Newport Pagnell	H'cp Ch	4m	£100 added	13.6	J. Mason	4/5f	2nd
Feb 17	Romford	H'cp Ch	4m	£100 added	13.1	J. Mason	5/6f	won
Mar 2	Liverpool	Grand National	4m	£100 added	13.4	J. Mason	5/1f	p.u.
Season 1842–43								
Dec 22	Brixworth	Selling Ch	4m	£50 added	13.0	J. Mason		2nd
Mar 1	Liverpool	Grand National	4m	£100 added	12.6	J. Mason	4/1	7th
Season 1843–44								
Oct 19	Edgeware*	Selling Ch	4m	Sweepstakes and Cup	11.7	J. Mason		2nd
Nov 16	Newport Pagnell	H'cp Ch	4m	£100 added	11.6	J. Mason	6/1	2nd
Jan 17	Tring	H'cp Ch	4m	£60 added	11.4	J. Mason	2/1f	5th
Feb 15	Hereford	H'cp Ch	4m	£150 added	11.2	J. Mason	7/2f	unpl
Mar 22	Swindon	H'cp Ch	4m	£100 added	11.0	J. Mason	6/1	unpl
Apr 8	Windsor	H'cp Ch	4m	£50 added	12.0	J. Mason		won

* As spelt in 19th Century

Authors' Note. There is no official *Calendar* covering this period: our statistics are taken from Mr. H. Wright's *Steeplechase Calendar, 1826–1844* (pub. 1845). The returns do not always tally with those published in *Bell's Life.*

TWO

The Lamb

THE 1860S; QUEEN VICTORIA, HER BELOVED ALBERT DEAD, IS IMMURED IN WINDSOR TRAILING YARDS OF BLACK CREPE; IN POLITICS, DISRAELI DUELS WITH GLADSTONE; IN IRELAND THE POTATO FAMINE BITES DEEPER – MISERABLE HUNDREDS DIE, THOUSANDS EMIGRATE TO AMERICA; AND AMERICA BLEEDS IN CIVIL WAR AS NORTH FIGHTS SOUTH OVER SLAVERY AND THE RIGHT TO SECEDE FROM THE UNION; FOXHUNTING SQUIRES SPUR ACROSS HIGH LEICESTERSHIRE AND THEIR STABLE-BOYS SCRAPE £12 A YEAR.

In the spring of 1862 a sporting farmer in County Limerick, by the name of Henchy, bred a grey colt foal by Zouave out of an unnamed mare distinguished only because she was by Arthur, the 1840 Grand National runner-up. The foal was beautifully made with the small, quality head and huge, trustful eyes of the Arab strain, which, coupled with his gentle disposition and his colour, earned him his name. Unfortunately for Mr Henchy, his decorative youngster was no bigger than a pony, and whether he could ever earn his keep seemed problematical.

By the time The Lamb was four he probably did not exceed 15 hands and some reports say he was not more than 14.2 hands – a suitable size for a 12-year-old child. When hopefully offered to Mr Edward Studd, a prominent English owner, as a hunter for his son, he was rejected out of hand. Mr Studd, whose Salamander had just won the National, scornfully declared that the little grey was 'not fit to carry a man's boots'. Five years later he was to watch his good horse, Despatch,

land in the lead over Aintree's last hurdle (as the obstacle then was), and his hopes of doubling his 1866 triumph leapt. But Despatch was not alone: shadowing him was a little grey carrying rather more than a man's boots in Lord Poulett's blue and cerise colours. Grimly the grey stuck to Mr Studd's hope, collared him, mastered him, and eventually drew away to win by 2 lengths. The Lamb had gained a sweet revenge.

As a youngster, however, Farmer Henchy had still to sell him, and when a purchaser was finally found for him, it was Mr Joseph Doyle, a Dublin veterinary surgeon, and for the insulting sum of £30. By some accounts Mr Doyle passed all or half of him on for 300 guineas to Mr William Long, but it was in Doyle's name that The Lamb made his first appearance on a racecourse in the Kildare Hunt Plate at Punchestown, worth the huge sum then of £285. Ridden by Murphy, The Lamb made the happiest of débuts and won unchallenged by 4 lengths.

His next two efforts, however, at the Louth Hunt meeting in May were unsuccessful, and he took ship for England.

He made his first acquaintance with Liverpool at the Autumn meeting, running unplaced to Lord Poulett's Benazet in a 3-mile Handicap Chase on Grand Sefton day. An attempt on the longer Grand Annual at Leamington was similarly unrewarded, the race being easily won by Lord Coventry's Chimney Sweep. But Earl Poulett had noticed him at Liverpool and was again impressed, and shortly afterwards leased him for his racing career.

William Poulett, the sixth Earl, was born in 1827, named after his godfather King William IV, and succeeded his uncle John in 1864. William, the third son of Vice-Admiral Poulett, inherited his father's love of racing. The old Admiral, in an age unlike ours when people did rather than watched, rode successfully on the flat and across country in India, Ireland and Gibraltar.

The family, a very old one, became extinct in 1973 (the last peer was an engineer apprentice on the Great Western Railway) and in 1968 offered for sale the estates in Somerset which had been in the family 550 years. Sir Anthony Poulett was Captain of the Guard to Queen Elizabeth I and Governor of Jersey. His descendant, William, who so fortunately discovered The Lamb, was married three times. When only 22 he married a sea-pilot's daughter at Portsea called Elizabeth Newman. When she died in August 1871, he married again six weeks later. That wife only lasted five years, but he waited longer after her death before, at the age of 52, marrying Rosa Melville.

When Lord Poulett died in 1899, his title was claimed by someone called William Turnour Thomas, born on 15 December 1849, less than six months after William Poulett married Elizabeth Newman, and who now claimed to be their son. After four years wrangling the House of Lords finally rejected the claim, but allowed the claim of another William, the son of the sixth Earl's last marriage to Rosa.

The Lamb's owner, having served in three regiments, settled on the family estate, Waterloo, in Hampshire, and found time to be Master of the Hambledon Hounds for nine years, to be a founder member of the National Hunt Committee, a keen yachtsman and a notable whip. He was assisted in most of his activities by his greatest friend, George Ede, a famous Hampshire all-round sportsman, who lived with him. Ede helped found the Hampshire Cricket Club, rode 306 winners in fourteen years under his *nom-de-course* 'Mr Edwards' and was killed in the 1870 Grand Sefton after a dreadful fall from a chance ride.

The Lamb's first run for Lord Poulett satisfied without startling. In the Grand Metropolitan Handicap at Croydon he again encountered Chimney Sweep, carrying a 10-lb. penalty for his Leamington victory. Although Chimney Sweep started favourite at 4–1, Lord Coventry curiously declared to win with his other runner Balder, ridden by stable jockey George Stevens, who was allowed to start at 10–1. The public were right; Chimney Sweep swept home a sparkling winner on the strength of which he was made favourite for the National. Lord Coventry, 11 years younger than Lord Poulett, was another racing Earl, a co-founder of the National Hunt Committee and another leading 'chasing personality of the era. His family still exists and he is reputed to have saved the estates from ruin by the successive National victories of the sisters Emblem and Emblematic.

The Grand National had been building up steadily in the 28 years since Lottery. Apart from being unquestionably the major event in the steeplechasing calendar, it had become one of the top sporting social occasions of the year. The 1868 meeting, however, opened on a minor chord: though the crowd was up to standard, the fields were meagre. The first non-race was a walk-over and in the fourth race all three runners refused the very first obstacle. The only good contest of the dreary day was the final hurdle won from nine others by a leading National candidate, Pearl Diver – a performance which was thought to augur well for his chance next day.

Liverpool, splitting its seams with a glut of visitors, stirred at cock-crow the next morning. As dawn broke palely a tidal wave of humanity flooded into Aintree. The race was strongly international. There were French and German horses among the entries and a great many foreign visitors – 'quite a babel of tongues on the roof of the grandstand' auntishly clucked *The Times*.

The public were confused by the number of fancied horses and Chimney Sweep, The Lamb and Moose all vied for favouritism. There was no reason why The Lamb should turn the tables on Chimney Sweep, but accounts of his 'high trial' coupled with his magnificent appearance – paddock onlookers voted him 'the picture of perfection' – aroused much enthusiasm. He was to be ridden by 'Mr Edwards', alias George Ede. Moose owed his exalted position in the market almost solely to the enormous respect accorded to anything carrying the red, yellow cap of Mr Brayley.

Steeplechasing had emerged from the backwoods of farmers and horse-copers and was extending itself into the parklands of the nobility. The list of stewards had the aristocratic resonance which was to set the tone for a century before lesser mortals were allowed to join the councils of the Turf. They included the 'Red Duke' of Hamilton, the Marquess of Hastings, the Earl of Westmoreland, Lord Coventry and Lord Poulett.

Lord Sefton drove a party of friends over from Croxteth and Lady Sefton took advantage of the fine weather and brought the ladies in a pair of carriages. As 3.30 approached, Chimney Sweep hardened to a firm favourite despite a last minute run on Mr Barber's mare Fan, who had been second the previous year. Mr

Barber, however, upset everyone's calculations by declaring, at the very last minute, to win with his other runner Helen. The pithy comments this drew from the press suggest it was typical of him and probably much glee was felt when Fan withdrew herself from the contest at the very first fence. Her jockey, loth to give up, tried in vain to induce her to continue and then Mentmore and Charming Woman (as such creatures will) followed her wayward example by sticking in their toes too and by obstinately, unreasonably, refusing to do what was not only their duty but what, in the past and without pressure, had so often seemed to please them. The approach to the fence, choked with obdurate horses and cursing flapping jockeys, foreshadowed a Thelwell cartoon of a Pony Club Hunter Trials. A little ahead, however, tragedy had smitten the race. Chimney Sweep struck a stone as he crossed the Melling Road and smashed a leg so badly that he had to be shot.

The Lamb, meanwhile, avoiding both comedy and drama, was right up at the front and led Pearl Diver by half a length over the water. At the start of the second circuit the 1865 winner Alcibiade took up the running from The Lamb, Pearl Diver, Moose and Colonel Crosstree, these five being about 100 yards in front of anything else. Alcibiade was done with a mile from home and The Lamb and Pearl Diver went on. They were still together approaching the last. 'Now you will see what the Diver will do to the pony,' exclaimed a knowledgeable bystander. But he was wrong and it was The Lamb who lasted out best on the exhausting ground to squelch home for a 2-length victory. Alcibiade was 10 lengths away third. Only three others finished.

The major credit for The Lamb's great win goes to his trainer Ben Land who had transformed the pretty rather too delicate little grey into a most imposing, muscular individual and produced him on the day ready to run for his life. Ben Land had been a Norfolk farmer so keen on hunting that he kept his own staghounds, and an enthusiastic, but unsuccessful rider. When he turned to training he produced marvellous results and was tremendously popular with all the young amateurs like George Ede who went to him, generally direct from lessons in less important subjects at Eton, to be coached in steeplechasing.

After The Lamb's great victory, Ben Land renounced steeplechasing to concentrate solely on the flat (as Vincent O'Brien was to do 90 years later). Four years later, however, he killed himself by cutting his throat.

The next year The Lamb had such a light season that he may already have been afflicted by the wasting disease in his quarters which was to lay him off for the whole of season 1869–70.

In December he ran a marvellous race for the £450 Metropolitan Grand Steeplechase over 3 miles at Kingsbury. Carrying 12 st. 3 lb. over a distance palpably short of his best he failed, only by half a neck, to give 4 lb. to The Nun.

His age was given wrongly when he was entered for the National and by ridiculous petty-foggery the authorities refused to let him run, so he had to go instead for the 2¾-mile Sefton which had been transferred from the autumn meeting. Nobody expected him to distinguish himself over this trip, and he started the outsider of Lord Poulett's troop of three. They finished consecutively but Roving Maid beat them all. The Earl's Benazet was second, his Endsleigh was third and The Lamb fourth.

That was The Lamb's last race for two years and at one time it was despaired of ever getting him back. Finally he was placed under the care of Mr Mannington who successfully treated him by blistering his quarters and by giving him one of the best, but not the cheapest cures: a long rest from work.

By the time the 1871 National came round The Lamb had acquired a new trainer. Chris Green, who had ridden two National winners, Abd-el-Kader (1850) and Half-Caste (1859), now nominally trained Lord Poulett's horses, although the Earl who was very knowledgeable in and out of the stable, did much of the training himself. The Lamb also found a new jockey.

George Ede had been tragically killed in the previous year's Sefton and his successor was engaged in a curious way. Tommy Pickernell was then the leading jump jockey. Born in Cheltenham. he was sent out to Tasmania as a young man and rode there with such success that the natives got up a petition imploring him to cease. He returned to England, was coached by 'Black Tom' Olliver and William Holman, and rode under both rules all over Europe. When he retired after a last terrible fall at Sandown in 1877 he had a Grand National record *par excellence*, having ridden in it 17 times and won three. He endured many bad falls but the last one smashed his jaw in three places and blinded him in one eye. He was a complete contrast to The Lamb's previous jockey, the cultivated Old Etonian George Ede, and must have only narrowly qualified as an amateur. The rules then insisted that to be a Gentleman Rider a man must either hold a commission, or have a title, or belong to a short list of predictable London clubs, including White's, Pratts, Boodles and The Turf.

On the night of December 14th, 1870, Lord Poulett dreamed two dreams, and

An interesting portrait of The Lamb normally depicted as a grey but who contemporary reports described as 'darkening like weathered leather'.

the following day wrote to Tommy Pickernell as follows:

My dear Tommy,

Let me know for certain whether you can ride for me at Liverpool on The Lamb. I dreamt twice last night I saw the race run. The first dream he was last and finished among the carriages. The second dream, I should think an hour afterwards, I saw The Lamb run. He won four lengths and you rode him, and I stood close to the winning post at the turn. I saw the cerise and blue sleeves and you, as plain as I write this. Now let me know as soon as you can, and say nothing to anyone.

Yours sincerely,
Poulett.

But the Earl was unable to be secret himself. The Lamb's preparation continued to please and Lord Poulett's confidence waxed. Having secured a brace of rich bets, one of £3,000 to £100 bolstered by a second of £1,300 to £100, he blazoned his hopes abroad and even sent circulars round to his friends. The Lamb as usual made no public appearance but reports of his work were widely circulated and his price continued to shorten.

In spite of its much criticized clash with the Lincoln, the National aroused more interest than ever. The 25-strong field was reckoned superlative, including, as it did besides The Lamb, two other previous winners in The Colonel (1869–70) and Alcibiade (1865). To these were added The Doctor, second last year, Pearl Diver, second to The Lamb in 1868, Mr Studd's promising Despatch and a highly-rated Irishman Wild Fox. The big day had been proclaimed a public holiday to celebrate the wedding in the Chapel Royal at Windsor of Princess Louise and the Marquis of Lorne. The novel idea of a princess of the blood being permitted to marry a subject of the Crown had been tremendously popular since its announcement, and the country was *en fête*.

Events conspired to promote The Lamb to favouritism. On the first day Lord Poulett's Broadlea, the outsider of five, won the Molyneux Chase. Then there was an eve-of-race panic when it was rumoured that the former favourite Pearl Diver had not arrived on the course and would not run. Scarcely had this been stifled and the excitement calmed, when a trainload of racegoers decanting on Liverpool Station saw a lamb leap out from a wagon in the sidings and run all the way down the platform. Immediately this tale uncorked a flood of superstitious silver half-crowns.

The Lamb's appearance in the paddock settled the matter. He was greeted with a round of applause. Profiting from his enforced rest, he had miraculously grown – if the racing correspondents are to be trusted – to a full 15.2 hands. Indisputably he had thickened into a magnificent individual. His diet must have been exceptional for his coat, astonishingly for a grey, shone like satin, and it required the united efforts of young Ben Land, the son of his former trainer, clinging to his head, and a light lad on his back, to restrain him. Even the hypercritical correspondent of *The Times* allowed that he presented 'the model condition', while dealing testily with his rivals. The Colonel *The Times* thought 'a trifle burly', Pearl Diver 'by contrast somewhat overdone', Dog Fox (The Lamb's not unfancied stable companion) 'looked a wretch' and Casse-Tête 'as though in training for an anatomical museum instead of a Grand National'.

Several inexpert current trainers prone to over-galloping their horses would die of apoplectic rage if they read such criticism over their breakfast-tables. Indeed, no trainer likes to have his skill ridiculed or his charges defamed. You may be ruder about trainers' wives than their horses, and not only because the former will give better than they get.

The weather, for once, relented. No one remembered such halcyon days in National week: and it was more like July than March. This, coupled with the fact that the enterprising Mr Topham had converted part of the Grandstand into private boxes *à l'Ascot*, induced the attendance of 'a galaxy of beauty and fashion seldom excelled on any racecourse not excepting the Derby'. The crowd was conservatively estimated at 45,000, and the course was testified to be in excellent order although The Lamb's connections had some qualms about the amount of plough land. There was a particularly heavy stretch spreading back 300 yards on the approach to Becher's Brook and another two fields by the Canal Turn.

The pace was a scorcher from the start: Rufus made the early running with The Lamb closely attending. Pearl Diver settled down in the middle while The Colonel, conserving his energies with 12 st. 13 lb., was held up. The special guard employed by Tophams to keep order and the fields clear, failed to drive thousands of Lancashire lads off the course in time, and the field, disregarding the lower orders, charged straight through them 'knocking them down like ninepins with severe injury to some'. Passing the stands on the first circuit, a sheet would have covered the first 15 horses and all the leading fancies were still in the race, apart from The Doctor, who had let down his profession and refused on several occasions, and Lord Raglan, who stumbled on some rough ground and broke a fetlock. On the second circuit, The Lamb lost his action and his place in the deep plough before Bechers. He was consequently behind as the field approached the Canal Turn. Here, to Tommy Pickernell's horror, two horses crashed to the ground immediately in front of him, but The Lamb, always an incredibly agile little horse, sprang blithely over both and continued merrily on his way. As they turned on to the racecourse, the issue clearly lay between him and Despatch. They jumped the last dead level. On the run-in Despatch momentarily threatened. But The Lamb quickened and went away to win a little cleverly by 2 lengths – not the 4 that Lord Poulett had envisaged in his dream, but it is not recorded that he quibbled.*

The Lamb walked in to a fantastic reception: not only was his owner universally popular, but he had carried the hopes, and cash, of the lusty Irish contingent, and 'the boys were ready to eat him'. Horse, jockey and owner were carried bodily into the unsaddling enclosure and in the scrimmage The Lamb was bereft of most of his tail, and Lord Poulett of his watch. The latter was later recovered; the former, in time's fullness, regrew.

* D. H. Munroe (a writer in whom we do not have implicit faith) in *The Grand National* makes the margin a head only, and describes in some detail the whirlwind finish and superior horsemanship of Tommy Pickernell. We are unsure where Munroe found that story: all the newspapers (including both *Sporting Life* and *The Times*) and the official *Steeplechases Past* carrying the comfortable 2-lengths version.

The Sporting Life, then a bi-weekly publication, appraised The Lamb's dramatic second victory – an astonishing comeback which ranks with Jerry M.'s and Mandarin's. It declared that a better field had never stripped and that the oft-bemoaned theory that the modern horse had deteriorated was all so much humbug.

The Lamb was perhaps the best winner until the extraordinary arrival of Red Rum. The little grey had been up in front the whole way, setting a clinking pace and attacking the fences with great determination, and had recorded an abnormally fast time. Indeed his 9 minutes 35¾ on the long plodding grips of plough compares excellently with modern times on famously fast turf.

Tough Tommy Pickernell was to ride yet another National winner, Pathfinder, four years later in 1871 . The horse, wags said, was well named, for his jockey was on the brink of becoming a very heavy drinker, and could be seen at the start to be far from sober. Pickernell had no doubt about The Lamb – 'The finest fencer I was ever on in my life – the best horse I ever rode'.

This was not the end of The Lamb's career. He was still only nine and in the following National he was to run one of his best races ever. At about this juncture he was sold for £1,200 to Baron Oppenheim, of the well-known German family of owner-breeders, who had also bought The Colonel. The date of the sale is uncertain: the newspapers regarded him as still belonging to Lord Poulett, but the official *Steeplechases Past* described him as the property of the Baron.

In whatever ownership he duplicated his previous programme. Again he came to Aintree without any preliminary race at all but in equally fine fettle and again he was ridden by Tommy Pickernell. There was one difference, however: the favourite now was Despatch and The Lamb was allowed to start at 100–8. Many pundits thought him a good each way bet at this price: he was a spring horse who would be suited by the prevailing hard ground and he was known to be very well. Ben Land even said he was 10 lb., better than last year. He needed to improve at least 16 lb., for inevitably he had shot to the top of handicap and now carried the crusher of 12 st. 7 lb. This, a bad enough burden for a full-sized horse, was a cruel task for a small grey pony.

His appearance in the newly constructed paddock was eagerly awaited and disappointed no one. He came in, coat gleaming, 'gay as a girl at a picnic', and lashed out exuberantly in all directions. 'Sure, you could crack a cob-nut with a hammer on his quarters', declared a fellow countryman as the little grey bounced by. Age, unusually, had instead of bleaching him to chalky white, darkened his coat like weathered leather.

The race was a rattle of accidents as many of the fancied horses crashed to the ground. The Lamb barely dodged disaster at the water and had to perform acrobatic convolutions to avoid the prostrate bodies of Primrose and Marin. Coming on to the racecourse for the last time, he was still in the fighting line, but he was in trouble two out and the unconsidered – indeed much despised – Casse-Tête drew clear to win by 6 lengths from Scarrington. The Lamb struggled on gamely but in the end had to relinquish third place to Despatch.

Astonishing to us, but not abnormal then, this double Grand National winner next ran at two up-country Hunt meetings which were no more than point-to-

points with a couple of open races thrown in. The first, at Abergavenny, was only a fortnight after the National and The Lamb, carrying 12 st. 10 lb. and starting odds-on was unplaced. He redeemed himself, however, two weeks later at the South Hampshire meeting at Emsworth, winning by 30 lengths, despite slipping and all but falling on the last bend.

Baron von Oppenheim, whose descendants were still racing and breeding successfully a century later from Schlenderhan, near Cologne*, then took him to Germany where his bright life was brutally snuffed. Running for the Grosser Preis von Baden-Baden in September and ridden by Count Nicholas Esterhazy, he was winning easily when he ran into a boggy patch barely 100 yards from the post and ground to a halt. His rider frantically urged him on and as he gamely tried to accelerate, one of his forelegs stuck in the mud and snapped. He was destroyed on the spot.

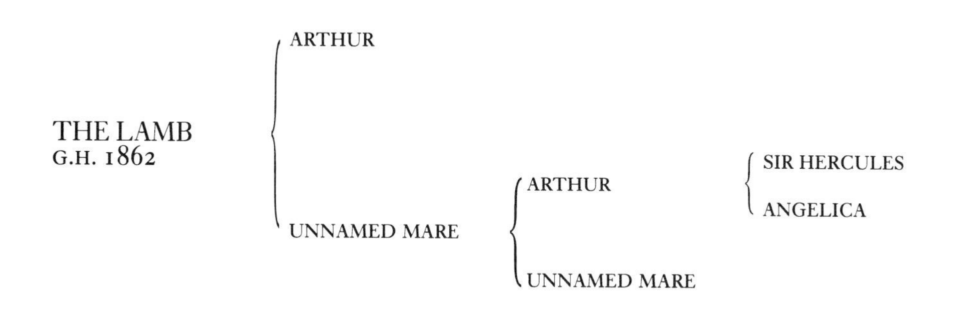

* They bred Sayonara, dam of 1985 Derby winner Slip Anchor, and Schönbrunn granddam of Arc de Triomphe winner Sagace. Gestut Schlenderhan is Germany's oldest private stud. Founded in 1869 it had produced 84 Classic winners up until 1988.

DATE	COURSE	RACE	DISTANCE	VALUE	WEIGHT	JOCKEY	PRICE	PLACE
Season 1866–67								
Apr 25	Punchestown	Kildare Hunt Plate	3m 4f	£285	10.7	Murphy	no prices	won
May 15	Mullacurry	County Louth Stakes	3m 2f	£165	11.7	Mr Long	no prices	unpl
May 16	Mullacurry	Ardee Plate H'cp	2m 6f	£100	10.12	Mr Long	no prices	4th
Season 1867–68								
Nov 7	Liverpool	H'cp Plate	3m	100 sovs	11.11	Wynne	100/8	unpl
Nov 22	Warwick	Leamington Grand Annual H'cp Ch	4m	£594	10.12	Wynne	unquoted	unpl
Nov 27	Croydon	Grand Met H'cp Ch	3m 4f	£670	10.5	Wynne	100/8	unpl
Mar 4	Liverpool	Grand National	4m 2f	£1,570	10.7	Mr Edwards	9/1	won
Apr 3	Bedford	Grand National H'cp Ch	4m	£840	12.1	Mr Edwards	6/1	unpl
Season 1868–69								
Dec 9	Kingsbury	Met H'cp Ch	3m	£450	12.3	Mr Edwards	5/2f	2nd
Mar 4	Liverpool	Grand Sefton H'cp Ch	2m 6f	300 sovs	12.0	Mr Edwards	unquoted	4th
Season 1869–70 – DID NOT RUN								
Season 1870–71								
Mar 21	Liverpool	Grand National	4m 4f	£1,665	11.5	Mr Thomas	11/2	won
Season 1871–72								
Mar 21	Liverpool	Grand National	4m 4f	£1,455	12.7	Mr Thomas	100/8	4th
Apr 5	Abergavenny & Monmouths Hunt	Abergavenny Open Ch	3m 4f	£190	12.10	Mr Thomas	5/6f	unpl
Apr 19	Emsworth	S. Hampshire Open Ch	3m	£60	13.0	Mr Crawshaw	7/4	won
Sept	Baden-Baden	Grosser Preis				Count Esterhazy		p.u.

THREE

Manifesto

THE 1890S; THE OLD QUEEN CELEBRATES HER DIAMOND JUBILEE: MARIE CURIE DISCOVERS RADIUM; MARCONI SENDS A MESSAGE ONE MILE BY WIRELESS; BRITAIN AND HER EMPIRE BRIEFLY CONTROL THE WORLD; THE WEBBS PROPOUND THE FIRST TENETS OF SOCIALISM; ELEMENTARY EDUCATION BECOMES FREE; IN SOUTH AFRICA THE HARRIED BOERS STAND AND FIGHT; AND IN IRELAND THE CRIES FOR HOME RULE GROW SHRILLER.

Fifteen years after The Lamb was killed in Germany, there was foaled near Navan in the green-and-gold of County Meath, a plain raw-boned colt out of Vae Victis, by the half-savage Man O'War. Named Manifesto, he was to become an Aintree legend and his record of two wins, three thirds and a fourth in eight Nationals remained for 70 years until wrested from him by Red Rum.

His breeder, Mr Harry Dyas, was a full-blooded character with a natural eye for a horse, to which inestimable gift he added the patience to wait and the skill to produce a good horse on the right day. (Fortunes are not made by allowing the rare swan to beat geese unsupported.) If all was to his satisfaction he believed in wading into the ring with great sheaves of money and the bookmakers, like wary hares, stood waiting for his thumping assaults. He never allowed his huge affection for his horses (the basic reason he was good with them) to cloud his businesslike mind (which was why he was financially successful). He would always part with a horse at the right price and such was his reputation that he demanded and obtained some staggering prices.

In the New Year of 1892 the four-year-old Manifesto was sent over to Manchester with a squadron of Mr Dyas' horses to make his racecourse debut in the Pendleton Chase. It was a gloomy one in the murk: he fell early on. But, before returning home, he recouped some of the slow boat's tedious expenses by winning a hurdle race worth 39 sovereigns. Back in Ireland after two unsuccessful runs he caused a sharp vibration in Irish circles by winning the Irish Champion Chase at Leopardstown in April. Perceiving seeds of greatness in Manifesto's gawky, unfurnished frame, Mr Dyas sagely resolved to give him every chance to develop. Nothing is better for a large young horse than time, and wise the trainers who allow it. But even Job may have thought Mr Dyas' patience excessive, for Manifesto ran only twice as a five-year-old, winning a little race at Derby, and again only twice the following year when he gained a momentous and totally unexpected victory in the valuable Lancashire Chase. At six he was finally judged ripe for his first visit to Aintree, which course, under the linked auspices of Mr Topham and a Mr Gladstone (*not* the politician off duty) had at last become very much as we know it today: all grass with an inside running rail and regulation furze fences. The fences were, however, toweringly and terrifyingly upright and so they remained for half a century until the National Hunt Committee decided there had been too many falls and, advised by the then Inspector of Courses, Brigadier Tony Teacher, instructed Tophams to slope them outwards to prevent horses getting under them. A simple, if tardy solution to the swift decline of the National was thus easily reached, and from that date, and injected with outside money, the National ceased to die.

His Lancashire Chase victory had forced Manifesto up in the handicap and his allotment of 11 st. 3 lb. was excessive for a relatively inexperienced young horse. Nevertheless, with Terry Kavanagh in the saddle, he attracted some attention at 100–8 and ran an excellent race, making much of the running until tiring and finishing fourth to the Widgers' Wild Man From Borneo. His only other outing that season was curiously in a two mile National Hunt flat race. He finished a close-up fourth.

His bid for the 1896 National was short, brutish and nasty: he overturned at the very first fence, bringing Redhill down over him, and apart from walking over for a little 'chase at Manchester, he didn't reappear that season. No one could say he was being over-worked and the following year Mr Dyas decided that the time had come for Manifesto to race in earnest. He was sent to the Eversleigh stable of Willie Macauliffe and for the first time in his life, put in an appearance before Christmas. It was in quite a valuable 'chase at Nottingham but, carrying 12 st. 7 lb., he ran as if he failed to carry stable optimism: he started unquoted and finished unplaced. Mr Dyas however was by no means despondent and with cheeky disdain for the authorities made no secret of his hopes for Manifesto in the National. He fancied too his other runner Gentle Ida, a slashing great mare who had won the 1895 Lancashire Chase. By some accounts he preferred the mare but as she is not quoted in any ante-post list and as Mr Dyas' convictions were usually conveyed to and closely mirrored in the market, this seems to be an unlikely tale.

It is true that he told Tom Vigors, a well-known Anglo-Irish agent (whose name

continues in the same trade today) that one of his was sure to win and that he would accept £5,000 for the pair. Although no taker could be found the public thought this confidence infectious and Manifesto's price shortened steadily.

The Grand National was now without question a great sporting event and racing correspondents arrived in Liverpool days in advance to report the latest progress of the runners. On 22 March, *Evening News* readers learned – for the sum of a halfpenny – that the original ante-post favourite Wild Man From Borneo had recovered from his slight mishap and – proof of his well-being – had done a rattling good gallop of 4½ miles 'across the flat'. Cathal, the new favourite, was led 3 miles at 'a slapping pace' while Mr Dyas' pair contented themselves with a mere 2½ miles. The days of long gallops are long over and no one can deny that this is because our horses are more frail. Tom Dreaper, when reflecting on his long training life, used to say, 'I'm getting progressively easier on my horses'. They stayed out for half an hour. Peter Cazalet used to have his string out for only 40 minutes, cantering twice up a two furlong slope. Leading Lambourn N.H. trainers, like 1986–87 champion Nicky Henderson, currently have their horses out for about an hour. To gallop a National contender 2½ miles – let alone 4½ miles – on the day before the race would, in the opinion of any competent modern trainer, leave the race on the gallops and a herring in the box. When horses were the sole means of transportation, when labourers jogged in traps and gipsies moved in caravans, horses were so commonplace that only the very best were regarded. The rest were no more than undergraduates' bicycles, and were treated not so much cruelly as with disdain. There were plenty more around, and if the brute didn't stand up to a few 4-mile gallops a week he usually wasn't up to racing, was he?

They were different then. Manifesto's appearance evoked much enthusiasm and his myriad Irish supporters threw out talk of defeat like waste paper. The narrow Lincoln victory of the Navan-born Winkfields' Pride with whom Manifesto had been expensively coupled threatened several bookmakers with possible bankruptcy and his odds contracted dramatically. The English press, however, while allowing him to be one of the fastest 'chasers in training, questioned his ability to last home and preferred Cathal.

On the eve of the race Mr Topham announced an innovation. For the first time each of the 28 runners would be provided with a white quarter-sheet, bound in scarlet and with their names embroidered across the corner. This was an Australian custom recently introduced to England by Sir Blundle Maple for his own horses and the executive's enterprise in adopting it generally and officially was widely praised.

The morning of the 26th crept out of the east under sullen pewter skies but later the sun popped out making 'the raindrops sparkle like dew on grass and hedge under an Italian sky', as the *Liverpool Courier* wrote with the unlikely lyricism of a hopeful poet getting something better than a rope of clichés past the dull minds and heavy hands of the sub-editors. Lord Derby brought a huge house-party over from Knowsley, adding a bevy of sartorial elegance to a scene already petalled and bejewelled by a drift of elegant ladies hemming the grandstand's lower steps. Steeplechasing had scaled the greasy slopes of social acceptability.

The artist, Bavarian Emil Adam (1843–1924) reputedly considered steeplechasers 'big, ugly and common' until he saw Manifesto! The then Duke of Westminster commented 'Emil Adam is the only artist . . . to put on canvas the thoroughbred as he really is.' Most photographs like the one below portray Manifesto less flatteringly . . .

There was a last minute sensation. Mr Dyas withdrew Gentle Ida and announced that Terry Kavanagh would ride Manifesto, now firm favourite at 6–1.

After jumping a preliminary hurdle, a sensible old custom allowing the horses to limber up and the crowd to measure their prowess, the field paraded and were shortly despatched without incident. Timon made the running from Manifesto and the pair galloped in this order round the first circuit. The previous year's winner The Soarer slithered over at Valentines second time round and at this stage Wild Man From Borneo could be seen steadily losing his position. At the second last obstacle Timon, utterly exhausted, crumpled up on landing, leaving Manifesto in a clear lead with the only conceivable dangers Cathal, Filbert and Ford of Fyne lurking behind him. Cathal fell heavily at the last and lay for dead (he had in fact suffered only the minor inconvenience of swallowing his tongue) and Manifesto strolled home by 20 lengths.

It was a smashing performance and the vast crowd gave him an enthusiastic reception. On the strength of it he was made 3–1 favourite to win a second Lancashire Chase (at £1,725 worth only £250 less than the National), but Manifesto found the fences small fry after Aintree. Treating one in far too cavalier a fashion, he tangled in its top and toppled over. He then made a rare journey into Southern England, and handsomely redeemed his name in Sandown's 3½-mile Grand International. Carrying 12 st. 5 lb. and starting 15–8 favourite he came right away from a good field that included Ford of Fyne and the maddeningly named Wild Man From Borneo.

Next year – as was the custom with most National candidates of his day – he didn't appear till February when he gave proof of his marvellous versatility by winning a 2-mile 'chase at Gatwick with 12 st. 10 lb. aboard conceding 37 lb. to the second. Before making his next appearance in a National Hunt Flat race at the Suffolk and Berkshire Meeting he was sold for a sum in the region of £4,000. His new owner, Mr Bulteel, whose son would become Sir John Crocker Bulteel and Clerk of the Course at Ascot, Aintree and elsewhere, had abandoned the Devon squiredom into which he had been born and had come up to London to try his luck on the Stock Exchange. The gamble paid off and he made a small fortune out of South African stock, some of which he decided to sink in the desperate hunt for a National winner. Alas for such hopes: a week before the big day one of the lads in Manifesto's new stable, managed jointly by Willie Moore and John Collins, inadvertently left his box door open. Entranced by his unexpected freedom Manifesto gaily essayed the gate out of the stable yard but, finding the top bar less accommodating than his accustomed birch fences, turned poll over frog and severely bruised his fetlock. The appalled lad slunk out of the stables with the eyerolling speed of a threatened whippet, and dreading that the label 'The Boy Who Let Manifesto Out' would besmirch him for ever, worked thereafter under an assumed name.

Manifesto could not run again till the following January when on the last day of the month he failed to carry the burden of nearly 13 st. into a place in a 2½-mile hurdle race at Gatwick. Ten days later he ran in another hurdle race at Sandown and this time, with 12 st. 7 lb. up, finished a good second. Then winter's talons froze life out of steeplechasing and with only a week to go racing at Aintree seemed doomed. Muffled travellers came huddled from the north with reports of 12 degrees of frost in Lincolnshire, of roads across Yorkshire choked with snow. Some Clerks of Courses never happily face the weather's facts, and their view of racing's prospects as an inducement to patrons to attend, often verges on the fictional. Sometimes when freezing fog hangs thick across ground hard as tarmac and twice as lumpy, when only in the Clerk's office does the thermometer read above 0°C, still rises the maddening parrot-cry: 'Racing is certain. Racing is certain!' How damned those Clerks with trainers' curses when after a long journey, racing is cancelled. Mr Topham, however, was telling the truth when on the 22nd he optimistically telegraphed that racing was on. The depressed market sprang to life and a feature of it was a mammoth punt on Gentle Ida. Mr Dyas had sold her to Horatio 'John Bull' Bottomley but she was still in his yard and he was adamant that no horse – Manifesto included – could possibly give her a stone. Six to one Gentle Ida was snapped up within hours of the market reopening and by the 24th no better than 4–1 was available. Manifesto, Drogheda and Ambush II were other popular orders around the 8–1 mark, but when word flew round about Manifesto's magnificent appearance thousands of new supporters rushed to back him. Despite his 12 st. 7 lb. (only once before carried successfully by Cloister in 1893) he ended up second favourite at 5–1. As a precaution against a return of savage frost, hay had been spread over the take-offs and landings and this nearly brought tragedy to the race.

The 19 runners filed on to the course and a shiver of anticipation flickered through the tightly packed stands. The early stages of the race passed without incident but as the field landed over the Canal Turn, Manifesto vanished abruptly from view. He had slipped on some hay wickedly left lying on the ground and, according to his new pilot George Williamson, came right down. 'I saw one of his legs sticking straight up over my head . . . the toe of my boot was on the ground and both irons were gone. I left everything to the horse and he recovered himself.' Williamson added laconically '. . . and I picked up the reins and went on'. Hardly had the crowd recovered their breath when Gentle Ida completely misjudged Valentines and crashed heavily to the floor, and only minutes later the good French mare Pistache dived through The Chair. She was leading at the time so the whole field galloped over her sporting owner-rider, the Comte de Geloes, while the crowd gaped in frozen horror. Astonishingly the Count escaped not only death but even minor injury and watched the remainder of the race on his feet.

George Williamson was biding his time on Manifesto but soon after Valentine's he decided to make a move. He hit the front shortly before the home turn and as he did so the cheering started. With every stride it swelled like a stormy sea and as Manifesto flipped effortlessly over the last and came home an easy 5-lengths winner from Ford of Fyne, it reached a deafening crescendo, which didn't drift away until after the 'Winner all right' signal had been hoisted. The Press outstripped themselves coursing like long dogs to snatch up new superlatives with which to deck this magnificent performance, the greatest, all reckoned, in the history of the race, surpassing even that of Cloister.

Manifesto was now 11 and with two Grand Nationals behind him might reasonably be supposed to have shown his best. But this was far from the case.

Back he came next year and humping the wicked load of 12 st. 13 lb., he so nearly achieved the historic treble. Before this attempt his first race of the season was delayed until the beginning of March: starting at odds on, he was beaten 5 lengths at level weights by Hidden Mystery. This good young horse by the strangely named Ascetic (who must after all have enjoyed some bodily gratifications to have sired him) belonged to the well-known racing family of Nugents. He was in the National and as a result was promoted favourite; the other public fancy, apart from Manifesto, was the Prince of Wales' Ambush II, a short-legged, deep-bodied six-year-old bought in Kildare for £500 and then trained at Eyrefield Lodge on the Curragh officially by Algy Anthony but in fact by Dan McNally.

It was announced that the popular Prince would stay with Lord Derby at Knowsley for the meeting: he had not attended since Hettie and Magic had unsuccessfully represented him in 1889. The Boer War was at its height and the Prince delayed his departure until the last minute in order to inspect Paget's Horse and the Sharpshooters battalion of the Imperial Yeomanry at Chelsea Barracks, before they sailed for South Africa. He was deputizing for his mother, then on her controversial visit to Dublin. Once the parade was over he sped to Euston, caught the 2.15 p.m train and arrived at Knowsley in time to dress for dinner. For Royalty, duties at one end of the realm and pleasure at the other had suddenly become possible in the space of hours rather than days, and the busy-ness of their lives, as of everyone else's, instantly expanded to fill the gaps which progress had won from time.

The Prince of Wales made a colourful and popular contrast with his solitary widow's-weeded mother. He kept mistresses, he snitched wives off husbands, loved gambling, ran up debts and opened up the Royal set to Jewish bankers who helped to finance his arrangements.

There was frost overnight but not enough to imperil racing and by mid-morning the sun was shining brightly. The combined attractions of Manifesto and the Prince had drawn a record crowd and Mr Topham, with his usual sense of showmanship had risen to the occasion. The Irish flag, *The Times* noted, flew proudly in honour of Ambush II and just before the race it was announced that the handsome white quarter-sheets made specially for each horse were a present to their owners. Ambush's was a particularly splendid affair edged with the scarlet, purple and black of the Royal colours and embroidered with not just His Royal Highness' cypher, but with the Prince of Wales' feathers, and a rose and a thistle and a shamrock.

The nineteen runners were despatched without delay and with the unimportant exception of Covert Hack, they were all standing after one circuit. Too often the innocent at Aintree are felled by riderless incompetents and at the water jump in front of the stands Covert Hack careered across the favourite, Hidden Mystery, barged into him and knocked him over. The other two public fancies were still galloping well, and turning for home Ambush II seized the lead from Barsac. Meanwhile Manifesto was making ground steadily and when he drew alongside at the second last a battle royal commenced. Stride for stride these two gallant horses bore down on the last and few of the hysterically cheering crowd knew which they really wanted to win, the green youngster owned by their Prince or the

battlescarred 12-year-old struggling heroically under his monstrous weight. As often happens, youth prevailed: on the flat Manifesto could struggle no longer and Ambush II forged triumphantly ahead to win by 4 lengths, and Barsac, coming again with a late run, overhauled the exhausted Manifesto and stole his rightful second place.

The scenes that then broke out were unbelievable. In an age governed by the strictest etiquette all formality went by the board. Led by wild whoops of the crazed, incoherent Irish, pandemonium exploded like shrapnel. 'The scene after Persimmon's Derby was nothing to that of yesterday . . . yet there were tears in men's eyes at the thought of the defeat of Manifesto. The Prince and his horse alike were mobbed and slapped on the back and an Irish dealer cried "Begorra', we'll beat the Boers as aisy".'

And still Manifesto was not done with. Incredibly this iron-legged old Trojan was to run in three more Nationals, never carrying less than 12 st. Twice he was third and in 1904, now aged 16 and ridden by Ernie Piggott, he made his farewell appearance. He was very much the Grand Old Man of 'chasing and treated as such. Crowds gathered round when he appeared for his early morning work to marvel at his youthful appearance and astonishingly clean legs. The famous flat jockey 'Morny' Cannon begged to be allowed just to hop up on his back and the privilege was granted. Manifesto went down to the post with his old rival Ambush II, who at a mere 10 years old, was also making his farewell appearance. Ambush this time failed to negotiate the particularly severe course, but it need hardly be said that Manifesto, as usual, did. Sadly, magnificently though, he finished last of the six to stand up behind the New Zealand giant Moifaa who bulldozed great gaps through the normally unyielding fences and won very easily.

Fittingly it was to Liverpool that Manifesto came one grey November afternoon in 1904, to sing his weary swan-song. After finishing a very remote fourth in the Valentine Chase he was at last retired, leaving a generation of sportsmen to declare into their dotage that there was never a peer to the 'Magnificent Manifesto!'

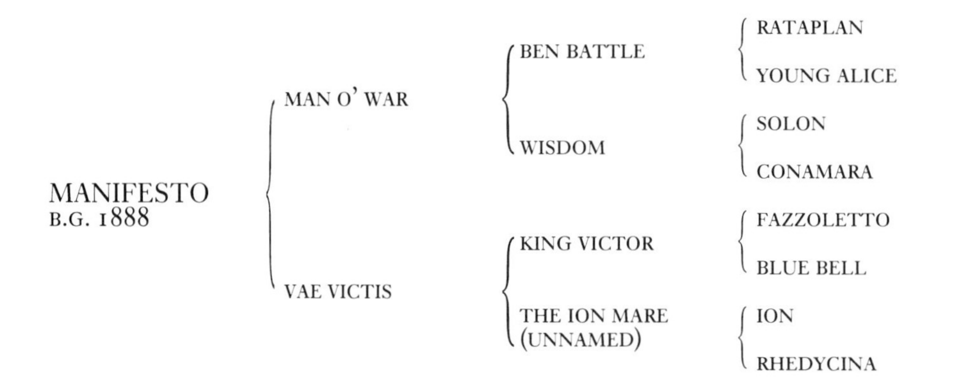

DATE	COURSE	RACE	DISTANCE	VALUE	WEIGHT	JOCKEY	PRICE	PLACE
Season 1891–92								
Jan 26	Manchester	Pendleton Ch	2m 1f	£39	10.6	Daniels	unq	fell
Feb 26	Manchester	M'dn H	2m	£49	10.7	T. Kavanagh	8/1	won
Mar 19	Derby Hunt	N.H. Juvenile Ch	2m 4f	£348	10.12	A. Skelton	6/1	4th
Apr 19	Manchester	Eastern H'cp Ch	2m	£239	10.7	Baily	unq	3rd
Apr 30	Leopardstown	Irish Champion Ch	2m 4f	£491	10.12	Baily	7/2	won
Season 1892–93								
Mar 15	Derby	Shipley Hall H'cp Ch	2m	£137	11.9	T. Kavanagh	3/1	won
Season 1893–94								
Dec 5	Gatwick	Winter Ch	2m	£162	11.2	J. Walsh	10/1	unpl
Mar 26	Manchester	Lancashire Ch	3m 4f	£2,170	11.3	T. Kavanagh	unq	won
Apr 21	Sandown	Criterion Ch	2m	£255	11.0	T. Kavanagh	5/1	2nd
Season 1894–95								
Mar 29	Liverpool	Grand National	4m 856 yds	£1,975	11.2	T. Kavanagh	100/8	4th
Apr 16	Manchester	N.H. Flat Race	2m	£173	12.6	Capt Woolmer	10/1	4th
Season 1895–96								
Mar 27	Liverpool	Grand National	4m 856 yds	£1,975	11.4	Gourley	100/7	fell
Apr 6	Manchester	Paddock Ch	2m	£173	11.9	Gourley		w.o.
Season 1896–97								
Dec 21	Nottingham	Gt Midland H'cp Ch	2m	£405	12.7	W. Hoystud	unq	unpl
Mar 25	Liverpool	Grand National	4m 856 yds	£1,975	11.3	T. Kavanagh	6/1f	won
Apr 19	Manchester	Lancashire Ch	3m 4f	£1,725	12.7	T. Kavanagh	3/1f	fell
May 1	Sandown	Grand International Ch	3m 4f	£412	12.5	G. Williamson	15/8f	won

DATE	COURSE	RACE	DISTANCE	VALUE	WEIGHT	JOCKEY	PRICE	PLACE
Season 1897–98								
Feb 2	Gatwick	Holmwood H'cp Ch	2m	£172	12.10	G. Williamson	4/1	won
Mar 11	Kempton	Suffolk & Berks Welter Flat Race	2m	£185	11.10	Mr Grenfell	6/1	2nd
Season 1898–99								
Jan 31	Gatwick	Gorse H'cp H	2m 4f	£87	12.13	G. Williamson	6/1	unpl
Feb 10	Sandown	Cardinal H'cp H	3m 2f	£92	12.7	G. Williamson	5/2	2nd
Mar 24	Liverpool	Grand National	4m 856 yds	£1,975	12.7	G. Williamson	5/1	won
Apr 3	Manchester	Lancashire H'cp Ch	3m 4f	£1,725	12.12	G. Williamson	13/2	fell
Apr 22	Sandown	Grand International H'cp Ch	3m 4f	£412	13.7	Mr Davies	5/2f	unpl
Season 1899–1900								
Mar 7	Hurst Park	Richmond Ch	3m	£87	12.5	G. Williamson	4/1f	2nd
Mar 30	Liverpool	Grand National	4m 856 yds	£1,975	12.13	G. Williamson	6/1	3rd
Apr 16	Manchester	Lancashire Ch	3m 4f	£1,725	12.13	Gourley	7/1	unpl
Season 1901–02								
Mar 20	Liverpool	Grand National	4m 856 yds	£2,000	12.8	E. Piggott	100/6	3rd
Mar 31	Manchester	Lancashire Ch	3m 4f	£1,725	12.7	E. Piggott	100/7	unpl
Season 1902–03								
Nov 6	Liverpool	Grand Sefton H'cp Ch	3m	£412	12.12	E. Piggott	10/1	2nd
Nov 29	Kempton	Richmond Ch	3m	£93	11.10	E. Piggott	1/2f	2nd
Dec 31	Hurst Park	Hurst Ch	3m	£100	10.12	E. Piggott	5/2	2nd
Mar 27	Liverpool	Grand National	4m 856 yds	£2,000	12.3	G. Williamson	25/1	3rd
Season 1903–04								
Mar 25	Liverpool	Grand National	4m 856 yds	£2,000	12.1	E. Piggott	20/1	unpl
Season 1904–05								
Nov 11	Liverpool	Valentine Ch	2m 6f	£123	11.7	F. Hartigan	6/1	unpl

FOUR

Easter Hero

THE 1920S; LLOYD GEORGE FALLS; RAMSAY MACDONALD HEADS THE FIRST LABOUR GOVERNMENT; GIRLS BOB THEIR HAIR – AND GET THE VOTE; SOUTHERN IRELAND AT LAST BECOMES INDEPENDENT; THE GENERAL STRIKE PARALYSES THE COUNTRY; AND THE GREAT DEPRESSION BRINGS UNEMPLOYMENT, STARVATION, DEATH AND THE HARD CORE OF SOCIALISM.

The stability which steeplechasing had laboriously achieved by the eve of the Great War collapsed during it and disintegrated in its aftermath. Enthusiasm certainly bubbled again in the 'Twenties' general effervescence, but the sport's integrity had never fallen so flat. Prize money was minimal and rich owners with flat-sized strings non-existent. Gambling was an economic necessity and where men *must* gamble with racehorses honesty snivels outside in the cold. 'Fiddling' became not only the rule rather than the exception, but everyone could see its blatancy. Old Stewards, it was widely said, told younger ones not to haul up non-triers but to watch, wait and next time back them. The dishonesty which usually crawls in a war's slimy wake was rampant. And the sport stank.

During the 1920s however, three largely complementary events helped to remedy the sickness. They were, first, the founding in 1924 of the Cheltenham Gold Cup, a level-weight classic at last providing a true championship for the best staying 'chasers; secondly, the advent of the Big Owners – at first American, but soon followed by wealthy British businessmen and aristocrats; and thirdly, the

appearance of a rakishly handsome, supremely elegant chestnut horse called Easter Hero, in whom the other two parts of steeplechasing's recovery were fused. His exuberant style of racing and sensation-strewn career were to illuminate 'chasing with a far wider spread of glamour. As the motor-car had succeeded the carriage, and the plane was starting to outstrip the car, Easter Hero became the first of the new-type 'chasers. And as usual with new forms of motion, his design – fleet and all quality – was regarded by a small dodder of reactionaries with dark scepticism.

Easter Hero was born four miles from Greenogue, Co. Dublin, where the great Tom Dreaper 40 years on was to train the champion Arkle. He had another link with Arkle too as we pass from history into the times of living men: his sire, My Prince, became Arkle's maternal great-grandsire. He was bred by an Irish farmer, known locally as 'Old Larry' King, a good judge who bred a number of horses, most of which he also trained and rode. Several, like Easter Hero were cleverly named after the Irish Rebellion and the ensuing Troubles: Easter Hero's dam was Easter Week and his uncle, Civil War, won the Irish Grand National.

As with most leading lights in men and horses Easter Hero took time to glow, and after Larry King had run him once unplaced at Baldoyle, he sold him cheaply to a Mr Bartholomew. In the view of one veteran Irish trainer, Mr Bartholomew, an Englishman, was 'a bit of a chancer'. He owned Easter Hero for about 18 months till he apparently went broke and had to sell up. During that time Easter Hero ran eight times. On three occasions he fell and once made such a blunder that he had to be pulled up. In between these spills however he showed ability: he won a good race at Manchester and was second at Sandown. These performances allied to his handsome looks made that shrewd judge Frank Barbour find him an excellent buy at a mere £500, despite his erratic jumping. Barbour was right in thinking this could be cured: the Hero's cavalier fencing tempered by experience was to prove a major weapon in his armoury and one of the keys to his crowd-appeal.

Like Desert Orchid sixty years on, Easter Hero at home was headstrong. When working he always ran away. Danny Morgan, who went on years later to train Gold Cup winner Roddy Owen, rode Easter Hero a lot. He discovered that the only way to stop him was to drop the reins, when he'd instantly pull up, turn round, and trot back to where his trainer waited by the gallops-side, hunched on his hack.

Frank Barbour was a very rich and endearingly eccentric linen-thread manufacturer from the north of Ireland. Once, at his own point-to-point when Master of the Westmeath, he fell off competing in his Members Race. Instead of going back to the paddock, he walked on to the road, thumbed a lift into Mullingar in a pony-and-trap, and caught a train to Dublin. There, still in his hunting clothes and without any luggage, he got on a boat and sailed off to New York for a short visit.

Barbour owned a huge place at Trimblestown, the front door of which was flanked by two huge mysterious barrels, which years later were discovered to be concealing the entrance into his secret cellars. Behind the house he had laid out magnificent gallops interspersed with replicas of a variety of fences. His steel and

vermilion colours were widely respected in England. As Paddy Sleator did later this century in Warwickshire, he would swoop over with a string of horses, then base himself on a pub in Tarporley and raid all the big English 'chases at the Autumn and Spring Liverpool Meetings and the National Hunt meeting at Cheltenham. He won the 1926 Cheltenham Gold Cup with Koko, one of Easter Hero's great rivals.

He wrought a remarkable improvement in Easter Hero's jumping: in his remaining races that season the horse was only once out of the first two. His five victories included good 'chases at Kempton and Manchester and the inaugural race for the Molyneux Steeplechase, a 2¼-mile handicap at the Liverpool Autumn Meeting. English racing correspondents were impressed: 'I have never seen a horse finish so fresh at Aintree', marvelled well-named 'Philippos' in *Country Life*.

But their admiration was qualified. They were accustomed to 'chasers built to carry 15 st. across Leicestershire and eyed Easter Hero's elegant frame askance; 'he is full of quality but rather lacking in substance', wrote one doubtfully. Another wondered 'where he finds all his powers of jumping and endurance'. Certainly no one considered the flamboyant newcomer as a likely Gold Cup or National prospect. Nor did they revise their ideas when (after a preliminary race at home in Ireland), he won the 2½-mile Becher Chase at Liverpool in November with the utmost ease, although most subscribed to 'Philippos'' view that 'he must be one of the handsomest horses ever to cross a fence'. He next gave the lie to those who said that he lacked the substance to carry big weights by winning a good handicap at Kempton under 12 st. 7 lb. But his next race really set the cocks crowing. On March 3rd, just a fortnight before the opening of the National Hunt Festival, he was saddled for the 3½-mile Coventry Chase at Kempton – an acknowledged Gold Cup trial – and, carrying 12 st. 7 lb. won by a neck and 5 lengths from Spear O'War and The Coyote, to whom he was conceding 29 lb. and 8 lb. respectively. The Ancils' National hope Carfax was fourth.

By suddenly proving he could stay the extra mile, Easter Hero became a serious contender for the Gold Cup. He had an alternative engagement at Cheltenham in the National Hunt Handicap Chase. He ran in neither. On the eve of the Gold Cup, without a heralding whisper, it was announced that he had been sold and would wait for the National. The news caused a sensation. Neither buyer nor price was disclosed and rumours ran yapping round like dogs. The staggering sum of £10,000 was suggested. One correspondent, irritated by the mystery, sourly remarked that he *could* reveal it was not the King of Afghanistan, the horse-loving potentate of enormous wealth then on his much-publicized visit to England. After the shouting had died down, the buyer turned out to be Captain Lowenstein, a Belgian financier, who had come into racing, aided by Captain Cyril Harty (the former Irish Army showjumper) via the Leicestershire hunting field. The price was the astronomical one of £7,000 plus a contingency of £3,000 should he win the National. This figure, the equivalent of £300,000 in the late 1980s, was all the more astonishing against a background of stable lads then earning £2 a week.

The qualities which made Easter Hero such a marvellous ambassador for widening the appeal of 'chasing were now apparent: not only was he beautiful to look at, intensely exciting to watch and a prolific winner of races but he had the knack of igniting publicity. He believed in doing the unexpected with a sudden clash of cymbals.

Aintree 1928 approached surrounded by even more excitement than usual. King Amanullah of Afghanistan and his lovely queen Suriya were attending and had booked an entire liner on Merseyside for their stay. Large numbers of Americans had chartered boats across the Atlantic to support their hope, Billy Barton. Croydon airport made history by arranging five chartered flights to the course and aided the *Evening News* to achieve an unprecedented feat of newspaper distribution: the sporting edition, rushed to the airport by 10.30 a.m. was being sold on the course at midday.

The weather quite failed to rise to the occasion: 'it rained, it blew, it hailed, it snew'. People made awful jokes about Raintree and the Grand Splashional. Queen Suriya braved the elements in a heavy sable coat and a tiny blue hat trimmed with an osprey feather. One of her retinue understandably confused by the mystique of English racing 'gear', blundered out on that mad March day in a grey top-hat. A fashion correspondent noticed with approval that most of the ladies (anticipating Courrèges and the Kings Road by 40 years) wore knee-high boots.

A last minute run on Master Billie brought him down to 5–1 favouritism, the ante-post favourite Trump Card was 11–2 and after that they went 10–1 Amber Wave, 100–7 jointly Easter Hero and last year's winner Sprig. The Hon. George Lambton summed up the cognoscenti's view of Easter Hero's chance: 'He is beautifully balanced and of great quality. He has proved himself to be a great horse and he has won over Liverpool. Yet he does not quite fill my eye as a National horse and I think he may fail in the last half-mile.' Certainly he was the most spectacular horse to grace Liverpool for years and everyone was agog to see how he would acquit himself. They had their spectacle but it was not one they had anticipated.

After three false starts the 42 strong field were despatched and, predictably, Easter Hero went straight into the lead and was soon bowling along, flicking over the towering fences in an insolent fashion to which they were not accustomed. All went well until he reached the Canal Turn, which in those days was an open ditch. This he completely misjudged, and taking off outside the wings, landed slap, crunch, grunt on the top. There he struggled, gasping and stuck. Within seconds there was a gigantic pile-up. To onlookers it seemed that horses and riders were being mown down by machine guns. Thirty-nine years later the desperate carnage was to be repeated. Now only nine runners emerged to continue the race. By the time the last fence was reached, these had been reduced to two: the American hope Billy Barton and a 66–1 outsider, the tubed Tipperary Tim.

Slowly the pair approached the last. Then a great moan went up: Billy Barton had capsized. He was swiftly remounted but by this time Tipperary Tim and his amateur pilot Mr Billy Dutton were home to record one of the race's most sensational victories until Foinavon, similarly profiting from others' mass misfortune, won in much the same way in 1967. The ditch, after Easter Hero's blunder, was removed from the fence . . .

Easter Hero brings down three-quarters of the field at the Canal Turn in the 1928 National. Reproduced from County Life *April 7, 1928.*

Mr Dutton, not long down from Cambridge, was articled to his uncle, a Cheshire solicitor, but his memorable victory disinclined him to persevere with the legal profession. Soon afterwards he took up training with marked success in every field. He won the 1956 Gold Cup with Limber Hill, and a host of sprints on the flat notably with Pappa Fourway.

Easter Hero was not done with sensation that year, but this time it was a tragic one. In July his new owner, Capt. Lowenstein was flying back to Brussels when, over the North Sea, he dramatically vanished. It was presumed he had fallen out of the aircraft, but no trace of the Belgian financier was ever found, and after six months his executors put his horses up for sale. Sixty years later the mystery remains unsolved. Murder? Suicide? A convenient escape? Nobody breathes a word.

Steeplechasing had now really seized the imagination of American sportsmen. One of the many American visitors to the 1928 Grand National, told a reporter 'Your style of steeplechasing is quite a new game to us. We like it tremendously. It has caught on as has nothing else English since the America's Cup.' And it was a young and then unknown American who now entered Easter Hero's life.

Easter Hero and another of the late Capt. Lowenstein's horses Maquelonne were bought for £11,000 by the American millionaire Mr 'Jock' Whitney. After the sale Easter Hero was transferred to Jack Anthony's yard at Letcombe in Berkshire and began his preparation for the 1929 Gold Cup and National. It was an unusual one, for in the months before Christmas he ran in four 2-mile hurdle races. On each occasion he was partnered by George Duller, perhaps the greatest hurdle jockey ever, started at odds on, and won cantering by up to 20 lengths.

But he had jumped not one fence in public that season till he arrived at Cheltenham for the Gold Cup on 12 March. In fact it had been a particularly bitter winter. There was no racing for a month, and racing correspondents had two main topics to fill their columns.

Lord Dewar propounded to his fellow peers the advantages of the new bill to legalize the Tote. It would, he said, promote order and comfort on racecourses – ladies would be encouraged to attend – and premiums to breeders would promote bloodstock, as in France. There the Pari-Mutuel enabled courses to provide big stakes to be run for small forfeits and the cost of keeping a racehorse was a third of the British level. Lord Dewar's arguments 60 years ago remain as valid as ever today, but the boons of a Tote monopoly as in France and America – where losing bets boost racing, not the bookies' pockets – are still denied to poor Britain.

The new Totalisator machine was tried out at the North Warwickshire point-to-point meeting on March 19th, and shortly afterwards was used at Hurst Park. Soon 51 of the 67 courses considered suitable for permanent buildings were clamouring for it. There were then two units only: 2s. 6d. and 10s. (12½p and 50p respectively) 10 per cent was deducted from the pool, of which three per cent went to the course and seven per cent to the Betting Board Control who paid the tax.

Mr Churchill's Betting Tax had proved a dismal failure. Bookmakers, by amalgamating themselves and their clients into 'Totes', could evade not only their tax, but also their licence. Mr Churchill was urged to withdraw his ill-conceived Bill.

The new Gold Cup had not yet built up enormous interest. Its value was still less than either the Champion Hurdle or the National Hunt Chase, and the whole

Easter Hero, going out to win the Gold Cup (then worth £670) ridden by T. Cullinan. It was Easter Hero's second Gold Cup victory. Installed favourite for the Grand National, he went lame.

meeting was considered inferior (at any rate socially) to Sandown's Grand Military Meeting. In fact this year's field was the best to date. The 10 runners included Koko (a previous winner and Easter Hero's former stable companion), Grakle and Bright's Boy, although last year's winner Patron Saint had unfortunately gone wrong.

Easter Hero was to have the priceless assistance of F. B. Rees, one of the very best and certainly the most elegant jockey of his age, of whom it was said that he even fell off gracefully. The morning papers frothed over the feat of a 20-year-old Australian. D. Bradman had made 109 not out in a record fifth wicket stand against England in the last Test. At home bad weather gripped the Cotswolds and the Cheltenham meeting was postponed a week.

In the race Easter Hero seized the lead after 50 yards and was allowed to stride on. In contrast, Koko, another front-runner, was restrained, which, as often happens with a fine, free horse, totally confused him. After several uncharacteristic muddled errors, he finally crashed at the water. Passing the stands on the first circuit Easter Hero was a staggering 30 lengths in front and although Grakle and Bright's Boy managed to close with him along the far side Rees was only giving him a breather. At the top of the hill he sent him on again and the increased pace was too much for Bright's Boy who fell at the third last, the plunging grave of so many Cheltenham hopes. Grakle gave chase vainly all the way down the hill but he

Easter Hero's 1928 Gold Cup pilot, F.B. Rees, in 1941. Rees and other Sussex horsemen formed their own Home Guard cavalry to defend Britain.

was never able to get on terms and Easter Hero coasted home unchallenged, quite assured by a damning 20 lengths.

Immediately he was declared an intended runner for the National for which he had been allotted top-weight of 12 st. 7 lb. The previous year's débâcle had induced Tophams to up the entry fee to £100 in the hope of pruning the field to a manageable size. It had the directly opposite effect. The increased forfeits swelled the first prize to the staggering sum of £13,000 (which was £2,000 more than the Derby) and the lure of such a prize which could obviously be won by hopeless scrubbers like Tipperary Tim, encouraged owners of anything to leave their rubbish in. A record field of 60 or so horses seemed likely to face the starter. Tremendous National interest leaped across the cold Atlantic. The Americans, spurred on by Billy Barton's bid last year, trooped over in greater force and noisy parties on the trans-Atlantic liners.

The day before the heavens opened. Heavy going and a huge field were scarcely propitious to the favourite, but it was hoped that his class would see him through and money continued to pour on him.

The morning of the 22nd broke fine. The morning papers carried the 'Cinderella' story of a 26-year-old miner's daughter called Jennie Lee who had romped home for Labour at the North Lanark by-election. But that day all roads led unpolitically to Aintree. Between 7 a.m. and 11 a.m. on the LMS line trains were departing at six minute intervals to the course. The approach roads were jammed with every sort of vehicle; limousines and noisy sportscars jostled with charabancs, pony-traps and natty tandems. Aeroplanes droned overhead and one man walked from London.

Newmarket trainer Tom Leader held what seemed a winning full-house in his hand: of his five runners Sprig, Grakle and Mount Etna were preferred to Gregalach and Sandy Hook.

As before, Easter Hero, ridden by Jack Moloney, set off in front on the first circuit. Playing to the gallery, he staged a particularly flamboyant leap at the water. He was still in front approaching the second last, but tiring visibly. It seemed as if George Lambton's prediction that the last half-mile would find him out was coming true. But, unknown to anyone in the stands, he had been handicapped since Valentines by a grotesquely twisted plate. He couldn't quicken when Gregalach, receiving 17 lb., swept by and went on to win by 6 lengths, thus recording the fifth Newmarket victory in the last seven years and the third for the Leader family – but not the one expected. Neither the winning owner, Mrs Gemmel, nor her husband were even present and their whereabouts was a mystery which the butler of their London house could not explain. Nor were the staff unequivocally delighted by the result. They had backed Mount Etna.

Of the 66 starters 56 had been felled to the ground and there were renewed cries for revising the conditions. One Jeremiah Socialist sold on the principle of levelling down suggested that the first prize should be reduced to £200. More practicable suggestions were that would-be runners must have been placed in a £500 race, or that the race should be turned into a condition 'chase with weights in a range of 11 st. 7 lb. to 12 st. The last measure would have ensured an élite field, but too small to provide the circuses the public wanted.

Messrs Tophams however, complacently pointed out – in the manner of County Councils over speed limits – that as there had been no serious accident yet, they were not disposed to make any alteration.

Easter Hero was given a long rest after his 1929 exertions. His preparation was different but again very light. He made his first appearance on Boxing Day in a little 'chase at Wolverhampton. His new partner was Tommy Cullinan, an ex-amateur who had been second in the 1928 National on Billy Barton. The pair started favourite at 30–100 and won by 15 lengths. He then went to Leicester for the 2-mile Wigston Chase for which he started 7–100 favourite and proceeded to thrill the crowd. 'Philippos' wrote of 'the astonishing speed of his jumping . . . making it all look so very simple. Everyone was delighted to watch so exhilarating a spectacle.'

But a young star, a potential rival was rising. The seven-year-old Gib had climbed rapidly to the top in the tough school of handicaps and on his last outing, under 12 st. 9 lb. at Lingfield, had given 6 lb. and a decisive beating to Gregalach, to record his seventh successive victory. He was not in the National so went to Cheltenham fully wound up, whereas Jack Anthony had Easter Hero's sights set on the infinitely richer Liverpool target. Moreover Gib would have the great advantage of Easter Hero's erstwhile partner F. B. Rees, known as Dick. Easter Hero was a year older, and he hadn't been asked a serious question this season till this one: had he deteriorated?

The problem was entrancing and the public flocked to Cheltenham for what they hoped would prove a ding-dong duel. Cheltenham's prestige had suddenly risen dramatically. It was now freely described as the Ascot of the 'chasing season and nothing further was said about it playing second fiddle to Sandown. Nor was

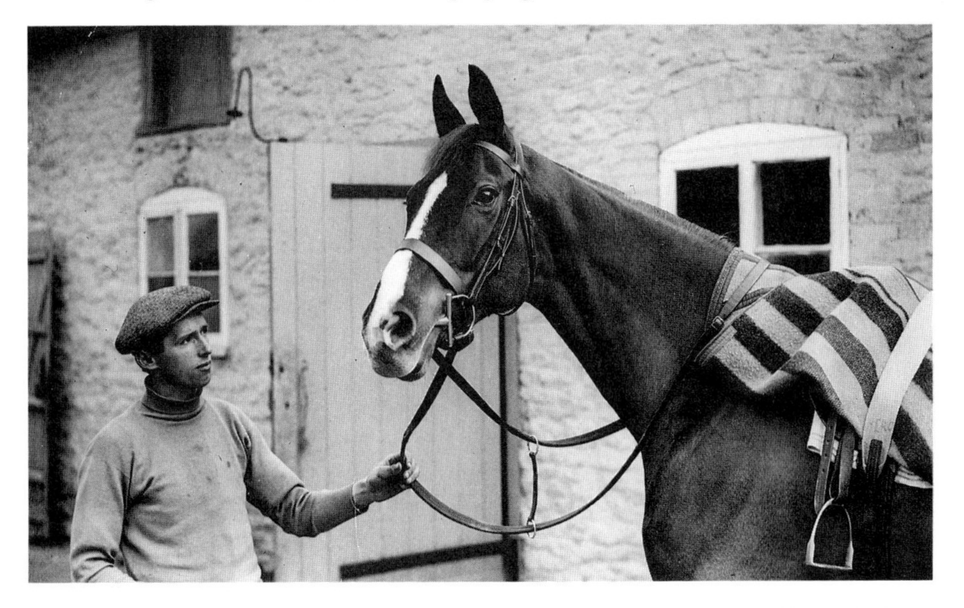

Easter Hero in Jack Anthony's yard at Letcombe Regis in the week before the 1931 Grand National in which he started favourite but got brought down. The type of bold head still sought by trainers nearly sixty years on.

there now any doubt about which was principal day although the National Hunt Chase ('the Amateurs Grand National') still offered the bigger prize.

The clash of champions had scared away all but two of the original entry, Donzelas and Grakle, and they too might just as well have stayed at home. The ring offered 8–11 Easter Hero, 13–8 Gib.

At flagfall Easter Hero dashed straight into the lead, and with his flair for the staggering, took the first fence by the roots. He repeated the astonishing blunder at the second. The crowd gasped, but Cullinan managed to steady him and he negotiated the third safely. After that he drew steadily ahead and by the end of a circuit was 10 lengths clear. All along the far side Gib gave chase: a couple of slight mistakes suggested that he was at full stretch, but as they began the turning descent for home Rees had driven him upsides his old ride. The pair rose together for the second last, but Gib struck it, reeled and came down, leaving Easter Hero to record his second successive 20-length victory. He was cheered from the last fence to the post and came in to a National type reception, which was repeated later that afternoon when Brown Tony completed a memorable double for Jack Anthony and Tommy Cullinan, by winning the Champion Hurdle.

Easter Hero was installed 5–1 favourite for the National for which he had again been given top weight of 12 st. 7 lb. Last year's winner Gregalach had gone up 10 lb. to 12 st. But disaster's hounds were on triumph's traces. Hardly had Easter Hero returned home when he went lame. The worst was feared and soon discovered. Heat and puffiness in a foreleg felt ominous. He had sprained a tendon. After a week of touch-and-go during which he had heat-treatment at the Cundells' Aston Tirrold establishment, he was withdrawn four days before the National. Immediately the Press declared that he would not have won in any case. Tommy Cullinan, left without a mount, came in for a chance ride on Shaun Goilin, and in a desperate finish, won by a head and 1½ lengths from Melleray's Belle and Sir Lindsay, giving him a magnificent riding treble.

The new decade, which had slunk in with slumps and was to get driven out by war, was under way as Easter Hero recovered from his injury. He began his 1930–31 campaign with Bob Everett replacing Cullinan as his jockey. They duly won the Penkridge Chase at Wolverhampton and the Wigston Chase at Leicester and on 28 January won a 2½-mile handicap 'chase at Sandown. But a month later, reunited with Rees, he was beaten a head by Desert Chief (receiving 23 lb.) at Lingfield. The public were stunned: he hadn't been beaten on a park course in six exciting years. It was planned to give the Gold Cup a miss this year in favour of the 2-mile Coventry Chase in which he was due to meet Captain Sassoon's flying mare West Indies, in what would have been a terrific contest. But it never materialized. The accursed weather stole away the entire meeting and only the National Hunt Chase re-opened in April.

For the National on 27 March Easter Hero again had top weight of 12 st. 7 lb. and again he started favourite at 5–1. Rees had the ride. He was knocked over at Becher's on the second circuit by Miss Dorothy Paget's Soldanum, but was not reckoned to have been going like a winner at the time.

The next day he came out again for the Champion Chase and at level weights only just managed to force a dead heat with a much inferior animal, Coup de

This stable portrait of Easter Hero taken four days before the 1931 Grand National shows the lads' uniform of boots and baggy breeches. Note the heavy wooden buckets.

Château. This was considered to be an irrefutable sign of decline and he was kindly and wisely retired forthwith. It is, though, hard to imagine a current National contender, trained for 4½ miles and having completed two-thirds of that most gruelling course being hauled out the next day to battle against fresh specialist 2-milers. Horses, like Britons before the comforting arrival of the featherbedding Welfare State, came tougher in those days.

Easter Hero was shipped across the Atlantic to retire to his owner's stud in Virginia when he lived on to the excellent age of 28. Steeplechasing's supporters on both sides of the sea for whom he had opened the windows on to a rising sport remembered him with gratitude. But they were not left long without an idol. His successor, although cast from a less glamorous mould, was to become, with the passing of years, more famous still and even better loved.

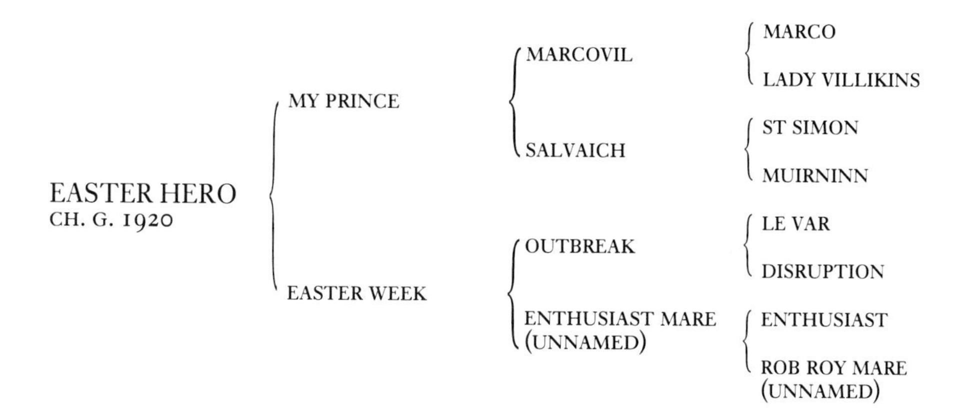

EASTER HERO CH. G. 1920	MY PRINCE	MARCOVIL	MARCO
			LADY VILLIKINS
		SALVAICH	ST SIMON
			MUIRNINN
	EASTER WEEK	OUTBREAK	LE VAR
			DISRUPTION
		ENTHUSIAST MARE (UNNAMED)	ENTHUSIAST
			ROB ROY MARE (UNNAMED)

DATE	COURSE	RACE	DISTANCE	VALUE	WEIGHT	JOCKEY	PRICE	PLACE
Season 1924–25								
Jan 1	Baldoyle	Killeston Plate	1m 4f	£83	10.5	S. Duffy	20/1	unpl
Feb 6	Manchester	Medlock Chase	2m	£100	10.11	S. Duffy	20/1	fell
Feb 20	Hurst Park	Novices Chase	2m	£162	10.11	S. Duffy	7/1	fell
Mar 7	Manchester	Ellesmere Chase	2m	£118	11.2	S. Duffy	4/1	won
Mar 10	Cheltenham	Cotswold Chase	2m	£415	11.10	S. Duffy	7/1	fell
Mar 19	Sandown	Novitiate Chase	2m	£163	10.11	S. Duffy	5/1	2nd
Apr 18	Fairyhouse	Irish G. National	3m 4f	£840	9.11	S. Duffy	8/1	unpl
Season 1925–26								
Feb 20	Leopardstown	Bray H'cp Ch	2m	£83	9.11	J. Hoylan	5/1	unpl
Season 1926–27								
July 15	Limerick	July Plate	2m	£46	10.4	Mr S. Dennis	7/1	p.u.
Aug 18	Mallow	Rakes of Mallow Ch	2m	£80	9.11	E. Foster	1/1f	2nd
Sept 2	Balinrobe	Mayo Plate	2m 2f	£88	10.0	E. Foster	4/6f	won
Sept 8	Dundalk	Ardee Plate	2m	£68	12.2	E. Foster	7/4	2nd
Sept 13	Mullingar	Stand Plate	2m	£83	10.11	J. Moylen	4/6f	won
Nov 12	Liverpool	Molyneux Chase	2m 2f	£415	10.0	P. Powell	5/1	won
Dec 28	Kempton	Gamecock H'cp Ch	2m 4f	£249	11.6	E. Foster	7/4f	won
Mar 4	Manchester	Waterloo H'cp Ch	2m	£319	12.7	P. Powell	11/4	won
Mar 18	Baldoyle	Metropolitan Chase	3m	£397	12.1	P. Powell		unpl
Season 1927–28								
July 27	Galway	Galway Plate	2m 4f	£492	12.3	P. Powell	1/1f	2nd
Nov 9	Liverpool	Becher Chase	2m 4f	£335	12.0	P. Powell	3/1	won
Dec 3	Kempton	Middlesex H'cp Ch	2m 4f	£253	12.7	P. Powell	9/4f	won
Mar 3	Kempton	Coventry H'cp Ch	3m 4f	£293	12.7	P. Powell	100/30	won
Mar 30	Liverpool	Grand National	4m 876 yds	£11,255	12.5	P. Powell	100/7	fell
June 9	Auteuil	Prix Ste Sauveur	4,500 m	25,000 F	75 k	F. B. Rees	5/1	unpl

June 17	Auteul	Grand Steeplechase de Paris	6,500 m	400,000 F	69 k	F. B. Rees	16/10j.f.	fell
June 22	Auteuil	Prix des Drags	4,500 m	75,000 F	66 k	J. Biarotte	27/10j.f	won
Season 1928-29								
Nov 28	Newbury	Hampshire H	2m	£118	11.10	G. Duller	1/2f	won
Dec 4	Leicester	Oadby H	2m	£73	12.2	G. Duller	1/10f	won
Dec 14	Lingfield	Crowhurst H	2m	£102	11.9	G. Duller	2/9f	won
Dec 26	Wolverhampton	Wyfold H	2m	£117	12.3	G. Duller	9/100f	won
Mar 12	Cheltenham	Gold Cup	3m 2f	£776	12.0	F. Rees	7/4f	won
Mar 22	Liverpool	Grand National	4m 876 yds	£13,000	12.7	J. Moloney	9/1f	2nd
Season 1929–30								
Dec 26	Wolverhampton	Penkridge Chase	3m	£132	11.8	T. Cullinan	30/100f	won
Jan 24	Leicester	Wigston Chase	2m	£88	11.11	T. Cullinan	7/100f	won
Mar 11	Cheltenham	Gold Cup	3m 2f	£670	12.0	T. Cullinan	8/11f	won
Season 1930–31								
Dec 26	Wolverhampton	Penkridge Chase	3m	£147	11.10	R. Everett	—	w.o.
Jan 20	Leicester	Wigston Chase	2m	£83	12.1	R. Everett	1/3f	won
Jan 28	Sandown	Mole H'cp Ch	2m 4f	£162	12.7	R. Everett	4/5f	won
Feb 27	Lingfield	Buckhurst H'cp Ch	2m 4f	£205	12.7	F. Rees	1/6f	2nd
Mar 27	Liverpool	Grand National	4m 876 yds	£9,385	12.7	F. Rees	5/1f	b.d.
Mar 28	Liverpool	Champion Chase	2m 7f	£1,650	12.0	F. Rees	9/4f	d.h. 1st place

FIVE

Golden Miller

THE 1930s; NAVAL MUTINY AT INVERGORDON; IN LONDON POLICE CHARGE HUNGER MARCHERS; FINANCIAL CRISIS – BANK RATE UP TWO PER CENT – £50 MILLION BORROWED FROM U.S.A. AND FRANCE. INCOME TAX UP TO 5 SHILLINGS; THE FIRST RADAR STATION OPENS AS HITLER BECOMES CHANCELLOR OF GERMANY; AND IN OXFORD THE UNION RESOLVES NOT TO FIGHT FOR KING AND COUNTRY; MRS SIMPSON THREATENS THE MONARCHY – EDWARD QUITS; ANOTHER BLOODY CIVIL WAR BREAKS OUT IN SPAIN.

March 1930: a lean young man walks into his large country house from going round Evening Stables. On his hall table a telegram: 'WOULD YOU LIKE TO BUY REALLY GOOD-LOOKING 3-YEAR-OLD OUT OF MILLER'S PRIDE? PRICE £500'. Promptly he wires back, 'WILL BUY HORSE FORWARDING CHEQUE'. Young Basil Briscoe, Old Etonian and recently down from nearby Cambridge, rich, talented and self-assured, has recently set up a large mixed stable at Longstowe, his family home. His unseen purchase is destined to dazzle the steeplechasing world of the 1930s with the glory of the greatest 'chaser yet seen: 29 victories including 5 Gold Cups and a Grand National. Basil Briscoe has blithely bought Golden Miller.

Briscoe had reasons other than his mercurial temperament for his apparently hazardous purchase. First, he had owned a half-brother to his new buy in May Court, on whom he had won point-to-points and under Rules. The horse, now owned by Mr Keber, had won five races in the current season and was well-fancied for the National. Secondly, the telegram's sender was a well-known Leicestershire hunter-dealer, Captain Farmer, who had already found Briscoe many a good horse.

The Captain had picked 'the Miller' himself from a huge flock of horses kept near Fethard, Tipperary, by that redoubtable farmer and dealer Paddy Quinn, who was to sell the winner of the English, Irish and Scottish Nationals, and another future Gold Cup winner in Linwell 23 years later for very little money to another young trainer. Quinn, whose sons were in such awe of him that they stood in his presence, had bought Golden Miller, (as he was to buy Linwell) for under 120 guineas at Ballsbridge Sales. For prospective purchasers he had his herd of youngsters driven across the valley field below his garden at Kilbragh. What caught the eye was caught by hand for closer scrutiny. Old Quinn used to say: 'I told Capt. Farmer there was a good one in this lot. "Is it that?" he asked. "No", I said. "That then?" "No, it is not." "It must be that then," said Capt. Farmer. "That is he," I said. And that's how the English Captain came to buy "the Miller".'

But Basil Briscoe's first reaction to his acquisition was one of horror, when he saw a gangling, mud-plastered three-year-old eyeing him gloomily from the corner of his box. Indignantly he rang Capt. Farmer to protest that he wanted a likely 'chaser, not a young carthorse. Farmer generously offered to take the horse back but Briscoe decided to give him a try. Come autumn, he was bitterly regretting his decision. Golden Miller's only racecourse venture had been a flop in a lowly hurdle at Southwell. Taken out with the Fitzwilliam hounds in the hope that it would arouse some interest in life, he had given his owner a wretched day, 'We went through the roots of every fence we jumped – he seemed so slow that we couldn't keep up with hounds', recalled his despairing owner. Meanwhile Head Lad Stan Tidey was relishing a great day on Briscoe's beloved pony. Nothing was glimpsed of the 'fluent jumping and amazing turn of foot', over which the racing world was soon to be enraptured. 'The Miller' believed in making his dislikes plain; patently hunting was a pastime he loathed. Later in his life he was to register the same disapproval about Aintree, the course which jockeys often liken to the hunting-field. To cap everything his antics out hunting left him with a badly filled off-fore leg which the vet pessimistically pronounced to be a sprained tendon. Stan Tidey caustically commented on Golden Miller: 'It's a damn'd good name for a damn'd bad horse!'

In the face of these calamities, Mr Philip Carr's sudden offer of £1,000 for the horse seemed heaven-sent. With his usual engaging candour, Briscoe told his owner exactly what he thought of 'the Miller's' abilities and the veterinary report, but Mr Carr was undeterred and went ahead with his purchase. He was a personal friend of Briscoe's as well as his oldest patron, and a great sportsman – his son Arthur was the famous Nottinghamshire cricketer who captained England. Carr's chocolate, scarlet cap had been seen on the Turf for 40 years, and although he hadn't had a lot of luck, Briscoe had great respect for his judgment. He was thus quite at a loss to understand his choice of the wretched animal.

Almost at once, however, Golden Miller vindicated Carr's judgment. A month later, he ran in a handicap hurdle at Newbury and finished an encouraging third to

two older horses, Black Armstrong and Young Prince. Jockey Bob Lyall enthused 'One of the best three-year-old's I've ever ridden.' The New Year brought twin victories: 'the Miller' hacked up at Leicester and Nottingham ridden in the latter by Ted Leader, a champion National Hunt jockey and later successful trainer to Mr Jim Joel. On this occasion he made a rare error of judgment, for, anticipating the start he got Golden Miller caught up in the tapes and lost a tooth in the process.

'The Miller' was then schooled over fences and made his 'chasing début in February with Gerry Wilson riding. Surviving a shocking blunder at the second last, the pair went under a short head to 15–8 favourite Rolie, ridden by six times champion jockey Willie Stott.

The following autumn he ran in four hurdle races, winning twice and being placed twice. But as winter closed in Mr Carr fell seriously ill. He feared that he would not see another spring and told Briscoe that he must sell his horses. At this time the Hon. Dorothy Paget, the unusual daughter of Lord Queenborough, had been intrigued by the steeplechasing triumphs enjoyed by Easter Hero, owned by her American cousin, Mr 'Jock' Whitney. She turned her close and lavish attention from the wheels and stench of motor-racing to the older equine sort. Brusquely she rang Briscoe and enquired if he had any good horses. 'Certainly,' he replied without hesitation, 'I have the best 'chaser in the world, Golden Miller, and the best hurdler in England, Insurance.' The temerity of this boast is probably unmatched even in a sport where pride and passions strike sparks off hotly competitive individuals. Certainly no other racing boast this large can ever have been so swiftly, triumphantly justified: within fifteen months Golden Miller and Insurance had won for Miss Paget two Gold Cups and two Champion Hurdles.

Dorothy Paget, 'the Miller's' new and final owner, was a splendid eccentric whose passion for steeplechasing was assuaged by her riches and often gratified in victories. Having inherited an American chain-store fortune, she diverted nearly all of it into racing. She was one of the last of the 'real big spenders' and hundreds of thousands of her pounds were transfused into steeplechasing. When she had a good thing to bet on colossal wagers walloped the bookmakers.

In her youth she had been beautiful, but by middle age, when her cortège of female secretaries, racing managers, trainers and trainer's assistants was clucking and twittering across English racetracks, she had grown exceedingly obese. In her perpetual ankle length, shapeless, shabby, flapping coat, squat beret pulled on to cropped hair, Miss Paget, cigarette holder jutting out of the strong-boned but pale face, would carve through little people like a battleship off Battersea, barking instructions and queries to the pattering retinue bobbing in her enormous wake.

Generally she slept all day, rising just before midnight. 'She used night for day,' recalled Charlie Rogers, who trained for her, ran her Irish stud and managed her racing interests from 1937 to her sudden death in February 1960. She had nicknames for everyone: Rogers was always 'Romeo', Gordon Richards who was training over 30 flat horses for her when she died was called 'Moppy'. Herself – she had a sharp sense of fun and was never pompous – she called 'Tiny'.

She spent thousands of night hours upstairs in her house, Hermit's Wood, at Chalfont St Giles, working at her papers from 2 a.m. to 5 a.m. and then

This picture vividly shows the tragic side of Dorothy Paget's eccentric character.

summoning her staff to the Bridge Room to play cards till the morning when she went to bed. An 'Iron Curtain' separated her quarters from her seven or eight servants and several cooks, one of whom was always on night duty to answer her calls for gargantuan meals at crazy times. Though she hardly ate anything herself she would call like a Roman Emperor for food enough for 20 at varying dark hours, pick at it and leave it. Sometimes she would simply fancy a boiled egg and bread and butter. Two would come up, be disregarded, then two more would arrive also to be ignored, until by dawn her room gleamed ovoidly with cold, vain eggs. She drank nothing except innumerable bottles of Malvern water.

In an upstairs room she kept every copy of *The Sporting Life* which mentioned her horses. Her squadrons ran frequently: soon thousands of copies of the racing man's *vade mecum* gathered dust in serried stacks yellowing to the ceiling.

At least three of her secretaries were always on duty to dispatch letters and do her bidding. Each secretary had a particular colour for the copies of her manifold dispatches. Pottering about Hermit's Wood all night she normally wore nothing but a woolly teddy-bear dressing-gown. When she wanted to summon someone from below (Charlie Rogers perhaps over from Ireland to discuss business at 4 a.m.) she'd stamp her foot on the ceiling – 'We'd hear bang-bang-bang and then up we had to go through the Iron Curtain', Rogers remembered.

She broke with many trainers and jockeys and moved her string in sudden swoops around the country. In some quarters she was regarded with awe, in others with near terror. But those who knew her best and served her longest spoke of her with a warmth transcending loyalty. Charlie Rogers said 'She was a wonderful person. When I was ill she sent flowers and the food I liked best and had me flown to Ireland and back. She sent me 99-word Christmas telegrams. She thought a lot of Gordon Richards,' Rogers recalled. 'She was a good judge of people and liked those who were straight. She was 100 per cent straight herself.' So much so that her bookmakers, knowing she usually slept by day, let her back horses in the evening after they had run, trusting her absolutely not to have found out the results.

Sir Gordon who rode for her on and off for nearly 30 years and then trained for her for six more recalled:

'One heard a lot of stories about her messing her trainers about, but that never happened to me. She left everything absolutely in my hands. I never want a better owner and she was the best loser I have ever known.

'If any of the boys got hurt while riding her horses and had to go to hospital, there were always parcels for them.'

'Frenchie' Nicholson who was the last of her many English jumping trainers thought her 'a marvellous owner, one of the best'.

When she died this eccentric part-recluse, half-terrifying, half-terrified person had won 1,534 races. No one has yet come along to fill the gap this vivid creature left.

Golden Miller's début in the blue-and-yellow hooped colours was dramatic. Starting 11–10 in the ill-named Moderate Chase at Newbury on 4 December, he passed the post in front of subsequent National winner Forbra and landed a hefty coup for the stable. The following day, however, Forbra's connections objected on the grounds that Golden Miller had, owing to Basil Briscoe's misinterpretation of the conditions, carried the wrong weight. The objection was upheld, 'the Miller' disqualified and Briscoe fined £50 and severely reprimanded. Losing the race proved a hidden blessing for the great bets stood but 'the Miller' was still eligible for novice 'chases. He ran in two,both at Newbury, winning one and finishing second in the other. On 27 January he won a 3-mile 'chase at Gatwick by a distance at odds-on. After that he was given a short rest before being prepared for his first assault on the Gold Cup. He was not given a great chance; while allowed to be a very good young 'chaser, he was thought to have little hope of beating Grakle at only 9 lb. difference. On a cold day and firm ground Grakle was odds-on favourite at 10–11 with Golden Miller (Ted Leader) at 13–2. However, Grakle fell a mile out and brought down Kinsford, leaving Golden Miller to win rather easily from Inverse. As Leader was pulling up after the post he saw the riderless Grakle galloping past him. He set off in pursuit, caught him and brought him back in tow. Thus the crowd were treated to the ironic spectacle of the young victor coming into the winner's enclosure like a Roman general with the conquered enemy reined behind his heels. Grakle's trainer the great Tom Coulthwaite presented Leader with an inscribed cigarette case.

Later that afternoon, Insurance settled the score with his old rival Song of Essex, and completed the best double of them all with a clear-cut victory in the Champion Hurdle. For both new owner Paget and young trainer Briscoe it was a memorable triumph, and for Ted Leader, who had been suffering a lean spell, it marvellously broke a bad run. But the papers did not enthuse over 'the Miller's' victory: he was considered to have been very fortunate.

To wind up the season Golden Miller was sent to Manchester for the valuable Lancashire Chase (at £1,725 it was the second richest race in the *Calendar*). Despite a 12 lb. penalty, he started favourite and, in atrocious going, ran moderately. The impetuous Briscoe, quick to blame others, was equally self-critical. He now damned himself: the horse had had a hard season, was stale, and should never have run.

Golden Miller enjoyed the gentle unwinding of a really good summering. Muscles and nerves at action stations during the battling winter now stood at ease and dozed. Briscoe believed passionately in this therapy and closely supervised every day of his horse's rest. This strange, sensitive, gifted young man was so dedicated he drove himself hard all year, and during the seven years 'the Miller' was in his care, he never took a holiday. Half a century later another brilliant trainer, but from a totally different background, went eleven years without a holiday, when David Elsworth, once a penniless market trader, was caring for Desert Orchid.

Golden Miller had for a close companion through the warm drift of summer not a pony, goat or lamb, but a large Great Dane, who grew so devoted to him that when autumn work restarted he used to pad down the schooling fences with him.

In the 1930s – and indeed until merry commercial sponsors started to burgeon after World War II – there were no rich races before Christmas. Every 'chaser with any pretensions to class therefore had his programme geared to reaching peak fitness in March. Golden Miller did not run again until 1 December, when he made a triumphant reappearance at Kempton. It was the start of a conqueror's progress. He won 'chases at Lingfield, Hurst Park and then Lingfield again, when in his winding-up race for the Gold Cup, he gave 31 lb. and a 1-length beating to Buck Willow. The press surprisingly still shuffled their feet about his brilliance, while conceding that nothing was likely to prevent Miss Paget repeating her big-race double at Cheltenham. The bookmakers, too, even more astonishingly failed to evaluate 'the Miller'. Briscoe, who revelled in knocking the books for six, continued to be happily astonished by the prices at which his champion was returned.

March blew in – windy, rough and wet. Longstowe was delighted and prayed for more rain. The deeper the going, the more opportunity for 'the Miller's' tremendous strength and stamina. Country house-parties assembled for the Festival, now the acknowledged show-piece of the 'chasing season, not caring that a little man called Hitler had just seized power in Germany. Sensibly shod women with regimental brooches, oblivious of the sounds of distant thunder, were escorted by tweedy country gentry in bowler hats and covert coats. All were being wafted towards the end of their long era. Clutching race-glasses, *Sporting Life*, race-cards, form books, gloves and other vital impedimenta, they lugged their hampers, green with champagne, pink with smoked salmon, heavy with plum cake and sloe-gin for their rich old voices and glossy cheeks, up the hill from the car-park and debouched into the enclosures in a cacophonic braying of upper-class vowels.

The day started well for Longstowe when Insurance, favourite at 10–11, won the Champion Hurdle in a rousing finish with Windemere Laddy. Nor did 'the Miller' long leave hopes hanging for the double. He took the lead five out and although 'fiddling' the second last, he put in an exhibition leap at the final fence and roared up the hill to win by ten lengths from Thomond, who that day only murmured of their epic duels to come.

Afterwards it was announced that Golden Miller would definitely run for the National, for which he had been given 12 st. 2 lb. Ted Leader had the mount and the pair started 9–1 favourite. For a circuit they were well in touch, but on the second time round Golden Miller blundered badly at Bechers. This so shook his confidence that he hit the next even harder and 'lost' his partner. After it was all over and the tumult died many correspondents discovered that his style of jumping – fast, low and off his forehand – was most unsuitable to Aintree's towering fences and massive drops. Although a magnificent-looking horse, he was rather straight-shouldered and while National winners come in most shapes and the full pony-to-monster range of sizes, they usually possess that common quality of comfort: a long sloping shoulder.

1933–34, his great season, rejoined Golden Miller with Gerry Wilson, then champion jockey. He started auspiciously at Lingfield on 25 November, when cantering in by 6 lengths and the same from Kellsboro' Jack and Mr 'Jock' Whitney's Thomond, both top-class horses. Then a reverse followed: at a difference of only 7 lb. Mr Whitney's great-hearted little horse turned the tables over 2½ miles at Kempton. 'The Miller' was beaten again at Hurst Park, this time by 3 lengths and a short head by Southern Hero and Persian Sun to whom he was conceding 2 st. and 2½ st. The stable lost its money and was bitterly disappointed, but it wasn't realized at the time just how good these two were. As is easy enough when training a champion who brushes aside most opposition, the stable had underrated the competition. Time passed, Southern Hero and Persian Sun

Cheltenham 1934. Golden Miller's third successive Gold Cup (worth £670) this time ridden by Gerry Wilson. He would win two more. The couple will go on to win the Grand National seventeen days later under 12 st. 2 lb. Note here the start was at the side *of the stands in a chute now buried beneath stands and car-parks.*

achieved other victories and hindsight recognized 'the Miller's' defeat by them at those weights as a splendid performance.

A dry spell at the beginning of March didn't increase Briscoe's confidence for the Gold Cup, but luckily the rain came in time to ease the sting out of the rattling ground. Golden Miller (although 6–5 favourite), started unusually at odds against. But there was money for El Haljar, a French horse who had won Kempton's Coventry Chase impressively, and for Avenger, a very promising five-year-old of Mrs Mundy's.

In brief, 'the Miller' was supreme; all the challengers had a go, all were beaten off before the last which 'the Miller' jumped immaculately and Gerry Wilson, seizing like an actor his vast audience's electric reaction, pushed him right out. The pair were cheered every stride to the post.

And so to Aintree. His adoring public would not hear of defeat, but the press were cautious. If he stood up they agreed he was a certainty. But it was mathematically 3–1 against any horse getting round, and Captain Coe's view – 'Golden Miller's style of fencing does not lend confidence' – was generally shared.

23 March dawned fine and dry. 'The Miller' had given every satisfaction since Cheltenham – 'he was a terribly fit horse that day', Briscoe remembered. Fortunately he was unmoved by the thronging crowds fighting to get a glimpse of him. The first fence scythed heavily through the 30-strong field and Mr Rank's Southern Hero was among the four fallers. Poor Basil Briscoe, panting in the Press-stand, with no time to reach the Owners' and Trainers' was told 'Golden Miller's down too' and endured several agonizing moments until, passing the stands on the first circuit, Golden Miller was seen well up there and Briscoe breathed again. So too indeed was Thomond. Golden Miller, always one to play to the crowd put in a particularly spectacular leap over the water. Off they went for the last circuit, with 'the Miller' up with the leaders as they came galloping homewards. Delaneige led him over the last, but once on the flat, he sprinted away to win easily by 5 lengths in the then record time of 9 min. 20⅖ sec.*

The gigantic crowd went mad. 'Never have I seen such a demonstration . . . there's a perfect tornado of cheers . . . Wilson's almost dragged from his horse' – the gasping *Evening News* reporter telephoned through to his office.

Miss Paget, so overwrought as to be deathly pale, shook hands formally with her father and then with the two lads in charge of 'the Miller'. She wore her thick lumpy tweed coat with its beaver collar, low-heeled shoes, very utility stockings and of course no lipstick. Someone called for three cheers, and agonizingly self-conscious, she bowed acknowledgment. Haltingly she told reporters, 'I have always had faith in my horse . . . I cannot adequately express my admiration. I am very proud of him.' Her father, Lord Queenborough, announced that there would

* Golden Miller's record time under 12 st. 2 lb. should be compared with Bogskar's 9 min. 20⅗ sec. under 10 st. 4 lb. in 1940, Reynoldstown's 9 min. 21 sec. under 11 st. 4 lb. in 1938, and E. S. B.'s 9 min. 21⅖ sec. in 'Devon Loch's National' of 1956. But all these times seem slow compared with Red Rum's 9 min. 1.9 sec. in 1973 when, under 10 st. 5 lb., he won the first of his three Grand Nationals, just catching front-running Crisp close home. It should be remembered, however, that until 1961 the Aintree fences were horribly upright.

Golden Miller wins the 1934 Grand National, ears pricked, though carrying 12 st. 2 lb. He was ridden by Gerry Wilson. The following year, with Wilson again, 'The Miller' refused in both the National and in the Champion Chase for which he was pulled out again the next day.

be a small, quiet celebration at the Adelphi, but as visitors to that hotel on National Night can imagine, it turned out to be nothing of the kind.

Miss Paget arrived at 10 p.m. swathed in red velvet to the neck. Her hair was, as usual, short, straight and parted in the middle. As always she wore no make-up. Mr 'Jock' Whitney proposed her health and she stayed till after midnight. Then, as racing journalist Sidney Galtrey recalls, she left the party by the back passages and the luggage lift up to her rooms, rather than face the crowds on the dance-floor.

By 1935, Jubilee Year, Golden Miller had risen swiftly to become another popular institution. His acclaim had leapt to unprecedented heights, putting a tremendous strain on his highly-strung young trainer. Miss Paget was in Germany but constantly on the telephone. Her telephone bills were astronomical. Charlie Rogers, for 23 years her trainer and stud manager in Ireland, estimated his calls for her to be in the region of £300 a month, and when she could not reach Fulke Walwyn when he trained for her, she sent telegrams in the middle of the night running to seven or eight pages and bristling with queries.

Briscoe's policy with 'the Miller' was to avoid the cracks and to bring him slowly to his peak. He made his first appearance at Wolverhampton on Boxing Day in the race that Easter Hero had won twice. One of Briscoe's lads, J. Baxter, on a red-letter day for him, had the mount. 'The Miller' was only half-fit but he started 1–4 favourite, duly collected, and went on to win little races at Leicester and Derby, at very long odds-on and by contemptuous distances. At Sandown he was asked more of a question. In the £500 Grand International Handicap Chase he had to give 18 lb. to a fair horse in Really True, and 14 lb. to his old adversary Delaneige, but he won nevertheless very comfortably by 10 lengths.

And so to Cheltenham for a nice exercise canter (as it seemed) to complete his National preparation. The going was firmer than Briscoe could have wished but he wasn't worried. He was sure 'the Miller' would not have to exert himself, and it is extension plus exhaustion on unsuitable ground which does the damage.

Thomond, who, getting 7 lb., had beaten him over 2½ miles at Kempton last year, was among the entries. 'Jock' Whitney's horse was little, light-framed, and rather delicate: his astute trainer, Jack Anthony, hadn't run him since December. It was generally understood that he would run not in the Gold Cup but in the 2-mile Coventry Cup.

'Jock' Whitney flew in from America a few days before the start of the meeting, and his horses obligingly started to win races. His Rod and Gun won the important National Hunt Chase on the opening day and his appetite was whetted. At any rate, meeting Briscoe leaving the course he told him that he had changed the plan for Thomond: his good horse would now go for the Gold Cup. Basil Briscoe was appalled. He had deliberately left something to work on 'the Miller' and a hard race on firm going was the last thing he wanted. In vain did he try to convince Whitney that a hard duel between the two could improve neither's chances at Aintree. He may have disclosed his agitation and thus strengthened the American banker's resolve. Whitney was immovable.

The public naturally was entranced. To the pleasure of enjoying 'the Miller' in action, was now added the thrilling prospect of a duel. Few people thought he

Golden Miller and Gerry Wilson in 1935. The combination began in February 1931 and continued off and on until the Newbury Chase in February in 1936 when 'The Miller', at even money, ran out.

would actually get beaten, but Thomond was reckoned a very good horse who, on ground that he loved, would take full advantage of any lapse, weakness, or lack of condition on the part of the champion.

Speed and records blew in the bright March air for Sir Malcolm Campbell had just broken the world land speed record.

The Gloucestershire weather smiled for the occasion. The cradling slopes round Prestbury Park lay dappled in spring sunshine and crowds surged down on Cheltenham in record-breaking numbers. The officials, gratified but bemused, completely lost control: the supply of racecards was exhausted an hour before the first race; desperate racegoers impatient of queueing stormed the hedges and handed their money to grinning policemen. And those who finally attained the haven of the enclosures, abandoned any notion of being able to bet. Miss Paget, just in time, flew in from Germany and landed dramatically on the course.

The race began. Southern Hero opened up by setting a cracking pace. Billy Speck on Thomond could be seen behind angling for the rails. Three fences from home Southern Hero could do no more. He had set the stage for the two great gladiators and the struggle now set its teeth in earnest. Stride for stride the stars hurtled down the hill, Thomond having the advantage of that inside elbow so that 'the Miller' had to come round him, a few feet extra each raking stride – those extras when the pace is cracking that may never be regrasped before the post. As they straightened up for the last, there was still nothing in it. Wilson and Speck, champions both, flung themselves and their horses like conquering centaurs at that last fence.

Together the twin pairs catapulted into the rushing air. Together four forelegs punched forward, necks stretched, knees gripped, and the turf rushed up at them. Four hindlegs bunched beneath, then touched down too, tightened again and launched the heavy bodies up the implacable hill. The jam-packed enclosures were utterly silent. Defeat, so long unthinkable, now suddenly loomed. Then, as 'the Miller's' superior strength and stamina began slowly to assert itself up the hill, a roar was let loose that reverberated to the surrounding hills, and echoed, and re-echoed and went on re-echoing long after the two principals had been unsaddled and led away.

The National was still to come, and as to Aintree, opinion divided: could Thomond, on 10-lb. better terms, turn the tables, or would 'the Miller's' superiority increase over the extra mile? No one questioned his ability to jump the course; he had answered his critics in magnificent fashion the previous year.

The fretting Briscoe felt Aintree drag towards him under a terrible welter of worries. Not only was Golden Miller the hottest ante-post favourite ever known, but Briscoe also trained Commander III, favourite for the Lincoln, the Spring Double's first leg. And Commander was beaten, finishing unplaced to Lord Rosebery's Flamenco. Stable confidence was only partially restored when Amaris beat a large field for the Eltham Plate.

Aintree was set fair to honour England's champion. The Prince of Wales arrived by train, and watched the racing from Lord Sefton's box. Ladies took advantage of the fine weather and ventured into spring tweeds and gay hats. A new fashion of jockey caps was noted – many of them gold in honour of the favourite.

The deluge of public money brought Golden Miller in to the fantastic price of 2–1, and few were to know – there being no racecourse commentary – how quickly the tens of thousands of pounds were lost. Wilson, hoping to avoid interference, tried to take a good position early on, but 'the Miller' ('never striding out') thwarted these intentions by climbing cat-like over the first three fences, and was thus well behind by the time he reached the Open Ditch after Valentines. Here he never attempted to take off, but bucketed through the fence, incredibly keeping his feet, but losing the hapless Gerry Wilson. It is worth recording that although he several times unseated his rider and was once brought down, he never fell in any of his 52 races, a remarkable record. Without the commentary it was not until the field streamed past the stands that a general rustle of panic rushed through the dense crowd like wind through a wheat field. Anxiety exploded. The blue and yellow colours were missing!

Owner, trainer and jockey alike were equally mystified. The public was stunned; its idol had fallen. Crowds in London that evening gaped incredulously at '3 Furlongs Triumph' blazoned across their evening papers. Everyone knew Golden Miller was the horse of the century but surely even he couldn't win by nearly half a mile. Sickeningly they discovered their mistake: the Furlongs were the remarkable sporting family who owned, trained and rode Reynoldstown, the winner.

A veterinary examination revealed nothing amiss with the favourite so it was decided to run him next day in the Champion Chase as a consoling formality. 'The Miller' however declined to view it as such. He not only repeated his blunder, but did so at the very first fence, and once more his jockey was shot off.

Then the fur began to fly. On Monday morning a statement issued by Briscoe appeared in the Press announcing that as a result of Golden Miller's failure in the Grand National, all Miss Paget's horses would leave Beechwood House, Exning, by the end of the week. Miss Paget didn't wait. The horseboxes were dispatched and the cortège left on Thursday. 'The Miller', for swift temporary lodgings, went first to Donald Snow, a cousin of Miss Paget's, and thence to Owen Anthony's stables.

Gerry Wilson survived the cataclysm, but not for long. For, after winning a little race at the end of December, 'the Miller' caused another sensation: five fences from home in a 3-mile 'chase at Newbury, he ran out. Another furore followed, and this time Gerry Wilson was axed. With the Gold Cup only a fortnight away, there was little time to find a replacement so Evan Williams, a little-known ex-amateur attached to Owen Anthony's stable, was given the double edged task of piloting the wayward champion on his bid for a fifth Gold Cup. However, back on his favourite course, 'the Miller' played no tricks. Jumping immaculately all the way he galloped home an easy 12 lengths winner from two National victors, Royal Mail and the unfortunate Kellsboro' Jack, who must by this time have grown heartily sick of the prospect of 'the Miller's' powerful quarters. The public, hugely relieved, were delighted to hoist their Miller back on his pedestal and sent him to Aintree second favourite at 5–1. Alas for such faith. 'The Miller' was bumped into at the first fence and made little effort to jump it, shooting his jockey off. The horrified Williams hastily remounted and set off in pursuit, but on reaching the

A dramatic action shot of 'The Miller' at full stretch, ridden by Fulke Walwyn on the Downs above Letcombe.

fateful fence after Valentines, his peculiar partner irrevocably stuck in his toes.

His dislike of the English Grand National did not extend to its equivalent at Cardiff. Starting odds-on, he ran a marvellous race for the Welsh Grand National, though not quite able to give away 23 lb. and 33 lb. to Sorley Boy and Free Wheeler.

The season 1936–37 was one of mixed fortune for Golden Miller. He won three Optional Selling Chases easily enough but in between turned in two drearier displays. Sent to Liverpool for the 2½-mile Becher Chase, this time with Fulke Walwyn aboard, he, for once, negotiated all the fences, but showed none of his customary finishing speed in going under by 12 lengths to Royal Mail. Even more disquieting was his performance at Gatwick on 9 January when he was forced to a dead heat by Drinmore Lad. His own race, the Gold Cup, went to steeplechasing's perpetual enemy, bad weather. This was a bitter blow to his new pilot 'Frenchie' Nicholson who was convinced he would have won, and furious to see, after racing had been abandoned, the sun pop out. By midday it had melted all the snow away.

On 19 March 'the Miller' was sent north for yet another final attempt on the National. 'Frenchie' Nicholson had been previously engaged for Didoric so Danny Morgan had the ride. Again 'the Miller' had top-weight of 12 st. 7 lb., again he started favourite (this time at 8–1) and again he refused the fence after Valentines. Onlookers reported that it was perfectly obvious from the moment he landed over Valentine's that he had not the smallest intention of essaying his bogey fence.

Regularly partnered by 'Frenchie' Nicholson for the following season, he opened encouragingly at Sandown, followed up by winning a little 'chase at Wincanton on Boxing Day in storming fashion, and then returned to Sandown for the Prince's Chase, a big race then worth £500, since renamed as a Memorial to Lord Mildmay after 'the last of the Corinthians' was tragically drowned in the sea

off his Devon estates. And later, when his life-long friend and successful trainer Peter Cazalet also died sadly young, his name, too, was added. By 1989 the value of the Anthony Mildmay, Peter Cazalet Memorial Chase had grown to £13,825. Nicholson recalled: 'It was January 13th, my birthday. We had a party the night before in the Café de Paris! Horrible day, it rained, snowed, hailed, the lot – 'the Miller's' weather, he loved it – hock deep, y'know. It was a slow pace, didn't suit him, so we went on from the water. They got to us between the last two, headed me over the last, but he wouldn't give in. That horse was like a good boxer, he'd *worry* them out of it. We won a length, maybe less giving the second Sporting Piper 34 lb. and he was a fair horse. I reckon it was one of the best races he ever ran. In the unsaddling enclosure Owen Anthony's brother Jack came across: "great race," he said, "but it'll finish him." '

It seemed as though Jack Anthony was right when next time out, in whirling snow at Hurst Park, Golden Miller showed none of his old fire and was beaten 5 lengths at level weights by Macaulay. However he refused to be written off just yet and back he came at Birmingham, bayonets fixed and colours flying to win by 25 lengths. And so to Cheltenham for the sixth and final time. Could he do it? The question's cud was chewed upon in pubs and clubs, in buses and in Rolls'. The hearts of the public would not hear of his defeat but the heads of the professionals racing wagged dubiously. It was no good pretending he was the horse he was. Why should he turn the tables on Macaulay? And what about Airgead Sios who had beaten Macaulay last time out? Moreover the old horse would loathe the firm going. The professionals were, however, conspicuously inaccurate at the meeting and by the end of the second day only one favourite had obliged them. The crowd was enormous. From all over the country extra trains were run, bringing people to honour the Grand Old Man of Steeplechasing. And honour him they could for 'the Miller' ran a marvellous race. A mile from home he drew alongside the front-running Airgead Sios and readily mastered him. Macaulay was clearly unable to get on terms and all seemed set for a famous victory. But suddenly a new danger loomed. The almost unconsidered Morse Code, who had been well behind Airgead Sios and Macaulay at Kempton, now ranged alongside, obviously full of running. As they jumped the last upsides, the crowd were willing their idol on, but saw in every stride that invincible enemy, Age, dragging back those flying feet. On the flat, the younger horse drew slowly, inexorably away with the finality of a judge's sentence, and at the post was two lengths clear.

'The Miller's' reign was over. It was his first and only defeat at Cheltenham. It should have been sad, but somehow it was not, for he had gone down fighting all the way, and, beaten at last by the dread, inevitable burden of the years, had been magnificent in defeat.

He ran one more race, at Newbury the following February, but he made no show and was immediately retired with Insurance to The Paddocks, Dorothy Paget's stud at Stanstead. Dorothy Paget took great care of her old servant, paying him frequent visits, insisting that a vet gave him a thorough check over every three months and arranging for a constant supply of apples. Golden Miller made guest appearances at various equine functions like the International Horse Show at Olympia and was finally put down in 1957 at the age of 30.

Fulke Walwyn at the unveiling of the Golden Miller statue at Cheltenham, March 1989.

There would, the racing world declared, never be another like him. 'The Miller' was dead, but his superiority would rule for ever. But in the year of his death in Essex, a few hundred miles westwards across the Irish Sea old Mrs Baker's mare Bright Cherry produced a bay colt foal by Archive.

GOLDEN MILLER B. G. 1927	GOLD COURT	GOLD MINER	GALLINULE
			SEEK AND FIND
		POWERSCOURT	ATHELING
			WATERFALL
	MILLER'S PRIDE	WAVELETS PRIDE	FERNANDEZ
			WAVELET
		MILLER'S DAUGHTER	QUEEN'S BIRTHDAY
			ALLAN WATER

DATE	COURSE	RACE	DISTANCE	VALUE	WEIGHT	JOCKEY	PRICE	PLACE
Season 1930–31								
Sept 1	Southwell	Farnsfield H	2m	£58	10.4	T. James	25/1	unpl
Nov 29	Newbury	Moderate H'cp H	2m	£162	10.0	R. Lyall	100/6	3rd
Jan 20	Leicester	Gopsall Mdn H	2m	£83	10.2	R. Lyall	5/4f	won
Jan 26	Nottingham	Annesley H	2m	£88	10.12	T. Leader	5/6f	won
Feb 21	Newbury	Spring Chase	2m	£312	10.5	G. Wilson	9/4	2nd
Apr 8	Warwick	Warwick Spring H'cp (F)	2m	£343	8.11	R. Dick	7/1	unpl
Apr 16	Newmarket	April Stakes (F)	1m 4f	£201	9.4	J. Leach	3/1f	4th
Season 1931–32								
Oct 12	Chelmsford	Witham H	2m	£63	11.10	W. Stott	4/11f	won
Oct 22	Sandown	Norbiton H'cp H	2m	£261	11.9	T. Leader	9/4j.f.	3rd
Oct 30	Manchester	Irish Hospitals H'cp H (Amateurs)	2m	£318	12.1	Mr R. Mount	3/1	3rd
Nov 11	Chelmsford	Chelmsford H	2m	£63	11.10	T. Leader	4/11f	won
Dec 4	Newbury	Moderate Ch	2m 50 yds	£332	10.5	T. Leader	11/10f	fin 1st, disq
Dec 30	Newbury	Reading Ch	2m 50 yds	£332	10.12	T. Leader	4/5f	won
Jan 20	Newbury	Sefton Ch	2m 50yds	£332	12.5	T. Leader	11/8f	2nd
Jan 27	Gatwick	Brook Ch	3m	£412	11.3	T. Leader	4/6f	won
Mar 1	Cheltenham	Gold Cup (Chase)	3m 3f	£670	11.5	T. Leader	13/2	won
Mar 19	Liverpool	Maghull Plate (F)	1m 6f	£150	9.5	H. Beasley	4/1	2nd
Mar 28	Manchester	Lancashire Ch	3m 4f	£1,725	11.10	T. Leader	9/4f	unpl
Season 1932–33								
Dec 1	Kempton	Middlesex H'cp Ch	2m 4f	£234	12.2	W. Stott	6/4f	won
Dec 10	Lingfield	Lingfield Open Ch	3m	£240	11.4	W. Stott	4/9f	won
Jan 19	Hurst Park	Mitre H'cp Ch	3m 180 yds	£245	12.7	W. Stott	6/4f	won
Feb 4	Lingfield	Troytown H'cp Ch	3m	£600	12.10	W. Stott	2/1f	won
Mar 7	Cheltenham	Gold Cup (Chase)	3m 3f	£670	12.0	W. Stott	4/7f	won
Mar 29	Liverpool	Grand National Chase (H'cp)	4m 856 yds	£7,345	12.2	T. Leader	9/1f	u.r.

DATE	COURSE	RACE	DISTANCE	VALUE	WEIGHT	JOCKEY	PRICE	PLACE
Season 1933–34								
Nov 25	Lingfield	Lingfield Open Ch	3m	£239	11.8	G. Wilson	8/11f	won
Dec 27	Kempton	Gamecock H'cp Ch	2m 4f 90 yds	£219	12.7	G. Wilson	4/7f	2nd
Jan 18	Hurst Park	Star & Garter H'cp Ch	3m 180 yds	£244	12.7	G. Wilson	1/2f	3rd
Mar 6	Cheltenham	Gold Cup (Chase)	3m 3f	£670	12.0	G. Wilson	6/5f	won
Mar 23	Liverpool	Grand National Chase (H'cp)	4m 856 yds	£7,265	12.2	G. Wilson	8/1	won
Season 1934–35								
Dec 26	Wolverhampton	Penkridge Ch	3m	£117	11.5	J. Baxter	1/4f	won
Jan 7	Leicester	Mapperley Ch	3m 50 yds	£83	12.0	G. Wilson	7/100f	won
Jan 22	Derby	Breadsall Ch	3m	£68	12.7	G. Wilson	7/100f	won
Feb 16	Sandown	Grand International H'cp Ch	3m 5f 25yds	£392	12.7	G. Wilson	40/95f	won
Mar 14	Cheltenham	Gold Cup (Chase)	3m 3f	£670	12.0	G. Wilson	1/2f	won
Mar 29	Liverpool	Grand National Chase (H'cp)	4m 856 yds	£6,545	12.7	G. Wilson	2/1f	u.r.
Mar 30	Liverpool	Champion Chase	2m 7f 110 yds	£1,480	12.0	G. Wilson	1/1f	u.r.
Season 1935–36								
Dec 6	Sandown	Arthur Coventry N.H. Flat Race	2m	£117	11.9	Mr J. Gordon	9/2	3rd
Dec 30	Newbury	Andover H'cp Ch	2m 50 yds	£122	12.10	G. Wilson	7/2f	won
Feb 26	Newbury	Newbury H'cp Ch	3m	£240	12.7	G. Wilson	1/1f	r.o.
Mar 12	Cheltenham	Gold Cup (Chase)	3m 2f	£670	12.0	E. Williams	21/20f	won
Mar 27	Liverpool	Grand National Chase (H'cp)	4m 856 yds	£7,095	12.7	E. Williams	5/1	b.d/ref
Apr 14	Cardiff	Welsh Grand National H'cp Chase	3m 4f 50 yds	£535	12.7	E. Williams	4/6f	3rd

Season 1936–37								
Oct 17	Wincanton	Lattiford Optional Selling Ch	2m 4f	£89	12.0	F. Walwyn	1/3f	won
Nov 11	Liverpool	Becher Ch	2m 4f	£415	12.0	F. Walwyn	7/2j.f.	2nd
Dec 26	Wincanton	Sparkford Optional Selling Ch	3m 50 yds	£89	12.0	E. Williams	1/5f	won
Jan 9	Gatwick	Crawley Chase	3m	£91 each	12.7	E. Williams	8/15f	d.h. won
Feb 22	Birmingham	Optional Selling Ch	2m 4f	£127	12.0	H. Nicholson	2/9f	won
Mar 19	Liverpool	Grand National Chase (H'cp)	4m 856 yds	£6,645	12.7	D. Morgan	8/1f	ref
Season 1937–38								
Dec 18	Sandown	Sandown H'cp Ch	3m 125 yds	£490	12.7	H. Nicholson	4/1f	unpl
Dec 27	Wincanton	Sparkford Ch	3m 50 yds	£82	12.0	A. Scratchley	1/4f	won
Jan 13	Sandown	Prince's H'cp Chase	3m 5f 25 yds	£332	12.7	H. Nicholson	1/1f	won
Feb 17	Hurst Park	Hampton Court Opt Selling Chase	3m 180yds	£417	11.10	H.Nicholson	4/6f	2nd
Feb 28	Birmingham	Optional Selling Ch	2m 4f	£124	12.0	H. Nicholson	8/100f	won
Mar 10	Cheltenham	Gold Cup (Chase)	3m 2f	£720	12.0	H. Nicholson	7/4f	2nd
Season 1938–39								
Feb 23	Newbury	Newbury H'cp Chase	3m	£415	12.3	G. Archibald	6/1j.f.	unpl

SIX

Prince Regent

World War II: Britain blacked out, Ireland stays neutral; Churchill in siren suit conducts the battle; Beveridge plans the Welfare State; 'The Few' save Britain; Spam and snoek fill British stomachs; The tide turns – 'Monty' wins in North Africa; Collapse of Germany and the first atom bomb; Peace creeps out.

Breeding pundits too often prove their point after the event, finding in the remote reaches of every famous winner's pedigree blood proof of why he won. So we can now say that if ever a horse was bred in the jumping purple it was Prince Regent. His sire My Prince, was the most influential jumping sire of his age; he was responsible not only for Easter Hero but also for Gregalach, that horse's conqueror in the 1929 National.

In 1936, when the My Prince yearling to be known as Prince Regent was sold at Goff's Sales in Dublin's pleasant suburb, another My Prince, Reynoldstown, won his second consecutive National. Thereby hangs a tale. Mr J. V. Rank, the millionaire miller, strode into 'chasing in the early 1930s, and had owned Southern Hero, the good horse who once beat Golden Miller. Jimmy Rank, like Dorothy Paget, was prepared to pour vast sums of money into racing: he desired passionately to win the Grand National. He had great regard for the stock of My Prince and was therefore keen to buy Reynoldstown when that horse came on the market as a youngster. He was, however, put off the horse by some trainer who was prejudiced against black horses. Now Mr Rank instructed his scouts to consider any nice young My Prince horse. In 1936 Harry Bonner of a well-known Oxfordshire hunting family, then acting as Mr Rank's racing manager, heard of one out of Nemaea, a flat-bred mare, whose dam Capdane had produced a champion sprinter in Diomedes.

He bought him, along with three others, for a total of £1,250 of which Prince Regent is said to have cost £350.

Mr Rank's racing interests were divided between England and Ireland. In England Gwyn Evans trained the National Hunt horses in a separate yard at the great private establishment Druids Lodge away on its own on Salisbury Plain. Bob Fetherstonhaugh from his neat bungalow behind the Curragh grandstand handled the Irish ones.

A few youngsters including Prince Regent were being broken in with a young Irish vet Bobby Power down in County Cork. Power was killed by a car as he was changing a punctured wheel on the road north to Dublin Horse Show and it was suggested to Mr Rank by both Judge Wylie and Harry Bonner that Tom Dreaper might take over. The illustrious Dreaper later drily remarked 'Both would say they discovered me!'. He was then principally a large farmer with a few horses and was threshing corn when he had the offer from Rank. He read the letter and went back to his threshing before he answered it.

So it was that in spring 1938, Prince Regent and another likely three-year-old Mayerling, both barely broken, arrived at Greenogue. By Christmas time Tom was taking them out hunting with the Fingal Harriers, across the land where 18 years and one world war later, Mrs Baker of Malahow was going to breed Arkle. Tom schooled Prince Regent backwards and forwards over any fence available, even when hounds were not running. The young horse thus acquired great experience of meeting obstacles at all angles, from varying take-offs, and was learning, what is more, while thoroughly enjoying himself.

In spite of the threat of war both horses went to Gwyn Evans at Druids Lodge in the spring of 1939, but shortly afterwards he too was killed in an accident. The war, which was to confine the scope of the horse Dreaper so long believed to be superior to Arkle, now erupted. The two youngsters sailed back to the land of their birth: Mayerling first to Bob Fetherstonhaugh, and Prince Regent to Tom Dreaper.

Prince Regent had his first run in a bumper at Baldoyle in March 1940, and Tom Dreaper gave him such a very patient introduction that Judge Wylie pulled his leg. Tom Dreaper riding himself was 'impressed' – but not as impressed as he was with Mayerling. Mayerling might have been even better than Prince Regent for he was then certainly faster over 2 miles. Later in the month Prince Regent was a good fourth in a 1½-mile bumper at Phoenix Park, and then in April he won one at Naas. It was to be Tom Dreaper's last winner as a rider. Judge Wylie watched the race with Harry Bonner. Prince Regent nearly ran away going down to the start and won terribly easily. Judge Wylie was hugely tickled – 'Wasn't I right now, to tell Tom to try a bit harder, then?'

He didn't run again until the following March when, ridden by Eddie Dempsey

(who won a sensational National on 100–1 outsider Caughoo) he finished close up at Baldoyle. The war which then looked likely to be won by Germany didn't stop racing in neutral Ireland. Representatives of the warring nations frequently stood side by side in the grandstands and bars, and German, British, French, Polish and Italian prisoners interned by the Irish often went racing together. A greater inhibition than war however restricted racing to the Dublin area: foot-and-mouth disease had broken out.

At the beginning of May, Prince Regent won a hurdle race at Phoenix Park, starting 100–30 second favourite. As a result, he, was made second favourite for the important Mickey Macardle Memorial Chase on Dundalk's sharp little track on the way to Ulster. Harry Bonner missed the submarines and came over, and was alarmed by the hard ground. Prince Regent won but Bonner wasn't happy till his protégé trotted out sound next morning. The third horse, Golden Jack (owned by Dorothy Paget) went on to win the Galway Plate with 12 st. 7 lb. so the form was good.

It was now, in the war's dark days when the bombs came crumping down on blacked-out Britain while Dublin's lights twinkled, that Prince Regent began to unroll his greatness. His canvas, like that of a few others, was constricted by the war for which he had been born precisely at the wrong time. The majority of his racing career was restricted to the one small island of his birth. Here the competition was fiercer than ever since all the best horses, unable to be exported into warring Europe, stayed at home and ran furiously against each other.

Because of this, and partly because he was the first great horse who made his name, Tom Dreaper held such a lofty opinion of Prince Regent that Arkle had to win two Gold Cups before Dreaper allowed that he might be 'the Prince's' equal.

In the season 1941–42 Prince Regent won five of his seven races, and was only beaten a short head by Golden Jack (gave 15 lb.) on his first outing. He won his next two, the second by 20 lengths. Jockey Jimmy Brogan was told not to win by too far but was totally unable to comply with his instructions. They all but made it a hat-trick, for next time out in the £550 Red Cross Handicap, then one of the biggest races in the Irish *Calendar* at Leopardstown, they were nearly a fence in front when they came down at the last. Next time, starting 4–6 favourite for the Ardmulchan Plate, Prince Regent won by half a length and six lengths from Simple Song and Brown Jack to whom he was conceding no less than 47 lb. apiece. All he got for his Herculean labour was £41. Just as Prince Regent was due to run for the Baldoyle Chase on March 18th, Jimmy Brogan was injured. A replacement had urgently to be found and Tom Dreaper grabbed Tim Hyde out of the changing-room to start a memorable combination that was to last unbroken through five seasons and 28 races. Tim Hyde was later paralysed as a result of a fall and spent his last years in a wheelchair. He died in May 1967.

Prince Regent wound up the season with one of the most startling performances of his career. Carrying top-weight of 12 st. 7 lb. he started 5–2 favourite for the Irish Grand National and won by a length from Golden Jack (receiving 12 lb.). Strictly interpreted, this represented an improvement of two stone on his first run of the season, and established Prince Regent as a great horse.

Mr Rank came to Fairyhouse for the race. It seems he always contrived to hold his Irish business meetings around Easter Monday, Irish racing's marvellous time of Punchestown and Fairyhouse. The Dreapers remember J. V. Rank with great affection: 'he was blunt and he called spades spades, but he was a *very* nice man'. He particularly enjoyed his Sunday lunches at Greenogue. He used to ask Tom Dreaper not to have anyone else, 'so we can just have a quiet day'. They talked racing and farming over lunch and spent the afternoon walking round Tom's fields appraising his cattle on the brilliant grass. He was godfather to Tom and Betty's son Jim, subsequently a good trainer himself at Greenogue.

From 1942 onwards, impediments mounted for Irish trainers, although of course they were in clover compared with their wretched counterparts in England. Only minute quantities of petrol were now arriving in the neutral island whose approaches were molested by U-boat sharks, and hawked at by long-range bombers. Few people drove cars. Ireland, land of the horse, turned back to horseflesh as a general mode of travel, and the green country which then preserved so much of the gliding peace of the past, seemed to have slipped back into the 19th century.

All horses were walked to race-meetings or to the railway station. They were meant of course to be led by their lads, who in the absence of the Guvnor's eye, would pop up on to their blanketed backs and take the heat out of their own little feet. Tom Dreaper recalled journeys to Kingsbridge station in Dublin following his string in a pony and trap, carrying all the fodder and clothing. 'Except for the trap, the only way Betty and I went the 15 miles to Dublin was on bicycles.' One day at a main crossroads he asked the policeman to hold up the traffic. 'Is Prince Regent there?' asked the officer. 'He is,' said Tom Dreaper, 'Right so,' exclaimed the policeman, lifting up his arms. 'I'll stop the *whole lot* of traffic, *both* ways.' Within the war-narrowed confines of his homeland, Prince Regent was, as Arkle was to become, a folk hero.

Oats were rationed, but the Dreapers had plenty from their farm. Bran was more difficult. But sources not unconnected with the Communion bread were reportedly available, and, racing being very dear to the hearts of the Irish clergy, supplies of bran were forthcoming. The only people allowed cars were doctors and priests, but others had to get to the races somehow: so the roads on racedays suddenly brimmed with strange horse-drawn hearses bulging with carousing race-goers playing poker on the coffin's plinth.

The following year the handicapper hammered Prince Regent with mighty burdens: in his seven outings he never had less than 12 st. 3 lb. and it was usually more than 12 st. 7 lb. He won a 2-mile 'chase at Baldoyle in February with 12 st. 9 lb., and the Hospitals Chase at Naas the following week with 12 st. 3 lb. He then failed, by a head, to give Heirdom 3 st. in the Leopardstown Chase and wound up the season by finishing second to Golden Jack (receiving 33 lb. – almost the full range of the handicap) in a sensational race for the Irish Grand National. It was a colossal performance. Golden Jack was trained by Charlie Rogers and ridden by Dan Moore and the stable was generally reputed to relish a gamble. On this occasion Golden Jack was hotly backed down to 5–2 second favourite. The local stewards immediately inquired into his running compared with that on 20 March at Leopardstown, but accepted the explanation given.

A study of exhaustion: Prince Regent (Tim Hyde) struggling over the last fence in the first post-war Grand National.

The stewards of the Irish National Hunt Committee however were not satisfied and most unusually intervened, summoning Charlie Rogers before them. They pronounced the matter 'most unsatisfactory'. While allowing Rogers the benefit of the doubt they 'severely censured him and cautioned him as to his future conduct'. They also considered handicapper Paddy Kirwan 'greatly to blame as he appeared not to have taken the horse's previous form into consideration'. In the winter of 1941 Golden Jack had given Prince Regent 15 lb. and beaten him a short head. The National weights, a turn round of 48 lb. in Golden Jack's favour, easily exceeded the full range of a handicap.

Next season Prince Regent had a lighter and less successful season. He ran only four times and on each occasion carried 12 st. 7 lb. and started favourite. He was third in the Naas Chase, and second in the December Chase at the Leopardstown Christmas meeting. He then won at Baldoyle giving the second and third, Ruby Loch and Knights Crest the best part of 3 st. apiece but the latter had his revenge in the Irish Grand National when, ridden by young Martin Molony and receiving 42 lb., he beat Prince Regent a length. Ruby Loch (9 st. 7 lb.) was a further length away third.

1944–45, Tom Dreaper recalled was the 'year of the warble': Prince Regent only ran three times. After an unplaced preliminary at Leopardstown in October, he returned there for the Bray Chase to meet his Irish National conqueror, Knights Crest (Martin Molony) on 7 lb. better terms for his one length defeat. Possibly needled at Knights Crest, being foolishly preferred in the betting, he produced one of his great races and won very easily by 5 lengths. Next time out at

Baldoyle, he was baulked and brought down by a horse called Whelan, who went on to win.

Then the warble arrived: 3 inches behind his withers it was, so it was impossible to put a saddle on him. 'He was very, very sore' Tom Dreaper remembered, and he did not run again all that season, thus missing the reopening of the Cheltenham Gold Cup (won by Lord Stalbridge's Red Rower) at the eve-of-peace one-day National Hunt Festival. He was out of action for nearly nine months.

By next season's start the dreary, murderous war was done. The armies gradually disgorged their conscripts and their heroes, their able commanders and their cheerful layabouts. A numbed and rationed peace shuffled blinking out from the wings and put on with stiff fingers its manifold disguises. Racing was replenished. Men came back to own, to train, to ride, to work in stables.

The armies shrank. The stables filled and only here and there were gaps and photographs of fallen friends and wistful rememberings as races Bob or Jack or Tom had won, were run again and won by someone new.

Prince Regent reappeared at Leopardstown in November and ran a tremendous race to be second, beaten a short head by Dorothy Paget's 1940 Gold Cup winner Roman Hackle, who was receiving no less than 3 st. – a colossal performance. Roman Hackle was the horse Charlie Rogers had so successfully bought for Dorothy Paget to replace Golden Miller when he started his long association with that rich and eccentric lady.

Then followed 'The Prince's' first visit to an English racecourse. Wetherby, one of the first four tracks to resume after the war, was chosen. His visit aroused tremendous interest for in spite of his legendary fame few Englishmen had been able to glimpse him. He was talked about as 'the horse of the century'.

English trainers, recently demobbed, wrestling with the problems of rationed fodder, untrained labour, petrol rationing, and lack of saddlery and clothing, were also in battle with a government which regarded racing as an anachronistic indulgence of the idle rich. English trainers soon realized that any old horse from Ireland with good grub inside and practical experience behind him had several lengths start over their horses. And Prince Regent was not any old horse. English prospects of retaining the Gold Cup and National seemed slim. Nevertheless, there was no ill-feeling. The race-starved public were only too pleased to see a champion horse in action and they flocked to see him. They were not disappointed. Prince Regent looked magnificent, jumped immaculately and won very cheekily by half a length. *The Times* was moved to devote half its back page to a photograph of the winner being led in. The short December afternoon ended on a less happy note for Tim Hyde who broke his collar-bone in a fall over hurdles.

He recovered in time to ride Prince Regent in the Baldoyle Chase in February. As was to be the case with Arkle 20 years on, Prince Regent carried his customary 12 st. 7 lb., giving most of his opponents the full 3 st. As usual he was an odds-on favourite but this time he could not quite win and in a desperate finish was beaten a neck and a head by Loyal King and Erinox. To go under at these weights only added lustre and he came to Cheltenham surrounded by all the panoply of greatness, including a special bodyguard.

The Gold Cup's value in that first year of anxious peace was £1,130, and a then

record crowd of 35,000* turned out to see Ireland's champion, a 4–7 favourite as most of the opposition had melted away. Among those brave enough to take him on were Poor Flame (Fred Rimell) a really promising novice but as yet a somewhat chancy jumper, Red April (Glen Kelly) and a French horse Jalgreya.

Prince Regent, a slashing great bay nearly 17 hands high and built on old-fashioned lines, dwarfed his rivals in the paddock. Elsich, who *The Times* thought had no business to be in the race (a view endorsed by the bookmakers who allowed him to start at 200–1) set a slow pace, but passing the stands on the first circuit Prince Regent and Poor Flame had taken it up, closely followed by Red April. The latter was beaten as they reached the top of the hill and although Poor Flame continued to make valiant efforts to get on terms with the champion, he never looked like doing so and was always struggling. He had been an expensive purchase, but this race brutally blunted his potential.

'Prince Regent, a slashing great bay nearly 17 hands high and built on old-fashioned lines . . .'

* The institution and rapid expansion in the late 1980s of Cheltenham's 'Tented Village' increased the crowds on Gold Cup day to 40,000.

Nothing is worse for the morale of a promising youngster than to be asked to strive against and struggle after something more fluent, faster, stronger, better than himself. A tender race behind such a paragon can be the best thing in the development of a young star to whom it is impossible to give too much attention. But a desperate tussle before heart and mind are ready can snuff out many bright hopes.

At Cheltenham the pressure brought on by 'The Prince's' superiority made Poor Flame misjudge the third from home and the last. Prince Regent, despite slipping on the final bend, won very easily by 5 lengths.

The press were eulogistic. Some correspondents declared that no Gold Cup winner – not even Easter Hero or Golden Miller, had been so impressive.

'T'at hoss could win t'National, t'Derby, t'Boat Race and t'London-to-Brighton Walk,' shrieked a jubilant Irishman as Prince Regent was led into the unsaddling enclosure.

'Thank goodness that's over, I feel better now,' disclosed Mr Rank on a note of suppressed triumph. But in the midst of the shouting, Tim Hyde slipped from his old friend's back and turning to Tom Dreaper said very quietly, 'It took me a moment or two to beat that fellow today, Tom'. In that instant his jockey grasped, ahead of everyone else, that peace had come too late and that Prince Regent, now 11, was just too old to stamp his glory on the English turf.

Hyde was alone in his views. Public money poured on Prince Regent for the National. Despite heavy seas the horse went home to complete his preparation in the green, grey peace of Greenogue. The critics discussed his chance in the National and not all were certain that Prince Regent's low-pitched, and sometimes cat-like jumping, would do for Aintree.

When he returned, it was under a maximum security guard which was further strengthened when Langton Abbot, with whom he was widely coupled in Spring Doubles, won the Lincoln. Should 'The Prince' bring off the other leg it was reckoned the bookmakers would be plundered to the tune of nearly £4 million, making him a frighteningly obvious target for would-be dopers.

Squads of policemen patrolled all approaches to the stables, officers kept constant vigil over his padlocked box and Paddy Murray, his lad for six years, and later Head Lad to the Dreaper stable, slept beside him in his box, as Desert Orchid's owner almost did on Christmas night before the 1988 King George.

Liverpool Corporation doubled their train services to the course to accommodate the thousands of people who wanted to catch a glimpse of the favourite. But they were doomed to be disappointed for they arrived to find the gates closed and the only horses in sight were those of the mounted policemen patrolling the entrance.

In his later years Prince Regent was to be bedevilled with kidney trouble and the first grave signs of the complaint showed themselves that National eve. On the morning Tom Dreaper met Harry Bonner and told him confidentially that he wasn't altogether happy: Prince Regent's box had been 'flooded'.

Afterwards some critics said Tim Hyde had made too much use of the favourite. Prince Regent went into the lead at Valentine's on the second circuit, and coming to the last he was well clear of the survivors. But the approach was

cluttered with the sweating jetsam of riderless horses and Tim Hyde was obliged to ride at least three finishes to get a clear run at the fence. He landed clear all right but his mammoth burden and previous exertions had taken their toll: he had no answer when first Lovely Cottage (amateur Bobby Petre) and then Jack Finlay forged past on the long haul home. Tim Hyde's own view (and Harry Bonner, an observer, supports him) is that Prince Regent was beaten not so much by the weight or the distance as by his own mistakes: he made enough to bring a lesser horse down ten times.

Bonner makes the point that Irish fences were then much smaller and softer and Prince Regent had been racing over them too long in the war years to change his style. Certainly when he came to be racing permanently in England, he fell a good deal.

From all parts of the globe letters of admiration and sympathy snowed upon Greenogue. A Catholic priest wrote of 'the heartbreak to myself', of 'my tremendous love and admiration for a truly grand and glorious racehorse. All over the long week-end a kind of weight of sorrow rested on me which I found hard to remove.' He concluded – 'In his defeat we are all the more proud of him, and please God shall the Prince come into his own in 1947'.

Another total stranger to the Dreapers, a suburban housewife, whose husband had gone to the races, related how she and her daughters had wept in their parlour after listening to the race on the wireless.

Prince Regent's defeat marked the start of the Grand National's decline as the prestige race of the season. Public interest in it, well whetted by television and press continues, and it remains a glorious gamble tinged with death. But it has lost for ever any claim to steeplechasing's crown.

Owners and trainers of class horses started to have second thoughts about Liverpool. Great horses like Prince Regent seemed always to be too heavily handicapped and too much the prey of blunders committed by fry so small as to have no place near them. The winners, often low class and singularly fortunate on the day, seldom confirmed the form. The race was getting won by rubbish: its professional status started to slide.

Later sponsors would emerge to stem, then reverse its decline. In spite of the great glitter of sponsored races all through the season, which have been an extraneous and a vitally needed blood-transfusion for racing's ailing frame, the amount added to the National still overtops the lot. Rubbish has been eliminated from entry by more stringent qualifications and by reducing the top weight to 12 st. But by far the most helpful step was the sloping of the fences which made those unique monstrosities fairer and easier to jump. The wise introduction of sloping aprons compelling horses to stand off where once they had been able to get damagingly under the bulge of the furze-clad fences was at the instigation of Brigadier Tony Teacher.

Of our 'Winter Kings' all the early ones were National horses and all but Easter Hero were winners there. After Prince Regent not one ran there till Red Rum a quarter century later.

Prince Regent began his 1946–47 campaign by winning a 3-mile 'chase at Leopardstown in October. For once he had to share favouritism with a horse

called Halcyon Home (receiving 27 lb.) but beat him a clear-cut length. Swindon's Glory (receiving 42 lb.) was 20 lengths back in third place. He then returned to Liverpool to record a bloodless victory in a three-horse affair for the Champion Chase. Starting at 1–6 favourite he won by a distance from the remounted MacMoffat. After that, winter set in with a vengeance. It was one of the worst on record and when the thaw squelched in the floods came roaring. A total of 67 days racing were lost including the National Hunt Meeting. The principal races were re-opened and added on to the April meeting, but Prince Regent was not among the entries. He was aiming for a second attempt at the National. The omens were not very favourable. Inevitably he had again been allotted 12 st. 7 lb. and the floods had left Aintree's usually well-drained turf a quagmire. Weighing-room morale on the opening day was not raised when not a single one of the 16 runners for the Becher Chase completed the course without mishap. Nevertheless, public faith in Prince Regent sent him to the post 8–1 favourite.

The huge crowd, shivering in Aintree's inhospitable stands, peered through the cold, murky mist and could make out very little of what was going on. They were not much enlightened when a huge sheepskin noseband and some unfamiliar colours emerged from the gloom, and there was much scuffling of racecards before the pair was identified as Caughoo and Eddie Dempsey, who went on to win by 20 lengths from a fellow Irishman, Lough Conn. Not a few tears were surreptitiously wiped away as Prince Regent, struggling gallantly under his huge weight, surrendered third place to Kami ridden by leading amateur John Hislop, as stylish a writer as he was a rider.

Prince Regent cannot have had much of a summer holiday that year for he was running again in July. He was made favourite at 4–5 for the Rathlin Handicap Chase at Leopardstown but *anno domini* was at last catching up with him and he made no show. A fortnight later he ran at Galway but was pulled up after 2 miles, and was not seen again until November when he came back to Liverpool for the 2½-mile Becher Chase. The ground was rock hard and Prince Regent, a warm favourite at 2–5, jumped cautiously and made several slight errors. Nevertheless he took the lead at the last and ran out a convincing 3-length winner from First of the Dandies. John Hislop wrote, 'Both in the paddock and in the race, he appeared past his best, and as he came past the post, a deservedly applauded but weary winner, there was a general feeling that honourable retirement should soon be his due.' In fact it was no mean performance, for First of the Dandies, trained by Golden Miller's partner Gerry Wilson, went on to finish a close second in the 1948 National. Prince Regent was also in the race but although his weight was now dropped to 12 st. 2 lb., he was allowed to start at 25–1 and was well behind when he was carried out by a loose horse at the fence after Bechers on the second circuit, the notorious 23rd. Sheila's Cottage went on to become the second mare of the century to win the race.

After this an attempt was made to retire Prince Regent but, like many a busy and successful man, he took a dim view of such a programme, and plans were changed. However it was felt that he should no longer be asked to carry colossal weights in Irish handicaps, and accordingly he came to England where more condition races

were available. He joined Mr Rank's magnificent establishment at Druids Lodge under the care of Head Lad and licence-holder, Fred Horris, who was known as the Professor (for the simple reason that he looked like one).

The policy proved a sound one and Prince Regent soon showed that though the edge might be gone from his brilliance, he was no back number. He had a new partner in veteran Jack Moloney, who had ridden Easter Hero on his gallant 1929 National bid, and in five outings the pair won at Lingfield and Cheltenham and on another occasion they were second at Cheltenham. Furthermore, in the other two races, they were leading when they fell at Sandown, and going well when brought down at Lingfield.

The following year Prince Regent, then 14, was third to Wot No Sun and Roimond in Manchester's important Emblem Chase and was finally retired after falling in the Blindley Heath Chase at Lingfield. The race was won by Coloured Schoolboy, a horse who had had several successful Gold Cup encounters with the new champion Cottage Rake.

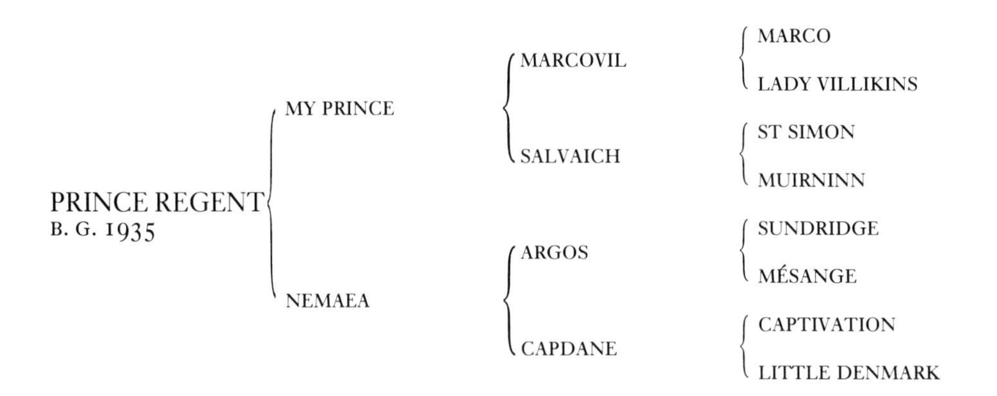

DATE	COURSE	RACE	DISTANCE	VALUE	WEIGHT	JOCKEY	PRICE	PLACE
Season 1939-40								
Mar 16	Baldoyle	Raheny Plate (Amateurs) (F)	2m	£78	10.12	Mr T. Dreaper	20/1	unpl
Mar 23	Phoenix Park	Ardsallagh Plate (Amateurs) (F)	1m 2f 50 yds	£83	11.0	Mr T. Dreaper	20/1	unpl
Apr 27	Naas	Maudlins Plate (Amateurs) (F)	1m 4f	£83	12.0	Mr T. Dreaper	4/5f	won
Season 1940–41								
Mar 17	Baldoyle	St Patrick's Ch	2m 2f	£146	11.7	E. Dempsey	100/8	unpl
May 7	Phoenix Park	Enniskerry Maiden H	2m	£123	11.7	E. Dempsey	100/30	won
May 16	Dundalk	Mickey Macardle Memorial Cup Ch	2m 200yds	£225	11.10	E.Dempsey	5/2	won
Season 1941–42								
Nov 22	Leopardstown	Avonmore H'cp Ch	3m 100 yds	£83	11.6	E. Dempsey	5/4f	2nd
Nov 29	Leopardstown	Webster Champion Cup H'cp Ch	3m 100yds	£83	11.5	E. Dempsey	4/6f	won
Jan 6	Naas	Press H'cp Ch	3m 76 yds	£41	12.2	J. Brogan	4/7f	won
Jan 24	Leopardstown	Red Cross H'cp Ch	3m 300yds	£555	11.8	J. Brogan	6/4f	fell
Feb 21	Navan	Ardmulchan H'cp Chase	3m	£41	12.7	J. Brogan	4/7f	won
Mar 18	Baldoyle	Baldoyle H'cp Ch	3m	£257	12.7	T. Hyde	4/6f	won
Apr 6	Fairyhouse	Irish Grand National H'cp Chase	3m 4f	£745	12.7	T. Hyde	5/2f	won
Season 1942–43								
Nov 21	Leopardstown	Avonmore H'cp Ch	3m 100 yds	£83	12.12	T. Hyde	3/1	3rd
Dec 5	Naas	Naas H'cp Chase	2m 2f	£475	12.7	T. Hyde	7/4f	unpl
Jan 2	Baldoyle	Baldoyle H'cp Chase	3m	£146	12.7	T. Hyde	6/4j.f.	won
Feb 6	Baldoyle	Stewards H'cp Chase	2m 1f 70 yds	£79	12.9	T. Hyde	1/1f	won
Feb 13	Naas	Hospitals H'cp Chase	3m 76yds	£370	12.3	T. Hyde	4/6f	won

DATE	COURSE	RACE	DISTANCE	VALUE	WEIGHT	JOCKEY	PRICE	PLACE
Mar 20	Leopardstown	Leopardstown H'cp Ch	3m 300yds	£367	12.7	T. Hyde	1/3f	2nd
Apr 26	Fairyhouse	Irish Grand National H'cp Chase	3m 4f	£745	12.7	T. Hyde	5/4f	2nd
Season 1943–44								
Oct 9	Phoenix Park	Wicklow Plate (Amateurs) (F)	1m 6f	£74	12.1	Mr T. Nugent	7/2	won
Dec 4	Naas	Naas H'cp Chase	3m 76 yds	£367	12.7	T. Hyde	1/1f	3rd
Dec 27	Leopardstown	December H'cp Chase	3m 100yds	£148	12.7	T. Hyde	4/9f	2nd
Feb 12	Baldoyle	Baldoyle H'cp Chase	3m 100yds	£740	12.7	T. Hyde	2/1f	won
Apr 10	Fairyhouse	Irish Grand National H'cp Chase	3m 4f	£740	12.7	T. Hyde	7/4f	2nd
Season 1944–45								
Sep 30	Phoenix Park	Templeogue Plate (Amateurs) (F)	2m	£74	12.8	Mr T. Nugent	2/1f	2nd
Oct 14	Leopardstown	Kilbride H'cp H	2m	£148	12.7	T. Hyde	6/1	unpl
Nov 4	Phoenix Park	Irish Cesarewitch H'cp (F)	2m	£367	8.7	T. Burns	100/7	unpl
Dec 27	Leopardstown	Bray H'cp Ch	3m 100yds	£148	12.7	T. Hyde	2/1	won
Feb 10	Baldoyle	Baldoyle H'cp Chase	2m 4f 130 yds	£740	12.7	T. Hyde	7/4f	fell
Season 1945–46								
Nov 10	Leopardstown	Leopardstown H'cp Chase	3m 100yds	£178	12.7	T. Hyde	2/1f	2nd
Dec 15	Wetherby	Bradford Chase	3m	£100	12.6	T. Hyde	1/10f	won
Feb 23	Baldoyle	Baldoyle H'cp Chase	2m 4f 130 yds	£296	12.7	T. Hyde	4/7f	3rd
Mar 14	Cheltenham	Gold Cup Chase	3m 2f	£1,130	12.0	T. Hyde	4/7f	won
Apr 5	Liverpool	Grand National H'cp Chase	4m 856yds	£8,805	12.5	T. Hyde	3/1f	3rd

Season 1946–47								
Oct 12	Leopardstown	Laragh H'cp Ch	3m 100yds	£223	12.7	T. Hyde	6/4j.f.	won
Nov 6	Liverpool	Champion Chase	2m 7½f	£2,825	12.0	T. Hyde	1/6f	won
Mar 29	Liverpool	Grand National H'cp Chase	4m 856yds	£10,007	12.7	T. Hyde	8/1f	4th
Season 1947–48								
July 12	Leopardstown	Rathlin H'cp Ch	2m 4f	£148	12.7	T. Hyde	4/5f	unpl
July 30	Galway	Galway Plate H'cp Ch	2m 5f 60 yds	£1,110	12.7	T. Hyde	8/1	p.u.
Nov 5	Liverpool	Becher Chase	2m 4f	£735	12.0	T. Hyde	2/5f	won
Mar 20	Liverpool	Grand National H'cp Chase	4m 856yds	£9,103	12.2	T. Hyde	25/1	p.u.
Season 1948–49								
Nov 26	Sandown	Withington Stayers' Ch	3m 125yds	£204	12.6	J. Moloney	3/1	2nd
Dec 9	Sandown	Ewell Ch	3m 125yds	£522	11.12	J. Moloney	11/10f	fell
Dec 30	Cheltenham	Bibury Ch	3m	£340	11.5	J. Moloney	4/5f	won
Jan 14	Lingfield	Godstone Ch	3m	£204	12.5	J. Moloney	13/8f	won
Feb 12	Lingfield	Manifesto H'cp Ch	3m	£1,128	12.7	J. Moloney	9/2	b.d.
Season 1949–50								
Nov 18	Manchester	Emblem Ch (H'cp)	3m	£1,412	11.8	E. Newman	100/8	3rd
Dec 9	Lingfield	Blindley Heath Ch	3m	£393	12.3	B. Marshall	7/4	fell

SEVEN

Cottage Rake

INDIA BECOMES INDEPENDENT AND PAKISTAN IS BORN; DIOR INTRODUCES THE NEW LOOK; NATIONAL HEALTH SERVICE FOUNDED; BERLIN BLOCKADED AND NORTH ATLANTIC TREATY ORGANISATION ESTABLISHED; THE SOCIALISTS DEVALUE THE POUND; WAR BREAKS OUT IN KOREA.

On the evening of 29 March, 1948, a number of people in the euphoric state which starts stealing over Dublin every lunchtime and envelops the lovely city every night, foregathered in Jammets, the late, famed French restaurant. After dispatching a cluster of Cocktails Brabazon, they dined. A choice of soups: Potage Vincent or Consommé Eileen, was followed by Smoked Salmon Churchtown, les Poussins à la Rake, Coupe Brenda avec les Poires Ardmore and finally Café Oonagh. Puzzled gastronomes will not find these recipes in contemporary cook books: the clue lies in the chickens. Cottage Rake's owner Mr Frank Vickerman was giving a dinner in honour of his beloved eight-year-old gelding, who that month had won the Cheltenham Gold Cup and that very afternoon had carried 12 st. 7 lb. into second place in the Irish Grand National.

The dishes' names were all associated with the famous 'Rake'. First the jockey, brilliant Aubrey Brabazon, most stylish of stylists with a clutch of Gold Cups and Champion Hurdles then unequalled. The trainer Vincent O'Brien, the greatest jumping trainer ever who, before he deserted the great sport for the Flat, had won within 12 years no less than four Cheltenham Gold Cups, three Champion

Hurdles, three Grand Nationals in a row, and ten divisions of the Gloucester Hurdle.

Frank Vickerman's daughters were Brenda and Oonagh, Churchtown was where 'the Rake' was trained, and Aubrey Brabazon's then fiancée (subsequently his wife and mother of seven) came from Ardmore, a lovely village on Ireland's southern coast.

The story of Cottage Rake came at the start of the astonishing success story of Vincent O'Brien, that small, shrewd and dedicated entrepreneur who would have hit the top in almost any business he essayed.

Suitably enough, Mr Vickerman was Vincent's first owner. He was a Bradford wool-merchant who had moved to Ireland and bought some horses to give his son an interest when he returned from the war. The son never came back. Far from the green fields of neutral Ireland, he caught malaria in the North African desert and died. A friend and namesake of Vincent's in nearby Fermoy was one of Vickerman's wool agents, so it happened that in 1943 three three-year-olds came to Churchtown. All turned out very moderate, but the two 'chasers that Vincent O'Brien bought him later both won good races: one, Con's Cottage, was later sold to Lord Mildmay and went to Peter Cazalet.

Cottage Rake didn't enter O'Brien's life till he was 6 years old. He was born in a little yard behind a doctor's surgery in the main street of Mallow – an attractive little town on the banks of the Blackwater. His breeder, Dr Vaughan, nicknamed 'Otto', was a great social character who liked parties, fancied himself with the girls, remained a bachelor, hunted twice a week and rode his own horses in local point-to-points. He was a very popular doctor.

Cottage Rake was sent up to Ballsbridge as a five-year-old but was not sold, so Dr Vaughan asked O'Brien who then had built up to about twenty horses, whether he would take him to train at Churchtown. He had already run in a bumper at Thurles, but without distinction. Vincent remembers him being very poor on arrival but was impressed with his size and quality. When he first ran at Limerick on 27 December in the County Plate – a valuable race for maidens – it was really to please Dr Vaughan as Vincent had not yet galloped him seriously and did not think him ready. However, ridden by Danny O'Sullivan, (later Vincent O'Brien's Assistant Head Lad) Cottage Rake made all the running and won in a canter by 6 lengths. When he followed up by winning a bumper at Leopardstown where the class is high and prospective buyers abound, people started to enquire about his price and several offers were tendered. Major 'Cuddie' Stirling-Stuart whose most famous horse was to be Cool Customer, bid £3,500 subject to his passing the vet, but to everyone's consternation, Maxie Cosgrove, later a world-famous horse physician who later cared for Arkle, spun him for making a noise. Major Stirling-Stuart did not therefore go through with the deal, and three years later had the chagrin of watching his reject beat his beloved 'Coolie' for the Gold Cup.

During the summer some old friends of Dr Vaughan, Mrs Lewis and her son-in-law 'Jock' Skeffington, who became 13th Viscount Massereene and Ferrard in the Irish Peerage, were interested but they too cried off when they saw their vet's report – although this one, from Alan Baker, believed the horse would not be affected unless he caught a bad cold. This was a great stroke of luck for Vincent

O'Brien, for had the deal gone through, Cottage Rake would have been sent to England, probably to Ryan Price.

In the end the fortunate Mr Vickerman only became his owner as a result of a misunderstanding: he agreed to buy the horse, subject to the vet, but paid a deposit of £1,000 as a security. Dr Vaughan took the deposit as finalization of the deal and although Cottage Rake again failed the vet, he nevertheless changed hands for £3,500

He ran his first few races for Mr Vickerman in the *nom-de-course* 'Mr G. D. B. O'Brien', the initials being an amalgam of those of the horses, Good Days, and Dry Bob, whose 800–1 double in the Irish Cesarewitch and Cambridgeshire of 1944 had launched Vincent O'Brien (then in his first season with only seven horses) on his rocket road to fame. Mr Vickerman's large gamble on the double funded his purchase of the future Gold Cup winner.

Cottage Rake ran next in the Irish Cesarewitch but was not greatly fancied. He was not 100 per cent ready yet, and was taking in the race *en route* for the 1½-mile Naas November Handicap. It put him right for it. 'It wasn't a *great* gamble,' says Vincent drily, 'but we fancied him quite a bit.' He started favourite at 3–1 and in the hands of J. Tyrrel won fairly comfortably.

The way to 'chasing often starts with amateur-ridden flat races for maidens over 2 miles. In Cottage Rake's time these took place only in Ireland where some could (and still can) be won with friendly co-operation by very slow horses indeed. The Naas race was a different kettle of fish – smart flat-racers professionally ridden, competing for the Irish equivalent of the old Manchester November Handicap, then the last big gamble of the flat.

It showed clearly how classy Cottage Rake was. Now he would turn this speed to fences if he could and at this stage Aubrey Brabazon came into his life. 'The Brab' knows everyone in Ireland, is a friend to all, a seeker-out of many top-class horses and an excellent companion. Many is the deal he brought about between English trainers with eyes bigger than their purses and an infinite variety of splendid Irish vendors. 'So, you've £10,000 to spend, and Mr Flaherty here is asking £25,000. Sure there's nothing between you at all that a "jar" won't settle.' Aubrey with cheerful generosity stands one 'jars' all across Ireland, leaning forward like a bird under his dark wavy hair, 'Look now, would you ever be interested in an unraced horse? I know of just the fellow'. And we would be off again, tyres hissing down the grey wet lanes of Ireland to some forbidding Georgian farm and depressing horse and a wonderful welcome and six new friends.

Aubrey Brabazon remembered riding 'The Rake' one school and not being hugely impressed, 'a very good jumper, but not a terribly nice ride over fences – he carried his head very high, not an easy horse to get down on and look neat'. 'The Brab', who held the reins as if they were thin silk, was the dapperest fellow on board you ever saw.

However, Vincent O'Brien thought Cottage Rake would be a very good horse, as he had taken to jumping naturally and was bred the right way. His sire Cottage dominated the breeding of jumpers in the 1940s and 1950s, as Vulgan and Deep Run would do in the following decades. Few jumping sires have time really to make their names before they are dead. Cottage Rake accordingly was aimed high

and sent for the Carrickmines Chase – at the Leopardstown Christmas meeting – one of the top-class novice 'chases of the time of year. Word that he should win was babbled everywhere and the stable backed him heavily. He started hot odds-on at 4–7. The race was merely a procession. Cottage Rake, never putting a foot wrong, won by 20 lengths which could, Aubrey Brabazon reported, easily have been 50. He was then put by for a bit and when he reappeared in April, a new partner had to be found for him as Aubrey Brabazon had broken his collar bone. Eddie Newman, who was at the time working for Aubrey Brabazon's father Cecil at Ranger's Lodge, thus came in for a couple of lucky rides. He narrowly won a valuable Maiden Chase at Fairyhouse then, with an 'impossible' 13 st., won the important Mickey Macardle Memorial Chase at Dundalk. He wound up the season starting 6–4 favourite for the Champion Novices at Naas, but, according to jockey Danny Morgan, was never really going and could only finish third to Fear Cruid and Coupe. The same afternoon, a young hurdler called Hatton's Grace had his first outing and finished a promising fourth in the Maiden Hurdle. A year later he joined Cottage Rake at Vincent O'Brien's and the material was ready for the double Gold Cup-Champion Hurdle double of 1949 and 1950 trained by Vincent O'Brien, ridden by Aubrey Brabazon.

Cottage Rake opened his 1947–48 campaign with an outing in a handicap Hurdle at Phoenix Park. Aubrey Brabazon chose to ride the favourite, Whale Harbour, who duly won, and Cottage Rake, ridden by E. Kennedy and quite unfancied at 20–1, finished unplaced. Nevertheless he ran sufficiently prominently to be noticed by *Chaseform* who reported sapiently 'good sort, better for race'. He then diverted to the flat to attempt an awkward double of the Irish Cesarewitch and a repeat Naas November Handicap. He won the first, started favourite for the second, but failed.

Then it was 'chasing again. He rejoined forces with Aubrey Brabazon for the December Handicap Chase at Leopardstown and won with consummate ease. Aubrey Brabazon held him up and in fact landed over the last only third, but the issue was settled with the flashing speed on the run-in which was the stamp of his greatness. A later, equally brilliant exponent of this style was John Francome, a genius of judgement who could comfortably 'see his stride' 25 yards from the fence, and never seemed to be 'booting' his horse at all.

This race at Leopardstown set the pattern for his future races. The tactics from then on were always those of the hawk: to wait, hover and strike. Vincent O'Brien recalls that all Cottage Rake's races were exciting because up to the last, the result always seemed in the balance, but 'with Aubrey Brabazon's brilliance and the horse's speed', says O'Brien, 'the race could always be won from the last'. It was of course to Cottage Rake's infinite advantage that he had, in Aubrey Brabazon, a partner who was as good on the flat as he was over fences and whose cool, tactical brain outfoxed most jockeys riding. Vincent O'Brien fully appreciated the fact. 'Aubrey is a really brilliant jockey, especially on the big occasion.' He also approved of Aubrey Brabazon's quiet style of presenting a horse at a fence –'Good hands and an understanding of the horse are far better than booting . . . it is not necessary to boot if they have been properly schooled.'

'The Rake' had made his name. He was a worthy successor to Prince Regent to

challenge Britain's best at Cheltenham. So it was a wretched disappointment when, starting favourite for his last Irish outing, the important Leopardstown Chase in February, he caught the top of the second last ditch and toppled over.

Cottage Rake went to Cheltenham with the faith of the Irish unfurled around him and blowing trumpets. But his arrival did not cause qualms in every English breast. Major Stirling-Stuart's Cool Customer was favourite at 7–2 and Happy Home, Klaxton and Red April were all preferred in the betting to Cottage Rake who started at 10–1. Due to the shortage of accommodation Cottage Rake was boarded at 'Frenchie' Nicholson's stables next to the course. Mrs Nicholson vividly recollected goggling in disbelief at Cottage Rake's pre-race breakfast which consisted of 'a great bucket of mash and half a bowl of hay!', and, after the race, at Mrs Vickerman pedaling round and round the yard on young David Nicholson's ancient tricycle.

Cool Customer's manifold supporters were soon knocked silly. Hardly had he started in his all-scarlet colours at the side of the stands than he capsized at the very first fence: a great moan rose from the crowd. After this Dorothy Paget's Happy Home made most of the running. A mile out, Aubrey Brabazon made a move to go after him and the pair came down the hill and round the elbow, stride for stride. Going for the last Martin Molony, realizing that his horse could not hope to match 'The Rake's' speed on the flat, drove on for all he was worth, hoping to take 'The Rake' along full tilt into the last and perhaps thus at least upset or overturn him. Aubrey Brabazon wasn't tempted. He not only refused to go along with Happy Home but allowed Cottage Rake to 'fiddle' the fence losing a length in

Mrs Vickerman leads Cottage Rake into the unsaddling enclosure after his Gold Cup win in 1949.

the process. Then, with impudent coolness, he waited till his horse was balanced and running before asking for an effort. The response was magnificent and although Happy Home fought on bravely, Cottage Rake drew away to win his first Gold Cup by a length and a half, and the crowd babbled about his fantastic turn of foot.

Cottage Rake returned to Ireland to face a champion's task of shouldering 12 st. 7 lb. in the Irish Grand National at Fairyhouse, a course which Brabazon believes he never really liked. It proved beyond him and he was quite unable to give 3 st. to the bottom weighted Hamstar who won by 15 lengths, and afterwards went on to win several good races.

Cottage Rake's next memorable season was a masterpiece of training. He ran four times only: a warm-up in Ireland and three big English 'chases, the Emblem at Manchester, the King George VI at Kempton and the Cheltenham Gold Cup, and won all four. Aubrey Brabazon, commenting on this comparatively light programme, points out that although not very experienced, he was not exactly a young horse. Furthermore, although he did himself quite well, he was inclined to run up light with a lot of racing and travelling from Ireland to England and back.

The first outing on 21 October at Limerick Junction was typical of Cottage Rake. Set to carry top weight of 12 st. 7 lb., he was favourite at even money, and although only fourth at the last, accelerated to win very easily by four lengths, conceding 35 lb. and 34 lb. respectively to the second and third.

Next time out at Manchester he gave his supporters a nasty fright for the £1,600 Emblem Chase, in which his opponents included Lord Bicester's immensely

Cottage Rake after his victory at Cheltenham.

popular Silver Fame, and Cromwell, on whom Lord Mildmay had been so unlucky not to win the 1948 National. As usual Cottage Rake carried 12 st. 7 lb., and as usual he started favourite, but on this occasion at odds against: 3-1. All seemed to be well, although he was challenging rather earlier than usual, when he took the lead two out, but approaching the last Martin Molony repeated the tactics that had failed at Cheltenham in March, and went for his life. This time it paid off and Cottage Rake made a mistake: thus Silver Fame started the run-in with a 2-length advantage. Worse still, Aubrey Brabazon lost his whip in recovering from the blunder. (It was a silver-mounted one, presented by a grateful English owner and must adorn today some small thief's mantelshelf.) The finish that ensued was something 'that people who saw it will never forget', says Vincent O'Brien with feeling. Cottage Rake had it all to do from his last fence blunder and none but the best can get up and do it from there. But with whipless Brabazon coaxing and pushing he got into his stride at last and set off up the run-in after flying Silver Fame. And closed the gap. And caught him. And held on and edged past and stuck out his neck and won by it.

Cromwell, to whom 'The Rake' was giving a stone, was 4 lengths away third.

The King George VI Chase was nearly lost to Kempton's old bugbear, frost. As it was, the Boxing Day programme had to be postponed and only that evening did the thaw set in. However the postprandial Stewards heroically staggered on to the course liverishly early, and the decision to race was announced in the chill dark at 7.30. Uncertainty had affected the attendance, but a large, vociferous Irish contingent had come to cheer their champion. Aubrey Brabazon, together with his fiancée Ethne, Stuart Murless (Noel's Irish-based brother) with his fiancée Beryl and Aubrey's mother, all had a memorable stay at Grosvenor House.

In the race, Silver Fame's stable companion, handsome Roimond (12 st. 1 lb.) set out to make all the running, often a successful manoeuvre on Kempton's sharp track. However Cottage Rake, (12 st. 6 lb.) although not jumping too fluently, never lost touch and getting on terms with a great leap at the last he sprinted clear on the flat to win by 5 lengths. Happy Home, now only a dilution of his old strength, finished a further 6 lengths back in third place, though receiving 12 lb.

It was a great victory and stamped Cottage Rake as likely to become the third dual Gold Cup winner. Only last year's favourite Cool Customer, trained in the north by Jack Fawcus, could be seriously fancied to give him a race. Cool Customer had redeemed his last year's lapse with four consecutive victories and his chances were further improved when Cottage Rake fell victim to a bout of coughing in February. However, he recovered quickly and travelled to Cheltenham together with Hatton's Grace and Castledermot, (destined for the Champion Hurdle and the National Hunt Chase), on the first equine racing air-lift from Ireland to England. They flew in a Silver City Bristol from Shannon to Whitchurch and were boarded with Gerald Balding, that popular trainer and world class polo playing father of two highly successful English trainers, Toby and Ian, winners between them of two Grand Nationals, a Derby and an Arc de Triomphe.

Tuesday's and Wednesday's cards ran to schedule and O'Brien's stable confidence soared when Hatton's Grace (Aubrey Brabazon) and Castledermot

(Lord Mildmay) carried off their respective races. However, on Wednesday evening the frost set in and by Thursday the course was no fitter for racing than the adjacent A.46. The race was immediately reopened for the original entries and the date fixed for 11 April. The postponement, which was inconvenient for some, did not upset 'The Rake's' training. It helped, for his programme had already been upset and delayed by coughing.

Hatton's Grace and Castledermot returned to Churchtown by boat. Cottage Rake remained at Devizes with the Baldings, and Aubrey Brabazon, sticking manfully to his original plans, got married and went to France for his honeymoon. He returned just in time for the big race, reckoned to be a renewal of the duel between 'The Rake' and 'Coolie'. None of the other four, Finnure, Red April, Royal Mount or Coloured School Boy, good though they were, seemed to constitute threats to the two kings. The books offered 4–6 Cottage Rake, 7–2 Cool Customer.

A pleasing irony was apparent to those who remembered how close Cool Customer's owner, Major Stirling-Stuart, had been to buying 'The Rake' three years before. In the small world at the top of 'chasing's tree, there was another inter-relation: 'The Rake's' jockey Aubrey Brabazon was also the regular rider of Cool Customer and had indeed won no less than 10 races on him. This placed Stirling-Stuart in Brabazon's debt and Brabazon in a position to know a great deal about both horses.

The pace began poorly, which Cool Customer did not appreciate: he made several early mistakes. On the second circuit, he was sent on from the top of the hill, and at the increased pace began to jump brilliantly. At the last open ditch Cottage Rake moved up to join him and the race was on in earnest. Cottage Rake's supporters began to get apprehensive for Cool Customer was gaining at every fence and came round the elbow 1½ lengths up and with the advantage of the rails. Dread surged when Aubrey Brabazon went for his whip. Never before had the pressure come on the champion so early. Worse still, there was no immediate response. Thundering up the rise towards the last and the steep hill and the post beyond it, Cool Customer was definitely still going the better. 'The Rake' seemed about to be beaten.

Cottage Rake, however, refused to give in, and under vigorous driving, he began to close the gap. Eighty yards from the post he found what separates good horses from the truly great, not so much an extra gear but a final rocket. Suddenly he accelerated and shot past Cool Customer to win, incredibly, by 2 lengths. Aubrey Brabazon thought it the hardest race of his career, 'hardest for horse *and* jockey', he emphasized.

Cheering erupted again as the two horses returned steaming to the unsaddling enclosure, where there occurred one of those incidents which make steeple-chasing a band of brothers. In recognition of Aubrey Brabazon's victories on his Cool Customer Major Stirling-Stuart had had a pair of cuff-links made for him suitably engraved with his and the horse's initials. He did not post them to Aubrey in Ireland, saying, 'We're bound to meet at Cheltenham, aren't we?' Thus it was that when his dream of winning the Cheltenham Gold Cup had seemed about to be realized and was then blown away in the pull of a few strides and a puff of

seconds, Major Stirling-Stuart remembered his present. He left the little group of dejection surrounding his own conquered hero, stepped into the champion's throng around 'The Rake', touched Aubrey Brabazon on the shoulder and handed over amid the heat and sweat the little box of cuff-links. He congratulated Aubrey, the O'Briens and the Vickermans and spent a special moment giving 'The Rake' several congratulatory pats on his damp, tossing neck. Aubrey weighed in with the cuff-links and the Major went back to Cool Customer.

Cottage Rake was now 11 years old but he had been lightly raced and showed little signs of wear. With the possible exception of Finnure, no younger rivals seemed likely to threaten his throne.

He started the season by repeating last year's victory in the Croom Chase and followed up by winning a long-distance 'chase at Sandown with an ease that belied the ¾-length verdict. Then the stage was set at Kempton in the King George VI for another attempt by young Finnure to unsettle the old champion. Lord Bicester's horse was truly brilliant, unbeaten in all his four starts that season and yet, by the conditions of the race, was set to receive 11 lb. The early pace was slow which did not suit Cottage Rake. Aubrey Brabazon thinks he may have given his horse a bit too much to do. 'But I didn't ride a *diabolical* race – nobody gave me a rocket for it.' At all events Cottage Rake failed by ¾ length to catch his young rival and met his first defeat for 18 months. No one could damn him. The Finnure stable considerably fancied their horse for the Gold Cup and this time 'The Rake' had been trying to give him nearly a stone.

The Leopardstown Chase was again chosen for his Gold Cup preliminary. Two years earlier, he had fallen in the race, and now he hit the turf again. Ridden by the then leading Irish amateur Mr 'Bunny' Cox, he was brought down at the 13th fence, when going well.

'The Rake's' third successive Gold Cup. It's 1950 and 'The Brab' on board not only gives another demonstration of how to sit safely and leave your horse alone – but gives a little smile, too.

The warsong of 'The Rake' preceded him to Cheltenham:

Aubrey's up, the money's down
The frightened bookies quake
Come on me lads and give a cheer
Begod 'tis Cottage Rake!

Indeed, the treble reputation of 'The Rake', 'The Brab' and Vincent O'Brien had driven the English defenders scuttling from the field. Except for Finnure, who had a conservative 7 lb. to make up, there was nothing in the top class to take him on.

The early pace was so funereal that at one stage Michael O'Hehir, whose galloping commentaries for decades much enlivened the 'chasing scene, likened the contest to a bicycle race. The crawl was a deliberate plot. Finnure's connections had instructed his brilliant jockey Martin Molony to slow the pace down so that with one quick unleashed arrow of late speed, the younger horse could 'blind' his elder. In doing so Molony was hoist with his own petard. At the top of the hill Aubrey Brabazon with quicksilver thought dashed Cottage Rake into the lead and kicked on furiously for home. Gathering momentum from the downhill gradient, he went further and further ahead. Finnure, undefeated all season till that afternoon, was never able to get in a blow and the official winning distance was 10 lengths. The dashing Spanish Marques de Portago who lived at speed like an old-time lord and who was killed by speed in a car crash, made his début on an English racecourse, and was third on his own horse, Garde-Toi. Boldly, he ignored even the warning in the horse's name: he never looked after himself.

Hatton's Grace again won the Champion Hurdle so O'Brien and Brabazon brought off 'chasing's classic double for the second year running. Aubrey Brabazon's hectic and triumphant week concluded on Saturday when he rode an odds-on favourite at Hurst Park. He appeared to be winning comfortably and nearing the post dropped his hands, only to be forced to a dead-heat by a fast-finishing outsider. The Stewards hauled him over the coals and fined him. The late editions of the evening papers carried the headline *'Brabazon caught napping'*. Commented Vincent O'Brien 'Alas poor Aubrey, the only sleep he got all week'.

In April Cottage Rake had another attempt on the Irish Grand National. He started favourite despite his strangely poor record in handicaps and the fact that he had top-weight of 12 st. 7 lb. He faded gradually over the last ½ mile and eventually finished a distant fourth to Dominicks Bar.

The race was the beginning of the end. From that point, Cottage Rake declined with terrible speed. And it is as true of mighty 'chasers as of human champions, that the greater they've been the swifter they fall. When speed starts falling off, a loss of a few m.p.h. means 50 yards difference at the end of a 3-mile 'chase: the yawning gap between a Champion and a plater. Cottage Rake had no summer holiday that year and was running again on 29 June in a peculiar flat race restricted to National Hunt jockeys at Limerick Junction.

In July he finished sixth in a handicap hurdle at Leopardstown starting at 10–1. Aubrey Brabazon rode in the race, but not on his old friend. He was wanted for the

favourite Alberoni. He did team up with Cottage Rake for the important Galway Plate, a £1,000, 2½-mile 'chase at the beginning of August. This was his last main target and the pair were made favourites at 2–1. They finished fifth to Denistown. Aubrey Brabazon knew that the horse had 'gone'. Leg trouble now developed and he had to be fired. He was off the course for 16 months, reappearing in a hurdle race at the Leopardstown Christmas meeting and coming in third to his old sparring partner Hatton's Grace.

In the spring of 1953 he joined Gerald Balding's stable where he had always stayed for his raids on England. He was now 14 years old but not yet finished. He ran a fine race over hurdles at the Cheltenham spring meeting, finishing second to Vistal, and had a final go at the 'cracks' in Hurst Park's newly instituted Queen Elizabeth II Chase. Aubrey Brabazon came over from Ireland and the crowd was delighted to see the old firm back in business. The pair carried, with the public's affectionate wishes, a lot of sentimental money; the starting price of 100–6 was not a true reflection of the horse's form in his last two declining years. Cottage Rake was in touch and going well when he fell at the last open ditch, giving Aubrey Brabazon an expensive broken arm, for he thus missed winning that sensational Irish Derby on O'Brien's Chamour, the horse that was alleged to have been doped to win a maiden race. The analyst then employed by the Jockey Club and Irish Turf Club produced some bizarre findings, claiming that samples taken from police horses in Athens, and the starter's hack at Plumpton were all positive!

Even then 'The Rake' was not retired, but brought out to run twice more the following autumn. In the first of these he came up against the new star who had burst like a rocket from the ranks of hunter-'chasers: Hallowe'en without his regular professional pilot Fred Winter won by 5 lengths.

On 8 December Cottage Rake ran his last race in heavy ground at Wolverhampton. Ridden then by royal jockey Dick Francis, he started second favourite but finished a remote third to Holly Bank and Mont St Michel.

He had been at it for eight busy and triumphant years since we first met him in that little hunting yard in Mallow. He was, by the lateness and devastation of his final run, one of the most exciting champions to watch. And he was a singularly great one. No horse since his reign, not even Arkle, has exceeded 'The Rake's' Cheltenham treble of three Gold Cups in a row.

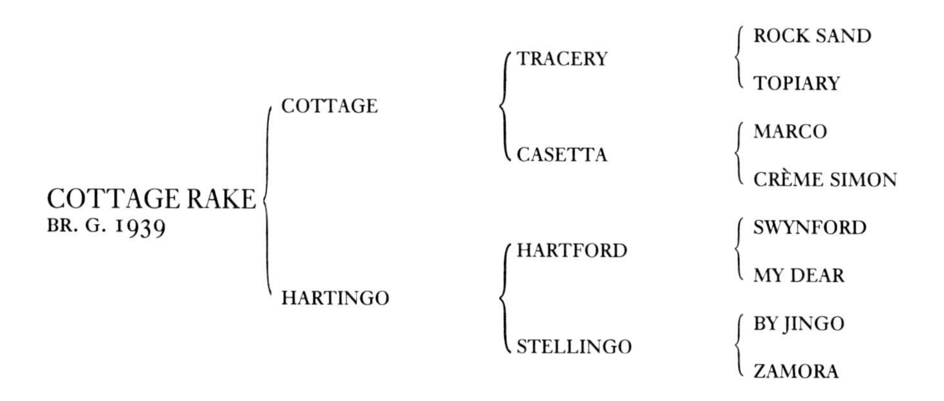

DATE	COURSE	RACE	DISTANCE	VALUE	WEIGHT	JOCKEY	PRICE	PLACE
Season 1944–45								
Mar 1	Thurles	Corinthian Plate (F)	2m	£74	11.9	Mr T. Bennett	100/8	unpl
Season 1945–46								
Dec 27	Limerick	County Plate (H)	2m	£178	11.0	D. O'Sullivan	10/1	won
Feb 16	Leopardstown	Corinthian Plate (F)	2m	£96	12.0	Mr P. Hogan	1/1f	won
Season 1946–47								
Oct 31	Limerick Junction	Emly H'cp (F)	2m 4f	£222	9.5	N. Brennan	7/1	unpl
Nov 9	Curragh	Irish Cesarewitch H'cp (F)	2m	£740	7.7	N. Brennan	100/7	unpl
Nov 23	Naas	Naas November H'cp (F)	1m 4f	£370	7.12	J. Tyrrell	3/1f	won
Dec 26	Leopardstown	Carrickmines Chase	2m 4f	£296	12.3	A. Brabazon	4/7f	won
Apr 5	Phoenix Park	Castleknock H'cp Plate (F)	2m	£370	9.2	M. Wing	7/4f	unpl
Apr 7	Fairyhouse	Maiden Chase	2m 2f	£444	12.0	E. Newman	4/1	won
Apr 18	Dundalk	Mickey Macardle Memorial Cup Chase	2m 200yds	£296	13.0	E. Newman	2/1f	won
Apr 26	Naas	Champion Novice Chase	2m 40yds	£296	13.0	D. Morgan	6/4f	3rd
Season 1947–48								
Sept 27	Phoenix Park	Tallaght H'cp H	2m	£222	11.0	E. J. Kennedy	20/1	unpl
Oct 30	Limerick	Garryowen H'cp Plate (F)	1m 4f	£111	10.12	G. Wells	4/5f	2nd
Nov 8	Curragh	Irish Cesarewitch H'cp (F)	2m	£740	8.2	G. Wells	5/1	won
Nov 22	Naas	Naas November H'cp (F)	1m 4f	£370	9.1	G. Wells	7/2f	unpl
Dec 27	Leopardstown	December H'cp Ch	2m 175 yds	£296	12.0	A. Brabazon	11/8j.f.	won
Feb 14	Leopardstown	Leopardstown H'cp Chase	3m 100 yds	£468	12.7	A. Brabazon	5/4f	fell
Mar 4	Cheltenham	Gold Cup Chase	3m 2f	£1,911	12.0	A. Brabazon	10/1	won
Mar 29	Fairyhouse	Irish Grand National H'cp Chase	3m 4f	£1,467	12.7	A. Brabazon	6/4f	2nd

DATE	COURSE	RACE	DISTANCE	VALUE	WEIGHT	JOCKEY	PRICE	PLACE
Season 1948–49								
Oct 21	Limerick Junction	Croom H'cp Ch	3m	£268	12.7	A. Brabazon	1/1f	won
Nov 6	Curragh	Irish Cesarewitch H'cp (F)	2m	£740	9.3	A. Brabazon	20/1	unpl
Nov 19	Manchester	Emblem Ch (H'cp)	3m	£1,616	12.7	A. Brabazon	3/1f	won
Dec 28	Kempton	King George VI Ch	3m	£2,486	12.6	A. Brabazon	13/8f	won
Apr 11	Cheltenham	Gold Cup Chase	3m 2f	£2,817	12.0	A. Brabazon	4/6f	won
Season 1949–50								
Oct 20	Limerick Junction	Croom Chase	3m	£256	12.8	A. Brabazon	1/4f	won
Nov 5	Curragh	Irish Cesarewitch H'cp (F)	2m	£740	8.11	A. Brabazon	33/1	unpl
Nov 25	Sandown	Withington Stayers' Ch	3m 125yds	£690	12.7	A. Brabazon	1/3f	won
Dec 26	Kempton	King George VI Ch	3m	£2,179	12.7	A. Brabazon	4/6f	2nd
Feb 18	Leopardstown	Leopardstown H'cp Ch	3m 5f	£740	12.7	Mr J. R. Cox	6/4f	b.d.
Mar 9	Cheltenham	Gold Cup Chase	3m 2f	£2,936	12.0	A. Brabazon	5/6f	won
Apr 10	Fairyhouse	Irish Grand National H'cp Chase	3m 4f	£1,485	12.7	A. Brabazon	1/1f	4th
Season 1950–51								
June 29	Limerick Junction	Santoi Cup (H'cp) (F)	1m 6f	£129	10.7	A. Brabazon	10/1	unpl
July 15	Leopardstown	Leopardstown H'cp H	2m	£478	12.0	R. J. O'Ryan	10/1	unpl
Aug 2	Galway	Galway Plate H'cp Chase	2m 5f 60 yds	£1,110	12.7	A. Brabazon	2/1f	unpl
Season 1951–52								
Dec 27	Leopardstown	Shankhill H	2m	£202	11.7	A. Brabazon	6/1	3rd
Season 1952–53								
Apr 15	Cheltenham	Painswick H	2m	£204	11.3	G. Kelly	100/7	2nd
May 25	Hurst Park	Queen Elizabeth Ch (H'cp)	3m	£3,735	11.9	A. Brabazon	100/6	fell
Season 1953–54								
Nov 5	Wincanton	Newquay Chase	2m	£136	12.0	B. Marshall	6/1	2nd
Dec 8	Wolverhampton	Shrewsbury Ch	3m	£204	11.10	R. Francis	9/4	3rd

EIGHT

Mandarin

THE SUEZ CRISIS: CONNIVANCE WITH FRANCE AND ISRAEL IN ALMOST THE LAST SAD POUNCE OF THE BRITISH LION; THE RUSSIANS BRUTALLY CRUSH THE HUNGARIAN UPRISING, BUT BULGANIN AND KHRUSHCHEV VISIT BRITAIN; THE FIRST SATELLITE LAUNCHED; ANOTHER BALANCE OF PAYMENTS CRISIS; AS BELGIANS QUIT THE CONGO CIVIL WARS RUN BLOOD; SOUTH AFRICA LEAVES THE COMMONWEALTH.

It is June 1962 and 52 years and two wars have passed since Jerry M. was over here at Auteuil, a green sprigged knot in the skirts of Paris, to win the 'Grand Steeple'. It is hot after scudding rain which wets the runway as Fulke Walwyn and Fred Winter, trainer and rider of Mandarin, fly in. 'Oh God,' groans Walwyn, 'the ground will be too soft.'

English hopes for a notable, immensely valuable victory in France rest on the slender frame and damaged legs of the 11-year-old French-bred, French-owned gelding and on the more robust, even more battered body of his partner. Not that Fred Winter was feeling particularly robust on race day. He had been nearly killing himself to do the 9 st. 10 lb. required for Beaver II in the Grand Haie de Quatre Ans later in the afternoon, more than half a stone less than his normal minimum. On the eve of the race he was attacked by a violent stomach upset, which kept him up all night. In the weighing room he had an attack of cramp and had to be dressed by Stan Mellor, and he finally tottered into the paddock feeling

like 'a bit of chewed-up string'. At least the Auteuil weighing-room was comfortable. English jump jockeys, then inured to the usually Spartan booths, where up till the 1970s muddy riders had to change on chilly afternoons, goggled at the rich leather-covered settees and luxurious tiled showers.

The scene outside too looked different to the small band of English supporters. Under the hot June sunshine the crowd was Ascot-clad. Clipped privet hedges glowed greenly against sparkling white railings. Curious obstacles abounded: the running brook in front of the stands with its resident family of ducks; 'Le Bullfinch'; white post-and-rails topping a little bank. The course, an intricate maze of peculiar jumps, might have been a show-jumping circuit: it looked nothing whatever like the tough but simple uniformity of any British 'chase track.

Fred Winter was no stranger to France: almost a South of France resident each summer between Whitsun's end and August's start of the jumping seasons, he had made himself felt along the Côte d'Azur and become a good, brave water-skier. He had also ridden horses in France: Lucky Dome for Vincent O'Brien, Retour de Flamme for Sid Warren, and he had won at Auteuil on Gold Wire. Now he twice walked the complex course, which consisted of two separate figures of eight in different directions, and then once round the outside, and wrote it all down four times. He hoped that he had got it right. He noted too that at the start the horses walked across the gate in Indian file, before they whipped right and jumped off. So, he reasoned craftily, if he could be at the back of the file, he would get the rails.

At first, all went to plan, but landing over the third of the 21 fences, the rubber bit which Mandarin always wore snapped in two leaving Fred to face 3½ miles of the twists and junctions with neither brakes nor steering. Afterwards he recalled: 'The first thought that went through my mind was "sabotage". The second was "Well, I'm not going to jump off. I never have, because I haven't the nerve".' Luckily the first four fences after the bit broke were straight ahead so there was less of an immediate problem. Fred went on: 'The *amazing* part was that Mandarin didn't try to run away. He was normally a very free little animal but he never attempted to go mad and never varied his speed one way or the other . . . This French rider Daumas was on my outside on a horse called Taillefer and he helped me round the first bend. He was about a neck behind and the pressure of his horse and my own efforts got us round.' Fred discovered he could move Mandarin about with the squeeze of his vice-like knees, the swing of his body, and some pressure on the horse's neck from the reins. But a more complex problem was now galloping towards him. 'There was a very tricky place with three courses to choose from. The one we had to take was in the middle. You've got about 50 yards without rails before the privet hedge which divides the thing up. Mandarin went a little to the left but I straightened him up fairly easily and took the middle course, and after that he had company and was never absolutely in front by himself. He made an awful mistake at the water the second time but this was a good thing! It left me fifth and the leaders gave me a lead round the bend!'

But another hazard loomed though, with nothing for Fred to do except wait as Mandarin came rushing down at it. Four fences from home they had to take a very sharp turn to the right and then pick the middle course. 'It's very open on the right and I had nothing on that side and he could easily have taken the inside course. In

fact for a couple of strides he *did* try to. I had to throw absolutely everything to the left and he came back. Then he broke down and from then on it was a struggle. Up till then he had been going terribly easily and I hadn't asked him anything. I lost about 3 or 4 lengths in the process and had a lot of ground to make up.' They made it up. Turning into the long home straight, they hit the front. Mandarin's loyal fans, few of whom were aware of the double penalties of broken bit and broken-down foreleg, watched on the rack as the French horse Lumino closed the gap inch by inch. The two struggled past the post. No one, not even Fred Winter, knew who had won. He had nothing to pull up with, but Mandarin dropped to a walk in a few strides. 'I've never known a horse so tired,' said Fred. And he himself was totally exhausted.

Half-way back to the unsaddling enclosure, the result was announced and general applause erupted. The French, who could claim credit for his birth, seemed equally delighted at Mandarin's astonishing capture of their richest 'chase. Fred Winter was touched by their generosity: 'Obviously one congratulates people but no one *likes* foreigners to come and pinch a £20,000 race. Yet all the French couldn't have been nicer.' The 'niceness' was further stretched only half an hour later when an exhausted yet invigorated Fred 'pinched' the £10,000 Grande Course de Haies des Quatre Ans on Ryan Price's Beaver II. Auteuil that day had been a little Waterloo.

For Mandarin it was the crowning achievement of his *annus mirabilis* in which he had won the Hennessy, the Gold Cup and then the Grand Steeplechase de Paris. The bare facts are an eloquent testimonial to his constitution and to the skill of Fulke Walwyn. To keep a horse at optimum racing pitch from November to June is good training; when that horse is 11 years old and has already had his legs fired, it is an astonishing achievement.

That season lofted Mandarin up from being a good, gallant but rather unlucky little horse to the ranks of the immortals. He belongs there. He might not have been the best horse of his decade at the time – Fred Winter rated Pas Seul and even Saffron Tartan his superiors – but when people have forgotten those good winners they will be regaling their grandchildren with Mandarin's epic victory in the 1962 Grand 'Steeple' de Paris.

A crystal ball would have been necessary to spot the seeds of greatness in the portly three-year-old who arrived at Saxon House in the summer of 1954. His half-brother Manuscrit – also owned by Madame Peggy Hennessy of the brandy family – was already there and highly regarded, having won the Cotswold Chase at the National Hunt Meeting at his first attempt over fences. Mandarin had been only partially broken, and what had been done to him had not been done too well. Fulke Walwyn started again from scratch, but no amount of patience and long-reining and rebitting could ever eradicate the 'woodeny' mouth which remained throughout his career. Even worse, he began as a really bad jumper. He was unable to right himself when wrong at a jump and could only smash straight on through. The two faults are interrelated: bad 'steering' usually causes bad jumping. The horse, resisting instead of responding to signals from on top, unbalances himself.

In spite of his defects Mandarin had at least speed; he won second time out at

Kempton, although Fulke Walwyn remembers that he only jumped two flights properly. It was then thought worth running him in Cheltenham's Gloucester Hurdle, later renamed by its generous sponsors The Waterford Crystal Supreme Novices Hurdle and worth £26,177 in 1989. But Mandarin didn't distinguish himself among the cream of the year's novices. His jumping failed to improve with experience and his first six outings the following season yielded only two places. There were other problems too. Since starting to race he had become very finicky about his food and the tubby youngster had developed into a very angular four-year-old who needed a breast-girth to keep his saddle in place. A variety of titbits and sweeteners was tried but the only thing that really worked was stout, not Guinness in his case, but the rival Mackeson brewed by Whitbreads. After his third consecutive defeat in the firm's Gold Cup at Sandown the then chairman Colonel Bill Whitbread (founder of this first sponsored steeplechase) presented him with two free bottles a day for life, delivered from a Lambourn pub. Mandarin was also a disruptive influence on the string at exercise and, when only a novice, had to be given V.I.P. treatment – sent ahead with a sensible old horse to lead him. One of Fulke's former apprentices 'Mush' Foster not only did him all the time, but also rode him regularly, and with particular diligence and tolerance. 'A lot of lads wouldn't have taken the trouble he did,' says Fulke Walwyn. 'Particularly before Mandarin got successful.'

A dashing steeplechaser on a winter's day in 1952 at Windsor. Mandarin and Fred Winter rocket over the last for an easy victory.

What with one thing and another he was nearly sent back to France. He wasn't doing well enough over hurdles and the normal progression to fences seemed in his case out of the question. He could hardly be expected to survive the bigger, thicker obstacles for long.

Then Fred Winter rode him at Sandown's Military Meeting. Fred used to declare proudly, 'I always claim to have been the beginning of Mandarin'. He had done little and his reputation of being a bad jumper was rife in the quick enquiries of the jockeys' changing-room. 'As I remember,' said Fred, 'he jumped very well indeed bar one mistake when he knocked a hurdle right out of the ground. He made all the running and won.' He then ran 'a hell of a race' over 3 miles at Ludlow. He set off in front and was taken on by one horse after another until he finally tired and finished third. Sandown had shown he *could* jump. Ludlow proved not just his stamina but his guts. The disappointing horse who had been on the transfer list was transforming himself. It was then wondered whether he would jump fences. Asked his opinion Fred rather naughtily said, 'Sure to', knowing that as he wasn't stable jockey, he was unlikely to have to ride him. Dave Dick, who was, thought Fred Winter was mad. It was Michael Scudamore, that tremendous horseman and top flight rider, winner of a Grand National and a Gold Cup and father of champion jockey Peter, who came down to Lambourn and got Mandarin jumping.

Much of Mandarin's astonishing development as a 'chaser was due to Scudamore's firm, balanced and courageous tuition. Scudamore had no superior in teaching a novice to jump: his early schooling helped turn his Gold Cup winner Linwell into a safe, and when unleashed, brilliantly fast jumper.

Mandarin's treatment was successful. Although he sometimes took chances and was inclined to get a bit close to his fences, on the whole he jumped very well and was placed in each of his nine races next season. He started off with an encouraging third at Ludlow, ridden by stable jockey Gerry Madden and a month later was second at Newbury. Then came his first success. With tutor Michael Scudamore up, he was started for the Coventry Novices Chase at Cheltenham, and won very easily by 4 lengths, despite hitting the last. He was then placed twice more, before galloping away with the Broadway Chase, subsequently the 3-mile 'Sun Alliance' – the staying novices crown at the National Hunt Festival. In hock-deep going the novices keeled over like drunks, but Mandarin jumped safely all the way and had his race won from the top of the hill, coming home 25 lengths clear.

He wound up the season by almost pulling off the first big post-war sponsored race – Sandown's Whitbread Gold Cup. As it was his first venture into top-class handicap company – a real leap even for a top novice – he hadn't many friends at 20–1. Only in the last stride though did the second favourite, Neville Crump's Yorkshire raider Much Obliged (Johnny East) pip him for the £4,800 prize. He had arrived among the élite, the top dozen 'chasers whose deeds and plans make the big news of the racing pages.

For next season he had a grand plan. His 1957–58 campaign opened with a pipe-opener over 2 miles at Newbury. He was quite unfancied at 100–8 and was unplaced to Kenure, but the race tuned him up nicely and he came to Cheltenham

for the first running of the Hennessy Gold Cup (sponsored by his owner's family firm) in the peak of condition. The star-studded field included that year's Gold Cup winner Linwell, the famed white Scottish hunter The Callant, the Whitbread Gold Cup winner Much Obliged and the speedy, elegant Lochroe.

The race had been Linwell's target too ever since it had been announced, for the dark brown horse with the broad blaze ran nearly 10 lb. better round Cheltenham than anywhere else. The course requires talents he possessed in abundance: stamina, sure, swift jumping off and onto varied gradients, balance and zip down hill, and acceleration and courage up the last awful climb.

Linwell's trainer reckoned he had a tremendous chance with a fair weight but when the handicap came out he vividly recalls choking over his Buckinghamshire breakfast-table: the others looked fairly handicapped but Mandarin stood out with no less than 16 lb. below Linwell.

His best friends could not describe Mandarin as an impressive horse but his trainer had done a magnificent job on him and he was a ball of muscle. Linwell too had been trained to the minute. Fulke Walwyn and Ivor Herbert, meeting the previous evening in the bar of the Queen's Hotel, both reckoned that if their horse didn't win, the other would.

The Hennessy was first run at Cheltenham before moving to Newbury. Here is its first running with Linwell, the 1957 Gold Cup winner, looking a consummate winner at the last. A superb jump after nearly 3¼ miles but the concession of 16 lb. to future Gold Cup winner Mandarin (Gerry Madden) proves just too much in what Ivor Herbert always maintains was Linwell's greatest performance.

So it proved: Linwell took up the running two out and he and Mandarin had a tremendous scrap all the way up the hill. Close home Mandarin's 16 lb. pull in the weights began to tell, Linwell weakened and Mandarin eventually won by 3 lengths. Ivor Herbert said on the day (and maintains now) that Linwell had run his best race ever. How many Gold Cup winners bar Arkle could give over a stone to another Gold Cup winner in their prime? Herbert's opinion got some support next month when Mandarin won a memorable race for the King George VI, giving 7 lb. and a 1-length beating to Lochroe.

Fulke Walwyn still finds it extraordinary that Mandarin should have twice won this 3 mile race, which is always run at a cracking pace round Kempton's sharp track, as he really needed longer distances. Indeed, he was rarely on the bit in the first 2 miles but ran on with great determination, displaying a toughness which his slender frame belied, and settled the issue with a great jump at the last.

On the strength of these performances, he started favourite for the Gold Cup for his return match with Linwell, but last year's great duellists now knocked each other out. Mandarin performed some extraordinary antics at the water, unseated Gerry Madden and, as he blundered about, knocked Linwell sideways. This left Linwell's cousin Kerstin (second to him the previous year) to become only the second mare to win the Gold Cup. The first was Ballinode, back in 1925 on the second running of the race. She was known as 'The Sligo Mare' and trained at The Curragh. There was no error when Mandarin returned in April and won the Golden Miller Chase in a cut and thrust duel with Lochroe, running on up the hill with the tigerish tenacity that he'd made his hallmark, to win by 1 length.

He then went to Sandown for a second crack at the valuable Whitbread but again he had to be content with second place, this time behind his 100–6 stable companion Taxidermist, ridden by that talented writer and worker for racing's good causes, John Lawrence, who succeeded his father, the Nuremberg war crimes judge, as Lord Oaksey.

In Mandarin's next season luck left him waiting. He started well enough at Newbury, failing by only 3 lengths to concede 22 lb. to Queen Elizabeth's course specialist Double Star over a distance palpably too short for him, but chosen like last year as a 'tuner-up' for his attack on the Hennessy. In his target race, unfortunately, he ran what Fulke Walwyn considers to be the only really bad race over fences of his life and it was ironic that it had to be in his owner's family race. Starting an odds-on favourite he could only finish a remote fifth to Taxidermist.

He went on to win a minor race at Sandown, then on to Kempton for a second crack at the King George VI. This offered one of the most stirring duels in modern 'chasing history, but Mandarin was not involved. The public weren't looking back at him as little Lochroe, owned by Lord Mildmay's sister Mrs Helen Mildmay-White, skimmed over the last and battled up the straight beating off the repeated challenges of the massive Irishman Roddy Owen, hot favourite at 7–4. Mandarin finished 15 lengths away third and then there was time to wonder what had happened to him. The mystery was partly solved when he limped into the unsaddling enclosure. By the time he got home, he was very lame indeed. An X-ray revealed a fractured fibula in his hind leg. He had no particular treatment, but was confined to his box for months while the bone set and healed, which it did

remarkably quickly. He was back on a racecourse in April, in a 2-mile hurdle at Cheltenham. As expected, he made no show but the fracture appeared to have mended, and he was prepared for his third shot at the Whitbread. There were 23 runners for the £6,240 prize (worth five times more in 1989) and the ground, desperately heavy, didn't suit Mandarin's small frame. The robustly handsome Irish horse Saffron Tartan was favourite at 5–2 – an amazingly short price in a big handicap. Mandarin was on the speculative mark of 100–7. For the third year running he landed over the last with a winning chance. This time in a desperate, driving struggle he went under by a few inches to John Baillie's Done Up who needed an almost demoniac degree of riding, entrusted that day to ace hurdle jockey Harry Sprague who seldom rode over fences. Back in the bourne of the weighing-room, Sprague, who was riding his last race, actually vomited from his exertions.

May came in abloom with chestnut candles and nearly every top-class 'chaser started to unwind for his summer holidays. But for Mandarin an ambitious venture had been planned. He was to return to the land of his birth and attempt to carry off the £20,000 Grand Steeplechase de Paris at Auteuil. In the 19th century such raids were common, but few English horses except Jerry M. and Easter Hero had been across since. In spite of improved transportation in the 1950s an insular attitude by the British racing authorities, and an unambitious one by British owners and trainers meant that horses ran for hundreds here rather than thousands in France. Furthermore, the race came in the middle of the close season for English steeplechasers.

Then air transport eased the journey and the difficulties were offset by the huge prize at stake. It was a bold gesture and it nearly collected. Coping manfully with the twisting course and unfamiliar obstacles, Mandarin managed to take up a position early on, and he hit the front landing over The Big Water, a formidable brook that has nothing to do with the shallow pan which caused such gnashing of teeth in England. He maintained his lead for some time, despite climbing over *'Le Bullfinch'* with extreme caution. Unlike some Irish 'chasers, he had never been hunting, and was therefore unversed in the technique of bursting through this odd obstacle. However it was the fifth from home which nearly finished him. Officially known as The Small Water, it was faced by glaring white, show-jumping post-and-rails, and rendered even more alarming by the sun's bright dazzle on the water. It was altogether too much for Mandarin who braked abruptly, finally hopped over it almost from a standstill, and lost some 10 places in the process. Pursuit seemed utterly vain. There were only four more fences to go. But Mandarin and Madden set off again and at the post had passed all but one.

It had not been a lucky year for Mandarin but his last two battling defeats had endeared him to the British public more than all his previous victories. Those racing devotees, not wholly concerned with their pockets, dearly love courage and generosity and simple guts. And if the end's a loser they can add to their admiration that other sort of love: sympathy.

Mandarin's 1959–60 campaign opened inauspiciously with defeat. Starting at 8–13 he was beaten 3 lengths by Pointsman at levels in a 3 mile 'chase at Worcester. Next time out Fred Winter rode him and remembered the occasion

Two great racing stars relax in summer as friends: Fred Winter and Mandarin.

well. 'I had a bad fall two races before, and hurt my hand but I wasn't going to give up the ride because I knew he was a bloody good horse. And he won very easily.'

Then came Kempton's King George VI. There were nine runners and the going was soft. Mandarin, ridden by Gerry Madden, was favourite at 5–2, the brilliant but erratic Pas Seul was at threes, and Pointsman, surprisingly in view of his previous form with Mandarin, was at nines. The flying 2-miler Flame Gun set a scorching pace but for once Mandarin was able to lie up. In fact he was never out of the first two. Four fences out he was joined by Pointsman and Tony Keen (later to be killed riding) and a tremendous battle ensued. Mandarin was fractionally the quicker away from the last and, all out, hung on to his advantage to the post. This gruelling race left its mark and soon afterwards he developed tendon trouble. He never actually broke down, but Fulke Walwyn and Lambourn vet John Gray decided to play safe. As was the custom with Walwyn, a wizard at training bad-legged horses, the decision was taken early to fire the leg and to put the horse away for a long rest.

These patient tactics were ill-rewarded; next season was his most disappointing to date. After an encouraging start (fourth to Blue Dolphin over 2 miles at Newbury) he took a horrible fall in Chepstow's Rhymney Breweries Chase. This knocked such a lot out of him that he didn't recapture his best form all season. He was well beaten by Frenchman's Cove at Kempton on 27 December, and although he won the Stanley Chase at Sandown in January, he was left with the race at his mercy when Peter Cazalet's brilliant young horse, King (favourite after his good second to Saffron Tartan in the King George VI), fell in the lead at the last. He was a somewhat remote fourth to Chavana in the Great Yorkshire, but ran very well in the Gold Cup to finish a close third to Saffron Tartan and Pas Seul. By now Gerry Madden was no longer riding for Fulke Walwyn, and Mandarin was reunited with Fred Winter for the Whitbread. He started second favourite in a glittering field that included Pas Seul, Nicolaus Silver, the Grand National winner and the Liverpool third Springbok who, defying the usual post-Aintree syndrome, ran really well and were both placed. Neither had any chance with a foot-perfect Pas Seul who carried his 12 st. to an effortless 4-length victory. Mandarin, weakening steadily, finished a distant sixth. He was 10 years old and had already been fired and had broken a bone. It was apparent his days were done. But Mandarin had no intention of bowing out.

The next season Winter exchanged his second retainer with Ivor Herbert's Linwell-Flame Gun stable for one from Fulke Walwyn's much larger establishment. Thus he rode Mandarin to an easy victory in his first race at Ludlow. But he then broke his collar-bone, so Willie Robinson had the ride in the Hennessy – transferred from Cheltenham to Newbury for business reasons. Onlookers in the paddock marvelled at the condition Fulke Walwyn had wrought. Never, they declared, had the finicky little horse looked better. He ran as he promised: always 'pulling double' he jumped into the lead a full mile from home and was eased before reaching the post 1½ lengths and a head in front of John O'Groats and his

At Kempton on Boxing Day in 1965, some old champions, some woolly, parade before the stands led by Mandarin. Other guests of honour include Pas Seul, Hallowe'en, Nicolaus Silver, Kilmore, Saffron Tartan, Taxidermist and Blessington Esquire.

old rivals 'Taxi' and John Lawrence. Few observed that Mandarin's old partner Gerry Madden was at Newbury that day. His only ride was on a 20-1 shot in a novice hurdle, and he finished tailed off.

Fred Winter wondered if he'd still keep the ride after Robinson's win. But 'I won the Walter Hyde on him at Kempton and so was reinstated'. The King George VI was snowed off, and Mandarin's next outing was the race that had so long eluded him, the steeplechaser's Derby, the Cheltenham Gold Cup.

Fred Winter, the future champion trainer eight times between 1971 and 1985, recaptured that race.

'Going into the water second time round, Mandarin was well off the bit. I jumped the ditch on the tail of the leaders and going down the hill I was getting nowhere. I gave him a couple of cracks and he *flew*! I had a wonderful run downhill

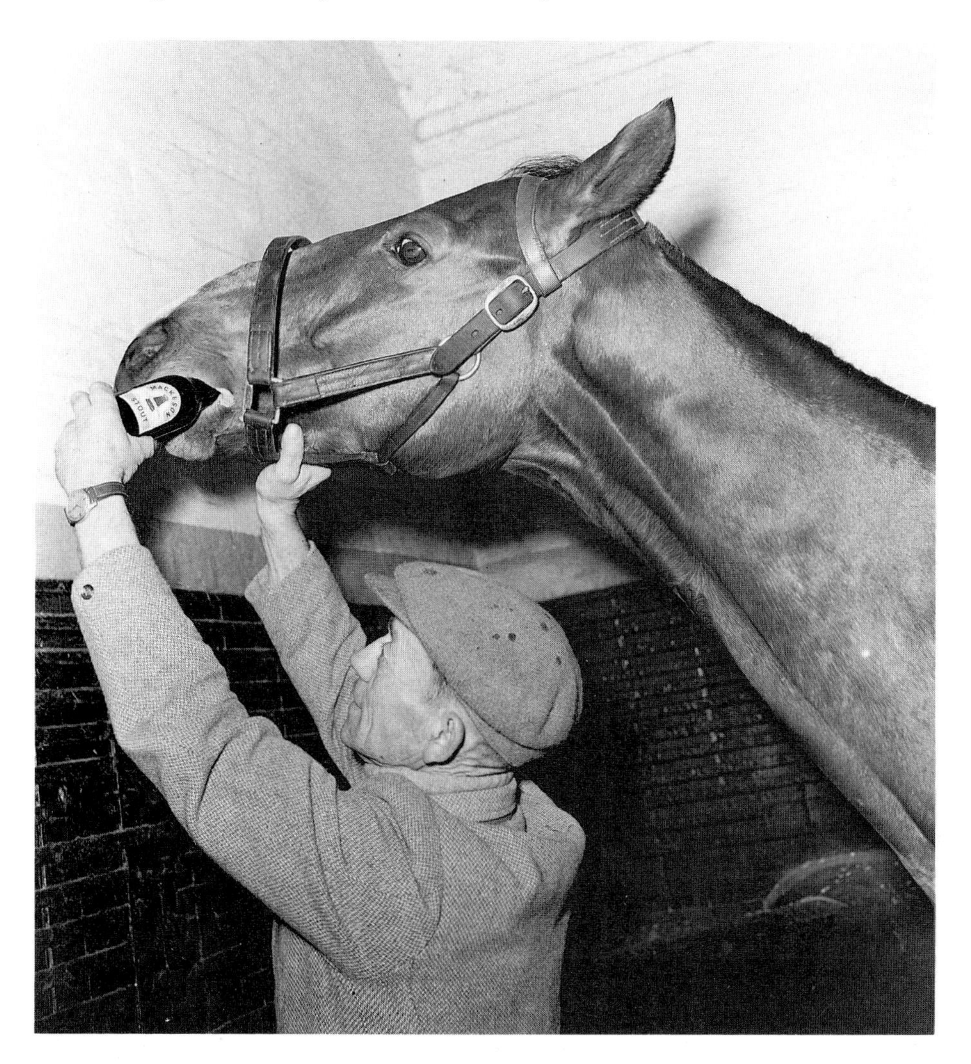

Mandarin receiving his daily gift of the 'black annuity of stout' awarded him by Colonel Bill Whitbread. Pouring the measure is Fulke Walwyn's famous old Head Man Joe Lammin.

on the rails, Fortria went a bit wide and I got through on the inside. I took off half a length behind him at the second last and that was the first time I knew I'd win.' The *Chaseform Notebook* comment, 'refused to give in and worried the second out of it close home', must be part of his memorial, for at the end of this, his *annus mirabilis*, he was retired. Mandarin caused a large section of the record book to be rewritten. His victories in England had earned Madame Hennessy £29,773, while his single French victory boosted the total over £50,000.

Fortified by Colonel Whitbread's black annuity of stout in his retirement, he paid daily visits to the training grounds where he observed, as old men will, the bumptious blunders of the younger lot, and then exploded into unseating gaiety.

He wasn't born to greatness, and he certainly didn't have it thrust upon him. He fought for it all the time, overcoming the handicaps of his lack of physique, bad appetite and clumsy jumping, and of his injuries and set-backs. Fortunately for him and his owner his courage was complemented by the patience and sagacity of his trainer.

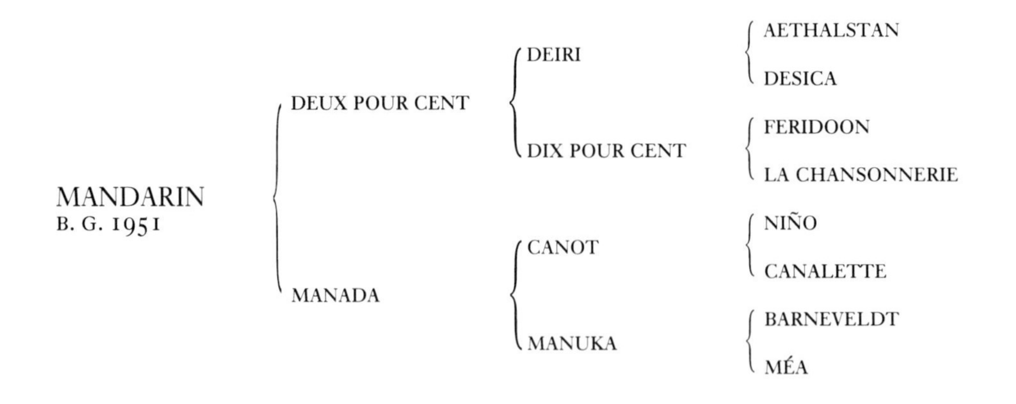

DATE	COURSE	RACE	DISTANCE	VALUE	WEIGHT	JOCKEY	PRICE	PLACE
Season 1954–55								
Dec 10	Newbury	Freshman's Hurdle (3yo)	2m 85 yds	£478	10.2	P. G. Madden	20/1	3rd
Jan 26	Kempton	Middlesex Novices Hurdle (Div 1)	2m 110yds	£204	11.3	J. Gilbert	4/1	won
Mar 10	Cheltenham	Gloucestershire Hurdle (Div 11)	2m	£685	10.13	B. Marshall	5/1	unpl
Season 1955–56								
Oct 20	Hurst Park	Hampton Court H'cp H	2m	£204	11.0	J. Bullock	20/1	unpl
Nov 19	Sandown	Esher H'cp H	2m	£572	10.5	J. Bullock	4/1	2nd
Dec 9	Newbury	Berkshire H'cp H	2m 85 yds	£204	10.8	J. Gilbert	7/2	2nd
Dec 26	Kempton	Kempton Park H'cp H	2m 110 yds	£1,541	10.0	J. Bullock	100/7	unpl
Jan 9	Leicester	Wigston H'cp H	2m	£173 (each)	11.6	J. Bullock	8/1	unpl
Mar 8	Cheltenham	Spa H	3m	£685	11.5	R. Emery	25/1	unpl
Mar 16	Sandown	Oak Open Long Distance H'cp H	2m 5f 75 yds	£204	11.5	F. Winter	10/1	won
Apr 25	Ludlow	Eardiston Stayers H'cp H	3m	£170	12.0	F. Winter	7/2	3rd
May 19	Towcester	Gayhurst H'cp H	3m	£204	12.0	B. Marshall	5/1	unpl
Season 1956–57								
Sept 26	Ludlow	Richards Castle H'cp Chase	2m 4f	£136	12.0	P. G. Madden	10/1	3rd
Oct 25	Newbury	Creslow Ch	2m	£685	11.5	M. Scudamore	8/1	2nd
Nov 15	Cheltenham	Coventry Novices Ch	2m	£272	11.9	M. Scudamore	2/1	won
Nov 21	Newbury	Hopeful Ch	2m 4f	£204	11.12	M. Scudamore	4/6f	won
Dec 1	Windsor	Dedworth Manor Ch	2m	£170	12.3	M. Scudamore	7/4j.f.	2nd
Dec 29	Newbury	Lambourn Ch	3m	£204	11.7	M. Scudamore	11/4	2nd
Mar 12	Cheltenham	Broadway Novices Ch	3m	£685	12.1	M. Scudamore	8/1	won
Mar 21	Lingfield	Shaun Spadah Ch	2m	£683	12.4	M. Scudamore	7/2	2nd
Apr 27	Sandown	Whitbread Gold Cup (H'cp Chase)	3m 5f 75 yds	£4,842	10.4	P. G. Madden	20/1	2nd

DATE	COURSE	RACE	DISTANCE	VALUE	WEIGHT	JOCKEY	PRICE	PLACE
Season 1957–58								
Oct 25	Newbury	Evenlode H'cp Ch	2m	£411	11.1	P. G. Madden	100/8	unpl
Nov 16	Cheltenham	Hennessy Gold Cup (H'cp Chase)	3m 1f	£5,272	11.0	P. G. Madden	8/1	won
Dec 11	Sandown	Sandown H'cp Ch	3m 125 yds	£505	11.10	P. G. Madden	11/10f	won
Dec 26	Kempton	King George VI Ch	3m	£2,983	12.0	P. G. Madden	7/1	won
Mar 13	Cheltenham	Gold Cup Chase	3m 2f	£5,788	12.0	P. G. Madden	9/4f	u.r.
Mar 19	Lingfield	Sussex Stks H'cp Ch	3m	£339	12.6	P. G. Madden	1/3f	won
Apr 2	Cheltenham	Golden Miller H'cp Ch	3m 2f	£461	12.7	P. G. Madden	8/11f	won
Apr 26	Sandown	Whitbread Gold Cup (H'cp Chase)	3m 5f 75 yds	£5,790	12.0	P. G. Madden	9/2f	2nd
Season 1958–59								
Oct 24	Newbury	Evenlode H'cp Ch	2m 160 yds	£414	12.9	P. G. Madden	15/2	2nd
Nov 15	Cheltenham	Hennessy Gold Cup (H'cp Chase)	3m 3f 100 yds	£5,302	12.0	P. G. Madden	10/11f	unpl
Dec 10	Sandown	Sandown H'cp Ch	3m 125 yds	£385	12.7	P. G. Madden	8/13f	won
Dec 26	Kempton	King George VI Ch	3m	£2,885	12.0	P. G. Madden	9/4	3rd
Apr 10	Cheltenham	Painswick H	2m 100 yds	£272	11.8	P. G. Madden	13/2	unpl
Apr 25	Sandown	Whitbread Gold Cup (H'cp Chase)	3m 5f 25 yds	£6,240	11.11	P. G. Madden	100/6	2nd
June 6	Auteuil	Prix Saint-Sauveur (Chase)	4,500m	1,200,000F	70 k	P. G. Madden	no s.p.	unpl
June 21	Auteuil	Grand Steeplechase de Paris	6,500m	12,000,000F	64 k	P. G. Madden	9/2	2nd
Season 1959–60								
Nov 18	Worcester	Holt Ch	3m	£204	10.12	P. G. Madden	8/13f	2nd
Dec 11	Windsor	Brocas Ch	3m	£204	11.0	F. Winter	1/6f	won
Dec 26	Kempton	King George VI Ch	3m	£2,919	11.5	P. G. Madden	5/2f	won

Date	Course	Race	Distance	Value	Weight	Jockey	Odds	Result
Season 1960–61								
Nov 26	Newbury	Theale H'cp Ch	2m 160 yds	£273	12.7	P. G. Madden	100/8	4th
Dec 10	Chepstow	Rhymney Breweries H'cp Ch	3m	£1,993	11.12	P. G. Madden	5/2f	fell
Dec 27	Kempton	Oatlands H'cp Ch	3m	£520	12.3	P. G. Madden	11/10f	2nd
Jan 13	Sandown	Stanley Chase	3m 125 yds	£491	12.3	P. G. Madden	13/8	won
Feb 4	Doncaster	Great Yorkshire H'cp Ch	3m 105 yds	£2,092	11.12	P. G. Madden	8/1	4th
Mar 9	Cheltenham	Gold Cup Chase	3m 2f 130 yds	£6,043	12.0	P. G. Madden	100/7	3rd
Apr 22	Sandown	Whitbread Gold Cup (H'cp Chase)	3m 5f 25 yds	£8,235	11.10	F. Winter	7/1j.f.	unpl
Season 1961–62								
Oct 25	Ludlow	Clun Chase	3m	£204	11.12	F. Winter	6/5f	won
Nov 25	Newbury	Hennessy Gold Cup (H'cp Chase)	3m 2f 82 yds	£5,230	11.5	G. W. Robinson	7/1	won
Jan 25	Kempton	Walter Hyde H'cp Ch	3m	£493	11.11	F. Winter	1/1f	won
Mar 15	Cheltenham	Gold Cup Chase	3m 2f 130 yds	£5,720	12.0	F. Winter	7/2	won
June 17	Auteuil	Grand Steeplechase de Paris	6,500m	250,000 N.F.	64 k	F. Winter	2/1f	won

NINE

Mill House

MASTER SPY VASSALL GETS 18 YEARS; MACMILLAN AXES SEVEN MINISTERS IN HIS JULY MASSACRE; HUGH GAITSKELL DIES – ALLOWING HAROLD WILSON TO BECOME LEADER OF THE LABOUR PARTY; LIBERALS WIN ORPINGTON; GOVERNMENT PUTS UP £350,000 TO BUY LEONARDO DA VINCI CARTOON; THE PROFUMO AFFAIR ROCKS THE GOVERNMENT; MACMILLAN RESIGNS; PRESIDENT KENNEDY ASSASSINATED IN DALLAS.

There hang about Mill House the trappings of a Greek tragedy. 'The Big Horse', pride of Lambourn's camp against Ireland's Arkle, was a star so early it seemed he must glow for years. But he was hammered down, rose again, and then once more the slings and arrows came whistling down.

His public, who made him their hero, called him British, hoped he'd keep the home side winning and turned out to bellow for him whenever he ran.

He had in his owner a sort of Greek Chorus too, declaiming the virtues of his Champion and the great deeds he was bound to do this year and the next and perhaps for ever. When a man showed what the Greeks called *hubris* their gods struck him down: no one but they could be arrogant. People who live in racing are still aware of the lurking threat to the cocky; few trainers or jockeys ever boast, but touch wood fervently and praise their luck. Poor Mill House was never proud at all, but the gods of racing gave him a regular tousing. Perhaps they may not have thought his owner modest.

It is a grey November afternoon at Sandown for the 1965 Gallagher Gold Cup. The stands are bursting, for Arkle is over from Ireland and 'The Big Horse' seems at last to be himself again. Mill House has been rejuvenated, we hear. Certainly he's been sharpened by 2 miles round Ascot in the wake of the flying Dunkirk, and his confidence must have been restored by a bloodless victory over Crobeg. If he *is* right again not even Arkle will give him 16 lb.

Applause smacks out, crisp on the grunts of approval as the two champions ping down the railway fences in great leaps. At the water Mill House is in front, pounding along like a giant panther, with the broad-shouldered, long-legged figure of David Nicholson hunched over him. This lead actually widens and in the stands there is a babble of astonishment, wild excitement, and from the Mill House camp – exultation. 'Mill House *is* as good as ever! He'll *beat* Arkle, he'll bloody beat him, man, you'll see! Look! He's going *away* from him!' Then in an instant, all is over. In a dozen swinging strides Arkle is alongside and has gone by, and as the English gape like yokels and the Irish loose their shrieks and roars, Arkle comes skipping over the last two fences and gallops lightly to the line.

David Nicholson simply couldn't believe it. He'd never ridden Mill House before (stable jockey Willie Robinson had broken his jaw at Hereford). He remembered the thrill of Mill House's jumping – 'down the railway he was gaining

Mill House, Willie Robinson up; 'The Big Horse', the pride of Lambourn.

at every fence but I couldn't take a pull, I had to keep on asking for a bit more. As we went round the top, I caught a glimpse of Arkle about 4 lengths behind, and thought well old chap, we've got you properly on the stretch; the next moment he was alongside with Pat Taaffe sitting bolt upright with his great gloves on . . . and then he just changed gear. Well, it broke my fellow's heart – all the fight went out of him after that.' On the run-in, Rondetto (receiving 10 lb.) passed Mill House to take second place.

The Lambourn camp was shattered. Arkle had made it cruelly clear that on no terms and in no circumstances would Mill House ever beat him again.

It was rumoured – and his admirers fervently hoped it was true – that he wouldn't be asked to try. No one likes watching a great horse almost literally gallop his heart out in a task beyond him. At any rate he was missing from the Hennessy line-up and didn't in fact run again for nearly two months, when he was sent to Cheltenham for the National Hunt Centenary Cup. The conditions of the race made it seem a gift to him. He wasn't invincible but few owners cared to oppose him on such favourable terms: only three turned out. A large Cheltenham 'county' crowd assembled – tweeds and regimental ties, but with the rare mini-skirt flashing through the sensible cashmeres and popping the ancient majors' eyeballs – swelled by swarming Christmassy schoolchildren come to goggle at the horse who had started a legend. All hoped that without the oppressive presence of his conqueror Mill House would again reveal his true self. The high hopes drooped like flags on a dull day: he won all right but gone was the spring from his heels and the fire from his belly, and as he heaved himself laboriously over the last and toiled up the hill, infinitely weary, it seemed that as far as the small top league was concerned, he was no longer in it.

Sadness wreathed the infinite post-mortems like fog in cemeteries. Pity and blame and knocking comments twanged through the little world of racing. Then, a week before the Gold Cup Mill House's legs, which had been giving Fulke Walwyn such headaches ever since he came to Lambourn three-and-a-half years earlier, finally gave way. A potentially brilliant young horse and an ambitious gambling owner can play a merry tune with the right conductor, but when the horse is of gigantic proportions and requires an abnormal amount of work, the problem is king-sized. In every race he had run, in every gallop he had done, in his box, morning noon and night, Mill House had worn supportive bandages. For three years they had kept his legs sound.

In any normal decade he would have won three Gold Cups, probably three King George VIs and certainly most of the big, sponsored handicaps, had not his four aces met four aces and the joker. The sad giant of Lambourn had been born in precisely the wrong year – Arkle's.

Mill House ran earlier and snatched a year's start, so he won one Gold Cup, one Hennessy and one King George VI, but on 7 March 1964, the day of reckoning came. By the end of it he was just another broken-down 'chaser, one of the thousand honest jumpers of all degrees who develop leg-trouble every season. In terms of finance what had then been worth probably £20,000 (or £150,000 in 1988) became with an 'iffy' leg, almost valueless. So it is with gelded jumpers of no stud value: the injury of a moment can eradicate the accumulated assets of years.

Like Arkle, Mill House came from Ireland. He was bred by the Lawlors, the hotel and catering family who lived in Co. Kildare. They had bred his dam, Nas na Riogh, who was supposed to be the product of a love-match between Breviary and Cariff. Jim Lawlor's Uncle Peter passionately believed in love-matches since he declared that Pretty Polly was the product of one. Nas na Riogh (the Irish for the town of Naas meaning 'Meeting place of the Kings') was named after old Mrs Lawlor's hotel there. The mare, though no Pretty Polly, was a useful one. Oddly enough, considering the mammoth proportions of her famous son, she was very small. Her early efforts didn't sparkle: in her first four outings – two on the same day – she fell three times, but later she went on to win eight races at Punchestown, Fairyhouse, Limerick Junction and Bellewstown. She proved rather a shy breeder but the results were worth waiting for. Lovely Polly, Mill House, Punchestown Lass and Ronan all won.

Mill House, named after old Mrs Lawlor's private house which used to belong to the manager of the carpet-mill, ran out until he was three in the park surrounding Jim and Vi Lawlor's remarkable hotel Osberstown House, near Naas. Here in the war Germans and English interned together on The Curragh and out on liberal paroles would drink together in the snug cellar bar and men who had been shelling, sniping and torpedoing each other made friends in neutral Ireland.

Several English trainers who knew the soft spots of Ireland always stayed at 'Oz' on horse-hunting forays, admired Mill House in the fields, but were always told by Jim and Vi that he wasn't for sale. Old Mrs Lawlor hadn't yet decided to part and she sent him to Tom Taaffe to be broken. Son Pat, who on top of Arkle was to 'hammer hell out of him', took on his early education, which included hunting with the surrounding packs – the Naas Harriers, the South West Dublin Harriers and the Kildare – a good apprenticeship for jumping.

He first ran at the end of January 1961 in a maiden hurdle at Naas. Ridden by Toss Taaffe, he finished an encouraging fourth to Away For Slates. A month later he returned to Naas for the Osberstown Hurdle and ridden this time by his mentor Pat, he won comfortably. It was a fair performance, but Willie Robinson who was there doesn't remember the occasion very clearly so he can't have been that impressive. He was, however, entered for the valuable Martin Mahoney Champion Novices Hurdle. A fleet of English horses, refugees from the foul weather, were over for this thousand pounder, including future Champion Hurdler, Anzio. Mill House, ridden by jumping's Lothario, bold Dave Dick, was still pulling Dick's arms out three from home but here he blundered horribly and fell. He had done enough though to impress Dick enormously and he told dealer Jack Doyle, the former Irish Rugby international, busy bloodstock agent, that the horse should be bought. Doyle touted Mill House unsuccessfully around the smarter trainers, including Ryan Price and Fred Rimell and then told Epsom trainer Syd Dale, formerly Price's head lad.

One of Syd Dale's owners was a wealthy advertising man, Bill Gollings, who had had three or four moderate horses and now decided on buying a good one. So that summer he and Syd Dale went over to Ireland, met Doyle and drove south out of Dublin to old Tom Taaffe's grey yard in Rathcoole village. Mill House was in a field, very muddy and the other horses had chewed off his tail. Mr Gollings was visibly shaken and audibly indignant – 'You've brought me all the way over here to look at this thing? What is it anyway – a ruddy great hunter?' Syd Dale admits, 'If he hadn't been broken you wouldn't have thought twice about him, but once he had a saddle on it was different. It was like getting into a Rolls after a Morris.' For racing purposes the way they move is so much more important than how they look: beauty, except in fast women, doesn't necessarily produce speed. Mr Gollings must have been considerably impressed by the horse's action because for a reputed £7,500 (about £50,000 in 1989 currency) Mill House changed hands.

He came to England with a formidable reputation. Pat Taaffe was on record as saying he would be the horse of the century and Dave Dick was inclined to agree. On the downs at Epsom he astonished Syd Dale by galloping over his two-year-olds. Schooling presented no problems at all: he was a natural jumper.

In this age of telephones and transport you can't keep a good horse dark, though it's only 60 years since a whole stable of lads and apprentices could be locked in their quarters for weeks while a mighty coup was plotted. Proud connections always boast about any promising newcomer and Mill House for his first race, a four-year-old hurdle at Newbury, opened 7–2 favourite. By the 'off' he had

Not the best start to an illustrious career. November 1961 at Newbury and Mill House crashes at the first hurdle . . .

drifted to 7–1 and ridden by pint-sized Ron Harrison, he caused a sensation by falling at the very first flight. After that he didn't bother with any more novice hurdles and on his next outing, at Sandown, he ran in a condition race against fully fledged stars like Champion Hurdle winner Another Flash. Not surprisingly he was run off his feet in the early stages, but made up an impressive lot of ground in the last half-mile to finish fifth. A glow of delight infused his supporters and he was launched at Wincanton for a little £170 race. The experienced Rondetto was odds-on favourite at 8–11 to beat him. Syd Dale found the recollection exquisitely humorous. 'Rondetto had won at Leicester and one of mine was second, so we knew the time of day nicely. 3–1 our horse! It was *giving* money away!' Mill House richly repaid his trainer's confidence and ran on strongly to win by 1½ lengths.

The fact that a horse of his size and scope should have the speed to win over hurdles as a four-year-old made an enormous impression on the racing public, but Mill House wasn't going to be allowed to run up a string of novice hurdle victories. It was learned with interest that the next step in an unorthodox selection of races was to be an instant switch to fences in a top-class novice race, the New Century Chase at Hurst Park. It was an inauspicious beginning: he and Ron Harrison made a nonsense of the sixth. This shook his confidence (novices first time out get rattled by a blunder) but given no chance to recover, he was driven up. This proved disastrous: two fences later he boobed again and came crashing down. It was a rotten start.

Although Cheltenham, by virtue of its shifting gradients is not an easy course for a novice to jump, this was the place picked for his recovery run. Tim Brookshaw, a notable horseman of the old school and later a heroic survivor from a paralysing fall, was engaged to ride. He had never sat on him before and gathered that although the horse was potentially top-class, his confidence had been badly shaken. The main object, he was told, was to get him safely round and thus restore his confidence. It was quite an assignment, as Tim Brookshaw soon discovered: 'he made two terrific mistakes at the first two fences and I had to pick him up off the floor. He had absolutely no confidence in himself, so I took him away from the others on the wide outside and started to school him as I would at home. Then he jumped better and started to regain his confidence and after six or seven fences, started jumping super. I wouldn't let him join the others as having got him going, I didn't want to undo the work I had done by having his attention distracted by the other horses jumping. It wasn't till coming down the hill the last time I got within striking distance of the leaders. Not that we accelerated – the others came back. He was still pulling very hard and he won very easily.' The official verdict was only 2 lengths but eagle-eyed Peter O'Sullevan informed *Daily Express* readers that he had never seen a horse win at Cheltenham so hard-held. O'Sullevan, shrewdest of observers, had seen hundreds of good Cheltenham winners.

It was then arranged that Tim Brookshaw should have the ride permanently, but, during the summer Syd Dale and Mr Gollings fell out and the owner removed the horse, saying that he wanted him trained by a stable who retained a top-class jockey. The reason was not completely acceptable to Syd Dale, but by the time the harvest was coming in Mill House was in Fulke Walwyn's yard, Saxon

House, at Lambourn. Mandarin had just retired but it did not immediately occur to anyone there that the big newcomer would so swiftly snatch the empty throne.

The coming season saw him shoot out of the bulging ranks of promising young novices and become a fully-fledged star, a crowd-puller and the most exciting English prospect since Golden Miller.

He began at Sandown in a handicap 'chase carrying the ludicrously low weight of 10 st. 7 lb. His new stable's own jockey Willie Robinson had the ride. 'He might have had a bash at the last, it was quite common in those days!' It was indeed: the young Mill House alternated his soaring race-winning leaps with monumental clangers which shook the black birch to its foundations. Such was his weight and strength though that these blunders, which would have sent any small horse reeling to the deck, barely checked him. Only once did one cost him a race. It was at Kempton and a stupendous leap three from home had landed him in the lead until a difference of opinion with Willie Robinson about take-off point at the last saw him on his nose. He was going again in a heaving moment but during it King's Nephew, wound up for the last in Stan Mellor's inimitable fashion, had shot past and was still half a length up at the line.

The result in some eyes diminished his Gold Cup chances and expert opinions were divided. He had brilliance, but he was erratic. He'd shown flashes of great form, but he was hardly out of the novice stage. He was those two things youth always resents in itself: young and inexperienced. These were the flaws, some thought, which would certainly crack in the great test of the Gold Cup.

The National Hunt Meeting opened in clouds of gloom. That winter's weather had been diabolical and Cheltenham moaned with frustrated trainers, browned-off lads, and purse-pinching owners. Hungry jockeys padded leanly round, the unfashionable from force of circumstance and the popular from shedding weeks of inactivity in Turkish baths. Ireland had as usual escaped the biting cold and their horses were presumably fitter. They'd scoop even more of the big prizes than usual, wagged English heads over mournful gin and tonics. In the event the Gold Cup was no race at all. Taking up the running over the water on the second circuit, Mill House was never headed again and came storming home 12 lengths ahead of Fortria. The Press were unanimously eulogistic. By Thursday evening the English were viewing the world through rose-coloured spectacles. The invasion had been largely withstood and the home side had produced a real champion – a horse to talk about, lingering over port in dining-rooms and beer in pubs in summer time while horses at grass grow fat and idle in the rook-caw and dove-coo of summer evenings. 'Nice young horse of Tom Dreaper's won the Broadway though. Arkle, wasn't it?'

The car-parks emptied. Bumper to bumper the house parties and coachloads crawled home. The sun slipped down behind the Malvern Hills darkening the stage for another year.

Mill House ran once more that year and royally endorsed his Cheltenham impression. He was saddled suitably for Newbury's rich Mandarin Chase (named for his stable's former star) and although set to carry 12 st. 5 lb. he started a warm favourite at 5–6. He soon powered his way to the front and his spring-heeled jumping and relentless gallop had his opponents gasping before the straight. 'A

Rolls,' said Willie Robinson emphatically, 'You have such *power*, everything else seems small.' He won devastatingly and was already likened to Golden Miller. He was, after all, only six years old. What mightn't he prove next year?

Mill House put his head down for a long summer and did not see a racecourse again until November's end. He reappeared on top of a mounting wave of enthusiasm for National Hunt racing stirred up by the recent spread of valuable sponsored races. No longer were the peak prizes of the season jostling each other in March, while the rest was a desert of moderate stakes. Interest whetted in dank November could now be kept sharp until the darling buds of May were on the point of flowering. Before Christmas there was the £5,000 3¼-mile Hennessy; the £4,300 2-mile Mackeson; the £2,500 2½-mile Massey-Ferguson. Then came the £5,000 King George VI, 3 miles; the £8,000 Gold Cup, 3¼ miles; the £20,000 National, 4½-miles; and finally the £8,000 Whitbread over 3 miles 5 furlongs*. Money's value had kept falling since Golden Miller, who had needed an astonishing 29 victories to earn him a mere £15,000. At last commercial sponsors were compensating for devaluation by using races to advertise their wares.

Television flung the interest nationwide. On 24 January 1948, three races at Sandown were covered. The experiment was an instant success, was extended more often on larger scales. The dashing, courageous world of steeplechasing came galloping into the sitting-rooms of Britain and brought a new taste to millions who till then had heard only of the Grand National and never seen 20 horses totalling 10 tons crashing down the fences at 40 m.p.h.

To sharpen appetites now came the spice of battle. From Lambourn poured forth glowing accounts of their champion's progress – paeans of praises rang round the valleys until the sober English became embarrassed by hyperbole. From Ireland – whispers first swelling to a confident battle-cry – came news of another champion – Arkle, the horse who had made such an impression at the National Hunt Festival. Perceptive spectators remarked that this horse's final turn of foot might find Mill House out. Mill House's protagonists laughed: what Arkle might do against a bunch of novices wouldn't be repeated when mighty Mill House had galloped him into the ground. So in a jumble of speculation and a drum-roll of boasts the two great horses approached their meeting place at Newbury for the Hennessy.

November 30th dawned grey and sullen, but the atmosphere round the paddock crackled – stout county ladies, of Newbury-Cheltenham type, much made-up and befurred, clacked on authoritively. 'My dear, doesn't Mill House look *marvellous* – he stands apart. Of course Fulke wouldn't run him if he weren't absolutely ready.' Arkle looked less impressive than the giant, but some who hadn't glimpsed him since last spring, observed too how much he was thickening and developing.

The race at first unfolded as expected: Mill House bounded to the front, bowling along and jumping like – 'Well,' said Fulke Walwyn, 'he's a great jumper

*Within twenty-five years the value of these races had reached a total of £200,000.

How styles change. This 1963 Hennessy clearly looks a race from a different era. The winner, Mill House (Willie Robinson) just leads over the first at Newbury.

at home and schools terrifically, but in his races he's fantastic. Half his brilliance is the way he gets ground when he jumps. The only way to ride him is have him in the first two or three – because he'll soon jump his way to the front!'

But Arkle was also going well, a few lengths behind. Four fences out, Pat Taaffe made a move, smoothly he went up almost to join the favourite. 'I did just sort of catch sight of Arkle coming at me,' Willie Robinson remembered. 'Then I lost him.' He didn't know why till afterwards. Coming in to the third from home, half a length behind, Arkle put in a huge leap, overjumped and sprawled on landing. Bystanders said it looked as if he'd got his foot stuck in a hole. In the time he took to recover Mill House had gone pounding ahead to win by an easy 8 lengths from Happy Spring who had overtaken Arkle on the run-in. The Arkle camp was shattered. Dreams of a champion had evaporated in two minutes: they had a very good horse, but no more. Would Arkle have made a race of it, but for his slip? Fulke Walwyn didn't think so. 'Mill House won terribly easily, you know. No, I think it was that Arkle made the most fantastic improvement between November and the following March.'

Before that March Mill House had two more races. Neither was more than an exercise canter. In Kempton's King George VI on Boxing Day he gave Christmas cheer to his triumphant fans and an object lesson in jumping to two-miler Blue Dolphin. Six weeks later he gave 24 lb. and a 12-length beating to tearaway Out And About in the Gainsborough Chase at Sandown. Almost everyone agreed this

Mill House leading Arkle – an early fence in the 1964 Gold Cup.

was the greatest horse since Golden Miller. Another Gold Cup lay within his grasp. And another and another, if owner Mr Bill Gollings was reported correctly. The British marvelled at their protégé, and the continuing Irish support for Arkle seemed a product more of Ireland's charming perversity than of logic.

Gold Cup day, 7 March 1963, is sharp and frosty and the pale sun silvers the coats over muscles as the four runners parade in front of the stands. Mill House, demonstrating his marvellous balance, treats the crowd to a show-hack's extended trot. Arkle sidles by, staglike, head held exaggeratedly high. 'They're off,' the loudspeakers crackle. Soon the runners are strung out in Indian file: Mill House, Arkle, Pas Seul, Duke of York. Starting the second circuit the order is unchanged. The two principals are jumping impeccably and going well within themselves. At the top of the hill Willie Robinson increases the pace, but Pat Taaffe and Arkle continue to shadow him with ominous ease. They reach the elbow together and Mill House's supporters are getting uneasy. Suddenly Willie Robinson's arm goes up as if he himself is doing the writing on the wall. With despairing courage Mill House hurls himself, tanklike, at the last and he lands on terms. But that is all. He has no answer when Arkle sprints away. Five inexorable lengths spread between them at the post. The margin between a great horse and a unique one gapes for all to see.

The defeat numbed. 'It is very depressing,' said Fulke Walwyn years later, 'to get beaten when you know you've got the best horse in Britain'. At the time he found it incredible that Mill House the unbeatable, the new Golden Miller, could possibly have been beaten by anything but a blow of Fate. 'No excuses,' said Willie Robinson sadly at first. Later he added hopefully, 'I might have reversed the result if I hadn't had to make all the running.' Mill House's groggy fan club, like lovers tasting disappointment, turned blind eyes to blunt truths and dug up excuses. There were still straws to snatch at: on softer ground, in a bigger field with something to make the running, it might be different. It *could* be different. A pacemaker was suggested, but Fulke Walwyn pointed out that the only horse in his stable who could live with Mill House over 2 miles was Richard of Bordeaux, whose popular senior owner Mr Jack Schilizzi (a generous private sponsor of the sport) was unlikely to spare him for the purpose.

Another blow from the gods followed in the Whitbread: in cloying mud Mill House tried to give 42 lb. to Mildmay winner Dormant round Sandown's gruelling 3 miles 5 furlongs. The task was too heavy. He lost the lead 50 yards from the post and was beaten 3 lengths. Some hardened racegoers actually wept and the sunken unsaddling enclosure was funereally wreathed in gloom. In this sepulchral atmosphere the winner's jockey missed a lot of praise: young Pat Buckley had wasted so stringently to get down to 9 st. 7 lb. that he could only just keep on his feet while Queen Elizabeth made the presentations.

Hope sprang up again like green corn the summer through, and old men fancied that next season somehow Mill House would be better. He was to open his comeback campaign in the Hennessy, this time receiving 3 lb. from Arkle. Although Arkle was favourite at 5–4, Mill House was strongly supported at 13–8, and not even the wildest Arkle-lover dreamed of the race that ensued. Taken on at his own game Mill House was so out-galloped and out-jumped that he was stone-cold before the straight, and finally finished a dispirited fourth, 28 lengths behind Arkle, with Ferry Boat and The Rip intervening.

Six weeks later he got home by a desperately short head from Dormant in the Mandarin Chase at Newbury. It was a magnificently courageous effort, and those who saw him, head low with fatigue, bulldoze his way through the last fence, incredibly gaining ground in the process, and then fight every inch of the way to the winning post, have not forgotten it. Because it seemed impossible that eight-year-old Dormant (who since the Whitbread had spent, it was joked, more time in transit between trainers' yards, than in any one) had suddenly improved 1½ st., it was plain that Mill House had deteriorated. He went on to win the Gainsborough Chase at Sandown, but at Cheltenham Arkle gave a further, crushing demonstration of his superiority and slammed him by 20 contemptuous lengths in the Gold Cup.

In the autumn of 1965 it seemed as if The Big Horse was a broken reed. The struggle against Arkle had evidently cracked his strength and his spirit. Something can occasionally be done about both. If morale needs building, easy races against rubbish is the treatment. But though it is easy to scare away all opposition with a healthy crack, a battered 'has-been' deters no one. Walwyn had Mill House well entered-up and picked his targets carefully. He ran against Dunkirk over 2 miles at Ascot and finished a creditable second; he then trotted up in a two-horse race at Sandown. Then, in the Gallagher came those few moments of hope restored

along Sandown's railway fences. And hope was finally snuffed out. On that day's running he could be rated no less than 3 st. below Arkle. The gods hadn't yet finished destroying their plaything: his legs finally went. He broke down in March 1966. He had reached a nadir totally unforeseeable on that glorious afternoon three years earlier when he had stood in the winners' enclosure at Cheltenham with the first of perhaps three or even four Gold Cups just won, and the steeplechasing world at his feet.

It now seemed as if Mill House had reached the end of racing's road. He might well retire. Certainly the chance of his running in any decent race for a year or so seemed quite remote. But he was being trained by a great master with bad-legged horses and incredibly, he was back in 10 months for Cheltenham's £4,000 Massey-Ferguson Gold Cup. Its 2½ miles were obviously too short for him, even supposing he were fit, but everyone was astonished and delighted to see him back in such fine fettle, galloping and jumping as zestfully as ever. Starting up the hill, he was still very much in touch and people suddenly wondered if the impossible was about to happen. A monumental blunder at the open ditch expunged such hopes. After that he weakened rapidly, leaving Charlie Worcester and The Laird to battle it out over the last three fences.

This encouraging come-back was followed by a good third to Spear Fir and Dormant in the Great Yorkshire Chase and a third successive victory in Sandown's Gainsborough Chase, this time at the expense of Ryan Price's course-specialist What A Myth. All of which encouraged his admirers to hope that profiting from Arkle's injury he might come back to win a second Gold Cup. On the rollercoaster of his fortunes Mill House was riding high again.

But for poor Fulke Walwyn another problem arose on top of the continuing headache of the big horse's forelegs. Mill House was now bedevilled with a muscle injury in his back. Ten days before the race he had a school on the racecourse at Newbury and thrilled everyone, but on the big day it was different. 'I knew the moment I got up that something was wrong,' said David Nicholson substituting for injured Willie Robinson. 'He was crippled, couldn't trot at all, only jumped one fence properly. I remember coming into the last first time round, in front with Terry Biddlecombe on Woodland Venture and him saying, "We'll do this one properly, 'Duke' – Christmas cards 1967" – then it was one, two, three – and we both missed! Coming in to that open ditch I asked him for a standback – first time in the race – and he couldn't.' Indeed Mill House failed to rise at all and crashed heavily through the fence. David had broken three ribs on Elan the day before and was, as he laconically put it, 'a bit sore'. Insult was added to injury when he heard the malicious rumour that his cracked windscreen, broken by a stone on the way to the course, was the result of a crash after a too-late-night party.

The five weeks left before the Whitbread were desperate ones for Fulke Walwyn. The ground was dreadfully hard for The Big Horse's delicate legs and there was the nagging worry of the recurring back trouble. But when David Nicholson was legged up on him at Sandown that late April afternoon among the flat-racers and the colossal crowd drawn by the last big steeplechase of the season, he could feel that Mill House was, 'quite different. At Cheltenham I'd been told to restrain him if I could – could? he wouldn't have pulled the skin off a rice-

pudding. But this time he pulled my arms out. Fulke told me to hold him up a bit to help him get the trip. He was gaining 2 lengths at every fence, so I kept checking after each one – "steady, old man – easy". I saw my way into the Pond Fence a long way out and asked him. He jumped it super and it carried him right round the elbow. As we came over the second last, I heard the commentator shouting, "And Mill House has gone clear", and I thought "we really might win". Then I saw San Angelo and Johnny Haine on Kellsboro' Wood and thought, "Christ, they're all coming at me and we're stone cold". By the time we got to the last he was drunk. It's funny, the pictures look super but he staggered through it really. It was a nightmare that last bit and I thought the post would never come. Two yards past it he had stopped to a walk and all the others came cantering past. I wondered if we'd ever get to the unsaddling enclosure, but when we got to the members they started cheering and he realized "this is for me", and he pulled himself together, pricked up his ears and when we came in he was stepping out like a show horse.'

His reception was almost hysterical, old men blinked eyes, blew noses, women snuffled, among the cheers. It exceeded anything at that time accorded Arkle. At last those gods had let The Big Horse have his day again.

There history – had it been a happy one – should have ended. But there were boasts again, one supposes, or something said to rile the really wise in Olympus. The come-back wasn't after all.

He only ran twice more before the Whitbread of 1968. His muscle noticeably twinged him during Cheltenham's Gold Cup, for after some sound, occasionally deliberate jumping in front, he made a terrific leap at the water, then at the next Open Ditch he stood back, seemed about to put in the necessary quick, short stride, failed to do so, failed to lift his great body, hit the fence's top and knuckled over.

And he ended where he had triumphed the previous year: at Sandown in the Whitbread. Well there, lying fourth or fifth when he came to the 13th fence, he got himself into a tangle of misjudgements, blundered badly, shot Willie Robinson off, and the season expired in bristling acrimony.

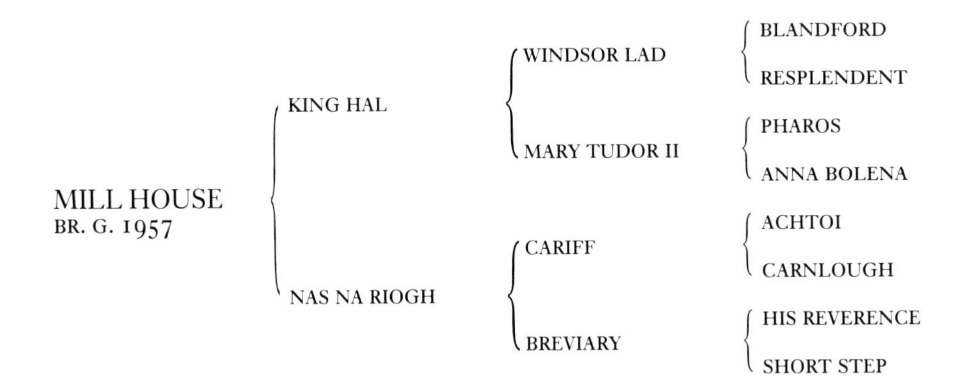

DATE	COURSE	RACE	DISTANCE	VALUE	WEIGHT	JOCKEY	PRICE	PLACE
Season 1960–61								
Jan 28	Naas	Sallins Maiden H (4–5yo)	1m 4f	£202	10.12	T. Taaffe	7/1	4th
Mar 4	Naas	Osberstown Maiden H	2m 1f	£202	11.2	P. Taaffe	2/1	won
Apr 25	Punchestown	Martin Mahony Champion Nov H	2m	£1,036	11.4	D. V. Dick	10/1	fell
Season 1961–62								
Nov 8	Newbury	Blewbury H (4yo)	2m	£276	11.0	R. Harrison	7/1	fell
Nov 18	Sandown	Black Hills H	2m	£273	11.0	R. Harrison	25/1	unpl
Nov 30	Wincanton	Castle Cary H (Div 1)	2m	£170	11.0	R. Harrison	3/1	won
Feb 17	Hurst Park	New Century Ch	2m 275 yds	£688	10.10	R. Harrison	2/1f	fell
Apr 18	Cheltenham	Ledbury H'cp Ch	3m	£340	11.0	T. Brookshaw	6/1	won
Season 1962–63								
Nov 10	Sandown	Walton Green H'cp Ch	3m 125yds	£374	10.7	G. W. Robinson	7/2	won
Nov 22	Kempton	Cottage Rake H'cp Ch	3m	£492	10.9	G. W. Robinson	4/5f	2nd
Dec 15	Sandown	Sandown H'cp Ch	3m 125yds	£510	11.2	G. W. Robinson	7/4f	won
Mar 14	Cheltenham	Gold Cup Chase	3m 2f 130 yds	£5,958	12.0	G. W. Robinson	7/2f	won
Apr 20	Newbury	Mandarin H'cp Ch	3m 2f 82 yds	£2,488	12.5	G. W. Robinson	5/6f	won
Season 1963–64								
Nov 30	Newbury	Hennessy Gold Cup (H'cp Chase)	3m 2f 82 yds	£5,020	12.0	G. W. Robinson	15/8f	won
Dec 26	Kempton	King George VI Ch	3m	£4,933	12.0	G. W. Robinson	2/7f	won
Feb 19	Sandown	Gainsborough Ch	3m 118 yds	£807	12.5	G. W. Robinson	1/7f	won
Mar 7	Cheltenham	Gold Cup Chase	3m 2f 130 yds	£8,004	12.0	G. W. Robinson	8/13f	2nd
Apr 25	Sandown	Whitbread Gold Cup (H'cp Chase)	3m 5f 18 yds	£8,235	12.7	G. W. Robinson	6/4f	2nd

DATE	COURSE	RACE	DISTANCE	VALUE	WEIGHT	JOCKEY	PRICE	PLACE
Season 1964–65								
Dec 5	Newbury	Hennessy Gold Cup (H'cp Chase)	3m 2f 82 yds	£5,516	12.4	G. W. Robinson	13/8	4th
Jan 16	Newbury	Mandarin H'cp Ch	3m 2f 82 yds	£1,980	12.7	G. W. Robinson	6/4	won
Feb 12	Sandown	Gainsborough Ch	3m 118 yds	£608	12.5	G. W. Robinson	8/13f	won
Mar 11	Cheltenham	Gold Cup Chase	3m 2f 76 yds	£7,986	12.0	G. W. Robinson	100/30	2nd
Season 1965–66								
Oct 7	Ascot	Frogmore Ch	2m	£796	12.3	G. W. Robinson	4/1	2nd
Oct 20	Sandown	Autumn Trial Ch	3m 118 yds	£426	11.7	G. W. Robinson	8/100f	won
Nov 6	Sandown	Gallaher Gold Cup Chase	3m 118yds	£5,165	11.5	D. Nicholson	7/2	3rd
Jan 26	Cheltenham	N.H. Centenary Cup (H'cp Chase)	3m 1f	£715	12.0	G. W. Robinson	1/6f	won
Season 1966–67								
Dec 10	Cheltenham	Massey-Ferguson Gold Cup (H'cp Chase)	2m 4f	£3,983	12.0	G. W. Robinson	100/8	unpl
Jan 28	Doncaster	Great Yorkshire H'cp Ch	3m 2f	£2,924	12.3	G. W. Robinson	8/1	3rd
Feb 10	Sandown	Gainsborough Ch	3m 118yds	£561	11.9	G. W. Robinson	6/5	won
Mar 16	Cheltenham	Gold Cup Chase	3m 2f 76 yds	£7,999	12.0	D. Nicholson	4/1	fell
Apr 29	Sandown	Whitbread Gold Cup (H'cp Chase)	3m 5f 18 yds	£7,350	11.11	D. Nicholson	9/2f	won
Season 1967–68								
Feb 9	Sandown	Gainsborough Ch	3m 118yds	£767	11.9	D. Nicholson	11/4	2nd
Mar 21	Cheltenham	Gold Cup Chase	3m 2f 76 yds	£7,713	12.0	G. W. Robinson	2/1f	fell
Apr 27	Sandown	Whitbread Gold Cup (H'cp Chase)	3m 5f 18 yds	£7,510	11.13	G. W. Robinson	13/2	u.r.
Season 1968–69								
Sep 26	Wincanton	Somerset Chase	3m 1f	£272	11.7	G. W. Robinson	8/13f	won
Oct 9	Ludlow	Clun Chase	3m	£511	11.12	G. W. Robinson	1/4f	fell

T E N

Arkle

De Gaulle vetoes British entry into Common Market; Labour sweep back to immediate financial crisis; International bankers save sterling from devaluation; Vietnam war starts; Swinging London is discovered; The rise of the mini-skirt, the fall of the pound.

The David to trump Mill House's Goliath arrived on the scene without ballyhoo. His elderly trainer, a dry, witty man, never believed in wasting words and took the mickey out of blatherers. His owner, though the widow of a famous public figure, the last of the great despotic aristocrats – has never been given to ostentation or public declarations. As for his jockey, few of the breed boast. Danger drives out braggarts and the only riders who swank are uncommitted amateurs who can stop when they like.

The famous triumvirate, the Duchess, formerly Miss 'Nancy' O'Sullivan from Co. Cork, old Tom Dreaper of Greenogue in Co. Dublin and lanky Pat Taaffe from Co. Kildare were all slow to enthuse about Arkle. Because for over a year he showed little to inspire them.

Arkle was foaled on 19 April 1957, and since this was an almost magic animal, astrologers can noted that his birthday fell exactly between those of the Duchess who cleverly bought him and the Irish farmer's daughter Alison Baker who patiently reared him.

His birthplace, never the Sunday place of pilgrimage his stables became, was the Ballymacoll Stud, then owned by Golden Miller's grand eccentric owner, the Hon. Dorothy Paget. Managed by Charlie Rogers it was the home of Miss Paget's Derby winner Straight Deal whom Bright Cherry, Arkle's dam, was vainly visiting.

She had been an excellent race mare, extremely fast over firm ground up to 2½ miles and she ended her career at the top of Irish 2-mile steeplechase handicaps. Bred by her owner, tall Mr Henry Baker, a Protestant farmer in the north of Co. Dublin, Bright Cherry was out of the marvellous brood mare Greenogue Princess (by My Prince) who was ridden in point-to-points by Tom Dreaper. She produced no less than twelve winning offspring.

Arkle's sire Archive had been selected by Henry Baker's sprightly widow because she thought he would give 'pep'. Superbly bred to win a Derby he was a racecourse flop, and thus stood at the 48 guinea fee the Bakers could afford for their old 'chasing mare.

No comet was observed in the Kildare sky the night of the birth (though Charlie Rogers sent the usual telegram), and after waiting several months while his mother failed to get in foal to Straight Deal, the young Arkle went home for the first time to Malahow. He did not particularly impress old Mrs Baker, who peeped down at him from her bedroom window. 'He wasn't so much gangling as "scopey".' By August he was weaned and next April so nearly cut his leg off on barbed wire across a gap that he showed the scar all his life.

Alison Baker broke him in when he was a two-year-old and except for the first time she had the long-reins either side ('fireworks then!') he was not troublesome at all. It had always been the Bakers' intention to sell Arkle as a three-year-old, although had old Henry Baker been alive he would have probably have sent him the few miles south, like his mother before him, to Tom Dreaper to be trained.

But farmers cannot keep every horse they breed, so he came up for sale at Goff's on 4 August 1960. Dreaper advised the Duchess to have a look at him – 'I don't say he'll stay more than 2 miles, though.' The Bakers confessed afterwards that they really did not want the three-year-old back. So they put on him the realistic reserve of 500 guineas, hoping he would make a bit more. They got 1,150 guineas, easily their highest price till then, and were all excitedly delighted.

The horse had found a new owner, but not yet a trainer. The Duchess, naming him after a mountain near her Scottish estates, had Arkle sent to her Cheshire home Eaton Lodge, and had him nagged about by William Veal, Lord Wigg's brother-in-law. He was 4½ when the Duchess asked Tom Dreaper to choose between Arkle and the other youngster she had bought at the same sales, Brae Flame. This slashing chestnut was much better looking, but – 'Blood's thicker than water', declared Dreaper, 'I'll take Arkle. I've had all his relations.' Loyalty to a family (plus intuitive judgment) was never better rewarded in the horse world. The beautiful showring winner Brae Flame went to the Duchess' other Irish trainer, Willie O'Grady: he ran but once, got leg trouble and retired . . .

Yet another youngster of the Duchess' arrived with Arkle at Dreaper's grey stone stables in August 1961. Ben Stack, similarly named after a Sutherland mountain, similarly outshone him on looks. But he turned out a good one: by next June he had won twice.

There was no rush among the lads to pick the unattractive Arkle to 'do', and so he fell to a new arrival, dark Johnny Lumley, 16 at the time, who came from a Dublin jewellers shop, and couldn't ride nor ever learned how to.

Paddy Murray the Head Lad who had arrived at Greenogue in 1942 to 'do his two' was frank about Arkle. 'He looked the worst of all the four-year-olds who arrived that season. He was unfurnished. And he moved bad.'

Stable jockey Pat Taaffe was even franker. 'He moved so terribly behind, you could drive a wheelbarrow through his hind legs!' From the start, however, he could do one thing well: jump; and he was jumping little fences really well before he ran in his first race. This, an amateur flat race, is the normal Irish introduction to 'chasing. His jockey for the 2-mile Bumper was the Earl of Donoughmore's son, the Hon. Mark Hely-Hutchinson, who came to ride work on Arkle several mornings a week before going off to his job at Guinness's Brewery. He says, 'My only claim to fame is that I'm the only man to have ridden Arkle and failed to win on him!' He was a far better rider than his modesty allows and recollects the orders for Arkle's first race: 'Lie third or fourth and see what happens.' He remarks that Tom Dreaper knew he could not give Arkle a hard race even if he had wanted to. It was 9 December 1961, on the country track of Mullingar, and the race the Lough Ennel Maiden Plate worth £133, in which the most marvellous steeplechaser ever first appeared.

The going, Pat Taaffe remembers, was 'like a ploughed field. One thing it did show us: he obviously stayed really well.' Arkle, outpaced early, ran on up the straight, passed half a dozen toiling runners and finished third, 9 lengths behind the winner.

The introduction took little out of him. Seventeen days later he ran in another bumper, but with better horses at classier Leopardstown. He finished fourth, showed improvement over one of his Mullingar opponents, and satisfied everyone. He did not suggest he was in any way outstanding, but, since he jumped well, he should win steeplechases. As a step towards that end (Dreaper never cared greatly about hurdlers) he ran in January as a five-year-old in a novice hurdle at Navan and, because he seemed to stay without being very fast, in a 3-mile one at that.

He was quite unfancied, ridden by a 26-year-old Dreaper lad, Liam McLoughlin, while Pat Taaffe rode his stable mate, the favourite, the good mare Kerforo. With 27 runners Arkle, having his first sight of racecourse hurdles, was ridden carefully along behind the main bulk of the field. McLoughlin remembers he was jumping superbly. For Pat Taaffe up in front, the race seemed either his or Lord Patrick Beresford's on Blunt's Cross as they galloped together at the second last flight. Taaffe weakened. Lord Patrick squelched ahead. Then, flabbergasted, he saw McLoughlin and Arkle 'absolutely *cruising* past me'. Smoothly Arkle went on to win at 20–1. There was no applause. Everyone was astonished. Four years later Taaffe still repeats bewildered 'We were at the end of the race. It was as if *he'd* just started!'

The thin lanky fellow had opened his account, but the magic story had not started in earnest: he was well beaten in two of his three remaining hurdle races that season. He won a small handicap with Pat Taaffe, who had to ride him very hard. He was not as impressed as he imagined he would be, having watched him fly past him in Navan's mud.

He spent the summer, as he was always to do, holidaying on the Duchess' farm Bryanstown, near Maynooth. There he so completely relaxed that he would bask on a warm bank, flat out, taking sugar from her hand. The summer's ease improved him. First time out next season round sharp Dundalk on fast ground – conditions he did not relish – he really impressed Pat Taaffe. But it was his next victory that first impressed the English. Ridden by stable work-rider Paddy Woods, because Taaffe had not got down to the weight, he won the important President's Hurdle, accelerating like a class horse. There was a valuable 'chase with some National hopes in it that day at Gowran Park so an observance of the English press attended. They took home and spread about news of Dreaper's smart young hurdler but without noticing that Arkle had cut himself really badly inside his hock. He often nicked himself when he jumped as his hindlegs, in the manner of a greyhound, flashed down outside his forelegs.

Tom Dreaper then decided it was high time to go 'chasing. He sent Arkle to trainer Dan Moore's old place next to Fairyhouse racecourse to school over some fresh fences. Warming up over hurdles first, Arkle made a shambles of the second flight, crashed to the ground and gave Taaffe such a badly cut eye that he could not see and had to have it stitched. It was his first fall, and his last. It was a colossal blunder and an astonishing one, but as Taaffe later said, 'I think that one fall at Fairyhouse taught him it all. I just feel now he can't ever fall, no matter what happened.' One of the strengths of that horse was that what he learned, perhaps hardly, had only to be learned once: he always remembered. His veterinary surgeon, brilliant Maxie Cosgrove reported the same of medical treatments. 'A fight first, perhaps, but after that never any trouble again.'

His first steeplechase venture was a bold one: it was to be in England where the fences are bigger and at Cheltenham which is not a novice's track. He accompanied his senior stable companion Fortria who was challenging for the Mackeson Gold Cup later that day, 17 November 1962.

Arkle's race was first. A gigantic gamble developed as the Irish walloped the money on. Never better than 6–4, Arkle started at 11–8. He jumped like an old hand against his useful English rivals. Turning for home against the dappled Cotswold backcloth he showed that magic acceleration, shot clear, sailed home and won by 20 lengths. Shrewd Frank Byrne of *The Times* observed, 'He won even more easily than the verdict of 20 lengths shows'. At home Paddy Murray was now convinced that he had in his care the possible winner of a Gold Cup.

The same notion had not escaped his trainer. With his customary planning Dreaper made Arkle's next objective the 3 mile Broadway Novices Chase at Cheltenham next spring – exactly the right rehearsal for a Gold Cup attempt the year afterwards.

Before raiding Cheltenham again he had to run at Leopardstown over 2 miles (possibly too short) carrying 12 st. 11 lb. (probably too much). This time he had the good ex-hurdler Rubor still with him at the last fence and the pessimists groaned. But on the flat Taaffe unleashed the tiger. Arkle shot away on the run-in to win by 6 lengths.

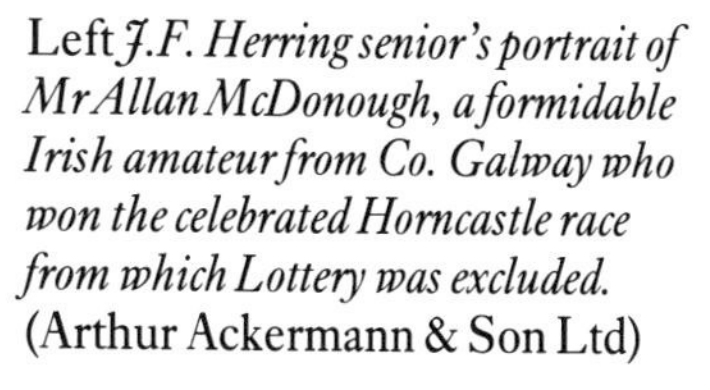

Left *J.F. Herring senior's portrait of Mr Allan McDonough, a formidable Irish amateur from Co. Galway who won the celebrated Horncastle race from which Lottery was excluded.* (Arthur Ackermann & Son Ltd)

Below *Dorothy Paget's great Golden Miller standing behind dual Champion Hurdler Insurance, as captured by Lionel Edwards.* (Richard Green)

Susan Crawford's famous portrait of Arkle and Pat Taaffe is reproduced here from the original which hangs in Anne, Duchess of Westminster's small study at Eaton.
(Anne, Duchess of Westminster)

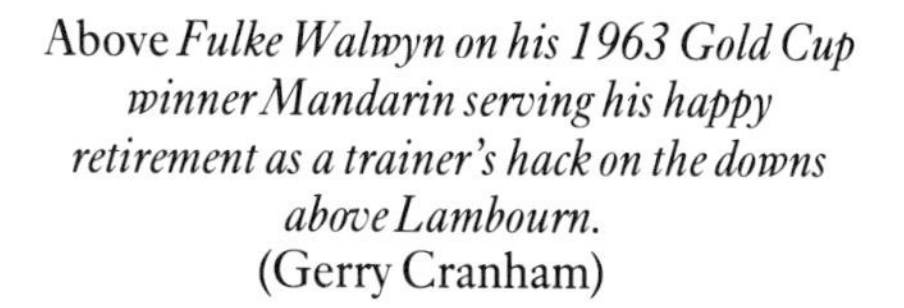

Above *Fulke Walwyn on his 1963 Gold Cup winner Mandarin serving his happy retirement as a trainer's hack on the downs above Lambourn.*
(Gerry Cranham)

Below *Peter Biegel's delightful studies of Arkle in retirement with his girlfriend Meg – 'a good hunter' – at Bryanstown, the Duchess's Irish farm.*
(Anne, Duchess of Westminster)

Above *Dawn at Aintree; L'Escargot and Tommy Carberry, Grand National morning 1975.*
(Gerry Cranham)

Left *Captain Christy. 'He was a free spirit' in the words of his jockey Bobby Beasley.*
(Gerry Cranham)

Above *On the day before the National Red Rum timed by ace photographer Gerry Cranham at 40mph galloping on the sands at Southport.* (Gerry Cranham)

Below *Red Rum and the Princess Royal together examine Philip Blacker's statue of the great horse.* (Associated Sports Photography)

Above *Wayward Lad winning the Lambert and Butler at Ascot after the drama of the punctured foot. He normally jumped with a beautifully rounded back and we do not think that 'Mrs D' would be particularly pleased with this photograph.* (Gerry Cranham)

Below *Silver Buck and Robert Earnshaw winning the Gainsborough Chase at Sandown 1980. The Dickinson family, who taught Robert from a sixteen-year-old school leaver, always commended his polished horsemanship.* (Gerry Cranham)

Above *The second statue to grace Cheltenham after Arkle's was that of Dawn Run and Jonjo O'Neill which stands at the bottom of the paddock where the winners come in.* (Gerry Cranham)

Below *Two Gold Cup winners contesting a Champion Hurdle: Dawn Run and Desert Orchid, 1984.* (Gerry Cranham)

Above *Yahoo and Tom Morgan over the last, touch down fractionally ahead of Desert Orchid in the 1989 Gold Cup.*
(Gerry Cranham)

Right *The cheering crowds begin to mass as Desert Orchid, lead in by his lass Janice Coyle, enters Cheltenham's winners' enclosure 1989.*
(Sporting Pictures)

Foul English weather before Cheltenham suggested that the Irish raiders would all be fitter. Their supporters started to count their chickens. As the meeting went on however, the English beat off the invaders, four Irish favourites failed in a row, but nothing diluted Ireland's wild optimism about Arkle. Punch drunk the punters were and Arkle, carrying 12 st. 4 lb. in almost impossible ground, was made 9–4 on. He pulled very hard, went second to Brasher at half-way, led hurtling down the hill, was joined by Jomsviking at the last, landed four square with him – and then, unbelievably, shot away up that muddy hill to win by 20 lengths.

Bold Tom Nickalls of *The Sporting Life* declared, 'Arkle seems likely to become a Gold Cup winner next year'. But, two days later he must have thought he'd over-egged it when Mill House in the Gold Cup gave Fortria a thrashing. Luminously, two great new stars shone east and west in 'chasing's firmament. Their meeting was anticipated with smacking lips and earnest discourse. 'Mill House will outdo Golden Miller!' rose Lambourn's cry. Arkle returned to Ireland and won two more races.

They were to meet next St Andrew's Day at Newbury in the £5,000 Hennessy Gold Cup. Mill House had to have top weight: 12 st. How far below him was Arkle? 5 lb., said handicapper Dan Sheppard and no one quarrelled. It was a difference attractive to both rival camps and no one momentarily suggested anything else could win.

Arkle opened this campaign with his only victory in a flat race. This fanned talk of what might he win at Royal Ascot? He then won in a steeplechase at Gowran. Mill House had no preliminary, but it was put about he might win five or six Gold Cups.

The result would have sprung from good plotting by a scriptwriter: an accident, a doubtful slip, elements of doubt, the twin protagonists survive unscathed, the pot keeps boiling, and there is a hint that pride goeth before a fall. Mill House leads through the murk, Arkle moves up third as they approach the fourth last, and jumps into second place. At the third last, the open ditch, Arkle, gaining, breathes on Mill House's quarters. The big horse rises, flings forward – Arkle rises, stretches, gropes, lands, blunders, checks . . . Mill House gallops away.

What happened? Taaffe said firmly: 'I was going extremely well coming up to the ditch, and I gave him a kick and he stood off a long way to be level with Mill House. He jumped the fence all right, but as he came down his forelegs stretched right out in front of him – slipping away. It really stopped him entirely.' A friend of Taaffe's standing by the fence saw Arkle slip and thought he stuck a foreleg in a hole made by hooves landing. Little was glimpsed from the stands. The Arkle camp walked down despondent. The Mill House camp crowed. It was a famous victory. One champion had emerged.

The return match at Cheltenham for the Gold Cup in which The Big Horse would be 5 lb. better off tantalized beyond the grip of winter. As people considered it calmly, the extent of Arkle's blunder was pondered. But the only person confident of a reversal of form was Pat Taaffe, and he said so a week later when schooling at Greenogue. The English camp were cock-a-hoop. Three months before the race Mill House was antepost favourite at odds-on.

Arkle, his record blotted, took on a tough task at Leopardstown giving the full range of the handicap away to all but one of his opponents on St Stephen's Day. He stayed his challenge till half-way up the run-in before shooting clear of Loving Record, a fancied National candidate, to win by 2 lengths.

They met again next month and the handicapper dealt with them to the pound. He lowered Loving Record's weight by 2 lb. to 9 st. 11 lb. Arkle had his now customary maximum of 12 st. In glutinous ground Arkle demonstrated another vast improvement: he now trounced Loving Record by an extra 8 lengths. How long, how far, one wondered, could the excellent continue to be bettered?

Tom Dreaper twinkled after the race: 'After another race at Leopardstown we'll confidently send him over for the Cheltenham Gold Cup.'

Because the grey mare Flying Wild fell when upsides Arkle at the second last at Leopardstown, he hacked home on the bridle. Pat Taaffe said dryly to the eager press, 'We'll worry Mill House a bit at Cheltenham'. Arkle, only three weeks before Cheltenham thus finished his particularly testing preparation: five steeplechases all under great weights, all in soft ground.

The Big Horse had gained two easy English victories winning the King George VI and cantering round in a condition race at Sandown. Giving less weight away, he had beaten less too, but he could not have won more easily.

The paths of the giants were about to cross again, and the drums of Lambourn rolled out loud and strong. Between the stables there was more than Arkle's Hennessy defeat to be avenged: in the two previous Gold Cups Walwyn with Mandarin, then with Mill House had beaten Dreaper's Fortria.

That Cheltenham the tide rolled with the Irish and proved Dreaper's horses fit. He and Taaffe won two races on the first day: in one the Duchess' Ben Stack beat Walwyn's odds-on Irish Imp, and the Irish seized this portent. They no longer considered Arkle's defeat a possibility, and they backed him down to challenge for favouritism. Only two opponents stayed to take the giants on, but both were good ones: Pas Seul, winner of the 1960 Gold Cup and second in 1961, and King's Nephew, recent winner of the Great Yorkshire and the conqueror of Mill House at Kempton the previous season. The superiority of the great pair was clearly shown: these other two good horses started at 50–1 and 20–1 respectively.

Bitter snow had whirled over the Cotswolds ten minutes before the Gold Cup and then suddenly, the wind whipped the spinning white curtain away. Behind, the sun beat out of an ice-blue sky, lighting the course with a rinsed brilliance.

From the start Mill House led, jumping beautifully as commentator O'Sullevan kept enthusing, attended by Arkle who was pulling hard for freedom. At the last open ditch, the 21st fence, Arkle had closed on Mill House and a long gap gaped to the others toiling behind. The stars swooped down the hill to the vital third last, Mill House still leading, and the Irish army raising the first screams for their hero to come. Still Arkle closed the gap, the crowd shrieked more shrilly and at the second last Mill House on the inside was only feet in front. They landed, thundered at the elbow. Then, flash, up shot Robinson's whip. Flash, it fell. Arkle was past. And on the run-in he galloped away. He had conquered in three strides. His superiority was damning. Fulke Walwyn, one racing correspondent reported, looked completely shattered.

Gerry Cranham's superb photograph of Arkle after his first Gold Cup win.

Both the giants ran once more, but where Mill House had to endure another defeat in the Whitbread, Arkle beat six opponents to win the Irish National, and made racing history. To allow for his literally immeasurable superiority the Irish Stewards changed their rules, instructing the handicapper to draw up two lots of weights: one with Arkle if he ran; the other without him.

He summered again on the Duchess' farm where a reception for 200 of his closest friends was given for him in the garden adjoining his paddock. After a while, party-suited Taaffe leapt onto his back and rode him bareback round his guests.

That season seemed the apex of Arkle's career, for he had overwhelmed a horse who, had he been born in another decade, would certainly have dominated steeplechasing perhaps as powerfully as Golden Miller. From now on, as the Big Horse drooped, Arkle simply soared.

When they met again eight months later in the Hennessy, the top weight had risen from 12 st. to a really punitive 12 st. 7 lb. This Arkle carried, with Mill House 3 lb. less – a change of 8 lb. on last year's race.

Arkle had thrived. The once dapper frame had developed. He seemed for the first time good-looking, even in Mill House's great handsome shadow. He was fresh, too. Tom Dreaper, struck down in hospital with a virus infection, had a problem: he wanted to run Arkle again only seven days later at Cheltenham in the Massey-Ferguson. This meant either contesting the Hennessy slightly 'under-done', or running 'stale' next time.

One excuse for Mill House was that he had had to make his own running at Cheltenham. Perhaps to puncture this or simply because he was ebullient, Arkle – under 12 st. 7 lb. – set out to make the running. We thought Taaffe mad, believing that this was the only way he could get Arkle beaten. Taaffe laughed last. The two Gold Cup winners jumped three fences 'upsides' along the back stretch applauded by the crowd. Then Mill House cracked and started toiling. In spite of bursting through the sixth from home and screwing over the second last Arkle won cantering. The Big Horse, totally eclipsed, trundled in 28 lengths behind, making Arkle technically his superior by over 2 st. The Queen Mother crossed immediately to congratulate the Duchess and three cheers were rousingly given.

Victory's penalty was a rise to 12 st. 10 lb. for the Massey-Ferguson next week. Most thought he wouldn't run so soon, particularly as the distance was only 2 miles 5 furlongs. He went off to the Duchess' place in Cheshire for the week, received a lot of visitors and fuss and not much peace and quiet. He ran at Cheltenham and just failed to give 32 lb. to Flying Wild, and 26 lb. to Buona Notte (the previous year's top novice). The press were generous – 'Arkle magnificent even in defeat' – while agreeing it had been a tactical error to run. Tom Dreaper made a strategic decision from hospital. Lest the race had harmed him, Arkle must rest. He did not run again for three months.

Before their next Gold Cup clash both he and Mill House endured hard races. Arkle had a battle at Leopardstown in February to give 2 st. 7 lb. to Scottish Memories, a star horse who would, without Arkle, have himself topped the handicap.

Again only two others took on the pair for the Gold Cup, run on fast ground dried by keen winds, but this time they were not much: a declining Caduval, and an unknown Three Day Eventer Stoney Crossing, sportingly ridden by his Australian owner. Caduval soon looked ridiculous, Mill House started to make blunders – two horrid ones – and Arkle simply cantered away with it. His victory broke Mandarin's record for stakes won: he'd now earned £36,818. And Tom Dreaper remarked that the Duchess could ride him herself in the Newmarket Town Plate. Very few critics did not agree that the pinnacle attained three decades earlier by Golden Miller had now been overtopped.

That spring he left the Irish National to a stablemate, and came back to England in April to run for the first time at a course other than Cheltenham or Newbury. With 12 st. 7 lb. to settle him he pranced off to make the running round Sandown's 3 miles 5 furlongs of the Whitbread Gold Cup. Aware now that we were watching a miracle horse we no longer thought anything – even this – impossible. He made one violent mistake at the fourth fence, taking off outside the wings, but when we opened our eyes we saw it had not checked him. On the run-in he accelerated from Brasher who'd headed him at the water, and won by 5 lengths. A minor riot occurred as the yelling crowd stormed from the stands to mob him as he came in, and to encircle him, roaring, as he was unsaddled.

Arkle jarred a joint in the race, was blistered before he was turned out and made an exhibition appearance before tumultuous fans at the Dublin Show in August. He footed it extravagantly round that lovely ground mimicking the action of the show horses, and lapping up the adulation.

A perfect example of the period of a great horseman, Pat Taaffe, on the greatest steeplechaser easily winning the 1965 Whitbread under the now unthinkable weight of 12 st. 7 lb.

For once Arkle didn't open at Gowran Park. His first race was Sandown again for the new-styled Gallaher Gold Cup. Mill House after two tune-up and morale-booster races took him on. This time the handicapper assessed him 16 lb. behind his old rival. He was backed too at 7–2; Arkle was 9–4 on as they went down to the post. What happened then made history: the pair were clapped as they wound down the Rhododendron Walk onto the course and cheered when they emerged on it. This extraordinary demonstration continued in the race: as the two stars sprang like Nureyevs down the fences, each bound was cheered and applauded.

Drama came at the water as Mill House surged ahead and it seemed as if Arkle would not catch him, that The Big Horse was king again, that a monumental turn-up was coming. Mill House goes 4 lengths clear . . . 'Pat! *Pat!*' scream Arkle's fans. And in a flash again, Arkle goes sailing past. At the end poor Mill House 24 lengths behind, receiving 16 lb., makes himself Arkle's inferior by nearly 3 st. That was the margin of Arkle. No other horse in steeplechasing history has proved himself even 1 st. let alone 3 st. better than another same aged Gold Cup winner.

Understandably Mill House declined the Hennessy, but Arkle had a struggle to win it, finishing – for the first time in his young life, dog-tired and slapped along by Pat. Taaffe blames himself for pushing on too fast after his cut-and-thrust with Brasher. Arkle screwed over the last ditch where he had lost the race to Mill

You wouldn't better this example of how champions jump. Yet another defeat of Mill House by Arkle, this time at Sandown in 1965.

House on their first meeting, and was exhausted coming to the last which he jumped clumsily to the right as the crowd started to press across the course. Old National hero Freddie came thundering after him on the run-in, and sweet relief flooded the crowd when the post was finally reached.

His next victory, the King George VI at Kempton on a Boxing Day so frosty that racing in general and Arkle's particular appearance hung dubiously in the cold, was earned cantering, and in sadness. The flying two-miler Dunkirk set a rattling spin, then suffered a lung haemorrhage, crashed into the fence and broke his own neck and poor Bill Rees' right thigh pinned beneath his body. It was then gravely suggested that Arkle's superiority ruined ordinary horses who opposed him. Mill House, Brasher, now Dunkirk were but the best known of a carnage of victims. Sensationalists queried: 'Arkle – A Killer?'

The star returned to Ireland for one Leopardstown race before his third Gold Cup. Ceaseless rain postponed the meeting twice as Cheltenham hurried closer, and Arkle, needing a race, waxed fatter. When it came old Mrs Baker was there as guest of the Leopardstown Club to watch him race for the first time and saw him scrape home by a neck. He had his hardest race so far when the tiny mare Height O'Fashion getting the full 3 st., raced at him from the last, caught him and nearly passed him. Taaffe remarked afterwards: 'Arkle was terribly unfit.' And to some of us not knowing then how brilliant the mare would turn out to be it seemed he was also, sated by victories, growing over-confident.

This and inattention nearly brought his downfall in the Gold Cup, for which he started 10–1 on (only three other winners in its history had previously been at any odds-on). At the last fence first time round, he never looked at all. He struck the birch with his chest, started blundering downwards, stuck his neck down and out to save himself. The crowd gasped gigantically and then somehow he had passed through the fence and was travelling on. 'But for the shamrock,' muttered his distraught lad Johnny Lumley 'he was gone for sure.' His admirers, it being St Patrick's Day, had pinned a sprig of Shamrock to his bridle. Again he won in a canter, this time by 30 lengths, the longest distance and at the shortest price of any Gold Cup winner. 'Sure,' shouted a brogue from the mill round the unsaddling ring, 'hadn't Saint Patrick himself had him well backed?' Behind him Hunch had fallen and been killed, and Snaigow was so exhausted that he had to be dismounted after the post. That Arkle murdered his opposition was again the cry.

Though intended, he did not run again that season. Torrential April rain which cancelled Epsom, put Sandown in doubt for the Whitbread, and Arkle stayed at home. If killer he was, Nemesis was only eight months away and had picked the place dramatically.

Arkle was six months off the course when he ran for his third Hennessy at Newbury in November. Though he bore his customary 12 st. 7 lb., only five opponents turned out. All had been set 10 st. bar What A Myth, a winner already that season and who would win the 1969 Cheltenham Gold Cup. He merely carried 10 st. 2 lb., another example of Arkle's superiority. The outsider was the grey Stalbridge Colonist who had been tailed off a fortnight earlier behind Arkle's inferior stablemate Dicky May. On yielding ground the great horse set out to make it all, but the grey caught him at the last, Arkle came again, and both horses at maximum extension strove for the line. Arkle was beaten half a length. It seemed that under these weights, in these conditions even he could now start losing to brilliant horses carrying little. Two years later Stalbridge Colonist was only beaten ¾ of a length in the Gold Cup. He was third in it, beaten only a neck and one length in 1968. He was a topclass horse. And Arkle had tried to give him 2 st. 7 lb. The public, only a tiny percentage of whom ever go racing, had long since taken Arkle to their hearts. But millions had seen Arkle struggling on TV and suffered with him. They were now audibly enraged with Stewards, handicappers, the racing authorities in general for what they regarded as malevolent cruelty to the greatest horse in the world. 'They're trying to kill him with those weights!'

Two-and-a-half weeks later he won a moderate race at Ascot (but worth nearly £3,000) with insulting ease and flew back to Ireland for a breather before Boxing Day. Frost put Kempton off and the King George VI was run in sombre chill on Tuesday, 27 December. Six opposed Arkle at 9–2 on, there being a nudge of support for Woodland Venture at 6–1 and Dormant at 10–1. The others ran for kicks or fourth money. It was a year since Dunkirk died.

Arkle led for just over the first circuit, then Dormant showed, then Arkle came again. He was not jumping spectacularly. Dormant blundered, then two fences later Arkle made a hash of the open ditch, striking the guard-rail. Woodland Venture passed him, but going to the second last Arkle was just in front again and the other fell. Coming clear at the last, you could see Dormant closing steadily but

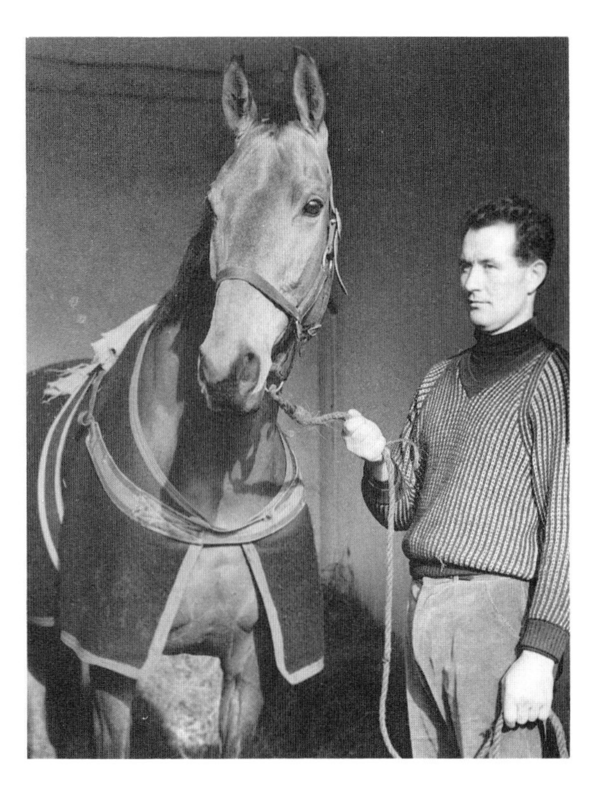
Arkle resting at Kempton Park in January 1967 after breaking his pedal bone in his last race on Boxing Day.

evidently hopelessly from behind. Then Arkle jumps crooked, seems to dwell, and we wait for the dazzling dash. Nothing happens. He is struggling up the run-in and Dormant catches him and goes past. Arkle is lame. He is very lame walking in. Standing to be unsaddled, he is crippled. Pat Taaffe whispers, his face twisted, 'His leg's gone, he's broken down'. It is unbelievable. He limps away into the grey dusk and the lights gleam like tears from the damp stands. A huge gloom washes over us all. It is the end of an era.

As the world was soon to know by radio, TV, and the front pages of newspapers, Arkle had not broken down. He had cracked the pedal bone inside his hoof, probably by striking it on the guard rail of the ditch where he blundered. He had completed the rest of the journey in sharply increasing pain, and though unable to stride out down the run-in had not flinched till the post was past.

He stayed at Kempton, held press conferences and photo calls, had the box next door set aside for presents from the world over and another for his telegrams and get-well cards. His progress, that of a star more than that of a statesman, was reported in the news headlines and in every paper. He had records played for him on request programmes and prayers said for him in distant churches.

Arkle spent a lovely summer at Bryanstown with old Meg. A television company was making another documentary about him. He received 160 letters on his birthday, and greeted visitors at Greenogue that spring from 10 countries.

During the summer the Duchess often rode Arkle round her farm. 'He was a lovely ride,' she says fondly. 'He'd shove himself into a ditch for me to get on. Or

How many other great horses – let alone the greatest steeplechaser – have been used as gentle hacks by their owners? The Duchess rides Arkle on a summer's day.

I'd get on him off the muck-cart – everyone used to laugh – or from the bumper of a car. He really did look after me.'

'Arkle would gallop and take a strong hold,' says the Duchess, 'but I never *ever* felt he'd run away with me. He really liked human beings, you know, much better than horses. Because he absolutely trusted everyone. He was an astonishing horse. When he was lying down in the field or in his box in the straw he'd never get up. He'd only lift his head just enough to lay it on my lap. He knew one's voice. He knew my car driving into the Dreapers and he knew my foot in the yard. He'd start banging on the box door with his toe . . .'

The Duchess so loved having Arkle at Bryanstown and so enjoyed the hours hacking him about and petting him in the field – 'She did spoil him dreadfully with those sugar lumps,' Johnny Kelly, the stud groom at Bryanstown remembered – that the decision which shook the racing world came to her quite gently.

On 9 October 1968, the Duchess formally announced the retirement of the greatest steeplechaser ever. 'Arkle is sound and very well,' she said, 'but, although his come-back had been planned for Leopardstown after Christmas that would be only just short of his 12th birthday. After a great deal of thought and discussions with Mr Tom Dreaper and Mr. Cosgrove,' she went on, 'we have decided to retire him. Not even Arkle, with his immense courage,' she concluded, 'could be expected to reproduce his old brilliance . . .'

'Not even Arkle . . .' how often in his life and afterwards that phrase has rung out like a trumpet of salutation, the declaration of a different breed.

It comforted us all that he had a gently caring last home in the best of hands. We thought happily and confidently that he would live on there for years and years, enjoying a quiet life and his contented recollections.

But as the winter of 1968 drew in, Arkle began to show more mysterious signs of stiffness. 'He seemed,' said the Duchess, 'to be stiff in his back, and it was then, I think, that Maxie Cosgrove began to talk about the possibility of brucellosis.'

The October of 1969 stayed particularly warm and the onset of Arkle's stiffness was kept at bay. So when the then Colonel 'Mike' Ansell asked the Duchess if Arkle could be paraded at Wembley at The Horse of the Year Show, she willingly agreed. As soon as his appearance was announced, advance bookings leapt 35 per cent on the previous year's.

Arkle, on what would be his last visit to England, stayed a full week. He was based at Lord Knutsford's home near Watford from the Sunday before the show until the Sunday it closed, and he drove in to meet his public every day. On the show ground he had a stable next door to Princess Anne's horse and she looked in to greet him and to talk to Kelly about him. His box was besieged by his admirers all six days and every evening. After the Monday he paraded twice daily. 'He was *delighted* with himself,' says Kelly who led him in, sometimes with Pat Taaffe riding, for the Parade of Personalities. 'Just like he was racin', he'd put his head up and have his ears cocked, lookin' at the crowds. The applause was so *enormous*, he'd give a jump when I led him in.'

Pat Taaffe remembers, 'He bowed to Her Grace, who loved it. When he was warmed up from the exercise he felt really well. It is unbelievable to think that he was really so bad.'

The Duchess says, 'All the clapping was right down his street! He adored it. There was a costermonger's cart there, piled with apples and pears. And Arkle absolutely stripped it. I wrote to the owner to apologize and he wrote me the most charming letter back, saying he was delighted and honoured that Arkle had eaten all his fruit.'

Arkle showed off excessively. One night, standing in front of the parade with David Broome's show-jumper, he set about the show's hydrangeas and munched them up.

Mike Ansell had asked the owners of all the personalities to select the tune they would like the band to play each time their horse paraded. The Duchess did not ponder long. She picked for Arkle 'There'll Never Be Another You.'

Arkle had always played to his public. Like a politician before a crowd and an actor in the theatre he needed acclamation. In his case he deserved it. But, just as public performers come off drained of nervous energy having given their all, so it was probably the reaction from that, coupled with the onset of the cold winter that brought on him very soon an increasing degree of stiffness.

This may sound more like the symptoms of arthritis, but it is true, too, that brucellosis in horses comes and goes in waves, flaring up and subsiding like the effects of glandular fever in humans.

Arkle grew stiff. The Duchess travelling back and forth that spring of 1970 says, 'We were pretty despondent. We'd con ourselves that sometimes he was a bit better, but . . . He'd go out for a few hours most days, but he'd lie down a lot . . .'

She had hardly gone back to Cheshire when Pat Taaffe called to visit his old friend. He came over with his daughter Olive, who loved feeding Arkle apples and pears. The great horse was having much difficulty moving. Pat telephoned the Duchess and Maxie Cosgrove. 'I rang Her Grace and said, "You'd better come over." '

Anne, Duchess of Westminster, unveils Arkle's statue at Cheltenham (now moved higher up the hill behind the new paddock) watched by Lord Willoughby de Broke and the Racegoers' Club's Tony Fairbairn.

Maxie Cosgrove examined Arkle yet once more, and telephoned the Duchess. She made the last, hardest decision in Arkle's life, and flew over from Cheshire to say goodbye to him. 'In the few days since I'd seen him, he was very much worse.' When she went in to see him for the last time, he was lying down.

It was Sunday afternoon, 31 May 1970. Johnny Kelly could not bear to stay with his horse, but went up to his house at the end of the yard and shut the door. He said, 'All through the years Arkle would trust you. He took all those injections, because he knew that we were doing it to him for his good. And so . . .' Five years later, Kelly bit upon his lower lip and his eyes blinked quickly.

It fell to James Kavanagh, who accompanied the miserable Maxie Cosgrove, to give Arkle his last injection. The great horse went down in his box and went to sleep forever.

As sometimes happens in loving human relationships, Arkle's old friend Meg did not long out-live him. By the end of August she was buried beside him in their grassy grave, surrounded by a banked hedge of daffodils halfway between their old stables and what is now called Arkle's Field. The stone above her grave read simply '*Meg A Good Hunter*'. Above Arkle's, facing the rays of the southern sun, was an even more simple memorial. Befitting the last home of the greatest steeplechaser of all time it just gave his name.

The years passed and the Duchess decided to sell her Irish farm. Bryanstown, like much else in the world of the thoroughbred, was sold to the Arabs from whose three original stallions the whole race began.

The Duchess then agreed to a proposal which shocked many of Arkle's legion of fans. She would let his skeleton be disinterred from its quiet grave, to be installed in the Irish Horse Museum at the National Stud at Tully in Co. Kildare. After all, the skeleton of the unparalleled flat racehorse Eclipse stands for all to see in the excellent Newmarket museum. So why not that of Arkle, in Ireland, if only to remind those who come after and who never had the joy of seeing him in life, that here indeed was a steeplechaser whose deeds will never be equalled?

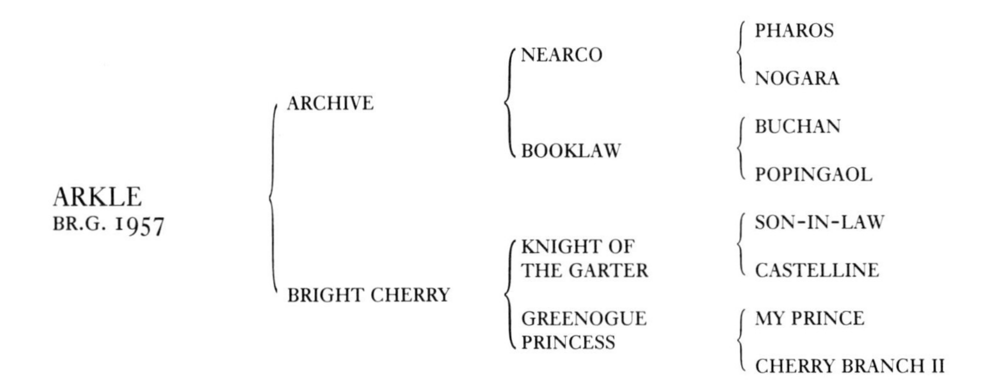

DATE	COURSE	RACE	DISTANCE	VALUE	WEIGHT	JOCKEY	PRICE	PLACE
Season 1961–62								
Dec 9	Mullingar	Lough Ennel Maiden Plate (Amateurs) (F)	2m 1f 160 yds	£133	11.4	Mr M. Hely-Hutchinson	5/1	3rd
Dec 26	Leopardstown	Greystones Maiden Flat Race (Amateurs)	2m	£202	10.11	Mr M. Hely-Hutchinson	5/1	4th
Jan 20	Navan	Bective Novice H	3m	£133	11.5	L. McLoughlin	20/1	won
Mar 10	Naas	Rathconnel H'cp H	2m	£202	11.2	P. Taaffe	2/1f	won
Apr 14	Baldoyle	Balbriggan H'cp H	2m	£387	10.1	L. McLoughlin	6/1	unpl
Apr 24	Fairyhouse	New H'cp H	2m	£742	10.5	L. McLoughlin	8/1	4th
Season 1962–63								
Oct 17	Dundalk	Wee County H'cp H	2m 216 yds	£163	11.13	P. Taaffe	6/1	won
Oct 24	Gowran Park	President's H'cp H	2m	£432	10.5	P. Woods	9/2j.f.	won
Nov 17	Cheltenham	Honeybourne Ch	2m 4f	£680	11.11	P. Taaffe	11/8f	won
Feb 23	Leopardstown	Milltown Ch	2m	£461	12.11	P. Taaffe	1/2f	won
Mar 12	Cheltenham	Broadway Chase	3m	£1,360	12.4	P. Taaffe	4/9f	won
Apr 15	Fairyhouse	Power Gold Cup (Chase)	2m 2f	£1,137	12.5	P. Taaffe	2/7f	won
May 1	Punchestown	John Jameson Cup (Chase)	2m 4f	£852	12.4	P. Taaffe	4/7f	won
Season 1963–64								
Oct 9	Navan	Donoughmore Maiden Plate (F)	1m 6f	£287	9.6	T. P. Burns	4/6f	won
Oct 24	Gowran Park	Carey's Cottage H'cp Ch	2m 4f	£519	11.13	P. Taaffe	4/7f	won
Nov 30	Newbury	Hennessy Gold Cup (H'cp Chase)	3m 2f 82 yds	£5,020	11.9	P. Taaffe	5/2	3rd
Dec 26	Leopardstown	Christmas H'cp Ch	3m	£846	12.0	P. Taaffe	4/7f	won
Jan 30	Gowran Park	Thyestes Park H'cp Chase	3m 170 yds	£899	12.0	P. Taaffe	4/6f	won
Feb 15	Leopardstown	Leopardstown H'cp Ch	3m	£1,671	12.0	P. Taaffe	4/7f	won
Mar 7	Cheltenham	Gold Cup Chase	3m 2f 130 yds	£8,004	12.0	P. Taaffe	7/4	won
Mar 30	Fairyhouse	Irish Grand National (H'cp Chase)	3m 2f	£2,630	12.0	P. Taaffe	1/2f	won

DATE	COURSE	RACE	DISTANCE	VALUE	WEIGHT	JOCKEY	PRICE	PLACE
Season 1964–65								
Oct 29	Gowran Park	Carey's Cottage H'cp Ch	2m 4f	£741	12.0	P. Taaffe	1/5f	won
Dec 5	Newbury	Hennessy Gold Cup (H'cp Chase)	3m 2f 82 yds	£5,516	12.7	P. Taaffe	5/4f	won
Dec 12	Cheltenham	Massey-Ferguson Gold Cup (H'cp Chase)	2m 5f	£3,989	12.10	P. Taaffe	8/11f	3rd
Feb 27	Leopardstown	Leopardstown H'cp Ch	3m	£2,583	12.7	P. Taaffe	8/11f	won
Mar 11	Cheltenham	Gold Cup (Chase)	3m 2f 76 yds	£7,986	12.0	P. Taaffe	30/100f	won
Apr 24	Sandown	Whitbread Gold Cup (H'cp Chase)	3m 5f 18 yds	£8,230	12.7	P. Taaffe	4/9f	won
Season 1965–66								
Nov 6	Sandown	Gallaher Gold Cup (H'cp Chase)	3m 118 yds	£5,165	12.7	P. Taaffe	4/9f	won
Nov 27	Newbury	Hennessy Gold Cup (H'cp Chase)	3m 2f 82 yds	£7,099	12.7	P. Taaffe	1/6f	won
Dec 27	Kempton	King George VI Ch	3m	£4,634	12.0	P. Taaffe	1/7f	won
Mar 1	Leopardstown	Leopardstown H'cp Ch	3m	£2,475	12.7	P. Taaffe	1/5f	won
Mar 17	Cheltenham	Gold Cup (Chase)	3m 2f 76 yds	£7,674	12.0	P. Taaffe	1/10f	won
Season 1966–67								
Nov 26	Newbury	Hennessy Gold Cup (H'cp Chase)	3m 2f 82 yds	£5,713	12.7	P. Taaffe	4/6f	2nd
Dec 14	Ascot	S.G.B. H'cp Chase	3m	£2,823	12.7	P. Taaffe	1/3f	won
Dec 27	Kempton	King George VI Ch	3m	£3,689	12.7	P. Taaffe	2/9f	2nd

E L E V E N

Captain Christy

ASTRONAUTS DRIVE ON THE MOON AND GOOLAGONG DRIVES TO WIMBLEDON VICTORY. ULSTER RIOTS OVER INTERNMENT; HEATH IMPOSES DIRECT RULE. INDIA DEFEATS PAKISTAN. AMIN EXPELS 50,000 ASIANS. ARABS STORM THE ISRAELIS' OLYMPIC COMPOUND AT MUNICH. NIXON BECOMES PRESIDENT, AND BETJEMAN POET LAUREATE. PRINCESS ANNE MARRIES. POMPIDOU AND PERON DIE. NIXON RESIGNS. LORD LUCAN DISAPPEARS, BUT MRS THATCHER LEADS THE TORIES

In March 1974, 38-year-old Bobby Beasley called at the Dublin surgery of Dr Austin Darragh, father of the international show-jumper Paul, and saviour of many jockeys' careers (including that of John Francome) through his treatment of weight control. Weight, sadly, was not Bobby's only problem, though that was formidable: at the start of his treatment he weighed more than 15 st. Alcoholism and its cure had induced not only dehydration but a massive crisis of confidence. To counter this he had been prescribed injections of parentavite, the short-term effects of which were violent, causing stomach cramps and a sensation of burning heat. That morning Dr Darragh gave the jockey the grim news: 'I can't give you any more. Your heart won't take it.'

In two golden seasons in his early 20s Bobby Beasley, born into an illustrious family of Irish jockeys, had won a Cheltenham Gold Cup on Roddy Owen, a Champion Hurdle on Another Flash and a Grand National on Nicolaus Silver.

He was the complete jockey: strong and stylish, a beautiful horseman and as brave as a lion. He was also startlingly good-looking with wide blue eyes and fair hair. He has a poetic turn of phrase and all the fabled charm of his race.

The gods perhaps had initially been too lavish with their gifts, for nemesis in the shape of alcoholism, seized him in his prime and brought him down. His marriage, his career and his confidence lay in ruins. His future looked piercingly bleak.

There then entered on his scene the skilful Dr Austin Darragh, the kindly and intuitive former top jockey Pat Taaffe and a lunatic horse, as brilliant as Bobby was himself, but wayward and unpredictable. Fifteen years later Bobby recalled affectionately, 'He was a free spirit'. The horse was Captain Christy.

Bobby Beasley was born to ride racing. His mother used to tell him how her Newmarket wedding was postponed for an hour while the frost came out of the ground so that her future husband could dash across to ride Golden Miller for Basil Briscoe in a final piece of Gold Cup work.

Bobby's father was 'H. H.' Harry, a top-flight flat jockey who rode principally for the great 'Atty' Persse. His grandfather, also a Harry Beasley, won a Grand National on Come Away in 1891, as well as a Grand Steeplechase de Paris and a Grand Course des Haies at Auteuil. He rode his last bumper winner at smart Baldoyle on Dublin's outskirts at the age of 85 the year before Bobby was born. Grandfather Harry's four brothers all rode too, the most famous being Tommy, who won three Irish Derbies, three English Grand Nationals and a French Grand 'Steeple'.

Captain Christy enjoyed no such illustrious ancestry. His sire Mon Capitaine was bred in France by that grand sire of French jumpers, Wild Risk, but he was himself a very moderate racecourse performer. He won but one race over a mile in France, before coming to Ireland as a four-year-old to be trained by the great Paddy Prendergast. He finished last in both his flat races. He then embarked on a long and rather unsuccessful hurdles career spanning six seasons: it yielded just two modest victories.

Captain Christy's dam, Christy's Bow, by the influential Blue Peter horse Bowsprit, did not run and Captain Christy was her first produce. With this sort of pedigree the offspring was likely to be almost given away, particularly if it was also unattractive in appearance. So it turned out. Breeder George Williams from West Cork sold the smallish, straight-shouldered individual as a foal at Ballsbridge for just 290 guineas. But though small, Christy was as agile as a cat. Like many of his sire's stock, he was also 'a bit of a boyo'. He passed through several hands and was reputedly 'a sod to break'. Human legs were broken in the process.

Eventually he came to belong to Tom Nicholson of Johnstown in whose wife's colours he first appeared in public. Ridden by Tommy Ryan, he ran in four bumpers, winning at Listowel and also at the big Galway Plate meeting which joyfully launches off the Irish National Hunt season. Captain Christy was also placed at Limerick and Tralee.

These performances disposed the racing fraternity to view his eccentricities in a favourable light, and he was bought for no less than £10,000 by Major Joe Pidcock, born in 1910, awarded the MBE and mentioned in despatches and then residing at Scarrough Lodge, Cahir, in Co. Tipperary. Reportedly a wealthy member of the Whitbread family, he was regarded as 'a right character' in Irish racing circles. His appearances in his 'straw and black cap' colours on the Curragh, clad in old-fashioned butterfly breeches that failed by 4 in. to make contact with his baggy boots, were treasured by the local fraternity for years. He was, after all, no longer in the first flush of fit youthfulness.

Major Pidcock was a man who enjoyed doing his own thing. He could not be described as a particularly distinguished amateur. Neither could his volatile, new purchase be regarded as a sensible conveyance for a middle-aged owner-trainer-rider.

Nevertheless the unlikely pair got on surprisingly well. There was an unfortunate start at Limerick when the steering of many of the youthful contestants was extremely erratic. Christy was one of four to run out, all earning their pilots a £25 fine. But he then won nicely at Baldoyle. Next time he nearly caused a sensation in the Scalp Hurdle, at the time to all intents and purposes Ireland's Champion Hurdle. Here he led until approaching the last flight, before weakening to finish third. He was also a respectable sixth in the 3-mile Lloyds Bank Novice Hurdle at Cheltenham's National Hunt Festival.

During the summer Major Pidcock moved Christy to Pat Taaffe, who had recently retired from the saddle and started up a small stable at his home Alasty, just down the road from the spanking new Goff's Sales complex at Kill.

Christy's first performance for his new trainer was remarkable to say the least: he finished last. But the race would have important repercussions. Sensing that

Daisies on the lawn; a contented Pat Taaffe with his daughter Elaine perched upon a remarkably relaxed Captain Christy.

the major might not persevere with Christy, whom he was finding increasingly moody and unpredictable, Pat Taaffe had it at the back of his mind that he might appeal to a new owner of his, Mr Pat Samuel. This dashing New Zealander, born in 1925, was a highly successful property developer and banker with world-wide interests and bases in Hong Kong and Majorca. In the former he lived in the prestigious Branksome Towers halfway up to The Peak. He would win top-class jumping races not only in England and Ireland, but also in Italy and the United States. He remains a formidable character and has always been, fortunately for the sport, a National Hunt fanatic. He had recently bought Ballinakill, at Kilfinny, near Adare, in Co. Limerick. His first horse with Taaffe, Beggar's Way, had won the monumental Conyngham Cup (it stands nearly 3 ft. high) at the big Punchestown meeting, and had then been quite fancied for the Grand National. Mr Samuel had indicated that he might be interested in a suitable young horse to go jumping.

So Pat Taaffe took him down to Tralee to watch Christy run. The prospective purchaser preserved a surprisingly restrained silence as Christy sulked round 30 lengths behind the last horse.

Finally, he burst out, 'And you want me to pay £10,000 for *that*?'

'Yes', responded Pat, unmoved by his charge's miserable performance. 'You should buy him'. So Pat Samuel did. And because Beggar's Way had run in his name and colours of 'cerise, gold Maltese cross, sleeves and cap', Christy was registered as the property of his wife, Jane.

Pat Taaffe now cast his eye round for someone to ride his temperamental youngster. Bobby Beasley, who considers that Pat Taaffe has never been given sufficient credit for his handling of Christy, thought that the major's loose-reined and slack-legged style had badly affected the youngster's discipline. Thereafter the horse furiously resented being organized. He was also hypersensitive to any movement from the saddle and would never let his rider 'place' him at an obstacle. These difficulties were exaggerated by the awkward combination of his small size and straight shoulders. 'You'd feel like John Wayne sitting on him,' commented Bobby.

For Christy's first outing in Jane Samuel's name, Bobby Coonan was engaged. Christy ran well enough to be second but was beaten quite comprehensively by Ballyowen. Four weeks later, again at Naas, Coonan was claimed by Paddy Sleator who retained him. Ironically Beasley had formerly been the skilful Sleator's stable jockey and had won the 1960 Champion Hurdle for him on Another Flash. Thus Pat again found himself in search of a jockey. Bobby Beasley had turned up at Naas in the hope of an odd spare ride. He had no rides booked. It was 11 years since his Grand National victory – a very long time in racing. His battle against the bottle had been initiated by Nicky Rackard, a trainer and neighbour of Beasley's. He had bullied him into joining Alcoholics Anonymous and later introduced him to Dr Austin Darragh. Then sporting Lord Fingall came to the rescue, too. Bobby had ridden Roddy Owen for him to win – somewhat fortunately – the 1959 Cheltenham Gold Cup. Pas Seul fell at the last when just ahead of Linwell, bringing the latter to a complete halt, but allowing Roddy Owen, then a distant third, a clear run up the hill.

Lord Fingall heard of Bobby's efforts to recover from alcoholism and to encourage him loyally offered him the ride on No Other in the Leopardstown Chase. His generosity was rewarded and No Other won. The second start of Bobby's career had begun.

Nevertheless the rides did not flow in. He was yesterday's man upon whom Celtic depression and horrendous loss of confidence lay dark and leaden.

It was trainer Paddy Murphy who suggested to Pat Taaffe that Bobby should ride Christy. 'You'll find no better,' he urged. Pat had ridden alongside Bobby for years. He took the chance. Christy struck up an immediate understanding with his new rider and won easily at their first attempt. It was the first leg of a four-timer which included a runaway win in the prestigious Scalp Hurdle, and a scintillating 6-length win over Comedy of Errors in Ireland's richest hurdle race, the Sweeps. Comedy of Errors, England's top novice of the previous season, had recently won the 'Fighting Fifth' at Newcastle and was well fancied. Hot favourite at 2–1 on was the dual Champion Hurdler Bula who, always labouring, finished a lack-lustre fourth.

The partnership of the young tearaway horse and the reformed tearaway jockey gripped the imagination of the racing Press. They hyped the dramatic situation to a pitch which Bobby found hard to cope with and in some perverse way resented. While admitting that but for Christy there would have been no comeback for him at the top, he still insists, 'Even without him, I'd still have gone on riding maybe three or four more years.'

Their winning streak ended abruptly in the Champion Hurdle, for which Christy started favourite at 85–40. In the opinion of Bobby, who travelled with him, the race was lost on the journey. He fretted and sweated. 'He must have lost half a hundredweight on the way over.' Bobby also felt in retrospect that his tactics were mistaken. Easby Abbey, tracked by Christy, set a moderate pace. Coming down the final hill Bobby realized it was not strong enough. But it was too late. The race turned into a sprint in which Comedy of Errors, by the sprinter Comedy Star, carried the most powerful guns. Four lengths covered the first six. Christy was third, 1½ lengths and 2 lengths behind Comedy of Errors and Easby Abbey.

Christy gained some compensation in the Scottish Champion Hurdle, where despite the concession of 6 lb. he put the best part of 5 lengths between himself and Easby Abbey, an improvement of nearly a stone on his Cheltenham running. His pursuers in Scotland declared that he demolished so many flights of hurdles en route to victory that he left behind him little for them to jump.

Despite the Champion Hurdle reverse it had been an ambitiously successful programme for a second season hurdler. Pat and Jane Samuel led a high-speed, glossy, jet-setting life and expected their horses to do likewise. Both liked being closely involved with their horses. Pat describes Jane as 'very knowledgeable and a fine rider'. He adores his jumpers – never the flat. 'I wouldn't bother to go. It doesn't interest me.' In the late summer and autumn of 1988 he was closely supervising his small team of jumpers based at the beautiful health and holiday resort of Merano in northern Italy some 30 km south of Bolzano on the road to Austria. The city is very *belle epoque* and the four-star Palace Hotel where Pat Samuel bases himself for his autumnal campaign stands full of antique furniture

in its own exotic park. The complicated racecourse with its figures of eight and different tracks lies less than 1 km from the city centre, and Pat Samuel was busy out there most mornings supervising work. In the autumn of 1988, his Grand Nudge proved best of all the European raiders at Nashville, Tennessee when finishing third in the first leg of the Sport of Kings series. Caution and patience never featured largely in the Samuels' lifestyle. Challenge did.

Christy's first season over fences was crammed with incident and drama. Those two imposters, Triumph and Disaster, were never far away and every move was being avidly pursued by the sporting Press. Everyone loved Pat Taaffe. Indelibly associated with the incomparable and much-mourned Arkle, Pat was amongst the finest of post-war jump-jockeys and one of the last of the long-legged breed. With it all he was modest, kind and unswervingly loyal. The racing world were united in wishing him well as a trainer. Some feared that he might prove too kind and gentle a man to prosper in that harsh profession. But it did not seem so at first. Like Fred Winter, a very different character when he began, Pat had the supreme good fortune of a star on which to start. Christy himself had all the attraction of wayward genius – unpredictable, spectacular, always exciting. Best of all was Bobby Beasley the reformed drunk now, at nearly 40, picking up the threads of a once brilliant but dissipated career. The scenario, and particularly the combination, were irresistable.

It began with a roll of drums and two devastating victories at Powerstown and Punchestown. 'He wasn't just *winning* novice chases', recalled Pat Samuel. 'He was winning them by a furlong!'

Christy then came to England to take on Fred Winter's star Bula, the dual Champion Hurdler, in Ascot's Black and White Whisky Gold Cup Novices Chase. Christy took a keen hold and made the running. Upsides with Bula two out he made a shocking blunder, giving Bobby no conceivable chance of staying on, and handed a bloodless victory to Bula. *Chaseform* considered him held at the time. All Christy's connections disagreed. Bobby still berates himself; 'I asked him to stand off too far.' Pat Samuel countered 'You couldn't dictate to Christy and no one could have survived the error he made.'

December proved a bleak month. As a preliminary race before the Irish Sweeps Hurdle, Christy reverted to hurdling for the Irish Benson and Hedges Handicap Hurdle. Inevitably Christy was burdened with 12 st. 7 lb. and the going was desperately wet.

Pat Samuel was abroad, but Jane came to Fairyhouse. 'Will you give a guarantee he'll win?' she queried eagerly.

Bobby couldn't. Not with that weight in the prevailing ground conditions.

He was quite right. Christy was second. Bobby maintains that Jane never came down to the unsaddling enclosure to see him in.

He also says that Pat Taaffe told him that before the Sweeps Hurdle Christy had been running a temperature, but that he would nevertheless have to run him. This seems unlikely. Possibly Taaffe had sensed that Christy was not 100 per cent, but had run him hoping for the best rather than disappoint the horse's owners.

It is easy enough, with hindsight and from the grandstand, to declare 'If in

doubt, don't run'. But a trainer's assessments are often as clouded in doubts as hills in winter mists. And the owner, paying the piper, can be felt to be calling the tune, even if he may restrain himself from doing so. If every trainer declined to run every horse about which he had a minor anxiety, many horses would never leave their boxes.

It was, however, generally accepted that Christy was below par that day. He ran a lifeless race to finish third, well beaten by his old rivals Comedy of Errors and Brendans Road. Bobby didn't even go through the motions of being hard on him.

Come January he was back to chasing, his immediate objective being the rich Wills Premier Chase Final at Haydock. Made odds-on favourite at 8–11, he set off jumping with the spectacular boldness which he loved. Bobby allowed him to stretch for home fully a mile out and he was nearly a fence clear when he ran into the bottom of the second last, belted it and gave Bobby again no chance whatsoever.

Bobby says, 'That race haunts me still. The Ascot thing came back – I let him fiddle. It's the oldest mistake in the world. When in doubt, ask!'

This view, considered in maturity, will cause surprise in many racing minds. Other top jockeys, riding a horse of Christy's wilful, sometimes erratic temperament, would be far more inclined to let such an animal fiddle his own way out of trouble. Fifteen years later, out of racing altogether and landlord of an old coaching inn, The Baiting* House in Upper Sapey, set in pretty rolling green country near Tenbury Wells, Bobby admits frankly and tragically, 'I was ten years too old. If I'd been in my prime Christy would have won both those races.'

Back in Ireland, the partnership hit the winning trail again, landing two novice chases with dazzling ease. Then it was Cheltenham, Mecca of every Irish jumper with any pretensions to class. The question was, which race.

Pat Taaffe favoured one of the novice chases, the Arkle or the Sun Alliance, seemingly Christy's for the taking, if he put in a clean round. Predictably, the Samuels opted for a bolder policy.

'He's well, he's winning novice chases by a furlong,' declared Pat Samuel. 'Next year he may be sick or broken down,' he argued reasonably enough. 'We'll go for the big one,' he decided.

So to the considerable surprise of the racing world and to its scant respect, the insouciant novice who had run in only six steeplechases (in two of which he had failed to complete) lined up for the Cheltenham Gold Cup with his has-been jockey. Pendil was hot favourite at 8–11.

Pat Samuel had another important Festival contender. This was the New Zealand-bred Yenesei, aiming for the Champion Hurdle. More recently several British trainers, notably Stan Mellor and David Barons, have imported horses from New Zealand to race over fences in Britain, but Pat Samuel was one of the first owners to do so. He was naturally keen to see how the tough, angular horses of his homeland (where the grass blessedly grows for nearly 11 months every year) measured up against the purpose-bred, expensively reared Anglo-Irish variety. Yenesei and Tinker Boy went first to Merano in Italy where they had a

* The name stems from an 18th-century word for feeding horses.

surprisingly tough introduction to racing in the northern hemisphere. Their intended target there was a valuable sponsored prize understood by the Samuel team to be a hurdle race.

The horses suffered a delayed and vexatious journey across the world, finally arriving only two days before the race. The Samuels, accompanied by Pat Taaffe, flew in to discover that the supposed 'hurdle race' was in fact to be run over fences and very substantial fences at that. Yenesei and Tinker Boy had never even been schooled over fences, let alone raced over them.

'They can't possibly run,' declared Pat Taaffe.

'They'll have to,' responded their owner robustly. 'There's several million lira starting money. They'll have to jump a fence or two and pull up.'

Italian jockeys were engaged and an English-speaking Italian amateur appeared to act as interpreter. English he might speak, but Pat Taaffe's soft County Kildare brogue was Irish miles beyond him. Incomprehension was writ large on all three Latin faces.

Pat Samuel grasped the situation and took control. A farcical three-way interpreting process ensued. Either the instructions became garbled in transmission or the Italian amateur decided that the truth was too awful to relay to his compatriots.

At any rate, Yenesei's Italian jockey, far from dropping his inexperienced mount out and getting a lead for a fence or two and then pulling up, instead set forth as boldly as one of Lars Porsena's messengers. He landed over the first in the lead and stayed there. Yenesei jumped like a kangaroo from his neighbouring Australia until his long journey and lack of fitness finally took their toll two out. He finished fourth. After this heroic start Pat Samuel had no hesitation in backing Yenesei each-way for the Champion Hurdle and, even more significantly, coupling him with Captain Christy for the Gold Cup in some huge each-way doubles.

He placed these bets with Ladbrokes and it was with their then long-serving and much loved rails representative, pink-faced, twinkle-eyed Dickie Gaskell that the owner travelled down to Cheltenham. Told that Yenesei was quoted at 200–1 he riposted 'You better give me another hundred then!'

Bobby Beasley arrived at Cheltenham in a state of acute depression. He knew that Austin Darragh's ultimatum effectively spelt the end of his second career. All his English ventures on Christy had ended in disaster. He had no outside rides. So

he was enormously heartened when his former guv'nor Fred Rimell, a kind man to many in adversity, offered him a ride in the Grand National. It was 13 years since Bobby had won the race for him on the grey Nicolaus Silver.

Yenesei was frankly ridden to get placed and land those doubles. Bobby dropped him out in the early stages and brought him with a sustained run from two out. He comfortably secured third place without remotely troubling Lanzarote and Comedy of Errors. Bobby afterwards reflected that if he had made more use of the tough New Zealand-bred, he could have finished closer. At any rate, the first half of the double was up and everyone felt more cheerful. A further bonus was the unexpectedly mild weather, which rapidly dried out the ground, producing going just on the soft side of good, and much to the liking of the light-actioned Christy.

Only seven runners faced the starter for the Gold Cup, with Captain Christy at 7–1, third favourite to the odd-on Pendil and then The Dikler at threes. As expected, the hard-pulling ex-West Country point-to-pointer, Charlie Potheen, made the early running. Somehow Bobby skilfully persuaded Christy to settle in behind and jump with unusual precision. These tactics, formulated more in hope than expectation, were nearly confounded at half-way when the American horse Inkslinger fell, almost bringing Christy down in his wake. In fact the incident served only to concentrate his mind. Turning down the hill, the race, as always, began to take shape. The classy but erratic High Ken, a 100–1 shot, led Pendil with The Dikler on his outside and Christy tucked in behind their heels. All three were pressing the leader like hounds on a sinking fox. Approaching the third last, the Almighty seems to have taken a hand in the affair. As Bobby put it, 'The chap I'd been praying to all last week said "pull out", so I did'.

Seconds later High Ken crashed, bringing down Pendil and the odds-on favourite for chasing's classic turned a desperate cartwheel over the fallen outsider. Terry Biddlecombe on the Queen Mother's Game Spirit says he had shouted an early warning across to Richard Pitman on Pendil – 'Don't get too near that bastard – he'll turn arse over head!'

But for that split-second decision of Bobby Beasley's, Christy would have joined that tangle of legs and oaths and shattered dreams.

Now only last year's winner The Dikler remained, twice the size of Christy, infinitely more experienced and certain to relish every yard of the final hill. The little horse jumped the second last with polished brilliance – 'He won it there',

Captain Christy's notorious last fence blunder before he recovered to win the the 1974 Gold Cup. As Bobby Beesley said 'He met it right but he didn't come up' and owner, Pat Samuel . . . 'Very few jockeys in the world would have sat on'.

reflected Bobby – and rounded the home turn with a fractional lead. 'He met the last right, but he didn't come up,' is Bobby's casual recollection of the nightmare of the next few seconds. Christy belted the last fence as only he could, yet with his unique, cat-like agility somehow survived the fearful blunder. Bobby braced his feet forward and sat like a limpet. He then coolly gave his mount a breather before gathering him up to pass The Dikler as if he was standing still. He won amazingly easily by 5 lengths. It was 15 years since his previous Gold Cup win, and the racing world probably thought that Bobby Beasley's miraculous come-back was at last complete.

'Very few jockeys in the world would have sat on Christy at the last', remarked Pat Samuel appreciatively.

The crowd was a little muted. Disappointment for the abrupt downfall of Pendil and the defeat of The Dikler hung like a pall over the unsaddling enclosure. The Press inevitably fastened on Bobby's resurrection in those 15 years since he had returned in triumph on Roddy Owen. Then he had been 23 and the blue-eyed boy of steeplechasing. This time the fruits of victory were not so sweet. He had beaten the drink, he was back in the saddle – back in the winner's enclosure by a great feat of horsemanship – but the savour was gone. 'He was a very brilliant jockey, but he always struck me as a most unhappy man', Pat Samuel reflected 14 years later.

Christy's reformed attitude to jumping did not survive the Irish National. He fell after 1¼ miles. He was quite unscathed and after examining him connections decided he could well turn out the next day for the rich 2½-mile Power Gold Cup. Bobby told Pat Taaffe bluntly that he wouldn't be coming to the races.

'He'll run,' replied Pat. 'If you're there, you'll ride him. If you're not, I'll engage someone else.'

This shows all of Captain Christy's wildfire, taken as he's led in by Jane Samuel, after his Gold Cup. Note the double-ringed snaffle – a bit preferred by Jem Mason when riding Lottery 135 years earlier.

Bobby was there. Going out on to the course someone booed. A voice from the crowd shrieked out 'You stopped him!'

'This'll be the last time,' Bobby told Pat.

Christy won by 15 lengths. In the unsaddling enclosure Bobby vowed, 'I'll be emigrating soon.'

He did. He left his wife, his children and his country and went to live in England. He never even told Pat Taaffe, who appears to be one of the few people whom he holds in unstinting respect and affection. He married again and began training a few horses. He never went back to Ireland. He says of his own people 'The Irish are a very cruel race. Look how they've treated Pat Taaffe. Oh, they'll sing songs about him till the end of time, but they never gave him anything.'

Bobby Beasley's training did not work out. 'To be a successful trainer,' he insisted afterwards, 'you need to be a hustler, a liar, a con-man or well-connected. I wasn't any of those things.'

So he gave up racing. Leaving the sport which had made him, broken him, made him again and then rejected him, made him suicidal for several weeks. But he swears he is over it all now. His marriage is happy. He has an engaging small son, who is clearly the apple of his eye. The Baiting House is welcoming and comfortable and pictures of Captain Christy and Nicolaus Silver adorn the bar.

He asked what other recent horses were deemed 'Winter Kings' and snorted derisively when told. 'Handicappers – not within 2 stone of Christy!'

Bobby Beasley's heroes, human and equine, died many years ago.

When Pat Taaffe realized that Bobby had indeed left racing, he turned again to his original choice for Christy, Bobby Coonan. It took Coonan a couple of races to fathom his brilliant but enigmatic partner. Furthermore, Christy began the new season with two problems. His Gold Cup victory had naturally shot him up to the top of the handicap, and the winter of 1974/5 was horrendously wet. Christy, with his spare frame and light action, found this combination very hard to cope with. Only twice did he find the good going he loved. Once in France, when he won, and once in the Whitbread when, carrying 12 st. he was beaten 1½ lengths by April Seventh to whom he was conceding the intolerable burden of 29 lb.

He came to England for Cheltenham's Massey-Fergusson Gold Cup, hit the seventh hard and thereafter, according to Pat Taaffe, sulked. Only one horse, the broken-down Denys Adventure, finished behind him. Those who had declared him a fortunate Gold Cup winner, one who owed his victory to Pendil's fall, found fuel for their argument. The racing press were unanimous in declaring that Pendil would easily win the King George.

These insinuations angered the Samuels and even goaded the gentle and modest Taaffe to retort. His pre-race instructions to Bobby Coonan were brief and to the point. 'Get out there in front and keep kicking. We'll show the bugger.'

They did. Pendil did his best to close as they raced into the final bend at Kempton, but once in the straight Christy quickened again and strode away to win by 8 convincing lengths. The critics were silenced, and some that day declared Christy to be the best 3-mile chaser in the world.

But not on heavy ground. The sodden winter squelched miserably on, sinking to its nadir at Cheltenham. The first day was washed out altogether and, although

the remaining two days were staged, *Timeform* declared, 'We'll probably have to wait till the next battle of the Somme before we see scenes and conditions similar to those at Cheltenham in 1975.' These were much to the liking of the powerful Dreaper-trained Ten Up who ploughed gallantly through to win. But they were entirely adverse to poor Christy who could never pull his feet easily out of the bog-like ground, made several mistakes and was pulled up over a mile from home. He pulled up again in the Irish National and not until the April sunshine shone warm upon his back and dried up the ground did he recover his form.

After his brave second in the Whitbread he went to France. Pat Taaffe knew that Christy could not last long if he continued to burn up the mileage at this rate. But if that was what Mr Samuel wanted, he after all was paying the bills. And Pat liked Pat Samuel. 'He was a nice man to deal with. And great fun.'

Christy made his bow to critical Parisian *turfistes* at pretty Enghien. They were apparently not wholly appreciative of his handsome victory. 'He never got a cheer,' remembered Pat Taaffe sadly. Nevertheless it was an encouraging dress-rehearsal for the big one, the Grand Steeplechase de Paris won by Manderin so memorably 13 years before. Unbelievably for June, the weather again did its worst. The rain descended in stair-rods and the well-watered Auteuil turf became as saturated as a heavy sponge. In fact, with only 10 st. 1 lb. on his back, Christy could handle it. 'He was almost going too well,' recalled Pat Taaffe regretfully. 'I remember The English Ditch – he jumped it great and went to the front. But he didn't quite last home.' He was second. The Grand Steeple is 4 miles 110 yards, and in heavy ground it was just too far for him.

In the autumn he went travelling again, this time across the Atlantic to Camden, South Carolina for the Colonial Cup. It was a great trip and a richly international gathering. But it turned out to be an unsuitable race for Christy. Pat Taaffe reckoned a 1½-mile flat horse that had been briskly schooled over hurdles would have proved the best type for those fences, though the course itself, set in pinewoods, is a galloping one. He schooled Christy himself over the large but flimsy Camden fences the day before, but the little horse could not adjust his painfully-learned technique to flicking though the fences American-style. He ran a gutsy race to finish fourth of the 18 runners.

Back in Britain the weather proved much more agreeable than in the previous year, and Punchestown surprisingly offered good ground in November. Thus assisted, Christy spreadeagled a high-class field, beating the future Cheltenham Gold Cup winner Davy Lad 6 lengths, with Ten Up, the 1975 Gold Cup winner, 24 lengths behind in fourth. It was a remarkable performance.

By this time Pat and Jane Samuel's jet-set marriage had dived towards the rocks. Pat spent most of the winter in Sydney, Australia. Jane was still based at Adare, and was by all accounts in an overwrought state. Even Pat Taaffe, most loyal of men, concedes that at this time he found her very difficult.

Ground conditions remained good for the King George and, with Pendil sidelined through an injury sustained on the road, Christy was made favourite at 11–10. He would probably have started odds-on had not an accident to Bobby Coonan rendered him unfit to ride. Instead of engaging a top, outside jockey, several of whom would have been eager to ride, Pat Taaffe elected to put up his

stable claimer, Gerry Newman. In a race of such value young Newman could not even claim his allowance. Pat Taaffe's decision was vociferously criticized.

But Gerry Newman refused to be overawed by comment or the occasion. He encouraged Christy to race as he loved best. He was never headed. Apart from a mistake at the 16th, Christy jumped with unflawed brilliance. He took his market rival Bula, England's leading staying chaser, by the scruff of the neck and beat him 30 lengths. He smashed the course record by no less than 4 sec. *Timeform* pronounced it 'One of the most exciting exhibitions of galloping and jumping ever seen on the racecourse.' Stately Peter Willett, never given to hyperbole, sonorously voted it 'one of the great performances of steeplechasing history.'

It was Christy's swansong. Pat Taaffe had been slightly anxious about a tendon ever since October. Working on Portmarnock Sands in February, the warm niggle became a hot reality. It was not a breakdown, but the vet counselled blistering and a year's rest.

Jane Samuel would not countenance this. After giving the horse a brief rest, she sent him instead to Francis Flood, a former leading amateur and a successful young trainer. But the vet was proved right: Christy did not stand training. Jane took him home to Adare, but he became very pottery and she had him put down.

Christy's exploits never gave Pat Taaffe's training career the tremendous impetus they deserved. 'I think he could have been a great trainer, but he never got the support. Even when Christy was flying he only had a handful of horses. I don't know why people didn't support him,' reflected Pat Samuel. He didn't say why he hadn't continued to do so.

Pat still lives at Alasty. He prepares point-to-pointers and breaks in young horses for Arthur Moore down the road at Naas, for whom his son Tom rides as first jockey. Tom, as lanky and courteous as Pat himself, is increasingly admired and clearly provides his father with a good deal of pleasure and pride.

Christy's brilliant career was effectively snuffed out before he had reached his ninth birthday. Edna St Vincent Millay, the 1920s American poetess, described as 'recklessly romantic, cynical and naughty,' wrote a much-quoted verse:

My candle burns at both ends;
It will not last the night;
But ah my foes, and oh my friends –
It gives a lovely light!

We think she too would have admired the reckless Captain Christy and understood the tragic Beasley. Half a century on her lines seem singularly apt.

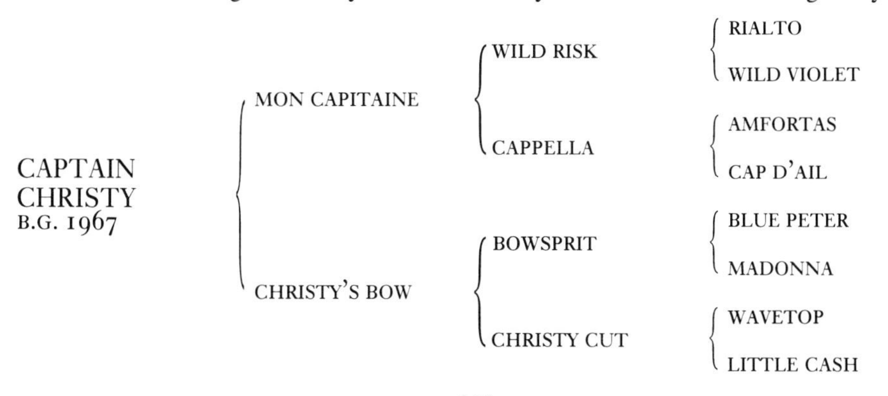

DATE	COURSE	RACE	DISTANCE	VALUE	WEIGHT	JOCKEY	PRICE	PLACE
Season 1971–72								
Jul 19	Limerick	Bruff Maiden Plate (Amateurs) (F)	2m 1f 147y	£202	11.2	Mr T. Ryan	7/1	4th
Jul 26	Galway	Lough Atalla Maiden Stakes (4–5yo) (Amateurs) (F)	2m 90y	£428	11.2	Mr T. Ryan	6/4f	won
Sep 9	Tralee	Havasnack Plate (Amateurs) (F)	2m	£800	11.2	Mr T. Ryan	5/1	3rd
Sep 29	Listowel	Newcastle West Plate (Amateurs) (F)	2m	£202	11.11	Mr T. Ryan	4/5f	won
Oct 24	Longchamp	Prix Gladiateur (F)	3m	£10512	8.13	J. Roe	no s.p.	unpl
Dec 27	Limerick	County Maiden Hurdle (Div 1) (4yo)	2m 1f 147y	£370	11.11	Maj. J. Pidcock	9/4f	r.o.
Jan 1	Baldoyle	Sutton Maiden Hurdle (Div 1)	2m	£734	11.10	Maj. J. Pidcock	4/1	won
Jan 29	Naas	Clane Hurdle	2m 1f	£960	11.6	Maj. J. Pidcock	4/1	unpl
Feb 19	Leopardstown	Scalp Hurdle	2m	£1450	11.6	Maj. J. Pidcock	20/1	3rd
Mar 15	Cheltenham	Lloyds Bank Hurdle	3m	£2131	11.9	Maj. J. Pidcock	33/1	unpl
Apr 4	Fairyhouse	Fingal Hurdle	2m	£1193	11.9	Maj. J. Pidcock	8/1	unpl
Season 1972–73								
Sep 7	Tralee	Havasnack Plate (Amateurs) (F)	2m	£1110	12.0	Maj. J. Pidcock	10/1	unpl
Oct 14	Naas	Saggart Hurdle	2m 1f	£904	11.9	R. Coonan	5/4	2nd
Oct 21	The Curragh	Irish Cesarewitch H'cp (F)	2m	£2174	7.7	J. P. Byrne	20/1	unpl
Nov 11	Naas	Rossmore Hurdle	2m 1f	£953	11.9	H. Beasley	2/1f	won
Nov 18	Leopardstown	Sandymount Hurdle	2m	£975	12.0	H. Beasley	6/4f	won
Dec 27	Leopardstown	Sweeps Hurdle	2m	£11045	11.6	H. Beasley	15/2	won
Feb 17	Leopardstown	Scalp Hurdle	2m	£1273	12.0	H. Beasley	1/2f	won
Mar 14	Cheltenham	Champion Hurdle	2m 200y	£14563	12.0	H. Beasley	85/40	3rd
Apr 14	Ayr	Scottish Champion Hurdle	2m	£1439	12.0	H. Beasley	2/1	won

Season 1973–74								
Nov 1	Powerstown Park	Magner, O'Brien & Moynihan Novice Chase	2m 2f	£690	12.0	H. Beasley	1/2f	won
Nov 7	Punchestown	Wills Premier Chase Qualifier	2m 4f	£1170	12.0	H. Beasley	1/2f	won
Nov 17	Ascot	Black & White Whisky Gold Cup Chase	2m	£4857	11.11	H. Beasley	11/10f	u.r.
Dec 8	Fairyhouse	Irish Benson & Hedges H'cp Hurdle	2m	£1977	12.7	H. Beasley	5/1	2nd
Dec 27	Leopardstown	Sweeps Hurdle	2m	£9769	12.0	H. Beasley	5/2	3rd
Jan 19	Haydock Park	Wills Premier Chase Final	2m 4f	£5736	11.7	H. Beasley	8/11f	u.r.
Feb 9	Punchestown	Poulaphouca Novice Chase	2m 4f	£690	11.7	H. Beasley	1/2f	won
Feb 28	Thurles	P Z Mower Chase	2m 4f	£690	10.11	H. Beasley	1/2f	won
Mar 14	Cheltenham	Cheltenham Gold Cup Chase	3m 2f 76y	£14572	12.0	H. Beasley	7/1	won
Apr 15	Fairyhouse	Irish Distillers Grand National H'cp Chase	3m 4f	£8916	12.2	H. Beasley	3/1	fell
Apr 16	Fairyhouse	Power Gold Cup Chase	2m 2f	£1783	12.0	H. Beasley	4/5f	won
Season 1974–75								
Oct 24	Punchestown	Free H'cp Chase	2m 4f	£862	12.5	R. Coonan	7/2	unpl
Dec 7	Cheltenham	Massey-Ferguson Gold Cup (H'cp Chase)	2m 4f	£5897	12.7	R. Coonan	9/2	unpl
Dec 26	Kempton Park	King George VI Chase	3m	£6963	12.0	R. Coonan	5/1	won
Jan 23	Gowran Park	Thyestes H'cp Chase	3m 170y	£1914	12.0	R. Coonan	4/6f	4th
Feb 22	Leopardstown	Leopardstown H'cp Chase	3m	£2507	12.0	R. Coonan	7/4f	4th
Feb 27	Thurles	P Z Mower Chase	2m 4f	£445 (each)	11.9	R. Coonan	1/2f	won (dead heat)
Mar 13	Cheltenham	Cheltenham Piper Champagne Gold Cup Chase	3m 2f 75y	£17757	12.0	R. Coonan	7/4f	p.u.

DATE	COURSE	RACE	DISTANCE	VALUE	WEIGHT	JOCKEY	PRICE	PLACE
Mar 22	Naas	Kildare H'cp Chase	3m 76y	£861	12.7	R. Coonan	2/1	won
Mar 31	Fairyhouse	Irish Distillers Grand National H'cp Chase	3m 4f	£8643	12.0	R. Coonan	3/1	p.u.
Apr 26	Sandown Park	Whitbread Gold Cup (H'cp Chase)	3m 5f 118y	£12383	12.0	R. Coonan	5/1	2nd
Jun 10	Enghien	Prix du Velay (H'cp Chase)	2m 3f	£2880	11.6	R. Coonan	no s.p.	won
Jun 22	Auteuil	Grand Steeplechase de Paris	4m 110y	£48,000	10.1	R. Coonan	no s.p.	2nd
Season 1975–76								
Nov 15	Camden (USA)	Colonial Cup International Chase	2m 6f 110y	£12818	11.6	R. Coonan	no s.p.	4th
Dec 13	Punchestown	Punchestown Chase	2m 4f	£1499	11.10	R. Coonan	1/2f	won
Dec 26	Kempton Park	King George VI Chase	3m	£6963	12.0	G. Newman	11/10j.f.	won

Career Record

Ran – Flat 7; won 2, £630. Hurdles 15; won 6, £16,419. Chases 24; won 12 (including 1 dead heat), £39,206

Total – Ran 46; won 20 (including 1 dead heat), £56,255

T W E L V E

Red Rum

TONY JACKLIN WINS U.S. OPEN AND LAURENCE OLIVIER A LIFE PEERAGE. OH! CALCUTTA! EXPOSES ITSELF. HIJACKED JETS EXPLODE IN JORDANIAN DESERT. MRS HAROLD WILSON PUBLISHES POEMS. BRITAIN'S MONEY GOES DECIMAL, BUT ROLLS ROYCE GOES BROKE. TURKS INVADE CYPRUS. SAIGON FALLS TO THE COMMUNISTS. SUEZ CANAL REOPENS AND NORTH SEA OIL TOO STARTS TO FLOW

Bred to be a humble sprinter on the flat, a runner in 'sellers'; sold for 400 guineas as a yearling but with one million dollars declined for him as a 13-year-old; handled by five trainers, ridden by more than two dozen jockeys from Lester Piggott to Tommy Stack; racing for 12 years from a two-year-old into his 13th year; 10 flat races then 110 under N.H. Rules. And in five glorious springs the ultimate Grand National hero: winner of three, second in the other two.

Red Rum was always and – as we write in his 24th year – still is a survivor. His name and deeds will never be forgotten, not just among racing people, but among millions for whom he was a real world hero of the 1970s. He achieved his triumphs against all the odds, without advantages 'and often', as his trainer 'Ginger' McCain used wonderingly to remark, '*in spite* of people.' He made it from rags to riches like his wonderful old last owner, Noel Le Mare, who had sold papers as a boy on Liverpool's cold wet streets and made a multi-million pound construction empire.

The late Mr Le Mare was Red Rum's last personal owner. But Red Rum Ltd.,

which started to handle his public appearances before his suddenly enforced retirement on the morning of the 1978 Grand National, was still busy making bookings for him in the spring of 1989. Quite early in this his last career – he adores crowds and adulation and is at home in hotels, TV studios and betting shops – Red Rum had earned many times more as a personality than his stakes on the course.

Nothing was ever ordinary about the public's beloved 'Rummy': neither how he was trained during the glory years, nor where, nor how he went about his business on the sands at Southport, bouncing through the traffic from his little yard tucked behind McCain's used-car salesroom on the wrong side of the railway crossing.

He used to work between the blowing sand dunes and the grey sea tide. Ahead of the beat of his feet the dunlins scampered for safety and the gulls rose in a white cloud shrieking. The wind brought a steely wall of rain racing towards the horse across the broad beach. The red danger flags were blown out stiff as scarlet boards, cracking in the wind like thunder.

The horse was bent over his bit like a bow. His head was tucked into his left and his mouth was open, showing his parrot-teeth in a snarl. The horse, as was his habit, led with his near-fore leg and, now that he was really galloping, the leg flicked outwards whistling through the air, the hoof thumping the ground, like a boxer again and again left-hooking. The action would have gained him no rosette in the show ring, but in a race, when the pressure was on, it showed clearly to those who knew him that the great horse had really begun to fly.

His front hooves hammered the sand, so that the shock was so great that you might think the feet would never stand it. Yet these were the feet which had in his mid-career been so crippled with a bone disease that he had only had a fifty-fifty chance of recovery.

Ginger McCain, who in Red Rum's retirement used him rather bravely for the first years as his hack – 'he'd go on blackguarding about!' – would stand very tall by the side of his old truck. Behind it were coupled the harrows with which he had just combed a 2-mile strip of wrinkled sand, just wide enough for two horses to work upsides. An old tweed cap, greasy-peaked, was perched atop of his very large head. Bursting out around it, the hair which had given him the nickname 'Ginger' flickered grizzled in the wind. His eyes, screwed up against sea-spray and the sting of sand, watched nothing but his horse. On his face burned the glow of exultation.

For this was the horse for which he had been waiting down all those dark years when he and his wife had camped in small rooms with a few sticks of furniture, and money was so short that he was down to borrowing a fiver to pay for a horse to run. Through all those years, driving a taxi, dreaming of finding one day, somehow, for someone 'The One Good Horse' which would make his name, the trainer had spent money he did not have on horses which were cheap and old and lame and bad. He bought experience most dearly, but he stored it up against the day when the one good horse would come.

McCain had been reared in a back street far from the open world of thoroughbred racehorses and rich friends and introductions into stables. He had no background of horses whatsoever. He had no relation in even the lowest echelon of the racing industry.

He had glimpsed hope winking fitfully at the end of a shadowy tunnel of setbacks and disasters. He had lost faith sometimes. He had thought the distant light beckoning him on might turn out to be only the winking eye of a harlot. But he, like the horse who now rushed past him like a conquering express into the lashing wall of rain, had struggled on against the odds. For the horse had received in his life much unjust punishment. He had been subjected to sufficient pain from whip and bone disease to make him, had he been human, turn crook or layabout.

The rain passed across the sea. The horse came back walking in the frothy rim of the tide. There, in the shallows a few years earlier, horses and carts had been drawing nets for shrimps and codling: horses with torn tendons and twisted joints had become remarkably sound again . . .

The horse played with his bit and splashed his now sound hooves against the sea's surface like a child larking. The horse knew that his work was done, for he was, as his trainer said, 'a true professional'. He was relaxed now. His arrogance had melted into a jaunty content.

He sprang up, plunged down the steep sand hills behind the Royal Birkdale Golf Course and made his way home, feet clipping the tarmac, leading the little string along the tree-lined avenues of Southport's smarter suburb. Here, where Victorian magnates had erected their red residences in ornate gardens with extensive coach-houses, mothers from flats and newly developed little homes bustled their children off to school. Because the horse was famous throughout the land commuters slowed to let him pass. Eyes followed his progress with awe from cars shuttling into Liverpool, where he had struggled for humble victory in his very first race, and later, achieved his glories.

In one commodious mansion in a tranquil street the horse's octogenarian owner would lie. The sprightly old gentleman's life had begun in poverty in the last century. For him, as for his trainer, victory at Liverpool, *the* racecourse of the country, in the Grand National, *the* great race of the whole year, had been a dream born in adolescence. The owner always remembered his mother running a school and teaching the children to sing each day, 'If at first you don't succeed, try, try, try again'. And Red Rum for the first time in the race's history, and almost certainly the last, had won it three times.

Red Rum waited at the level-crossing while a Liverpool train clattered past. The gates opened. He crossed and was in his humble street again. On his left lay, in a long and rather dingy row, a sweet shop and tobacconist, a pet centre, a Chinese fish-and-chip shop, a butcher, a small wholesale grocer. On his right, behind the bus shelter, behind the row of parked secondhand cars belonging to his trainer and partner, lay the alley leading into his cosy stable-yard, overlooked by the backs of houses and embracing one solitary tree.

Beryl McCain used to look up and out from her modern kitchen into the yard to watch Red Rum walk in. All those years when weeks were hard and months a struggle, and she had been worried sometimes close to breaking point, her husband had said 'All we need is one good horse'.

They had Red Rum.

The first of the weird coincidences which lace the horse's history began when he was a yearling. Bred by Martyn McEnery in Co. Kilkenny, he was out of

Mared, a mare rejected by her trainer 'Phonsie' O'Brien (Vincent's younger brother) as being 'mad'. Trained by a neighbour, and so crazy before her race that they had to throw a bucket of water over her before she came into the parade ring, she managed to win a little £202 maiden stake at Galway in August 1961.

When Mared retired to McEnery's stud he chose Quorum to cover her, simply because friends of the family owned the sire. Red Rum's now world famous name, though 'Murder' spelt backwards, was made from the last syllables of his parents'. The yearling and a filly subsequently named Curlicue were sent for sale in Goff's pleasant old Ballsbridge ring. 1966 was a wretched year for breeders. A Labour Government had imposed a credit squeeze, a new Betting Tax and Capital Gains Tax. And, just before Red Rum was due to be sold, through overfreshness when being shown to a possible client, he fell over and slightly lamed himself, thus putting off the only person, Yorkshire trainer Pat Rohan, who had shown the faintest interest in lot 201. Red Rum went for 400 guineas to the bid of former champion jump jockey Tim Molony, then training in a small way near Melton Mowbray. Molony had been instructed by a gambling owner, Maurice Kingsley, to buy a cheap one 'to win that 2-year-old seller at Liverpool next March.'

Red Rum did so. He dead-heated with the very filly from McEnery's stud who travelled up to Dublin to be sold as the very next lot at the very same price.

At Liverpool, after the seller, there was no bid for the filly Curlicue trained by the late Major 'Ginger' Dennistoun (a sporting character, later John Oaksey's father-in-law). Someone ran Molony up to 300 guineas to buy Red Rum back.

Red Rum takes Billy Ellison briskly back to breakfast.

The taxi-driving Ginger McCain, just struggling to start training, was at Liverpool that day. It was his local course and even then his favourite. He watched the race and the auction. But what good was a two-year-old seller to a man seeking jumpers?

Red Rum had a busy two-year-old season, suitable for a precocious youngster, but destined (one would have thought) to spoil the horse's long-term prospects. He won a 'nursery' at Warwick, was third at Newcastle and Pontefract. First time out as a three-year-old he just won a seller at Doncaster and, suitably enough, was only beaten a short-head while carrying a 10 lb. penalty and Lester Piggott, in a decent handicap at Liverpool on Grand National day. Even the judge and Piggott at first thought he had won.

Tim Molony had not only bought him well and trained him well, he briefly owned him. He bought him in after the Doncaster seller for 1,400 guineas only to have Maurice Kingsley explode, 'I'm not having him!'

He changed his mind the next day and Molony was planning to send the horse jumping. Out of the blue he got a telephone call from that shrewd old Yorkshire trainer Bobby Renton. 'I've bought Red Rum.' The yard was 'disgusted' at Red Rum's removal. He was even then a personality and loved by the lads. Six years later Molony said glumly, 'I was heart-broken.'

Renton had bought the horse for his particularly close friend and owner Mrs 'Muffie' Brotherton to whom Red Rum had been recommended by Kingsley. Renton in his heyday at Oxclose near Ripon had trained 30 horses, including Freebooter. On Red Rum's arrival in 1968 there were only eight, all owned by Mrs Brotherton who had been trying since 1950 to win a National.

She sold Red Rum seven months short of her dream. 'If Bobby had given up training earlier, I'd have sold my horses earlier,' the formidable old lady declared just after her one-time hope had won his second Grand National and the Scottish National. 'Red Rum was my oldest, so he had to go.'

Old Bobby Renton, good rider, good trainer, loyal friend said proudly, 'He won eight races when he was here: three hurdles and five chases.' Equally proudly, 'Muffie' Brotherton lovingly declared, 'At 83, Bobby used to get up at crack of dawn to feed his horses . . .'

Of Mr Renton, his old Head Lad, Charles Wright, who cared for 'Rummy', darkly opined, 'He was a cunning old fox, he was,' adding, 'Still waters run deep, and the devil lives at the bottom.'

But the person who cared for her beloved 'Rummy' absolutely to distraction was his stable girl Sandra who as a horse-mad schoolgirl had been hanging round the stables since she was 14. She was so heart-broken when Mrs Brotherton dispatched her horse to Doncaster Sales that she cried for days, quit racing for ever, and married the kindly Ripon builder who had been the second person in her young life after she fell for 'Rummy'.

Sandra Kendall started at Oxclose at £6.50 a week – 'Mr Renton liked to start you low!' She worked long hours and had some rough rides on her horse, particularly on the roads. 'He kicked out at cars. He'd buck and fool around . . . murderous he was at times . . .'

The future champion jockey Tommy Stack (subsequently a most shrewd breeder, investor, stud manager and trainer) was working as a lad at Oxclose 'doing his two' when Red Rum arrived. 'I hated riding him out! Really no one rode except for Sandra. There'd be big trouble from Sandra if she saw anyone else riding her Rummy!'

Bobby Renton pitched the horse in at the deep end, running him first over hurdles at Cheltenham. He told Josh Gifford to 'give him a very hard race'. The horse finished second. But Gifford's powerful riding (which he subsequently regretted) had absolutely no effect upon Red Rum's courage. 'He had stripes on him that lasted weeks,' Sandra recalled. 'He didn't much care for Cheltenham after that.'

Despite that introduction, despite a series of severe rides from Tommy Stack – 'driven out', 'hard ridden', *Chaseform* kept on reporting, together with, almost always, their rare accolade 'looked well' – Red Rum kept on racing: over all sorts of distances, both sorts of obstacles, all sorts of ground.

In the spring of 1969 gallant Paddy Broderick got the last three rides on Red Rum. 'He won three on the trot!' Sandra rejoiced. The warmth of the spring sun and fast ground, these he needed. And his trainers should have heeded. The following season Tim Molony watched his ex-horse's disappointments so critically that he told Bobby Renton, 'You must be mad to keep running that little horse on the soft. He hates it.'

Bright Tommy Stack, sharp of face and quick of wits, who had started life as an insurance clerk, briefly took over from retiring Renton. In his turn he was succeeded by his friend and neighbour Anthony Gillam, with whom he'd lodged as a jockey and who was training nearby across the river under permit.

Stack quickly discovered that, with all the racing there is in England compared with his native Ireland, it was impossible both to train and continue riding. Bluntly he told Renton so. As a trainer he had found Red Rum 'disappointing'. As a jockey, years later, he would have a startling change of mind.

During Sandra's month's absence after a fall, her 'Rummy' missed her so much she found him on her return 'a shadow. Gone to nothing.' Mr Renton had declared, 'If you're not coming back we're taking Red Rum out of training.'

Gentle Anthony Gillam now stepped into the breach, offering to take over the licence. Three years later he said, 'I wish in retrospect I'd never done it. I'd bitten off more than I could chew.' Old Bobby Renton with his shrewd eye and decades of knowledge was still living on the place observing the young man. So were the staff Renton had engaged. And Gillam, living miles away, felt out of touch with the yard, and out of sympathy with the powerful Mrs Lurlene Brotherton, and her close confidante, her ex-trainer, the foxy Mr Renton.

Red Rum had suffered changes and hardship. Then fell the first grave blow: the dreaded bone disease of pedalostitis set in. This in an ordinary horse would fairly rapidly have ended his racing career. It remained a closely guarded secret in the yard. But when three leading vets were told, after the horse had won his first Grand National, that he had suffered this crippling disease, they either would not believe it or regarded him as still doomed.

When Red Rum came back a winner from Catterick on New Year's Day 1972,

it was his 4th race in a month. He was lame for several days. The stable's vet took X-rays of his feet and pronounced 'I'm very sorry to say he has chronic pedalostitis in his off-fore. Very few horses, I'm afraid, get over it.'

Red Rum was put on a course of intra-muscular cortisone to relieve the pain, and given ultrasonic treatment by Mr Ashby, a blunt equine physiotherapist from Richmond. His feet were fitted with Swedish hoof pads. Long, slow gentle exercise was prescribed while treatment continued, so as winter yielded to spring Sandra rambled the countryside on her 'Rummy', 'even rounding up bullocks on him – he loved that!'

'And eventually,' said Anthony Gillam, 'he came right.' Or so it seemed. They ran the horse in the 1972 Scottish Grand National, and he finished fifth weakening from three out when he took the lead. The Scottish vet from Hawick who had treated him was watching. He noticed that in the last ¾ mile Red Rum kept changing his legs, and hanging unusually towards the rails, away from his damaged foot. 'He's still feeling it, I'm afraid,' he told Gillam.

Ginger McCain, too, saw the race. He knew nothing about any foot trouble, but noted, 'This is a real stayer . . . could be a National horse . . . I'll mention him to Mr Le Mare' (whom Ginger was often driving in his taxi), 'in case he'd ever be for sale.'

And Mrs Brotherton decided to send Red Rum to Doncaster's August Sales. 'I've some bad news for you, Sandra,' Gillam began. 'That's it then,' Sandra burst out. 'I'm going!' 'I might buy him. I'll try,' said Gillam. He had two friends who might help him buy the horse. He asked the vet, 'Will he stay right?' 'Fifty-fifty. I wouldn't spend too much money on him.'

Gillam soon had even more nasty news for the miserable Sandra. 'They're not going to let you take him to the sales,' he said acutely embarrassed. 'They' always meant the Mrs Brotherton-Mr Renton pair. They feared Sandra would betray her 'Rummy's' secret foot disease to prevent his sale. 'It was the way they treated me after 11 years. That's what upset me!' Sandra cried. 'So I went down into Wales on a holiday with Brian.' And there she was in a hotel with her ardent, faithful future husband when Rummy came up for sale.

On the sale's eve, hunched up old Mr Renton led tall young Anthony Gillam into Red Rum's box for one long last look. He said, 'Remember him. This is the most perfectly balanced and best proportioned horse you'll ever see.'

'So why the ---- are you selling him?'

'Well, Mrs Brotherton says . . .'

Gillam at least persuaded her at that eleventh hour to raise the reserve from 3000 to 5000 guineas. 'At that I didn't think I'd lose him.'

Ginger McCain thought otherwise. Till then the humble trainer had only once spent more than £1,000 on a horse. Now he had 7000 guineas from bold 84-year-old Le Mare. Captain Tim Forster, subsequently trainer of three Grand National winners, thought Red Rum might prove 'a fun horse' for his owner Mrs Henriques. He and Anthony Gillam, anxious to keep his horse, kept duelling across the ring up to the 5000 guineas level. Then McCain held up a spread hand and a thumb and mouthed 'six'.

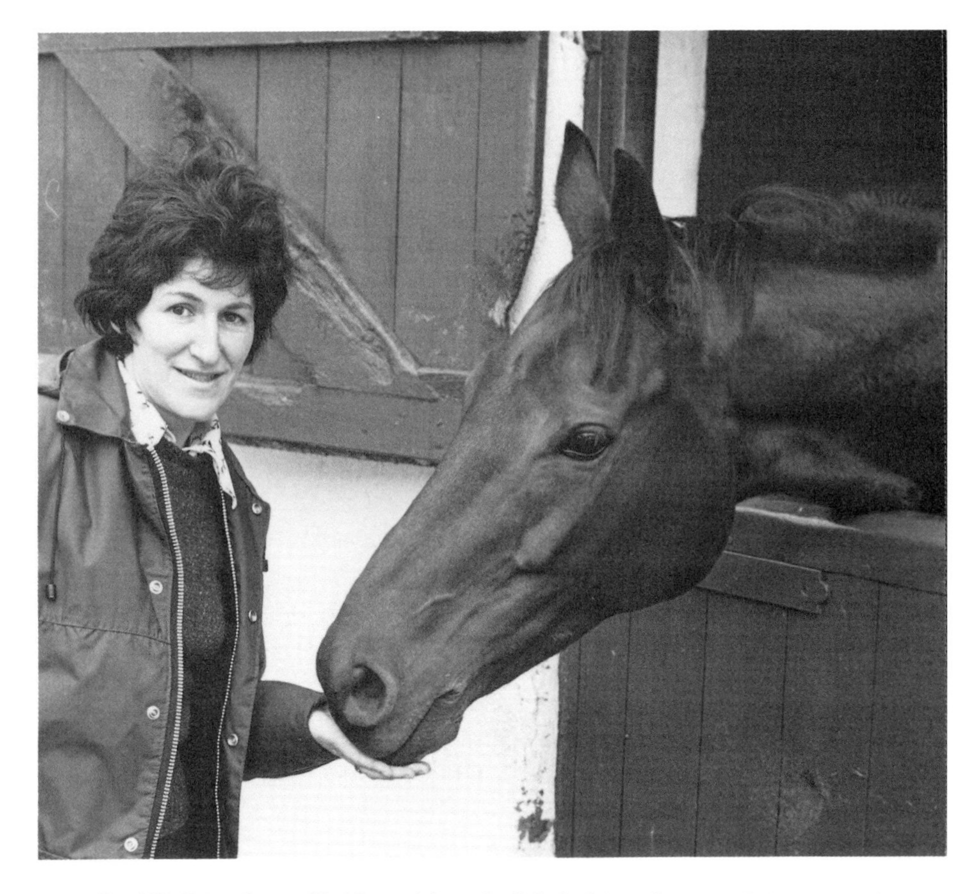

Beryl McCain who stood by 'Ginger' through all the bad times from taxi-driving upwards.

'I got him. Six times more than any other horse I'd had. I was delighted, but scared to death. And poor old Tony Gillam looked so sick. He told me what he knew about the horse's feet. "Don't bash him on hard ground", he warned me. "I don't think he'll stand up to it.".'

And so, by another of those astonishing coincidences which, in old Bobby Renton's words, 'make it all a fairy story', Red Rum went to the only stable in England which had no ordinary gallops, but only the soft sea shore and the cold and bracing salt water to soothe the damaged foot.

Without this combination, the horse's career must soon have ended. Indeed, on the very first day – 'as soon as we started to trot on the beach,' recalled McCain, still appalled, 'I thought, "My God! I've bought a lame horse". I felt sick. I shouted, "Bugger off with him into the tide then!" The others worked. Red Rum just walked about in the sea. And when he came out of the water, he trotted sound!'

Noel Le Mare recalled, 'Ginger had worried the bloody life out of me. Every time I came home, he'd say, "I would like to train horses for you". He taxied for us. Then after he'd brought us home he'd have a whisky with us and a conversation.

Ginger's stable is the happiest stable I've been near. Climbing up those sandhills with Ginger's children playing football in the yard, it keeps the horses fresh. If you can get happiness in your business,' declared the man who started one with £40 in a Liverpool teashop and turned it into £5 million, 'you don't need to bother with anything else! And I'd soon found out Ginger was solid gold.'

Everything worked out like a miracle. Red Rum won all his first five races. The ground varied between hard and good, his jockeys included Stack, Ron Barry and then Brian Fletcher. Sports headlines bellowed: 'SEASIDE SCENE'S SUCCESS SECRET', 'TIDE TURNS FOR GINGER' and 'MCCAIN SWEARS BY SEASIDE TRAINING'. On the morning of 31 March 1973, he started 9–1 favourite for his first Grand National.

'Don McCain,' said Brian Fletcher, 'did not give me any orders. I just said I was going to sit in the middle on the outside on the first circuit and hunt round. Then ride a race past the stands.' We pick up Peter O'Sullevan as they turn onto the racecourse: 'Crisp, well clear, over from Grey Sombrero who jumps it second, Endless Folly jumps it third, then Great Noise fourth, five is Black Secret, six is Rouge Autumn, seven is Spanish Steps and eight Tarquin Bid and nine is Red Rum . . . Coming to the Chair now – this is one of the biggest, Crisp, his ears pricked, jumps it beautifully in the lead – he just pecked a little bit, but got away with it. Grey Sombrero's gone at that one. Grey Sombrero's a faller, Glenkiln's a faller.'

Beryl McCain was staring from the top of the stand. 'I saw Red Rum on the wide outside all the way round. I saw Crisp. Then I saw poor Glen fall. We'd all got soft spots for him, 'cos he's a super and very kind horse. I hadn't watched Red

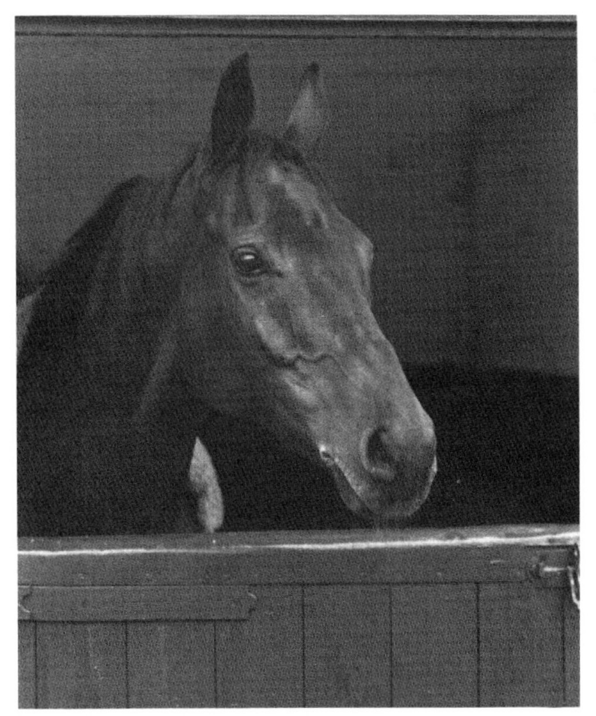

The splendid look of the 'living legend' who in five years won three Grand Nationals down the road at Aintree and was second in the other two.

Rum. And by the time Glen was out of the water, they'd jumped the first fence second time round and Crisp was still in the lead, but Red Rum was second!!'

'I just thought at the Canal Turn,' says Ginger McCain, 'that we'd be second and how unlucky we were to meet Crisp . . .'

John Hamner called quickly: 'Crisp has got three to jump, he's well clear of Red Rum, who's made a bit of ground. Spanish Steps is third, Hurricane Rock is fourth. Over the third from home, Crisp over safely. Red Rum in second place, then Spanish Steps, Hurricane Rock just passing Spanish Steps. As they go across the Melling Road, with two to jump, it's Crisp with Red Rum in second place making ground, but a very long gap after that to Hurricane Rock, Spanish Steps and Rouge Autumn.'

Peter O'Sullevan takes up the saga of the slowly shrinking lead, Crisp conceding 1 st. 9 lb. to his pursuer. 'It's Crisp in the lead from Red Rum, but Red Rum still making ground on him! Brian Fletcher on Red Rum chasing Dick Pitman on Crisp. Crisp still well clear with two fences left to jump in the 1973 National and this great Australian 'chaser, Crisp, with 12 st. on his back and 10 st. 5 on the back of Red Rum, who's chasing him and they look to have it absolutely to themselves. At the second last, Crisp is over. And clear of Red Rum who's jumping it a long way back. In third place is Spanish Steps, then Hurricane Rock and Rouge Autumn and L'Escargot. But coming to the final fence in the National now, and it's Crisp still going in great style with 12 st. on his back. He jumps it well. Red Rum is about 15 lengths behind him as he jumps it. Dick Pitman coming to the elbow now in the National. He's got 250 yards to run. But Crisp is just wandering off the true line now. He's beginning to lose concentration. He's been out there on his own for so long. And Red Rum is making ground on him. Still as they come to the line, it's a furlong to run now, 200 yards now for Crisp, and Red Rum still closing on him, and Crisp is getting very tired, and Red Rum is pounding after him and Red Rum is the one who finishes the strongest. He's going to get up! Red Rum is going to win the National. At the line Red Rum has just snatched it from Crisp! And Red Rum is the winner! and Crisp is second and L'Escargot is just coming up to be third . . .'

The time, 9 min. 1.9 sec., set a record knocking nearly 20 sec. off Golden Miller's previous best under 12 st. 2 lb. in 1934. The record was still standing 16 years later. The strange, knocked about, unlucky Brian Fletcher had won on his first ride on Red Rum in November 1972. The partnership, ending in complaints and recriminations would run for three years.

The very next season, that of 1973–74, was Red Rum's classiest. He gave the lie to those who said, and who still maintain, that 'he was only a Liverpool horse', for he failed by only a whisker to win the first half of the season's highest-class handicap. In the Hennessy at Newbury, carrying 11 st. 4 lb., he was beaten a shorthead by Red Candle who was receiving 1 stone. Furthermore the winner had been specially readied for the race by Colonel Ricky Vallance, skilfully assisted by David Elsworth, who would later achieve great public fame as a trainer in his own name.

Never carrying less than 12 st., Red Rum won four races before his second National in which he was set exactly that, the maximum weight. He was giving 1 lb

to the Cheltenham Gold Cup winner who should be the year's top chaser. This was the blue-hooded L'Escargot. Red Rum started third favourite at 11–1 – he had risen nearly 2 st. in the handicap – behind Scout (7–1) and L'Escargot.

Chaseform's invaluable 'Notebook', seldom given to hyperbole, summed up this second successive victory: 'Red Rum, a tough, relentless galloper and a much improved chaser made this look incredibly easy. Very much at home on the fast surface, he was going so easily that his rider had to let him hit the front approaching Becher's the last time round. Cruising in the lead coming on to the racecourse, he quickened appreciably and, with his race won long before the elbow, his rider was able to salute the crowd and then ease him back before the post. This was a fantastic performance and Red Rum, whose win last year was rather overshadowed by the gallant efforts of the second, now dominates the Aintree scene as a figure of heroic proportions in his own right. Such dramatic improvement reflects the highest credit on his trainer.'

To this victory, only three weeks later our hero under 11 st. 13 lb. and hot favourite at 11–8, added an easy Scottish Grand National. By the spring of his nine-year-old year, Red Rum had done a tough eight seasons racing. To his two-and-a-half victories on the flat, he had added 20 wins and 23 places under N.H. Rules from 68 starts. He had so far won £69,320.

At this point, having reached the prime of his life after a long, arduous ascent, it was generally assumed that Red Rum had no more peaks to scale. It was felt that his future path, after a plateau of a year or so, would in the nature of life gently, then swiftly, decline.

Over the next seasons between the autumn of 1974 and the spring of 1976, he ran in 18 more steeplechases, winning twice, and getting placed seven times. But behind the last bald phrase lie his exceptional two successive seconds in Grand Nationals. These came after periods when the public, his lad and his jockey had all begun to regard him as finished. In fact they ensured his unassailable position as the Aintree hero of all time.

There were less happy moves at home. Ginger McCain sacked his head lad Jackie Grainger. He installed in his place Red Rum's lad, Billy Ellison, he of the shock of black hair and arms and legs extended on the fiercely pulling horse along the beach. Then he fell out with Billy and then with poor, muddled Brian Fletcher.

In front of these backstage scenes, the horse's television and public career had taken off. His triumphs, then his appearances, had made him a national celebrity. Jockey Fletcher was simultaneously sliding into struggling obscurity. In 1972 he had fallen out with Denys Smith, the nearby Bishop Auckland trainer, his parents and other relations were in trouble with the police, charged with handling stolen goods, he had broken his pelvis and a leg and fractured his skull. By the end of January 1975 he had ridden only six winners that season. It was a black descent since he'd been champion northern jockey back in 1967–68.

And the Grand National, with the course then uncomfortably owned by a recalcitrant developer called Bill Davies, was itself in doubt. It might be run instead at nearby Haydock, the Jockey Club announced in a move to trump Davies' threats. This prospect shattered McCain.

The race was at least temporarily saved by the good offices of bookmakers Ladbrokes, who annually made huge profits from the race. L'Escargot had been specially prepared for it all year. At the third last Tommy Carberry was sitting still as a mouse on him while Fletcher was desperately booting Red Rum along. Going to the last, Fletcher, frantic for victory to solve his private problems, knew he was beaten. 'Go on!' he screamed at Carberry as a victim might beg his executioner to grant him a swift end. 'It wasn't the weight that beat him,' Ginger McCain went on explaining for three months. 'It was the going. He was hating the ground nearly every yard of the race. It was only his courage kept him going.'

Extraordinarily, in what he himself called 'a diabolical boob', McCain then sent the weary Red Rum up to Ayr to try to win a second Scottish National. He had fallen victim to his horse's fame. The world expected Rummy to run on the course where his latest statue had been unveiled. McCain concurred. The horse ran poorly. Flushed and furious Fletcher burst out on dismounting, 'The horse was *never* going! He *never* gave me the right feel.'

The following autumn the apparent decline continued. McCain came in for more criticism for running Red Rum too often. 'People began to query the horse,' he hurtfully remembered. At Haydock Red Rum jumped poorly, and then slipped up on the flat. McCain was thinking of a jockey change. At Newcastle he saw 'Brian sitting absolutely bloody still' at the last fence. 'I thought he'd give him just one slap. But no!'

To Fletcher he snapped, 'At least you should have been second.'

Red Rum, blazing away down Southport's beach, towing his lad, Billy Ellison, along at a furious pace. Feeling in charge always made 'Rummy' feel better.

Fletcher retorted, 'The horse isn't the same. I'm not knocking him around for a few hundred quid.'

'It's not the bloody money. I'm not having him made *non-competitive.* That's the bloody point!'

'Why don't you retire him?' snapped little Brian Fletcher, walking dejectedly away. His view was shared by many others that day, and by many newspapers on the morrow. Soon the general public followed suit, deluging McCain with exhortations to retire the horse. Many were abusive.

So after their three-year partnership Fletcher was jocked off. Not much has gone well with him since, and it is only the slimmest consolation in hard times that the racing world will always connect him with Red Rum.

Big Ron Barry had the ride in the Hennessy and McCain had declared to one of the authors that if Barry confirmed the horse had 'gone', then he would retire him. But Red Rum ran an excellent race under top weight, running on strongly up the straight to finish sixth. McCain and Le Mare had their 'second opinion': their horse, despite the mounting disappointments, was not yet finished, not yet prepared to call it a day.

For the 1976 National Red Rum's weight had dropped 4 lb. to 11 st. 10 lb. 'I was happy enough,' said McCain. 'I thought the horse was possibly as well as we'd ever had him.' But he had not won for a year. McCain had again stuck out his bold

Probably the oddest urban approach to Red Rum's unusual gallops – the beach at Southport . . .

neck. If Rummy didn't win or nearly win, the racing world would be baying for Ginger's blood. He would be vilified for ruining the most popular jumper Britain had known since Arkle, and subsequently the most famous steeplechaser the world has ever known.

Tommy Stack, who had ridden him years before and thought little of him, had the ride. The rejected Fletcher rode the unfancied Oxfordshire mare Eyecatcher.

For the third incredible year running Red Rum, with a staggeringly long leap, landed first over the final fence of the Grand National. Tommy Stack thought afterwards the length of this leap might have checked him on landing. But his trajectory took him well clear of the mare. Fletcher saw Le Mare's old colours and his old yellow cap now on top of Tommy Stack's neat taut frame and he says he thought then, 'The old horse has done it. Good luck to him.' He declared later, that, in spite of all the bitterness of their parting, he wished that Red Rum would win a third Grand National, if he, struggling at the end of his jockey's life, could not win a fourth.

Then on the bright green turf between the last fence and the white rails of the elbow, all changed. Rummy was not accelerating away. Under 11 st. 10 lb he was staying on, but Rag Trade with nearly 1 st. less on his back for 4¼ miles was joining him very wide on the stands side, was passing him, was clear of him, was cutting across Rummy's old head to make for the white rails after the elbow, to have them to guide him on and on up the long run-in.

And then, as Tommy Stack drove Red Rum on with all his renowned vigour, the scene once again changed. 'Red Rum', shouted Peter O'Sullevan to millions round the world, 'Red Rum is fighting back!' From 4 lengths clear by the elbow and with the race apparently well won, Rag Trade's lead was being, stride by stride, slowly bitten back. Rag Trade looked exhausted. He rolled. John Burke's whip was whirling. Red Rum's bay neck was stuck out horizontally like a ramrod and he was closing perfectly evenly, closing with desperate resolution, closing that gap of green.

There were tears in Ginger McCain's eyes as he watched; there were very few dry eyes in the stands. For what we were watching was the superlative Grand National horse of all time, fighting back in the last panting, pounding, sweating seconds, to keep what he must have felt he had won again after the last fence, his own throne at Aintree.

Closer and closer he galloped. The screams and bellowings from the gigantic crowd reverberated like the battle cries of manic hordes. 'Ah yes,' said 23-year-old John Burke afterwards with a wry smile, 'Red Rum was going well. I knew he was coming at me when I heard the crowd roaring, really *roaring* for him! And I didn't dare look behind.' The winning post came too soon for Rummy. He was a short and shrinking 2 lengths behind Rag Trade on the line. Eight lengths back came Eyecatcher and Brian Fletcher.

'He's a *marvellous* ride round there,' said Tommy Stack to David Coleman. 'He's like a cat, because twice goin' to Becher's, horses fell in front o' me, and he's like a ballet-dancer – he just side-steps 'em. I thought,' said Stack, 'that comin' across the racecourse I was goin' better than anythin' on the inside o' me. And I looked on me right-hand side and there were two going better, I thought. I jumped

the second last and I thought I'd a real good chance. And fractionally, after the last, I thought I was goin' to win.'

Tommy Stack, back in the days of the late Mr Bobby Renton, had met Red Rum as a three-year-old, eight long years ago. 'No,' said he, grinning, 'I never thought then that he'd develop into an Aintree horse; *the* Aintree horse.'

The Scottish National came too soon that year to tempt another blunder. Instead Red Rum was sent south to Sandown to run in the Whitbread. 'He looks a picture', John Oaksey proclaimed on television. 'There he is, the great, *immortal* Red Rum!'

The public's darling was rashly made favourite. But he ran pretty well to finish fifth after blundering at the open ditch. Ginger McCain running across the paddock to him before the race, had nearly blundered over the Queen Mother. 'Typical of you,' complained a friend. 'Only thinkin' about that horse!'

In August, poor Fletcher, domestically in crisis, was failed by racing's doctors. Steeplechasing had finished with him at the age of 29. He wanted work. McCain wrote kindly to him, asking if he'd like to partner Red Rum in the Parade of Champions at Cheltenham. Fletcher didn't reply. McCain engaged Stack. Parades and adulation were part of Red Rum's life now. He was acclaimed at Wembley at the Horse of the Year Show.

Now in that uncertain limbo outside the glow and warmth and lights in the arena, Red Rum waited to be summoned in. Ahead of him the more normal equine personalities had passed through the divide into the ring, were illuminated and introduced at length. His time was coming. He would come, in pride of place, at the end. His great ears were cocked. His huge eyes stared, peering ahead for the next adventure, as they gaze up into the changing skies over Birkdale. He drew close to the curtains and hesitated. Then he sprang through them into the celestial beam of the sole spotlight. The announcer needed no words to introduce him. 'Red Rum,' he simply said, and the cheers reverberated like thunder around the bowl of heaven.

He ran at Kempton, a foolish choice of a quite unsuitable track for a dour stayer. 'We'll learn one day, I suppose,' Ginger remorsefully remarked afterwards. He ran better round Haydock, where Ron Barry made the old horse jump as a skilled child might reschool an idle pony. He ran wretchedly on dead ground at Newcastle, his 100th race, and afterwards McCain said grimly, 'Bloody awful. I did think then that the horse *could* be finished.' Red Rum had mooched home last of three, beaten a dreadful 28 lengths.

A foul winter gave the horse a miserable time during his annual mid-season holiday in Cheshire on vet Ted Greenway's farm. 'When he came back, he wasn't sparkling,' McCain recalled. 'His coat had gone'. The weather, too, wrecked Southport sands. For the first time in the 25 years McCain had been training on them, 'for nearly three bloody months, I couldn't even prepare a gallop, the beach was that waterlogged. I could only canter steadily.'

Pressures squeezed in from all sides. Ginger and Beryl McCain suffered a furious quarrel and he actually walked out on her for a night. Then Red Rum's usual National 'prep' race, the Greenall Whitley at Haydock, showed at last a real return to form. But wasn't he too fat? Ginger round with 89-year-old Noel Le

Mare compared Rummy's old photographs with the 12-year-old's present bulk. But his last gallop turned out to be a blinder.

Red Rum 'hit his stride', caught the others like an eagle and swept ahead with Billy Beardwood jack-knifed in the horse's now famous 'stopping position'. 'They went just over 4½ furlongs. And the other two were niggling and pushing to try and *keep* with him!' McCain adds, typically, 'I thought first the other two were *sick*, he was going that much better! Then,' recalls Ginger warmly, 'as Red walked back through the sea with the press people running after him, I could see he was that well! He was full of himself. He was lit up and dancing. His legs just flowed. And he walked out clear.'

So he set forth for his fifth and final Grand National. 'It was landing over Becher's,' said Stack, 'that I began to hear this *extraordinary* roar. Everyone at every fence began to shout "Come on Red Rum! C'm on Red! Rummy c'm on! RED RUM! RED RUM!" It was quite fantastic!' Eight fences more to go for the legend. Leading the remnants now of his pursuers. But the horses of the fallen were everywhere charging about. Tommy Stack bellows back to Jeff King on What a Buck, 'C'm on, we've got to dodge these!' and then an astonishing event occurs. As Stack for the first time kicks Rummy firmly on, the horse shoots forward like the 5-furlong sprinter he was 10 tough years and 105 races ago. The loose horses were smoothly overtaken. The ridden pursuers were devastatingly outpaced. Red Rum, unhampered, swerved nonchalantly round the Canal Turn to head for home and glory.

People at every fence would relate how, as commentaries and radios reported the hero's progress, spontaneous cheering erupted and continued louder and louder into a continuous roar all round the course. His caution and Stack's calm were not affected. He was carefully, wisely, popping homewards towards the colossal clamour of the grandstands. He had, as his busy stride and flickering ears showed, an important job on hand.

Then there appeared behind him Chantilly-based Yorkshireman Martin Blackshaw, who had so adroitly snapped up the ride on Churchtown Boy, easy winner of the Topham Trophy here 48 hours earlier. Churchtown Boy moved closer, ready to pounce. It seemed for one doubting furlong as if the L'Escargot conquest of 1975 was about to be re-enacted. 'Certainly,' claimed a disconsolate Blackshaw afterwards, 'I thought I could eat Red Rum any time I chose.'

For Stack the main dangers appeared to be the glancing loose horses, as unpredictable as sticks on a river's current. This superb jockey has repeatedly said with the modesty of the truly great, that Rummy did it all. But Stack's avoidance of these uncontrollable hazards around him was the work of a cool quick expert. There was no question this year of Stacky sitting quietly waiting to make his run. He drove Red Rum along all the way. But still Churchtown Boy moved smoothly closer.

Then, in one ecstatic instant the battle was won. At the third last fence Churchtown Boy blundered, grunted, lost momentum and lost the race. Rummy skipped over the last two and then the roaring to which each stride had brought him closer boomed to such a crescendo that Stack dreaded that his horse might stop. 'It was like going into a funnel – a narrowing funnel,' he kept repeating, moving his arms together like a press. 'People everywhere seemed to be leaping up and rushing in. I thought we'd stop.'

But Red Rum never wavered.

A final astonishing thing happened. It is well said that no horse can sprint twice in a race. Red Rum had sprinted clear of the loose ruck of horses a mile away after Becher's. Then he had settled down again for a long slog home. Now, unbelievably, as Stack urged him, he sprinted again up the long run-in, accelerating away from the weary Churchtown Boy like a class horse leaving a plater. And did the tumult worry him? He gloried in it. These were his people screaming him home. He spurted for the post like a bright bay arrow.

'Couldn't pull him up,' said Stack marvelling. 'He'd have gone on galloping – oh, at least as far as Becher's once again.'

In 1976 Red Rum had given the brave mare Eyecatcher 17 lb. and beaten her 8 lengths. In 1977 he gave her 21 lb. and beat her 31 lengths, an improvement at the age of 12 of nearly 2 st. His victory, run at 28.42 m.p.h., had broken the prize money record over jumps with £114,370.

Weights and measures. The treble after five years was at last accomplished. A horse had been witnesed unlike any other in anyone's lifetime, in anyone's memory. And suddenly everyone was crying.

Cool little Tommy Stack cried. Great Ginger McCain came bursting through the crowd shouting 'Bloody marvellous, just bloody marvellous!' And tears rolled down his face. Old peers in tweeds cried. Trendy lads in jeans cried. A wet-eyed bookie burst into the pressroom blubbing out, 'We've lost a quarter of a million quid and we don't care!'

The horse, cool as always, walked into Southport's The Bold Hotel that night. On the left in the restaurant people leapt whooping upon the tables. Out of the bar on the right, applause roared and another crowd rushed forward. He walked on calmly, on past the other crammed bar ahead to the swing doors into the ballroom. A strip of red carpet had been unrolled for him across its glossy surface.

Tommy Stack was watching, eyes agog, Beryl McCain watched anxiously. Both saw one hoof for an instant come off the carpet. It tested the floor, found it slippery, and stepped back carefully on to his special red strip. He progressed to the ballroom's end and turned and posed himself for his photographers. The lights flashed. The crowd shouted. They milled all round him, pressing against him. He never shifted. Someone stood upon a table above the throng and declaimed a long paean of praise in his honour. The horse turned towards him and listened attentively.

And the modest Tommy Stack, who had declared at Aintree that there could never be another horse like Red Rum, suddenly realized, staring at our hero in the clamourous ballroom on Grand National Night, that this was really more than just a horse. 'He is,' said Tommy Stack simply, 'a different *being*.'

But the greatest Liverpool horse of all time was not yet done. Red Rum would be 13 if he ran in his sixth Grand National and, up till the very morning of the race, he was being prepared to do so.

'He was that well,' says Ginger McCain, 'we'd no thought of retiring him. We even were thinking, if he kept well and Mr Le Mare was well, too, of running the following year as well!' He ran five times in his last season of racing. The pattern was as before, with three early races before his mid-winter break. In all he carried 12 st. 2 lb or more, was described by *Chaseform* as 'looking well and jumping well,' and he ran well too: 2 seconds and a fourth, before his customary winter holiday.

But this year he did himself too well. He had grown very portly before his two comeback races at Haydock. He was tailed off in the first in February, and then in March got well behind after blundering badly. 'But that was Tommy Stack's first ride since he badly fractured his pelvis,' explains Ginger McCain. 'He was bound to be a bit rusty. The horse really middled that last open ditch on the far side. You could count Tommy's toes pushing through his boots! But Tommy was very enthusiastic about the horse.'

During the last weeks before the National, Ginger thought one day on the beach that Red Rum was slightly lame in his off-hind. 'Looked like a touch of string-halt. I kept him in the sea and we called in Ted Greenway. Couldn't find anything then. But we thought something must have happened to him either at Haydock, or just after. I worked him a couple of miles on the course at Haydock. Fine. Then on the Friday before the National, I worked him 5 or 6 furlongs on Aintree racecourse. He was that well he was running away with Billy Beardsley – Billy had to aim him at the stables' wall to stop him! But as he walked away from us he was definitely a touch lame. The only other person out there that morning to notice was Peter O'Sullevan.

'Then back at the stables the horse pulled out lame. We had his foot nerve-blocked. That proved it was definitely in his foot: it was a stress fracture, a hairline fracture. Ron Barry said "Forget it. When he warms up in the race, he'll be OK". But we couldn't. When he paraded he jumped and kicked and I wondered whether we should have run. But he was intermittently lame afterwards for 5 or 6 weeks. Well, if he'd run and won, we'd have gone on. We'd talked about it. He was

Red Rum (Tommy Stack) lands over the last fence of his life. This was at Haydock, his other nearby course. Picture taken by one of his legion of fans, Miss M. Hilton

all the Guv'nor had left – Mr Le Mare lived till he was 92, and died on the Isle of Man. He was alert as always, just physically more frail.

'A big Japanese-American restaurateur called "Rocky" Aoki came into my lounge one day and offered us $1 million for the horse as a personality. His firm was Benihana of Tokyo with offices in Florida and New York. He said "I open a new restaurant every week!" And he'd estimated the horse could earn him $1 million in 18 months! We said, "No", of course.'

Until the spring of 1986 McCain used him as his hack: 'He was a bloody old idiot at times! Then sometimes he'd come in sweating, a bit distressed. We found that an artery had contracted in that off-hind leg. He was getting a blockage. So I haven't ridden him since. He's led out, of course. But not ridden.

'He's still in his same box. He's led out First Lot to keep up the rhythm of his life. We'd put him back to Third Lot after his lameness, after the off-hind trouble. He didn't like that at all. He missed going out on his engagements. He started going back. He was unhappy. Then his leg got right – he still has 8 grammes of Warfarin daily – and we put him back in his old routine again – led out First Lot as he should be. And he has a couple of engagements every month booked up to a year ahead. He lives for those engagements. He needs them.

'You know when he started going back on us that time in 1986, and I thought for the first time there'd be a time we would lose him forever. He'd be the big part of my life gone, wouldn't he? A part of all our lives.'

But in the spring of 1989 – 'he's grand,' says Ginger McCain – the greatest Grand National horse of all time, that great survivor, was at the age of 24 full years, most happily still alive, and very often kicking.

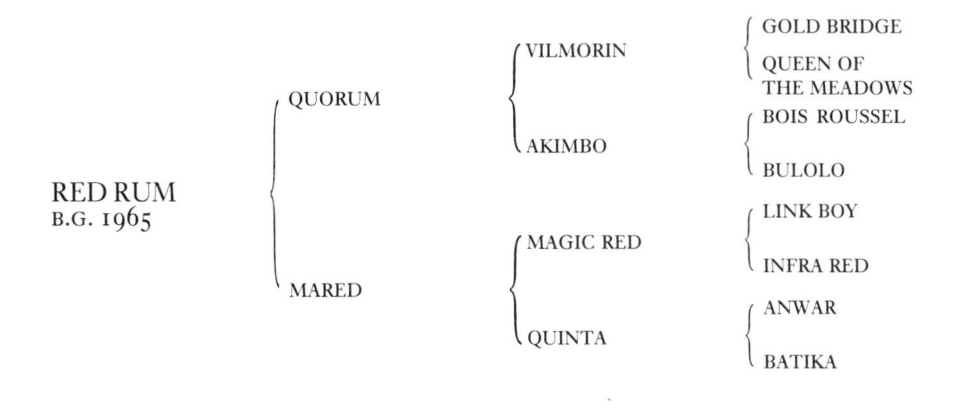

DATE	COURSE	RACE	DISTANCE	VALUE	WEIGHT	JOCKEY	PRICE	PLACE
Season 1967								
Apr 7	Liverpool	Thursby Selling Plate (2yo) (F)	5f	£133(each)	9.0	P. Cook	5/1	won (dead heat)
Apr 29	Beverley	Tickton Juvenile Stakes (2yo) (F)	5f	£364	8.10	J. Sime	10/1	unpl
June 19	Teesside Park	Vane Arms Plate (2yo) (F)	6f	£345	8.7	E. Larkin	100/7	unpl
Jun 30	Newcastle	Angerton Stakes (2yo) (F)	6f	£415	9.0	G. Cadwaladr	33/1	3rd
Aug 28	Warwick	Pinley Nursery (2yo) (F)	7f	£467	7.11	D. W. Morris	6/1	won
Sep 7	York	Bishopthorpe Nursery (2yo) (F)	7f	£598	7.11	G. Sexton	100/8	unpl
Sep 20	Pontefract	Minor Nursery (2yo) (F)	1m	£414	8.5	L. Piggott	6/1	3rd
Sep 25	Leicester	Nanpantan Nursery (2yo) (F)	1m	£345	8.9	D. W. Morris	10/1	4th
Season 1968								
Mar 27	Doncaster	Waterdale Selling H'cp (3yo) (F)	7f	£370	9.2	G. Lewis	11/4f	won
Mar 30	Liverpool	Earl of Sefton's Stakes (3yo H'cp) (F)	1m	£437	8.12	L. Piggott	11/4f	2nd
Season 1968–69								
Sep 18	Cheltenham	Junior Novices Hurdle (Div 2) (3yo)	2m 200y	£340	10.10	J. Gifford	8/1	2nd
Oct 19	Market Rasen	Hainton Hurdle (3yo)	2m	£272	10.7	A. Turnell	5/2	4th
Nov 18	Nottingham	Merit Hurdle (3yo)	2m	£837	10.7	J. Cook	100/8	3rd
Nov 22	Doncaster	Plant Novices Hurdle (Div 2) (3yo)	2m 150y	£272	10.10	T. S. Murphy	5/2f	3rd
Mar 8	Wetherby	Harewood Hurdle (4yo)	2m	£340	10.7	J. C. Doyle	10/1	unpl
Mar 27	Liverpool	Lancashire Hurdle (4yo)	2m 100y	£690	10.7	P. Broderick	100/8	2nd
Apr 7	Wetherby	Bilton Hurdle	2m	£204	10.11	P. Broderick	15/8f	won

Apr 15	Nottingham	Bradmore H'cp Hurdle (4yo)	2m	£340	11.5	P. Broderick	5/1	won
Apr 25	Teesside Park	Teeside Celebration H'cp Hurdle	2m 176y	£340	10.10	P. Broderick	5/2	won
May 20	Ayr	Orchardton H'cp Hurdle	2m	£340	11.4	P. Broderick	6/1	unpl
Season 1969–70								
Sep 18	Cheltenham	Andoversford H'cp Hurdle	2m 200y	£510	10.9	T. Stack	100/6	unpl
Oct 24	Doncaster	Town Field H'cp Hurdle	2m 150y	£449	11.3	J. C.Doyle	100/8	unpl
Nov 8	Wetherby	Tadcaster H'cp Hurdle	2m	£580	10.5	J. C.Doyle	9/1	unpl
Nov 22	Doncaster	Dormer Drill H'cp Hurdle (4yo)	2m 150y	£858	11.0	P. Broderick	100/8	unpl
Dec 31	Catterick	Dick Whittington H'cp Hurdle	2m	£340	11.5	T. Stack	6/1	2nd
Jan 20	Wetherby	Tockwith H'cp Hurdle	2m 4f	£442	10.13	T. Stack	6/1co-f	3rd
Jan 23	Doncaster	January H'cp Hurdle (Div 2)	2m 4f	£443	10.11	T. Stack	11/2	unpl
Feb 7	Wetherby	Bishopthorpe H'cp Hurdle	2m 4f	£680	10.6	R. Edwards	6/1	unpl
Mar 13	Teesside Park	Long Dog H'cp Hurdle	2m 5f 104y	£340	11.11	B. Brogan	11/2	unpl
Mar 18	Cheltenham	George Duller H'cp Hurdle	3m	£1365	10.4	R. Edwards	25/1	unpl
Apr 11	Cheltenham	Ronald Royds H'cp Hurdle (Div 1)	2m 4f	£540	10.7	T. Stack	6/1	unpl
Apr 21	Perth	Perthshire Drag Hunt H'cp Hurdle	3m	£544	11.2	T. Stack	6/1	2nd
May 6	Wetherby	Church Fenton H'cp Hurdle	2m	£442	10.0	T. Stack	10/1	fell
May 18	Ayr	Milsington H'cp Hurdle	3m	£442	10.13	T. Stack	5/1	unpl
Season 1970–71								
Oct 28	Newcastle	Vittoria Novices Chase	2m 120y	£272	£11.9	T. Stack	7/1	3rd
Nov 6	Doncaster	Town Moor Novices Chase	2m 150y	£580	11.9	T. Stack	100/7	won
Nov 13	Cheltenham	Borough Chase	2m	£442	11.8	T. Stack	9/2	3rd
Nov 20	Wetherby	WD & HO Wills Premier Chase Qualifier	2m 4f	£860	11.13	T. Stack	100/8	3rd

DATE	COURSE	RACE	DISTANCE	VALUE	WEIGHT	JOCKEY	PRICE	PLACE
Dec 5	Sedgefield	Hope Inn Chase	2m 250y	£272	12.5	T. Stack	4/5f	won
Dec 26	Wetherby	Rowland Meyrick H'cp Chase	3m 100y	£2040	10.8	M. Gifford	10/1	3rd
Feb 5	Ayr	Girvan H'cp Chase	2m 4f	£442	11.6	T. Stack	4/1	won
Feb 13	Newbury	Compton Chase	3m	£445	12.2	T. Stack	7/2f	4th
Feb 26	Teesside Park	Facey Romford H'cp Chase	3m 31y	£340	11.5	T. Stack	4/1	3rd
Mar 18	Cheltenham	Mildmay of Flete Challenge Cup H'cp Chase	2m 4f	£1020	10.3	T. Stack	16/1	4th
Apr 12	Wetherby	Crossley H'cp Chase	2m 4f	£442	10.12	T. Stack	7/2	3rd
May 5	Wetherby	Rigton H'cp Chase	3m 100y	£442	10.6	T. Stack	7/2	unpl
May 20	Perth	Spittalfield H'cp Chase	2m 4f	£272	11.2	T. Stack	5/2	3rd
Season 1971–72								
Oct 12	Southwell	Col. R Thompson Memorial Trophy H'cp Chase	3m 110y	£1192	10.12	T. Stack	16/1	4th
Oct 23	Kelso	Anthony Marshall Trophy H'cp Chase	3m	£837	10.4	T. Stack	12/1	unpl
Nov 6	Newcastle	John Eustace Smith Trophy H'cp Chase	3m	£510	10.4	T. Stack	16/1	2nd
Dec 1	Haydock Park	Sundew H'cp Chase	3m	£911	10.1	T. Stack	10/1	unpl
Dec 11	Catterick	Charles Vickery Memorial Cup H'cp Chase	3m 300y	£930	10.7	T. Stack	9/2	won
Dec 22	Catterick	Denby H'cp Chase	3m 300y	£340	11.0	T. Stack	15/2	3rd
Jan 1	Catterick	Zetland H'cp Chase	3m 300y	£551	10.10	T. Stack	7/2	won
Mar 6	Catterick	Busby H'cp Chase	3m 300y	£510	10.7	T. Stack	4/5f	bt dn
Mar 21	Nottingham	Trent H'cp Chase	2m 6f	£442	10.9	M. Gifford	5/1	3rd
Apr 3	Wetherby	Wetherby H'cp Chase	3m 100y	£2385	10.1	T. Stack	9/1	3rd
Apr 15	Ayr	Scottish Grand National H'cp Chase	4m 120y	£5137	9.8	M. Blackshaw	33/1	unpl
Apr 29	Market Rasen	Champagne H'cp Chase	3m	£594	10.4	T. Stack	7/4f	4th

Season 1972–73								
Sep 30	Carlisle	Windermere H'cp Chase	3m	£622	10.13	T. Stack	6/1	won
Oct 11	Wetherby	Gordon Foster H'cp Chase	3m 100y	£680	10.10	R. Barry	3/1	won
Oct 25	Newcastle	Salamanca H'cp Chase	3m	£715	10.11	T. Stack	9/4	won
Nov 3	Haydock Park	Southport H'cp Chase	3m	£684	11.10	T. Stack	2/1f	won
Nov 13	Ayr	Mauchline H'cp Chase	3m 3f 40y	£695	11.9	B. Fletcher	11/8f	won
Jan 31	Carlisle	Cumberland Grand National Trial H'cp Chase	3m	£632	11.9	B. Fletcher	7/2	3rd
Feb 7	Haydock Park	Haydock Park National Trial H'cp Chase	3m 4f	£1266	10.12	B. Fletcher	5/1	2nd
Mar 3	Haydock Park	Greenall Whitley H'cp Chase	3m	£4985	11.2	B. Fletcher	5/1f	4th
Mar 31	Liverpool	Grand National H'cp Chase	4m 865y	£25486	10.5	B. Fletcher	9/1j.f.	won
Season 1973–74								
Sep 26	Perth	Perthshire Challenge Cup H'cp Chase	3m	£576	12.4	B. Fletcher	4/1	2nd
Sep 29	Carlisle	Windermere H'cp Chase	3m	£405	12.4	B. Fletcher	8/13f	won
Oct 13	Ayr	Joan Mackay H'cp Chase	3m 110y	£1551	12.4	B. Fletcher	10/11f	won
Oct 31	Newcastle	John Eustace Smith Trophy H'cp Chase	3m	£860	12.1	B. Fletcher	13/8f	won
Nov 10	Doncaster	Doncaster Pattern Chase	3m 2f	£1763	11.10	B. Fletcher	5/2	2nd
Nov 24	Newbury	Hennessy Cognac Gold Cup H'cp Chase	3m 2f 82y	£7435	11.4	B. Fletcher	8/1	2nd
Feb 20	Catterick	Brettanby H'cp Chase	3m 300y	£939	12.7	B. Fletcher	3/1	won
Mar 2	Haydock Park	Greenall Whitley H'cp Chase	3m	£4638	12.7	B. Fletcher	5/1	u.r.
Mar 30	Liverpool	Grand National H'cp Chase	4m 856y	£25102	12.0	B. Fletcher	11/1	won
Apr 20	Ayr	Scottish Grand National H'cp Chase	4m 120y	£7922	11.13	B. Fletcher	11/8f	won

DATE	COURSE	RACE	DISTANCE	VALUE	WEIGHT	JOCKEY	PRICE	PLACE
Season 1974–75								
Sep 25	Perth	Perthshire Challenge Cup H'cp Chase	3m	£535	12.7	B. Fletcher	5/4f	2nd
Oct 12	Ayr	Joan Mackay H'cp Chase	3m 110y	£1507	12.7	B. Fletcher	5/4f	won
Oct 19	Kempton Park	Charisma Records H'cp Chase	3m 4f	£2310	12.0	B. Fletcher	9/4f	unpl
Nov 27	Haydock Park	Sundew Chase	3m	£1951	11.12	B. Fletcher	3/1	3rd
Feb 5	Haydock Park	Haydock Park National Trial H'cp Chase	3m 4f	£1646	12.0	B. Fletcher	6/1	won
Mar 1	Haydock Park	Greenall Whitley H'cp Chase	3m	£4576	12.3	B. Fletcher	13/8f	4th
Apr 5	Liverpool	News of the World Grand National H'cp Chase	4m 865y	£38005	12.0	B. Fletcher	7/2f	2nd
Apr 19	Ayr	Scottish Grand National H'cp Chase	4m 120y	£8107	12.0	B. Fletcher	3/1f	unpl
Season 1975–76								
Sep 27	Carlisle	Windermere H'cp Chase	3m	£502	12.7	B. Fletcher	7/2	3rd
Oct 11	Ayr	Joan Mackay H'cp Chase	3m 110y	£1453	12.7	B. Fletcher	6/4f	4th
Oct 15	Haydock Park	Peacock H'cp Chase	3m	£793	12.7	B. Fletcher	2/1f	s.u.
Oct 30	Newcastle	John Eustace Smith Trophy H'cp Chase	3m	£680	12.7	B. Fletcher	evens f	3rd
Nov 22	Newbury	Hennessy Cognac Gold Cup H'cp Chase	3m 2f 82y	£7360	11.9	R. Barry	8/1	unpl
Nov 26	Haydock Park	Sundew Chase	3m	£1829	12.0	T. Stack	6/1	3rd
Feb 11	Haydock Park	Haydock Park National Trial H'cp Chase	3m 4f	£1710	11.7	T. Stack	7/1	unpl
Mar 6	Haydock Park	Greenall Whitley Breweries H'cp Chase	3m	£5796	11.13	T. Stack	6/1	unpl
Apr 3	Liverpool	News of the World Grand National H'cp Chase	4m 4f	£37420	11.10	T. Stack	10/1	2nd

Apr 24	Sandown Park	Whitbread Gold Cup H'cp Chase	3m 5f 118y	£12487	11.10	T. Stack	5/1f	unpl
Season 1976–77								
Sep 26	Carlisle	Windermere H'cp Chase	3m	£651	12.7	T. Stack	2/5f	won
Oct 16	Kempton Park	Charisma Records H'cp Chase	3m 4f	£2560	11.7	T. Stack	13/2	unpl
Nov 5	Haydock Park	Cheltenham H'cp Chase	3m	£1245	12.7	R. Barry	5/1	3rd
Nov 20	Newcastle	Salamanca H'cp Chase	3m	£966	12.7	T. Stack	11/8f	3rd
Dec 1	Haydock Park	Sundew Chase	3m	£2280	12.0	R. Barry	12/1	3rd
Feb 9	Haydock Park	Malcolm Fudge National Trial H'cp Chase	3m 4f	£2461	11.7	T. Stack	9/1	unpl
Mar 5	Haydock Park	Greenall Whitley Breweries H'cp Chase	3m	£6310	11.6	T. Stack	16/1	unpl
Apr 2	Liverpool	News of the World Grand National H'cp Chase	4m 4f	£41140	11.8	T. Stack	9/1	won
Apr 16	Ayr	Scottish Grand National H'cp Chase	4m 120y	£9674	11.11	T. Stack	100/30f	unpl
Season 1977–78								
Sep 17	Carlisle	Windermere H'cp Chase	3m	£616	12.7	R. Barry	2/1j.f.	2nd
Oct 12	Wetherby	Gordon Foster H'cp Chase	3m 100y	£855	12.2	R. Barry	4/5f	2nd
Oct 29	Catterick	WL & Hector Christie Memorial Trophy H'cp Chase	3m 300y	£1038	12.2	R. Barry	13/2	4th
Feb 8	Haydock Park	Malcolm Fudge National Trial H'cp Chase	3m 4f	£3007	11.13	R. Barry	25/1	4th
Mar 4	Haydock Park	Greenall Whitley Breweries H'cp Chase	3m	£7780	11.13	T. Stack	33/1	unpl

Career Record
Ran – Flat 10; won 3 (including 1 dead heat), £970. Hurdles 24; won 3, £884. Chases 76; won 21, £113,380
Total – ran 110; won 27 (including 1 dead heat), £115,234

T H I R T E E N

L'Escargot

THE QUEEN LAUNCHES THE QE II, AND THE POUND SINKS. VIVIEN LEIGH AND THE BEATLES' BRIAN EPSTEIN DIE. ENOCH POWELL FORETELLS HIS 'RIVER OF BLOOD'. BOBBY KENNEDY IS SHOT AND RUSSIAN TANKS CRUSH PRAGUE'S SPRING. CONCORDE FLIES. DE GAULLE DIES.

So far as his athletic prowess was concerned, L'Escargot was singularly ill-named. There was nothing snail-like about his performances. Some were those of eagles. He was the classiest horse to win the Grand National in the 41 years since Golden Miller. But in capturing the imagination and love of the public he was indeed a snail. Despite the great popularity of his American owner and Irish trainer, he reached stardom only towards the end of his long career, and then only in a very brief flame. Charisma, that sadly abused donkey of a word, can neither be learned nor even earned. Great horses, like most of our Winter Kings, have it in abundance. L'Escargot had not. Even his name was not glamorous though neatly constructed, as he was by a French sire, Escart III, out of What a Daisy.

Other good horses have lacked charisma, like those rather forgettable brace of Derby winners both bred and owned by their trainer. How many men in the street could name the only steeplechaser since 'The Miller' to win both the Cheltenham Gold Cup and the Liverpool Grand National? We do not think a repeat of L'Escargot's double is likely, any more than another, similar Morston-Blakeney

double will be brought off by such a pleasant, honest and most retiring flat trainer as Arthur Budgett of Whatcombe.

Horses or people with charisma excite and attract. L'Escargot did not. In the minds of supporters of other great horses of his time, like the millions of fans worldwide who adored Red Rum, L'Escargot, clad in his evil-looking blue hood, galloping with his head stuck out like a snake, was the villain of several dramas. He should have been the dashing hero, like Raymond Guest, his owner, or Dan Moore, his trainer, or Tommy Carberry, his jockey. All played those rôles with dash and charm.

And the horse possessed tremendous speed in the highest class. He won a bumper first time out and a division of the 2-mile Gloucester Hurdle, the equivalent of the Waterford Crystal Supremes Novices, in only his second run over hurdles. But he took years to prove the truth of Dan Moore's positive response to Raymond Guest's oft-repeated request to find him a National horse, 'You've already got one'. It took L'Escargot four attempts to do it – itself a badge of courage – by which time he was a 12-year-old. Yet the fickle-hearted jumping public seemed only to recall, when he did it, his wicked defeat of Red Rum.

L'Escargot was bred in Mullingar, Co. Westmeath by Barbara O'Neill. His dam, What a Daisy, did not race, but was a half-sister to the National winner Mr What. One of the authors then in the business of buying jumpers called at that time on Mrs O'Neill to look over some of her young stock out of What a Daisy. He also visited the late Jimmy Brogan's place and saw a youngster for sale out of What a Daisy. He has occasionally felt with a shudder since then that this was probably L'Escargot he let slip, partly through not being enchanted by the young horse, and mainly through not having at either time an owner keen enough to override his tepid praise and rich enough to buy in spite of it.

What a Daisy was a prolific brood mare producing no less than seven winners. L'Escargot's sire, Escart III, one of a number of French stallions shrewdly acquired by former North Countryman Frank Latham of Blackrath to add quality and speed to the big, rangy Irish jumping mares, stood for only five seasons before dying of a thrombosis in the autumn of 1966. Despite this sadly truncated career, he made a tremendous impact, siring hundreds of winners. L'Escargot was one of his first crop. Jimmy Brogan, father of that brilliant but flawed jump-jockey Barry, bought him as a foal for 950 guineas, but Jimmy suddenly died three days later at the end of his morning gallop. His widow 'stored' the youngster and sent him to Ballsbridge in November 1966. The previous year, What a Daisy's first foal, Havago, ridden by Bobby Beasley, had won a division of Cheltenham's ace Gloucester Hurdle. At Ballsbridge, notwithstanding his crooked front action, he caught the eye of Tom Cooper of the B.B.A. (Ireland), a prótegé of the dashing and much decorated Wing-Commander Tim Vigors, an astute picker-out of multi-million dollar yearlings for the attentions of Vincent O'Brien, Robert Sangster, John Magnier *et al.*, and a friend of leading Irish trainer Dan Moore from their students days at Trinity College, Dublin. They bought L'Escargot for 3,000 guineas, a good price then, on behalf of Raymond Guest, the American Ambassador to Ireland. He was an exceptionally tall, good-looking man, with great charm, a millionaire, an Anglophile and a phenomenally lucky owner.

He had tried jumpers, not very successful ones, with the young Vincent O'Brien and when O'Brien switched to the flat he had asked him to buy him a potential Derby winner. As with L'Escargot later, Guest always urged his trainers to go for the top. O'Brien found him Larkspur at Ballsbridge and later Sir Ivor at Keeneland. Seeking another jumper, Raymond Guest turned, on Tom Cooper's advice, to Dan Moore.

Moore's large, bluff, gregarious figure was misleading. He had been a most distinguished jockey in his youth, first as an amateur, then as a professional. He was the third member of a most feared triumvirate with Dorothy Paget and Charlie Rogers, whom Miss Paget dubbed 'Romeo'. They had pulled off a memorable coup in 1943, when steeplechasing in the neutral Republic of Ireland continued rather more briskly than in war-blitzed Britain. They won the Irish Grand National with Golden Jack, who beat Prince Regent. The stewards of the Irish National Hunt Committee subsequently censured the handicapper, 'as being greatly to blame as he appeared not to have taken the horse's previous form into consideration'.

Dan Moore had been Leading Jockey in Ireland no less than six times and had come tantalizingly close to winning the 1938 Grand National on Royal Danieli, being beaten a short head by 17-year-old Bruce Hobbs on the diminutive full horse Battleship. He continued to ride after the war, but retired in 1948 and took out a licence to train. He was based initially at Fairyhouse, but moved in 1967 to Ballysax Manor on the Curragh. He was actively and most ably assisted by his dark-haired, attractive wife Joan, a keen hunting lady and a beautiful horse-woman, and later by his quiet and intelligent son, Arthur.

Dan Moore possessed such an intuitive eye for a young horse that he had already bought both Freebooter and Team Spirit as unbroken three-year-olds. Freebooter had been passed on to Mrs Brotherton, sometime owner of Red Rum, after winning his bumpers. He won the 1950 Grand National for her carrying 11 st. 11 lb. But Team Spirit had stayed in the yard to win numerous races, including the Mildmay Memorial and the Hurst Park Grand National Trial. Only then was he transferred to Fulke Walwyn, at the suggestion of Dan Moore, to profit from the increased opportunities in quantity and in value then available to high-class steeplechasers in England.

With Dan Moore at the time of L'Escargot's arrival was a young Englishman, not quite 21 and just learning his trade. The immaculately dressed Ben Hanbury is now a distinguished Newmarket trainer and married to the sister of Mrs Sonia Rogers of the Airlie group of studs. He spent three years with the Moores, 'the best years of my life. They were smashing people and wonderful to me. Dan helped so many young people, he taught me everything and gave me two or three hundred rides.'

Ben, with his enthusiasm and his tremendous sense of fun, was much liked in Ireland. To his duties with the Moores he added the agreeable task of escorting Mr Guest's attractive and vivacious daughter, Virginia. He helped Joan break L'Escargot and although the young chestnut was plain and immature they realized very quickly that he was a racehorse. One day he worked exceptionally well with previous bumper winners and it was decided he was ready for a run. Ben would ride. It was quite a responsibility, for Dan had always liked a bet and Raymond Guest, as he showed over a huge bet on Sir Ivor at long odds ante-post, was an intrepid gambler.

'Raymond was always someone who loved to have a bet,' Vincent O'Brien warmly recalls over the second Epsom Derby winner he trained for him. After Sir Ivor's first race as a two-year-old, Guest decided to back him for the Derby. He was in Deauville, found William Hill the bookmaker on his yacht and struck a bet of £500 each way at 100–1. The bet, worth some £650,000 in terms of 1989 currency, terrified Hill who tried a number of ploys and pleas to get it cancelled or reduced.

The first target for L'Escargot was at Navan in February. The money was got on in Northern Ireland, some of it at 20–1, and L'Escargot brought it safely home. Six weeks later he upgraded to a winners' bumper at Phoenix Park and ran another excellent race to be second.

He won a second bumper at Naas in October and then had his attention switched to hurdling. At this juncture L'Escargot teamed up with a brilliant young jockey who was to attach himself permanently to the Moore establishment by marrying the guv'nor's daughter Pamela.

Tommy Carberry did not come from a horsey background. His father farmed. However, at 15, 'mad about horses' and weighing less than 6 st., the obvious choice for the academically undistinguished school-leaver was to go 'down the road to Fairyhouse', to Dan Moore. 'D.L.' as he came to call him, taught the boy to ride but, appreciating his potential and talent and lightness, arranged for him to be apprenticed to a flat trainer. Carberry, as he is universally known, joined Jimmy Lenehan at The Curragh in February 1958. He rode his first winner three months later and finished the season as Champion Apprentice with twenty winners.

He returned to the Moores in 1961. He was still light enough for the flat and good enough to be put up in three Irish Derbies. But his heart lay in jumping. The following season, when stable-jockey Willie Robinson left for England and Fulke Walwyn, the twenty-one-year-old Carberry took his place. His first winner over hurdles for his new stable was a division of the 1962 Gloucester Hurdle on Tripacer.

He has a hawk-like face with a quite misleading touch of arrogance about it, a deprecating manner and a graphically vivid turn of phrase. He has the reputation of being a very cool customer with a flair for the big occasion and for many years was regarded as outstandingly the best jockey in Ireland.

L'Escargot's sights were set high. He won the Osberstown Hurdle at Naas at a longish price and was promptly dispatched across the channel to try and emulate his half-brother in the Gloucester Hurdle. L'Escargot rewarded Raymond Guest's bold tilt at a big prize with an emphatic 6-length victory over the Rimell-trained favourite, Pick Me Up.

Thereafter his fortunes dipped. He was losing his form when finishing only fourth in the Martin Mahony Champion Novices Hurdle at Punchestown and second when odds on at Down Royal. L'Escargot was thereupon sent to Jeffrey Braine, the Gloucestershire veterinary surgeon whose expertise on wind infirmities was world-famed. Jeffrey confirmed what Dan Moore had for some time feared, that L'Escargot had a partial paralysis of the larynx, which thus impeded the free flow of air into his lungs. Jeffrey Braine hobdayed the horse, an operation which, when done by him, normally proved successful.

L'Escargot's first target as a six-year-old was the valuable Scalp Hurdle. A couple of preliminary outings were satisfactory, if not scintillating, and he completed his preparation, threatened by frost, on the sands of Port Marnock beach. A sparkling piece of work with the useful Beau Chapeau convinced the stable that he was on target and he went to Leopardstown with much confidence behind him.

So well did he bear out his confidence that it was decided to have a crack at the Champion Hurdle. It was the era of Persian War, however, and although L'Escargot ran well to be sixth, he did not jump hurdles well enough to be a factor in that class of company.

As a result he was directed to fences, for he had always looked every inch a chaser. Wasting no time in preliminaries, he found himself up against Kinloch Brae for the prestigious Power Gold Cup at Fairyhouse. The Duchess of Westminster's fluent young horse had made a profound impression at Cheltenham, winning the Cathcart Cup by no less than 20 lengths. He had no difficulty in conceding 12 lb. to Mr Guest's novice and beating him 10 lengths. No such formidable opposition threatened L'Escargot in his next two races and he won them both, as an odds-on favourite should.

He did not enjoy a peaceful summer holiday in Ireland, but instead flew out to contest the top American steeplechases. Although a steady stream of horses – and occasionally jockeys – from the U.S.A. had been crossing the Atlantic to challenge for the Grand National since Billy Barton in 1928, no British chaser had made the opposite journey. Raymond Guest was naturally keen for his young star to shine in his native land. Apart from the fierce fixed-timber obstacles of such astonishing one-off races as the Maryland Hunt Cup and the occasional mixed race at other American jumping meetings, American fences are generally standardized, plastic and moveable objects, about as high as a hurdle, but with a big green canvas belly causing horses to stand off, and surmounted by black plastic 'twigs' through which horses can brush. Falls are infrequent, but when they do occur take place at fearsome speed. L'Escargot, with his hurdling technique fresh in his mind, coped well with the fences at his first attempt and won the Meadowbrook Chase in such good style that he was made favourite for the Grand National.

To the bitter disappointment of his connections, he was found to be lame on the morning of the race and could not run. The problem was temporary and never explained. Perhaps a rap or even a sharp stone bruising the foot.

At the beginning of the 1969/70 jumping season the tobacco company W. D. and H. O. Wills announced their sponsorship of a series of 2½ mile races for young steeplechasers culminating in a rich final at Haydock. This seemed an ideal target for L'Escargot and he duly won it, producing a fine turn of speed in the closing stages to beat East Bound and the mare Young Ash Leaf.

This victory certainly made him a rising star in the steeplechasing firmament, but it did not suggest that the seven-year-old would yet have a very realistic chance in the Cheltenham Gold Cup. Defeat in heavy ground in the 3-mile Leopardstown Chase served to harden Moore's opinion that L'Escargot would not be suited by 3 miles. He preferred a challenge for the Two Mile Champion Chase. Raymond Guest, although not believing that 'there was a horse in the world to beat Kinloch Brae', was made of sterner stuff. 'Hell! We have a good horse! Let's go for the big pot!'

His boldness paid off. Kinloch Brae, hot favourite at 15–8, was ridden by Timmy Hyde, now a breeder of top-class yearlings for the classic market. His father had ridden Prince Regent. The pair were cruising in the lead at the top of the hill but the wily Pat Taaffe on French Tan was sitting on their heels. Reasoning that the coming downhill fences would prove extremely tricky for a novice, and that Kinloch Brae was unused to being bustled, he boldly drove French Tan alongside. Kinloch Brae hit the third last hard, pitched, slithered and capsized. L'Escargot tracked French Tan until approaching the last, jumped it upsides and he whose stamina had been doubted stayed on just the better up the hill to win by 1½ lengths. Edward Courage's Spanish Steps, strongly fancied by the English to keep the Cup at home, was a disappointing third, 10 lengths behind.

The result was greeted with stunned silence. L'Escargot had started at 33–1 and Carberry was little known outside Ireland. The Press focussed on the cruelly

L'Escargot (no blinkers yet) lands level with French Tan over the last fence in the 1970 Gold Cup, before going on to win. The two high class jockeys are Tommy Carberry, going that much better, and Pat Taaffe.

disappointed but unhurt Hyde. 'Would you have won?' they queried. Timmy Hyde ignored any opportunity for blarney. 'Well, I was going terrible well. But there was some way to go and I daresay Tommy and Pat would say they were going pretty well too'.

L'Escargot made a second trip across the Atlantic in the autumn. After a couple of warm-up runs on the flat at The Curragh, he challenged for the newly-instituted Colonial Cup to be run at Camden, South Carolina. The race was proposed and entirely sponsored by Mrs Marion du Pont Scott, owner of Battleship and wife of the film star Randolph Scott. This splendid and much admired lady from one of America's richest families lived till a great age, in a beautiful colonial mansion set in a huge garden outside the pretty ante-bellum town of Camden. The racecourse and its training grounds (used in winter by New York trainers to escape the northern cold) were all laid out on her land. She extended boundless hospitality to all owners, trainers, jockeys and their friends. As on his previous trip, a preliminary race was planned for L'Escargot, this time the Temple Gwathmey Chase in which he finished a pleasing third. But in the rich Colonial Cup he fractionally disappointed his connections when finishing fourth to Mrs Ogden Phipps' Top Bird.

Back in Ireland, L'Escargot continued to be frustrated. He ran respectably to be fourth in the Sweeps Hurdle without remotely troubling the triple Champion Hurdler, Persian War, and then blundered, unseating Carberry, when favourite at Punchestown. Dan Moore then privately resolved against any more trips to the States, considering that those expeditions, in spite of successes, certainly spoilt L'Escargot's jumping over the very different Irish and British fences.

As if to prove the theory that practice makes perfect, L'Escargot jumped better in the Leopardstown Chase. But top-weight and bottomless ground anchored him into third place behind Mahoney and King's Sprite.

Gloom was cast over the preliminaries for the 1971 Gold Cup by two withdrawals. The first, due to recurring leg-trouble, was that of Kinloch Brae, who had transferred to Toby Balding over the winter, and the second was that of Spanish Steps, whom Mrs Courage had inadvertently removed by an incorrect four-day declaration. No clear market leader emerged following these important defections, and in the end L'Escargot, Leap Frog and Into View all shared favouritism at 7–2.

It rained so solidly for 15 hours before the race that the stewards had to abandon the proper start and use the Old Course 3¼-mile start. Thereafter the Gold Cup proceeded remarkably similarly to the previous year. This time the easy leader at the top of the hill was the mare Glencaraig Lady but she, for no apparent reason, dived headlong through the third last and crashed out of contention. L'Escargot led into the last challenged by Leap Frog and, though patently weary, stayed on stoutly up the hill to see off Leap Frog and The Dikler, and to gain his second Cheltenham Gold Cup. He returned to a reception not much more enthusiastic than his previous victory had earned. It was much more muted than he deserved. Up till 1989 only five horses have won more than one Gold Cup. Furthermore, L'Escargot had two future winners behind him that day. Glencaraig Lady, appropriately a daughter of Luckibash, put in a rare clear round to win in

1972, while The Dikler, so long the *enfant terrible* of British steeplechasing, finally got his act together to beat Pendil a short head in 1973. With hindsight L'Escargot's second victory in 1971 was first class. But few said so.

Dan Moore, however, now said firmly that L'Escargot was making no more transatlantic ventures. 'He'll have a summer in Ireland.' He also made his oft-quoted prophecy to Raymond Guest's repeated enquiries that Mr Guest already owned the horse with which he would win the National. This was remarkably percipient in view of the horse's rather confused background of running over different types of obstacles. And few trainers would contemplate risking a double Gold Cup winner round the hazardous mêlées of Aintree.

He meant the English Grand National but L'Escargot's immediate target was the Irish equivalent at Fairyhouse, traditionally run on Easter Monday. Inevitably he was burdened with 12 st. 7 lb. and he ran a brave race to finish a close third. The winner, receiving no less than 36 lb., was King's Sprite, ridden ironically by Dan Moore's fair-haired, lanky son Arthur, who had been closely involved with L'Escargot and travelled with him on both his trips to the States. Arthur, a man of vision and quiet efficiency, is now himself training with great skill. He has inherited his father's eye for a young horse and commands much of the same respect.

L'Escargot returned to Cheltenham the following year. Indeed, after his first season, he never missed a Festival in eight tough years. But this time his luck did not hold. He blundered at the crucial second last and could only finish fourth behind the blanket finishers, Glencaraig Lady, Royal Toss and The Dikler, who after a thrilling tussle were separated only by ¾ length and a head.

The edge had just gone from his speed and Dan Moore would now be confronted with two serious problems in placing and training him. Firstly, the handicappers would give the dual Gold Cup winner little chance in normal races, and secondly the bold-faced chestnut was developing his own ideas about the game. Against this Dan Moore could pit the skill of Carberry and himself and his knowledge that the horse would blossom with the spring. Henceforth he began to concentrate L'Escargot's still considerable abilities on winning the race that had so narrowly eluded him in 1938. It would prove a marvellously plotted campaign over the years.

L'Escargot's first experience of Aintree very nearly put him off for life. Despite the inevitable top-weight of 12 stone, he started favourite of the 42-strong field, but his supporters' hopes were swiftly and brutally snuffed when he was knocked over at the third fence, the mighty open ditch. He did not forget it. In future years Carberry had to exert every ounce of skill and psychology to eradicate the horrid memory.

Season 1972–73 was a frustrating one for L'Escargot. Invariably heaving burdens of 12 st. or more, he finished in the first four in seven of his nine runs but won only once and that by a short head. This was the Sundew Chase at Haydock at the end of November. Three consecutive seconds caused him to start favourite at 10–11 on. L'Escargot and Spanish Steps engaged in a tremendous battle over the last three fences. On the run-in Spanish Steps edged right under extreme pressure and Raymond Guest's distinctive blue and chocolate hoops inched home. Mr Jim Joel's good horse The Laird trailed in 30 lengths behind in third place.

L'Escargot was then fourth in another Cheltenham Gold Cup on fastish ground, outpaced in the closing stages behind The Dikler and Pendil, before returning to Liverpool, again with 12 st., for the National. Memories of the previous year's indignity returned with a vengeance. 'He was outraged!' recalls Carberry. It was not a year for the less than whole-hearted. The joint-favourites, Crisp and Red Rum, smashed Golden Miller's 39-year record by 19 sec. Apprehensively jumping much too big, L'Escargot was back in 17th place by the water. Encouraged by Carberry's consummate horsemanship he made steady headway from the second Canal Turn but the leaders were gone beyond recall and he could only finish a respectful third, 25 lengths behind the gallant and shattered Crisp. The way he ran on in the final stages suggested to some observers that, given half a chance by the handicapper, the Grand National victory forecast so long ago by Dan Moore could become a reality.

1973–74 was the only season in his long and honourable career that L'Escargot failed to win a race. He did nevertheless run three marvellous ones and he was, belatedly and slowly, gaining a little of the public's affection. Like Christmas, he came every year and he was so commendably tough. The British often prefer a familiar, gallant loser to a cocky, unknown victor. Even the handicapper was becoming a little kinder. Only once did he have to carry 12 st. The tide might now be turning. But the years might be running out too fast.

His early efforts were not especially exhilarating. But the impression was growing that his astute trainer was carefully programming his veteran to peak in the spring. It is likely that his chosen Festival race, the Cathcart Challenge Cup over 2 miles, was not so much an easier alternative to the Gold Cup as a sharpener for a horse who appeared to have lost his once formidable turn of foot. In fact L'Escargot, equipped with a hood to concentrate the mind, ran a terrific race to finish second, beaten just four lengths by the former Colonial Cup winner, Soothsayer, who had crossed the Atlantic to Fred Winter.

L'Escargot's hood, a vivid pale blue to match part of his owner's colours, combined with his habit of racing with his ears back, gave him a slightly sinister appearance. So when the thing was removed in the unsaddling enclosure the sight of his bold, generous head and keenly pricked ears came as a welcoming surprise.

That year Red Rum was set to carry top-weight in the National and the senior handicapper had generously dropped L'Escargot below 12 st. He allotted him 11 st. 13 lb. Dan Moore's preparation had plainly been timed to the hour, for L'Escargot earned the coveted *Chaseform* accolade 'l.w'. There was significant late money for him and he started second favourite at 17–2. He wore his blue hood and Carberry persuaded him to take a sharply keener interest in proceedings than in the previous year's race. He was always prominent and never further back than fifth or sixth from the first Canal Turn onwards. Coming to the second last he loomed menacingly alongside Red Rum. Brian Fletcher, giving a pound to the dual Gold Cup winner, glanced anxiously across. Carberry went hard at work, but could not persuade his enigmatic partner that Liverpool was a place where he should safely give his all. L'Escargot's effort petered out and Red Rum went away to score a memorable second victory by 7 lengths.

Following this fine effort, L'Escargot returned home to try his luck in the Irish equivalent. Here the handicapper had surprisingly given him a real chance with only 10 st. 9 lb. His task was lightened when the young Gold Cup winner, the brilliant but erratic Captain Christy, crashed out of contention at half-way. But yet again he had to be content with second place, 5 lengths behind Colebridge, trained by young Jim Dreaper.

By the time the new season came round L'Escargot was approaching his 12th birthday. 1975 had to be recognized as his last chance in the long-awaited National. The Moore family were frankly concentrating their efforts to producing him on 5 April fit to run for his life. It was in every sense a family effort. Carberry was now married to Pamela Moore. His home at Ashbourne lay to the north of Dublin with the city between him and Ballysax. He was riding most of the horses of his near neighbour Jim Dreaper, in addition to the Moores'. It was a very amicable arrangement. Dan Moore would let his son-in-law off to ride a Dreaper horse if it was really fancied.

Joan Moore had always played a major part in the stable's running. She was a beautiful horsewoman and was clearly much loved by the owners. The American consortium who owned Team Spirit gave him back to her to hunt after the chunky little bay, originally bought and trained by her husband, had won the National. With her husband's health becoming less robust, she played an increasing part in L'Escargot's preparation.

Arthur, now 26 and married, had assisted his father for the last six years while building up his own breeding and dealing interests. Having burnt his fingers in the bloodstock slump of 1974, he had diverted to training. In 1975, for the first time, he took out a licence of his own, but he was still closely involved with L'Escargot.

L'Escargot's efforts in Ireland were confined to three runs. He could not be said to have distinguished himself and was placed only once. He paid his customary annual visit to Cheltenham, this time for the National Hunt Two Mile Champion Chase 'to sharpen him'. No one was under any illusions as to the purpose: he started at 20–1. He wore his hood and, although he never troubled the leaders, he ran most respectably to finish fifth to Lough Inagh. A few watchers thought they recognized distinct promise for Liverpool in this run. Carberry was delighted. 'He's just coming right'. Indeed, before this race Arthur Moore had remarked with his usual quiet but great confidence that he was sure L'Escargot would run really well at Cheltenham. Even more significantly, Arthur murmured that the Two Mile Chase would put him spot on and give him a tremendous chance in the National. In view of Arthur Moore's remarks before the race, one of the authors with a particular interest in Red Rum, telephoned the public hero's trainer Ginger McCain on two occasions, telling him of his fears that L'Escargot, specially prepared, might now well beat Red Rum. 'He'll be a real danger'. McCain, in jovial mood, optimistically waved these gloomy doubts aside. 'Nothing to fear there. We've beaten him before.' 'But Ginger, he's been specially prepared.' 'We'll beat him!'

Carberry, now 33, was riding at the height of his powers and was enjoying a purple patch. He won the Gold Gup on the Duchess of Westminster's Ten Up and the Irish National (an early Easter made it run before Liverpool's) on Brown

Lad. Could he make it a historic treble? The public money was for Red Rum, also trying for an unprecedented three-timer, but he was now meeting L'Escargot on 10 lb. worse terms than when he'd beaten him last year. Much would depend on L'Escargot's attitude, as well as the precise timing of Dan Moore's preparation for the great goal.

The National was suffering a period of hideous uncertainty. The awkward Bill Davies, an outwardly unprepossessing property developer who reacted grittily to the urbane but steady approaches from most of racing's Establishment figures, was struggling against hopeless odds to make Liverpool a commercial proposition. Jacking entrance prices up to £20 for the member's enclosure had the effect of driving the public to their television screens in droves.

The going was however good on Aintree's legendary turf, though the day was bitterly cold. Flurries of snow scudded through the deserted enclosures, and whipped into the shabby old stands. The 15-minute delay while Junior Partner was replated was intensely disagreeable. The contest that was about to unfold was worthy of a better audience.

It was a National littered with grief. Of the 31 runners, no fewer than 15 fell or were brought down. A further five pulled up or refused.

There was nearly a leading addition to this inventory of woe: L'Escargot blundered horribly at the seventh. Nearly a foot smaller than its notorious predecessor, Becher's Brook, and with no juddering drop, it often catches horses unawares as they touch down unexpectedly quickly. On the second circuit it becomes the infamous 23rd which caused the spectacular carnage in 1967 letting in tailed-off Foinavon to lollop past the mêlée of huge swerving horses and frantically scampering little jockeys to plod on amazingly to win.

This year Carberry was skilful – and lucky – to survive. 'I so nearly fell off. I was round his neck and it took me three strides to get my stirrups back.'

This setback might have killed L'Escargot's tenuous enthusiasm for Liverpool stone dead. Luckily he had enjoyed two safe trips round since his unfortunate introduction in 1972 and Carberry's confidence flowed sweetly through hands and legs along the reins and down the old horse's flanks. This time it was going to be all right. The mistake in fact could have been opportune, because it was obvious earlier that the frighteningly large number of early fallers jostling loose must cause havoc as they scrummed towards the narrow Chair. The field were led into it by four loose horses who jinked first left towards the rails and then, at the last minute, darted right-handed across the fence in a pack. Miraculously only two horses came down, but one of these, Land Lark, was killed. 'I was far enough behind to go whichever way they didn't', reported Carberry cheerfully.

From then on everything went to plan. The pair made ground steadily and cruised up to the leaders at the Open Ditch four fences from home. As he crossed the Melling Road onto the racecourse, John Francome, some way behind on last-to-finish Rag Trade, vividly recalls how well L'Escargot was going. 'I've never, ever seen a horse going so easily at that stage! He was literally cantering!' The same thought communicated itself twitchingly to Brian Fletcher who had ridden a perfect race on Red Rum.

'You'll win five minutes! Go on!' Brian swore across to Carberry.

Brian Fletcher on Red Rum has just desperately shouted across to Tommy Carberry on L'Escargot 'You'll win five minutes! Go on!' But here, at the last fence of the 1975 National, the wily Carberry still bides his time.

'He was going', reflected L'Escargot's jockey, 'as a Gold Cup winner should, against a bunch of handicappers'. Carberry didn't heed Fletcher's exhortation or avail himself of the invitation. He intended to keep company with Red Rum until landing on the flat. Then he released the brakes to allow L'Escargot to stride home in triumph by 15 lengths, and to become the first horse since Golden Miller to achieve the Gold Cup-Grand National double.

The crowd though small and cold compensated with a loud and warm reception for the old trier, the horse of class who had finally brought off his trainer's promise. At 12 years old L'Escargot had at last crept into the hearts of the jumping public. Dourness and perseverance were celebrated, if his brilliance round Cheltenham had been largely overlooked. There were of course waves of sympathy for Red Rum. But he at 10 years would have other chances and more years to go. For L'Escargot old time had run out. In he walked to a happy, cheering crowd. His wicked blue blinkers were whipped off and replaced by Arthur's battered felt hat. Much of the goodwill and bursts of cheering were directed principally towards the Moores. As Dan Moore said 'I've been waiting 37 years to prove that this is not an unlucky course for me.'

In the post race euphoria Raymond Guest announced that he would retire

The blue-hooded L'Escargot and the darkly-goggled Carberry win the 1975 National. But almost everyone is looking back 15 lengths to find their hero, Red Rum.

L'Escargot and give him to Joan to hunt 'with Paddy Powell's Harriers'. The horses were led away, the Press and television crews dispersed, the champagne was opened and L'Escargot's supporters settled down to celebrate.

When the shouting was over and L'Escargot back in Ireland was enjoying himself out at grass, the implications of Raymond Guest's spontaneous gift began to dawn.

There had been no formal agreement. Mr Guest – 'not a generous man', said Arthur diffidently – had made no provision for the upkeep of his horse, who, sound and in excellent health, might reasonably expect to enjoy life for many years to come. Joan, playing an increasing part in the training, had little time to enjoy hunting. And L'Escargot, like an old war horse lonely for the sound of trumpets, did not appear to be relishing the programme of retirement so thoughtfully proposed for him.

In the end the Moores thought he might well enjoy himself and contribute a little towards his keep by contesting a few small races in Ireland. He went down to Kerry, enchantingly sited on the Dingle peninsula, to contest their indulgently-styled Kerry Grand National. He was beaten a short head.

Hardly had the result reached the U.S.A. before rumbles of discontent began to thunder across the Atlantic. Mr Raymond Guest had decided after Liverpool to retire his great steeplechaser. He had said so. The racing public knew it. He had said the famous horse could enjoy himself out hunting. He had not wished L'Escargot ever to run again. Now he found that he had done so. Raymond Guest, former Ambassador, big gambler, was absolutely furious. His horse should return forthwith to a real retirement in the U.S.A. Joan and Arthur felt that Dan Moore, not in the best of health, did not want this sort of wrangle. They sent L'Escargot back to the States.

Virginia Guest, Raymond's stylish daughter who has a network of racing friends all round the world, warmly remembers L'Escargot's retirement. 'In that bar under the old Grandstand at Liverpool we were all together before the race, and my father said "Win, lose or draw, it'll be the horse's last race." It was left just like that.

'So after the race when Pop came to wonder where the horse should retire, I simply said, "Look, he's spent nearly all his life since he was a three-year-old at Ballysax" – and my father immediately agreed to leave him there. Joan Moore used to ride him out and we thought she'd probably hunt him. But it's difficult, isn't it, when you're training, to have a horse in the yard who isn't actually *racing*.

'Anyway, when someone called me from Ireland to say he was amazed to see L'Escargot was racing again, we were pretty amazed, too. So my father said to the

L'Escargot with Raymond Guest and his trainer, Dan Moore, after winning the 1975 Grand National. Without that sinister-looking hood, the horse shows his handsome head.

Moores "I'll pay all his training bills since you've had him, and send the horse straight over and I'll pay the flight".'

So L'Escargot, now indeed retired, arrived at Raymond Guest's beautiful old farm, Powhatan Plantation, at King George in Virginia. The place was named after the Indian chief, the father of Princess Pocahontas who saving the Virginian colonist John Smith from her father's braves, finally married him, became a Christian, went to England and died of smallpox in 1617. Raymond Guest's first good filly was called Pocahontas.

At Powhatan, L'Escargot was Raymond Guest's 'pride and joy and treated better than a child,' Virginia recalls. 'Pop got a great deal of pleasure from him. Adored going to see him with apples and carrots – he didn't like sugar and he preferred women to men.

'We took him down one year to be paraded at the Colonial Cup at Camden, South Carolina – the year Grand Canyon won. Carberry was over to ride Casa Mayor (a horse of my father's who ended up in your Household Cavalry), and he rode L'Escargot in a parade before the race. The old horse was so well. I remember thinking "He may put Carberry down!" But he didn't quite!'

In the summer of 1989 Raymond Guest, at 81, was holding grimly onto life in a wheel chair and helped by an aspirator. L'Escargot had died aged 21. It reflects exactly how highly his owner rated him that he placed him among the three best horses he had owned in all his long life in racing: the other two were Tom Rolfe (whom he bred), Champion American three-year-old in 1965 and the 1968 Epsom Derby winner Sir Ivor. L'Escargot, winner of the Cheltenham Gold Cup, the Liverpool Grand National, the Meadowbrook Steeplechase and voted Jumper of the Year in the U.S.A., stands worthily right up there.

L'ESCARGOT CH.G. 1963	ESCART III	TURMOIL II	TOURBILLON
			BLUE IRAS
		ESCALADE	ESCAMILLO
			CLE DE MI
	WHAT A DAISY	GRAND INQUISITOR	HIS REVERENCE
			HIGH PRESTIGE
		LADY SUNDERLIN	J'ACCOURS
			DUCHESS OF PEDULAS

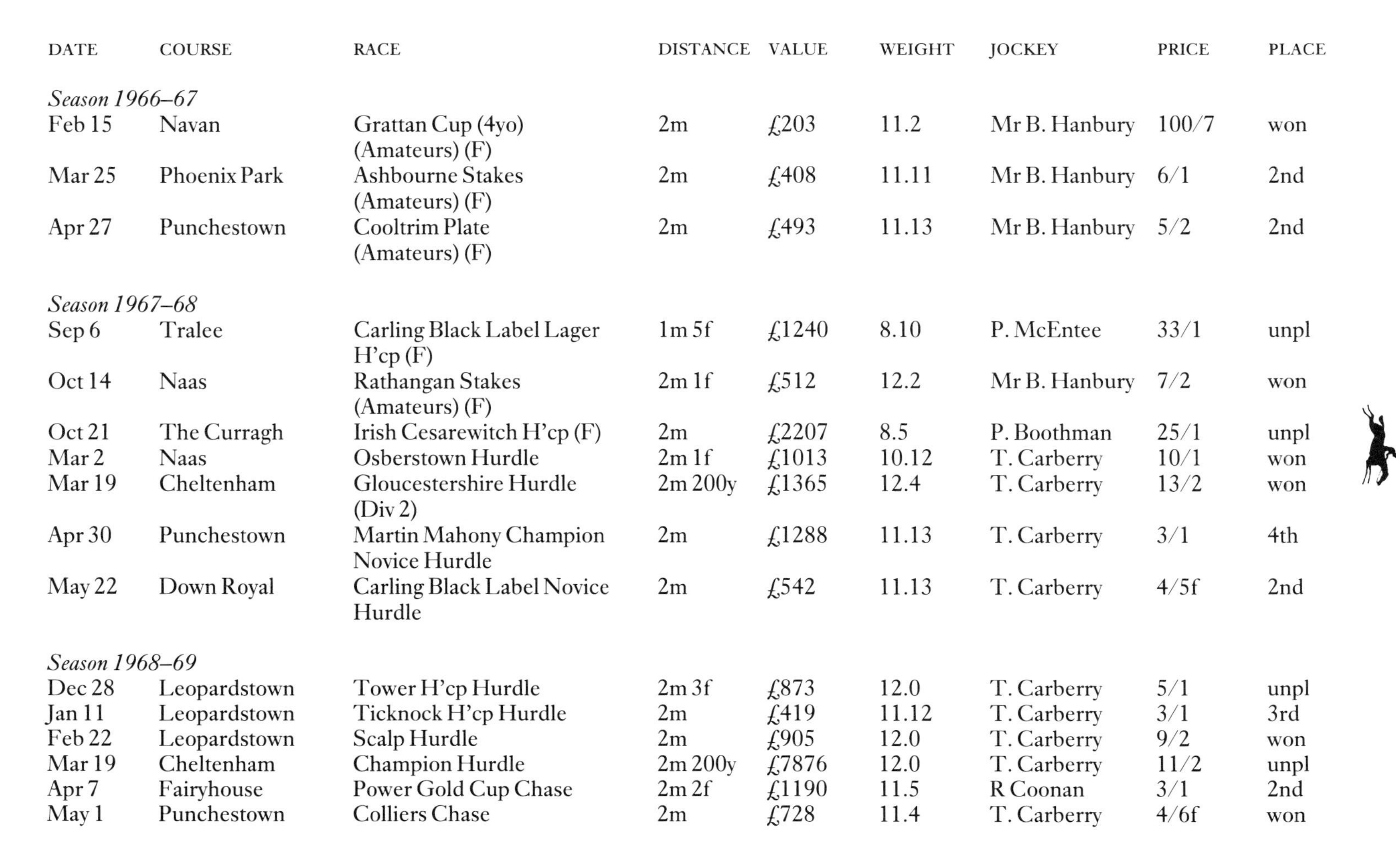

DATE	COURSE	RACE	DISTANCE	VALUE	WEIGHT	JOCKEY	PRICE	PLACE
Season 1966–67								
Feb 15	Navan	Grattan Cup (4yo) (Amateurs) (F)	2m	£203	11.2	Mr B. Hanbury	100/7	won
Mar 25	Phoenix Park	Ashbourne Stakes (Amateurs) (F)	2m	£408	11.11	Mr B. Hanbury	6/1	2nd
Apr 27	Punchestown	Cooltrim Plate (Amateurs) (F)	2m	£493	11.13	Mr B. Hanbury	5/2	2nd
Season 1967–68								
Sep 6	Tralee	Carling Black Label Lager H'cp (F)	1m 5f	£1240	8.10	P. McEntee	33/1	unpl
Oct 14	Naas	Rathangan Stakes (Amateurs) (F)	2m 1f	£512	12.2	Mr B. Hanbury	7/2	won
Oct 21	The Curragh	Irish Cesarewitch H'cp (F)	2m	£2207	8.5	P. Boothman	25/1	unpl
Mar 2	Naas	Osberstown Hurdle	2m 1f	£1013	10.12	T. Carberry	10/1	won
Mar 19	Cheltenham	Gloucestershire Hurdle (Div 2)	2m 200y	£1365	12.4	T. Carberry	13/2	won
Apr 30	Punchestown	Martin Mahony Champion Novice Hurdle	2m	£1288	11.13	T. Carberry	3/1	4th
May 22	Down Royal	Carling Black Label Novice Hurdle	2m	£542	11.13	T. Carberry	4/5f	2nd
Season 1968–69								
Dec 28	Leopardstown	Tower H'cp Hurdle	2m 3f	£873	12.0	T. Carberry	5/1	unpl
Jan 11	Leopardstown	Ticknock H'cp Hurdle	2m	£419	11.12	T. Carberry	3/1	3rd
Feb 22	Leopardstown	Scalp Hurdle	2m	£905	12.0	T. Carberry	9/2	won
Mar 19	Cheltenham	Champion Hurdle	2m 200y	£7876	12.0	T. Carberry	11/2	unpl
Apr 7	Fairyhouse	Power Gold Cup Chase	2m 2f	£1190	11.5	R Coonan	3/1	2nd
May 1	Punchestown	Colliers Chase	2m	£728	11.4	T. Carberry	4/6f	won

DATE	COURSE	RACE	DISTANCE	VALUE	WEIGHT	JOCKEY	PRICE	PLACE
May 12	Leopardstown	Woodbine Chase	2m 2f	£666	11.12	T. Carberry	1/2f	won
June 3	Belmont Park (USA)	Meadow Brook H'cp Chase	2m 4f	£6366	10.8	T. Carberry	no s.p.	won
Season 1969–70								
Oct 17	Belmont Park (USA)	Temple Gwathmey H'cp Chase	3m	£15713	10.12	T. Carberry	no s.p.	3rd
Nov 15	Punchestown	Sandymount Chase	2m 4f	£1049	11.10	T. Carberry	4/5f	2nd
Dec 26	Fairyhouse	Paddock H'cp Chase	2m 2f	£677	12.3	T. Carberry	11/4	won
Jan 17	Haydock Park	WD & HO Wills Premier Chase Final	2m 4f	£4493	11.0	T. Carberry	9/4f	won
Feb 21	Navan	Leopardstown Chase (H'cp)	3m	£2745	11.13	T. Carberry	6/4f	2nd
Mar 19	Cheltenham	Cheltenham Gold Cup Chase	3m 2f 76y	£8103	12.0	T. Carberry	33/1	won
Season 1970–71								
Oct 17	The Curragh	Irish Cesarewitch H'cp (F)	2m	£2312	8.6	L. W. Johnson	33/1	unpl
Oct 31	The Curragh	Crotanstown H'cp (F)	1m 4f	£468	9.3	T. Carberry	100/8	unpl
Dec 28	Fairyhouse	Sweeps Hurdle	2m	£10982	11.8	T. Carberry	4/1	4th
Jan 9	Punchestown	Rathside Chase	3m	£821	12.0	T. Carberry	7/4f	u.r.
Feb 20	Leopardstown	Leopardstown Chase (H'cp)	3m	£2617	12.2	T. Carberry	12/1	3rd
Mar 18	Cheltenham	Cheltenham Gold Cup Chase	3m 2f 76y	£7995	12.0	T. Carberry	7/2j.f.	won
Apr 12	Fairyhouse	Irish Distillers Grand National H'cp Chase	3m 2f	£9917	12.7	T. Carberry	8/1	3rd
Season 1971–72								
Nov 3	Fairyhouse	Donaghmore H'cp Chase	3m	£679	12.7	T. Carberry	6/1	fell
Nov 27	Newbury	Hennessy Cognac Gold Cup H'cp Chase	3m 2f 82y	£6132	12.7	T. Carberry	10/1	unpl

Dec 27	Kempton Park	King George VI Chase	3m	£3821	12.0	T. Carberry	6/1	4th
Feb 5	Leopardstown	Foxrock Cup H'cp Chase	3m	£672	12.7	T. Carberry	4/5f	2nd
Mar 16	Cheltenham	Cheltenham Gold Cup Chase	3m 2f 76y	£15255	12.0	T. Carberry	4/1	4th
Apr 8	Liverpool	Grand National H'cp Chase	4m 856y	£25765	12.0	T. Carberry	17/2f	bt dn
Apr 27	Punchestown	Guinness H'cp Chase	3m 132y	£1761	12.1	T. Carberry	8/1	p.u.
Season 1972–73								
Sep 26	Listowel	Kerry National H'cp Chase	3m	£1069	12.7	T. Carberry	5/2co-f	2nd
Oct 28	Liverpool	William Hill Grand National Trial H'cp Chase	2m 7f 110y	£4802	12.3	T. Carberry	9/2f	2nd
Nov 8	Punchestown	Donaghmore H'cp Chase	3m	£677	12.4	T. Carberry	2/1	2nd
Nov 29	Haydock Park	Sundew Chase	3m	£1214	11.7	T. Carberry	10/11f	won
Dec 30	Punchestown	Morgiana Hurdle	2m 4f	£959	10.11	T. Carberry	5/2f	2nd
Feb 17	Leopardstown	Leopardstown H'cp Chase	3m	£2658	12.0	T. Carberry	6/1	unpl
Mar 15	Cheltenham	Cheltenham Gold Cup Chase	3m 2f 76y	£15125	12.0	T. Carberry	20/1	4th
Mar 31	Liverpool	Grand National H'cp Chase	4m 856y	£25486	12.0	T. Carberry	11/1	3rd
Apr 23	Fairyhouse	Irish Distillers Grand National H'cp Chase	3m 2f	£9305	11.9	A. L.Moore	9/1	unpl
Season 1973–74								
Sep 25	Listowel	Kerry National H'cp Chase	3m	£889	12.0	T. Carberry	7/4f	fell
Dec 29	Punchestown	Morgiana Hurdle	2m 4f	£827	11.4	T. Carberry	3/1	3rd
Feb 1	Sandown Park	Gainsborough Chase	3m 118y	£1487	11.0	T. Carberry	5/2j.f.	4th
Feb 23	Leopardstown	Leopardstown H'cp Chase	3m	£2469	11.6	A. L.Moore	16/1	unpl
Mar 14	Cheltenham	Cathcart Challenge Cup Chase	2m	£1618	11.3	T. Carberry	10/1	2nd
Mar 30	Liverpool	Grand National H'cp Chase	4m 856y	£25102	11.13	T. Carberry	17/2	2nd
Apr 15	Fairyhouse	Irish Distillers Grand National H'cp Chase	3m 4f	£8916	10.8	T. Carberry	4/1	2nd

DATE	COURSE	RACE	DISTANCE	VALUE	WEIGHT	JOCKEY	PRICE	PLACE
Season 1974–75								
Oct 24	Punchestown	Free H'cp Chase	2m 4f	£862	10.11	T. Carberry	6/1	3rd
Nov 7	Thurles	Molony Cup H'cp Chase	3m	£690	12.2	T. Carberry	5/1	unpl
Feb 22	Leopardstown	Leopardstown H'cp Chase	3m	£2507	10.4	M. Ennis	16/1	unpl
Mar 12	Cheltenham	National Hunt Two-Mile Champion Chase	2m	£4316	12.0	T. Carberry	20/1	unpl
Apr 5	Liverpool	News of the World Grand National H'cp Chase	4m 856y	£38005	11.3	T. Carberry	13/2	won
Season 1975–76								
Sep 23	Listowel	Kerry National H'cp Chase	3m	£1484	12.0	T. Carberry	12/1	2nd

Career Record
Ran – Flat 8; won 2, £715. Hurdles 11; won 3, £3,283. Chases 41; won 9, £68,207
Total – ran 60; won 14, £72,205

FOURTEEN

Silver Buck

JOHN LENNON SHOT. PRINCE OF WALES MARRIES. BRIXTON BLAZES. POPE SHOT IN ROME AND SADAT KILLED IN CAIRO. LAKER AIRWAYS CRASHES. UNEMPLOYMENT BREAKS 3 MILLION. ARGENTINA INVADES FALKLANDS. AND GETS EVICTED. ISRAEL INVADES LEBANON AND MICHAEL FAGAN THE QUEEN'S BEDROOM. 20,000 WOMEN ENCIRCLE GREENHAM COMMON.

The scene is one of those vigorously bucolic Irish point-to-point meetings. In the paddock, making his debut on the first of many more glamorous racecourses he was destined to grace, is a smallish brown gelding with a particularly sharp, bright look about his head. His intended jockey is Mr Timmy Jones, the talented amateur rider, brother of Arthur Moore's pretty, dark-haired wife, Mary. He approaches him in the paddock, eager to mount. He is riding, after all, for the well-known Irish racing family, the Doyles, whose father Jack, a former Rugby international for Ireland, then race-horse trainer, was now established as an international bloodstock agent.

But Timmy Jones looking forward to his ride on this neatly attractive novice, was painfully disappointed. The horse totally refuses to allow him even to be legged up in the paddock. Finally mounted out on the course the horse then hurls himself and the hapless Jones into a wire fence. After a lengthy, painful extraction the pair have to be withdrawn. Timmy Jones' father is heard to remark that whereas he had no objection to a horse having a 'school' on a racecourse, he thinks

that breaking one in on the track is over-doing things!

Such was the extraordinary, violent and depressing start to the career, glorious and tragic, of Silver Buck.

Those who guided the youngster through his early years cannot possibly have dreamt of the steeplechasing heights he would scale. Apart from being by Arkle's classically-bred but useless sire Archive, there was little to recommend his dam, Mrs Samuel Booth's Choice Archlesse, whose best effort had been to win a little hurdle race at picturesque, but hardly classy Cartmel. His sire, Silver Cloud, had been quite a useful racehorse, but of suspect enthusiasm. Furthermore he wore blinkers, swallowed his tongue, needed top-of-the-ground and wanted things his own way, none of which traits particularly attracted breeders of prospective jumpers. He hadn't proved very successful in siring flat horses, which was why in 1972, he came to be based at veterinary surgeon David Clyde's Craig Stud near Mrs Booth's Co. Antrim home.

Mrs Booth sold the resulting brown gelding, not very big but beautifully made with a bright and eager head, privately to Brian Bamber of the well-known horse-dealing Ulster family, who at one point might show a man 60 or 70 hunters or young racehorses in a morning.

The youngster passed twice through the Ballsbridge Sales ring, in November as an unbroken three-year-old for 1,000 guineas and the following June, doubling his value as a supposedly broken four-year-old, for 2,000 guineas. In each case the purchaser was Jack Doyle, acting for different clients. But the first couldn't manage his new purchase and the second couldn't pay.

So Silver Buck came to Jack Doyle's Shankhill yard, managed by his son Peter, who swiftly discovered that the Sales description of 'broken' was at best an inexactitude. Breaking the newcomer proved a long and wearisome task and backing him a hazardous one. When finally he was handed on to Peter's sister-in-law, Katy, it was to school for show-jumping. She worked him on the flat and over poles and took him hunting with the Bray Harriers.

It proved an excellent education which would pay off when he came to jump steeplechasing fences. But that prospect was the last thing the Doyle family then had in their minds. The youngster's promotion to racehorse came quite by chance. He was used one morning merely to accompany a winning point-to-pointer from the stable in a spin up a bank. Far from being left behind as expected, he soon sprinted clear and in consequence rapidly found himself in transit to brother Paul Doyle's Curragh training establishment with quite a different purpose in life. Now named Silver Buck, he began his career as a prospective steeplechaser in point-to-points.

And so the disaster on that first appearance. Better things however had to come. Of his remaining four point-to-points, Silver Buck won two and was placed twice. He would have won a third had he not been impeded on the run-in by an over-zealous hunt servant. His last victory landed a substantial gamble for the Doyles.

Silver Buck then had a few weeks good grass in Tipperary before returning to the Curragh to be prepared for a bumper. As the Dickinsons were to discover later, he needed little work, and was thought to be ready enough for his first attempt in a flat race at Clonmel. But once again there was an immediate problem

in the jockey, Mr Magnier, getting on. He barely touched the saddle before being ejected with violence. After that Silver Buck wouldn't let him anywhere near him. Finally Noel O'Toole, Paul's claiming jockey who was leading the horse up, hopped on with no trouble and rode him out of the paddock. Going down to the start, Noel slid off the wrong side as the jockey vaulted on the right. This time he stayed there. Silver Buck gave no more trouble either before the race or during it: he won very easily by 8 lengths.

Irish bumper winners have always been a valuable, sought-after commodity. Within three days of victory, Silver Buck had been sold to that outsize character, gambler and entrepreneur, Barney Curley.

By July he had crossed the Irish Sea and was installed in one of the racing family Dickinson's spanking new yards at Gisburn, added to the west of the original hunter-livery yard which they rented from the Hindleys.

It seems still generally unknown that the somewhat eccentric Irishman, Mr Curley of the close-cropped head and broad-banded wide-brimmed hat had kept several horses with the Dickinsons over the years. The man who raffled his Irish mansion (a former Boyd-Rochfort home, no less) to make a dashing profit, who had several times won packets from bookmakers and on occasion fallen foul of Jockey Clubs, knew a good thing when he saw one. He knew the Dickinsons could prepare jumpers. He knew they could tell when a horse was ready.

Nothing quite like the Dickinson triumvirate had been noted till then on the British racing scene. Their rise to prominence had been steady, largely unpublicized (few of the racing press had sought them out), but it was total. There had been and are plenty of helpful husband-and-wife teams but not a family threesome all playing integral parts in a stable's success. And what a success it had been. From small beginnings with a permit and four horses for their lanky amateur son, Michael, to ride, they had grown in the last 10 years to a 32-horse public stable regularly turning out over 50 winners a season (some 35 per cent above the average) and with a string of big races under their belt. They were now highly and widely regarded. For they weren't merely potting 'sellers', but winning major races like the Arkle Challenge Trophy, the Mildmay Memorial and the Scottish Champion Hurdle. In 1976 the Horserace Writers Association had voted Tony Dickinson, known in the yard as 'The Boss-man', National Hunt Trainer of the Year.

The Horserace Writers couldn't know that the racing family Dickinson were poised to break into an even bigger time. The arrival of Silver Buck heralded the start of a period of dominance scarcely equalled in the annals of steeplechasing since Vincent O'Brien had switched to the flat.

They were quiet, unpretentious people with their feet firmly on the ground and their heads steeped in horse lore. They had grown up with horses: they had hunted, shown, show-jumped, point-to-pointed and dealt, all with conspicuous success. They understood horses through and through.

The Boss-man's instinctive feel for the make, shape and, most vitally, the action of horses made him a renowned judge. His selections may seem to a casual observer to conform to no pattern. But none were heavy or cumbersome. They tended toward the light, athletic type. They all had superb sloping shoulders.

Tony Dickinson, whose shrewd sharp eyes selected so many winners.

They used their hocks. They had that boldness of outlook without which the prettiest machine lacks motive power. 'Mrs D', as she was affectionately but respectfully called, had an encyclopaedic knowledge of feeding. She had always been a fine horsewoman, riding out every day, and thus could see, and feel, the results of her endeavours. As Monica Birtwistle she had show-jumped at national level and been a most successful point-to-point rider in those days when far fewer opportunities existed for girls. Michael, the only son of three children, was not only the stable jockey, but also contributed his passion for detail, order, and planning. Only adequately intelligent at school, he had developed an analytic brain driven forward by a restless energy. Nothing really sufficed. Under pressure he became in stable terms 'a box walker'. He had experience, and had garnered tips, methods and sayings from his spells with Frenchie Nicholson, Kevin Prendergast and Vincent O'Brien.

Michael likes to be drily self-deprecating. His manner fooled enquirers. Faced with racing correspondents pressing him for information, he would respond with a question himself. 'Do you fink ven' (he has a little difficulty with 'th') 'that the horse would be suited by Ascot?'

Pressmen, flattered by the enquiry, would ponder a good answer and forget their own question till too late.

Michael summed up his family's attitude to their job. 'We didn't try to do anything particularly well, but we did try *very* hard not to do anything spectacularly badly. We worked very hard and we *lived* for training'.

So it was a happy, confident and successful yard in which Silver Buck arrived in the summer of 1977. The Boss-man and Michael liked his make and shape; 'he's not very big but he's big enough', was their assessment. They liked his quality and

his action. What they did not like was his temperament. 'He was absolutely *terrified*', recalled Michael. 'Terrified of people getting on and pretty bad about them getting off.' He pulled very hard, propped and spooked in his work and was apt to duck out at his hurdles, particularly if in front.

For these reasons they selected for his first race a 2-mile Novice Hurdle at Carlisle. They realised from his point-to-point and bumper victories that he would be better suited by 3 miles, but they feared that at the slower pace of the longer trip, he might take off, shoot to the front, and then run out. Fortunately the pace was brisk and Michael had no difficulty in settling him. He denies that this was a schooling run, emphasising their worries that the horse might duck out, so that he was determined to keep the erratic youngster well covered up throughout the race, aiming him for the very middle of the flights of hurdles. Everything went to plan and Silver Buck finished seventh.

Part of the deal with Barney Curley had been that the Dickinsons would let him know the first time Silver Buck was fancied. They had done this before for their Irish patron. They were never asked to stop horses, just to let Mr Curley know when they were fancied. Curley would get the money on in Ireland spread among a number of bookmakers. He would do so this time, given the nod. Silver Buck had worked very well at home and the Dickinsons felt that, provided he didn't do anything silly, he would win next time. Plans were made accordingly. A 3 mile race was considered essential on not too soft ground. Not an easy combination to find in December but free-draining Catterick provided the answer. The race was for amateur riders so Thomas Tate, husband of Michael's sister Hazel, was called to the colours with explicit instructions to come up the centre of the track and not to hit the front too soon. With Yellow Fire trained by Josh Gifford dominating the market at 1–2 favourite, Silver Buck opened briefly at 12–1. But the punt was on and he quickly shortened to 5–1 as Barney Curley's wagers were recorded. Mrs D never bet, but the Boss did and very shrewdly too. One year, Michael remembered with admiration, his father had executed nine gambles and eight of them had been successful.

At Catterick Thomas Tate had only one anxious moment when the leader folded rapidly four flights from home, and Silver Buck pulled his way powerfully to the front. Yellow Fire obligingly took up the running, allowing Silver Buck to be restrained until the last. He quicked nicely but, as feared, idled as soon as he hit the front and had to be kept going to win by a length.

Michael could now resume the ride, and did so gloriously, to make the horse's hurdle victories four in a row. The last of these races, a novice handicap at Haydock in which, carrying 12 st. 7 lb., he was giving weight to everything, shows not just how good a novice he was but also how deceptive Silver Buck could be once he hit in front. The winning margin was just a length and *Chaseform*, that famously accurate publication, describes him as being 'all out'. Yet Mrs D, who recalls the race clearly because it was the first time they *knew* they had a good horse, says he won easily and Michael treasures the memory of 'one of the best rides a horse has ever given me'.

Everyone who rode him made the point that once in front he would idle and spook and drop his bit, so that his reins suddenly fell loosely.

For the Haydock race Silver Buck, who had previously run as the property of Mrs D, wore the colours of the family solicitor, Jack Mewies. But the lawyer's taste of glory was cruelly brief; his new acquisition disappointed in his last three runs. Heavy ground was blamed for a lacklustre performance at Haydock at the end of January but the ground was good for the novice championship, the Sun Alliance at Cheltenham's National Hunt Meeting. Silver Buck could not be said to have run badly to finish fourth but he hung and produced little up the hill. The family were sure he was feeling something. The vets could find nothing wrong, so after a week's rest and a sparkling piece of work he was allowed to go to Liverpool. Here it was the same story. After appearing to hold a good chance three flights out, he jumped to the right and hung all the way up the straight and actually finished lame. They never did find out what ailed him. Mrs D thought it might have been muscular, perhaps shoulder or back. Whatever it was, Mother Nature, Doctor Green Grass and doses of rare English sunshine effected a cure during our brief summer.

There were other changes at Gisburn that summer, two of which had a bearing on Silver Buck's future. The most important was that Michael had suffered appalling injuries in a fall at the Whitsun meeting at Cartmel, damaging his liver and rupturing his spleen. After a week in intensive care and a painfully slow recovery, he accepted medical advice that to continue his riding career would be suicidal.

So for the first time the family found themselves in urgent need of an outside and outstanding jockey. They needed, and their successes could command, a top-class one. They did hear that John Francome *might* have been available and *might* have been interested. But it was only racing hearsay, and so notoriously suspect. They never pursued the rumour. Michael, a long-time profound admirer of Fred Winter, said they would never have dreamt of approaching his jockey.

Their choice fell upon a 22-year-old Irishman, who had recently forced himself upon English reckoning by winning two races at the National Hunt Meeting. Tommy Carmody came from a flat race background. He had indeed been Champion Apprentice on the flat three times and ridden 158 flat winners before increasing weight forced him to switch to jumping. His arrival in the closely-knit family yard where everyone mucked in and mucked out as necessary, caused something of a stir. Mucking out, he made plain, was not something he was prepared to do. The Boss and Mrs D were amazed. Tony Dickinson, in relaying the tale to friends, would add caustically, 'It must be nice to be semi-retired at 22!'

Michael defended Carmody's stance; 'We'd never employed a top jockey; we didn't understand.' He thought Carmody 'one hell of a nice guy; he was great with the lads'. Tommy shared the flat Michael rented in the big house, the imposing but plain Gisburn Park.

The second change affecting Silver Buck was that of his ownership. Jack Mewies sold out to Mrs Christine Haggas, who would later become Mrs Feather, of Otley, West Yorks, a vivacious lady, much loved by all the Dickinsons. Her distinctive colours of black, white braces, and scarlet cap, Silver Buck would carry for the rest of his career. Mrs Haggas' marriage had just broken down. After a long period of uncertainty, it had come to a shockingly abrupt end. It was hoped that

Silver Buck would give her a new distracting interest and some much needed fun.

Tommy Carmody's introduction to Gisburn was painful. During his first week the Dickinsons planned a school over Michael's meticulously maintained fences on their own land on the other side of the road. Robert Earnshaw, Silver Buck's lad, was slightly disappointed when told to follow on over with two hurdlers half an hour later. He had been longing to watch his beloved 'Bucket's' first school over fences. When he arrived he saw the wing of the first fence smashed to the ground, and Tommy crouching under its remains looking very sorry for himself. The Boss thereupon told Robert to get up on Silver Buck and to school him. At the time Robert had only been schooling over hurdles. His experience over fences was confined to a couple of spins on board an old handicapper. The battered state of Tommy and the wing did not fill him with confidence. Silver Buck again attempted to run out. This time he darted the other way, bringing him directly at the much larger adjoining plastic fences. These, to everyone's astonishment, he jumped. But the air rang blue with imprecations till Tommy defused a distinctly tense situation by remarking that at least the horse had jumped something, after all. From that day on the Dickinsons left all Silver Buck's schooling to Robert, realizing that the pair enjoyed a mutual understanding.

Robert Earnshaw, who was to play so important a role in Silver Buck's career, was in his third season when the young horse arrived. Robert came as a 16-year-old straight from school and the pony club – just the background Dickinsons liked. 'If they've done a bit of show-jumping or eventing, learned some basic horsemanship, then you're half way there,' explained Mrs D. He was given Silver Buck to do and set about the uneasy task of winning his charge's confidence. Silver Buck bucked and kicked both in his box and out of it. He wouldn't be caught. He fought against having his feet picked out and was a nightmare to tack up. Over-zealous psychiatrists might well have described him in human term as having paranoid tendencies, verging towards juvenile delinquency. A packet of mints provided the breakthrough. He didn't dare take one from Robert but a couple left in his manger would vanish overnight. Gradually he developed a taste for them which led him to overcome his fears and accept them direct. Finally they became the key to his good behaviour. One mint and Silver Buck would stand good as gold – even for the blacksmith. Robert recalled 'it took years of patience so that I could go and brush his head, and even then I had to work quite a while to do his ears.'

After his unpleasant experience schooling, Tommy Carmody approached their first outing over fences with trepidation. It was to be at Teesside. Michael's instructions were to steer the horse to the centre of the track and to keep him covered up as long as possible so Tommy was horrified to be jumped to the front at the second. However Silver Buck behaved and jumped impeccably and won without being remotely extended.

Succeeding wins at Stratford, Wetherby and Leicester went just as smoothly and the hope, springing eternal in every trainer's heart, that they just *might* have a very good horse, could no longer be suppressed.

Particularly impressive had been his Wetherby win when he beat the later Gold Cup winner, Alverton, 6 lengths in the Embassy Chase qualifier.

The final at Haydock in January became his objective but jumping's old enemy the weather intervened. Torrential rain followed bizarrely by severe frosts caused the race to be postponed till March.

The freeze dragged on, and the Dickinsons grew desperate to find a prep race for Silver Buck who had become very idle at home. Finally and with reluctance, he was despatched on the long trek south to Windsor, just nine days before the postponed Embassy Final. It looked a formality and Silver Buck was cruising when he was brought down by the falling Purdo three fences from home. He was unscathed but it was not the happiest preparation, and it could only be hoped that he had done a searching enough gallop for his big-race encounter with the dual Champion Hurdler, Night Nurse.

The contest was keenly anticipated and the principals let nobody down. Night Nurse, as was his wont, went straight to the front but, as planned, Silver Buck challenged him at the start of the backstraight second time and from that moment the battle was on. Michael reflected years afterwards, 'They called it "The race of the century". It probably was. They say that about big flat races – and that's if two horses are battling it out over the last 2 or 3 *furlongs*! But this was over 1½ *miles*. It was over eight fences. They were together all the way. It was tremendous.' So they strove. Every time Silver Buck jumped to the front, he stopped, allowing Night Nurse and Ian Watkinson to get back on terms. Neither horse would give way and neither deserved to be beaten. At long last Silver Buck wore his rival down and finally won by 2½ lengths. Michael confessed afterwards to being more shattered than the horse.

Eleven days later Silver Buck turned out again for the Sun Alliance Chase at the National Hunt Meeting and got beaten. The ground was forecast good at midday on Sunday but torrential rain over the next 48 hours changed it to heavy and Silver Buck could not handle it. He weakened up the hill to finish a tired third behind the mud-loving Master Smudge. In retrospect the Dickinsons believed the race had come too soon after his titanic efforts at Haydock. He never was a robust horse.

The Boss used to say that the big thing about training was to keep a horse so that he loved his racing. Abiding by this dictum, he roughed Silver Buck off and turned him out to grass.

Earlier that year the Dickinsons had won their first King George VI Chase at Kempton with Gay Spartan. Unfortunately the horse tweaked a suspensory on his first outing in the autumn of 1979. But here was Silver Buck stepping forward to wait in the wings in the hope of keeping the famous trophy at Gisburn. Tommy Carmody had predicted after the Embassy Final 'Silver Buck will win the King George'. He now said, 'If both horses had gone to post, I'd have chosen "Bucket" anyway'.

In the autumn of 1979 the Dickinsons pulled up their red rose roots (the parents were Lancashire-born, though Gisburn lay just in Yorks) and the family crossed the Pennines to their handsome, purpose-built complex Poplar House, not far from Leeds in white rose country.

It lies on flattish ground below the bluff on which stands Harewood House. The river bounding their property follows the high ground. On the Dickinsons' side is a huge river meadow, 'useful for cantering the horses about', said Tony

Dickinson. Closer to the stable block and the neat new red-brick house are the wide-railed circles of the artificial gallops. The low land lacks trees, but the house is surrounded by a brilliant garden. Mrs D somehow found time to be a skilled and ardent gardener. As Henry Cecil has shown, training and gardening grow together. Both need an understanding of nature. The surrounding lanes are reasonably quiet up gentle slopes through a small village. The entrance, spanking new, is instantly impressive and all the facilities were greatly superior to those of Gisburn, where training even 35 horses had felt cramped.

Silver Buck's 1979–80 campaign was forged round the twin objectives of the King George and the Gold Cup. He had two little races within a week at the beginning of November, both of which he won comfortably, before resuming hostilities with Night Nurse in the Edward Hamner Memorial at Haydock. Border Incident, then in his prime, was the third member of this select field. All three were there with a chance at the second last. Here Border Incident fell, so once again it was left to Night Nurse and Silver Buck to fight it out. Once again Silver Buck proved just stronger than the former Champion Hurdler. He inched ahead on the run-in and won by one and a half lengths. Years later Michael declared 'Haydock in November was a good track and a good time for Silver Buck'. He was to win this race an amazing four years in a row.

His preparation for the King George met with a set-back when no one ventured

Silver Buck and Tommy Carmody (riding as short as a flat race jockey) come in at Kempton after winning their 1974 King George. Often criticised for the shortness of his leathers, Carmody stuck to his style and has, since his return, been thrice champion jockey in Ireland.

to take him on for his preliminary race at Nottingham, thus giving him an unwanted walk-over. There was nearly another set-back when Tommy Carmody, who had arranged a lift down south to Kempton with fellow Irishmen Jonjo O'Neill and Ron Barry, waited anxiously on the North side of the Knutsford Service Station on the M6 while his compatriots fumed impatiently on the South Side. As Jonjo said ruefully later, 'We should have left the beggar behind'. They should indeed. Jonjo on Jack of Trumps and Ron on Border Incident finished second and third respectively but neither could get in a blow at Silver Buck who thus easily won his first and the Dickinsons' second King George.

The rest of the season went much less smoothly and ended in a row.

The Dickinsons were troubled to hear that their star's blood count was low before his Gold Cup 'prep' race at Hereford. But, taking their vet's advice, they ran him none the less. Michael explained 'So many of our horses in the past had poor blood counts but ran well, that we sometimes wondered why we had them tested at all!'

But Silver Buck was clearly trying to confirm the clinical verdict at humble Hereford. He ran and jumped moderately and had not Portway Nick obligingly made a nonsense of the last, he might not have scrambled home by an undignified ½ length.

Over at Newbury a gloomy and anxious day for Harewood was compounded when their rising star Wayward Lad got beaten. Even worse Silver Buck also appeared to be troubled by some back problem. None of the family was happy with his final preparation.

Apparently these worries had not been communicated either to Christine Feather or to Tommy Carmody. Both were looking forward excitedly, keenly to the Gold Cup. They were both thus stupefied when, on arriving at the course on the morning of the race, they found that their horse had been withdrawn and was actually on his way home. Reports of rain and inevitable heavy ground had proved the final straws. Christine Feather for once in her racing life was furious with the Dickinsons and Tommy was close to tears. Michael sympathized with these reactions but stoutly maintained that the decision was in the horse's best interests. He agrees that it was wrong that they hadn't been able to let Christine know.

'But she was out partying somewhere in Cheltenham or near it. The Boss-man and I spent nearly an hour on the telephone ringing various places. We simply couldn't contact her. Yes, we did feel bad. Rightly. But I'm sure those were the only cross words Christine Feather – a marvellous owner – ever had with us.'

In the autumn of 1980 Michael took over the licence from his father, as had always been the plan. Tommy Carmody continued as stable-jockey but pressing behind him there was now a quintet of young, home-produced claiming riders anxious to get on. In the previous season Chris Bell, Graham Bradley, Robert Earnshaw, Chris Pimlott and Kevin Whyte had ridden no less than 50 winners between them and they were all hungry for more rides.

Silver Buck's autumn campaign, much as before, proceeded smoothly enough. He was particularly impressive winning Haydock's Edward Hamner for the second year running, bearing out Michael's assertion that the course and the time of year particularly suited him.

He did get beaten at Catterick but the concession of 34 lb. to Sunset Christo, the winner of five consecutive races that season including the Greenall Whitley and then third in the 1982 Gold Cup, proved in Michael's opinion, 'the sort of task which even defeated Arkle when he got beaten by Stalbridge Colonist. I'm not saying "Bucket" was the equal of Arkle. Nothing is. But it was a marvellous performance.' His 1-length defeat lost Silver Buck none of his innumerable fans.

The King George signalled another clash with his great rival, Night Nurse. The tearaway Irish mare Anaglog's Daughter was certain to add zest to the mixture. Expectedly the mare set a ferocious pace and was at one stage a fence ahead. This created tactical problems for Tommy who dared not let so classy a pace-setter go beyond recall and so gave chase fully a mile from home. He reached her four fences out but the mare ran pluckily on. At the next, Night Nurse appeared on the scene but, asked too mighty a question by Alan Brown, he ploughed through the fence and was lucky to stay on his feet. Gamely Night Nurse renewed his challenge but another, even worse error at the last shed his rider leaving Silver Buck, idling in front as usual but in no danger of losing his King George double.

The band of dual King George winners till then was very select comprising only Hallowe'en, Mandarin, Pendil and Captain Christy. Later another Dickinson horse was to join the élite group of dual winners and then surpass them.

Michael was hugely relieved to have won so prestigious a race in his first season. The Dickinsons, perhaps because of their extraordinary record in the Kempton race, have always rated it as one of the twin pearls of the entire British and Irish seasons. Not every N.H. trainer would set it quite as high as the Gold Cup. With Michael it rated equally.

He said years afterwards, his face again reflecting those earlier anxieties. 'It was quite something taking over from the Boss-man. People would say I wasn't as good as my father. And so after Kempton I could say to myself, "Well if I never win any other good race, at least I've won a King George".'

The Gold Cup was to have no such happy ending. The weather was kinder than in recent years and the going was no worse than soft; but the majority of racegoers doubted whether Silver Buck would stay the extra quarter mile up Cheltenham's testing hill.

They felt their point made when he hit the second last and weakened steadily thereon to finish third, beaten 1½ lengths and 10 lengths by Little Owl and his old rival Night Nurse. '3¼ miles round Cheltenham is far tougher than 3 miles round Haydock,' commented the experts. Michael said afterwards 'I was probably the only man on the course not to believe that Silver Buck wouldn't stay.'

Already worried by the below-par runs of Wayward Lad and Badsworth Boy, 'I was afraid,' he said, 'that all the horses might be afflicted by some mild bug.' Silver Buck's performance (Tommy described graphically the stables' runners as having 'cut out' suddenly when apparently cruising) bore this out. Confirmation was provided when Silver Buck was found on his return to Harewood with blood in his nostrils from a broken blood vessel.

At this juncture Tommy Carmody decided to return to Ireland. One senses that this decision was not entirely regretted by the Dickinson parents. He was just not their style. They perpetually lamented his short stirrups and although Mrs D was unwilling to be drawn on the subject, she did say that she thought him 'better over hurdles than fences' and that 'the horses jumped much better for Robert Earnshaw.' Few would disagree. Michael's own careful view was that 'Tommy did ride very short. But he was a very good jockey.' Left unsaid was any reference to Carmody's horsemanship. But, back in his homeland, his career swiftly bloomed. In 1988 he was champion jockey for the third time.

Robert was just one of the gaggle of five fledgling jockeys at Harewood and Michael announced that he would henceforth rely on them although he might engage John Francome or another available top jockey for important races. A later champion trainer, Nicky Henderson, made the same type of announcement in the summer of 1988 when stating that he would no longer be retaining the remarkable Steve Smith Eccles, but would be sharing the races out generally among his up-and-coming young riders, calling in a top jockey when the occasion demanded.

Michael's decision flung up into public prominence two young men who between them rode all Silver Buck's work at home and had been largely responsible for his transformation from terrified lunatic to the mighty mature racehorse he had become. Quiet, diffident Robert Earnshaw had started as a lad; bright and bouncy Kevin Whyte, known as 'Sooty', had crossed from a tiny hamlet in Co. Meath Ireland as a claimer. Both idolized 'Bucket' and neither had dared hope they might get to ride him in public. For Kevin the opportunity was confined to the small condition races that Michael used to prime his best horses without imposing too much strain. He rode him three times, all at Market Rasen. Each time Silver Buck carried 12 st. 7 lb., started favourite and won easily. Kevin did say wistfully, 'It would have been wonderful to ride him in a "proper" race.' But he wasn't really repining. 'It was a privilege to ride him; he was one brilliant racehorse. I used to get so mad that he never got the recognition he deserved until he won the Gold Cup. Think of the races he'd won up till then.'

Both Bucket and Wayward Lad had their fervent fans at Harewood. Rivalry split the camp. In America in 1988, witty Kevin Whyte and the quietly responsible Brian 'Beano' Powell, the Head Lad, were arguing just as furiously in Michael's office in one of his large cool barns at the Fair Hill Training Center on the borders of Maryland, Delaware and Pennsylvania.

They were two of the eight lads and stable girls who had not lost faith in Michael Dickinson after his year as private trainer to Robert Sangster had ended in tears. Michael needed to prove he could train flat-race horses. After his much publicised rupture with the Isle of Man based pools heir, he felt he had no future in Britain. He chose the USA and the new, highly competitive and initially almost friendless world of American East Coast racing. His old staff in these very different conditions – racing on dirt, training on drugs, huge prize money, a shared training complex – came with him to help him. They were rather enjoying themselves. 'Feels like England,' remarked Tony Dickinson on a visit. And Michael's first two seasons, starting with a handful of horses, proved most successful from his first runner onwards – a stakes winner. His string soon expanded from eight to thirty.

In the Silver Buck days the departure of Tommy was a chance for Robert

Earnshaw to taste such stuff that dreams are made on. Not that things started on quite such a lofty plane. For their initial outing at Wincanton, Robert was afflicted by all the normal anxieties and apprehensions – and flu. 'I am plagued with flu', he lamented. Perhaps Silver Buck felt he owed his devoted henchman a favour. At any rate, he took a good hold, soon jumped his way to the front and won comfortably.

Their next outing at Chepstow had no such happy outcome. Silver Buck was never going and was literally out on his feet when he subsided at the 15th. Plainly he was not right but exactly what ailed him was obscure. When he reappeared at his favourite Haydock, John Francome was in the saddle and although his style of winning did not impress everyone, there was nothing wrong with the form of giving Sunset Christo 13 lb. and a 1½-length beating, with the blundering Night Nurse, favourite at 11–8, 30 lengths away third. John Francome remarked 'He's a super horse till he hits the front. Then he wants 10 men on him!'

The King George was frozen off, and had it not been Silver Buck could not have run for he was found crippled lame in his box with a damaged hind foot on the morning of the race. There he was confined for a month having treatment night and morning from the skilled George Foster who fulfilled a special role created by the Dickinsons as the stable's medical officer in charge of Harewood's walking wounded and of any horse requiring veterinary care. It became a

Silver Buck ridden by Robert Earnshsaw jumps the last to win the 1982 Cheltenham Gold Cup from stable companion, Bregawn (Graham Bradley). Earnshaw reported that giving 'Bucket' a kick at the elbow was 'like waking a sleeping giant'.

desperate race against the clock now to get 'Bucket' fit for another attempt on the Gold Cup.

In spite of the hold-up, the Dickinsons became very hopeful. They had always known their horse didn't need a lot of work: the enforced rest might, they thought, even prove beneficial. His blood count was especially good and his last two pieces of work positively sparkled. The betting public did not share this confidence, particularly after 13 hours of non-stop rain put the meeting in jeopardy and rendered heavy going again inevitable. Night Nurse, Royal Bond and Venture to Cognac were all preferred in the market. But the Dickinsons had been much cheered by the storming success of their Rathgorman in the Two Mile Champion Chase. He had gone through the ground all right and Silver Buck had worked the better over a mile in their last gallop.

Robert Earnshaw was by no means confident he would get the Gold Cup ride on Silver Buck. If he rode in the race at all it would more probably, he thought, be Bregawn. However a week before the race, Michael told him, 'You'll be riding Silver Buck,' and so began the most exciting and nerve-racking week in his life. Christine Feather was in a similar state and on the day of the race, overstrained by the lengthy preliminaries, she rejected the proffered hospitality of a private box and struggled with Mrs D into the cramped, inadequate stand reserved for owners

Silver Buck and Robert Earnshaw return triumphant after their 1982 Gold Cup victory, as photographer Ed Byrne scuttles out of the way – the snapper snapped.

and trainers. Here they watched in stoical silence, gulping as Silver Buck nodded on landing three out. Slightly anxious at this point, Robert gave him a kick. He exclaimed later, 'It was like waking a sleeping giant!' Suddenly 'Bucket' was cruising in front of his sweating, striving pursuers. As this glorious truth became clear in the owners' stand, Mrs D could contain herself no longer; 'We're going to *win*!' she cried with a triumphant swing of her handbag which caught Mrs Feather a resounding blow in the stomach. As the dark brown horse touched safely down over the last, she completed a right and left with the whirling handbag before, shrieking her head off, she hurtled joyously off the stand to greet him. Bregawn was well in pursuit now and by the post was only 2 lengths behind but the family knew that Silver Buck, once in front would do just as much – if no more – than was necessary.

'He'd never win going away' reflected Michael, 'and because of this people never believed how good he really was.'

The triumphant return to the winner's enclosure with first and second was exceptionally sweet. Here at last was proof incontrovertible to the doubting Thomases of the press that Silver Buck *did* stay 3¼ miles, *at* Cheltenham *and* on bottomless ground. More mixed feelings must have been harboured by the watching Tommy Carmody, who yet was sportingly among the very first to come forward to congratulate Christine Feather.

Like his father, Michael was not one to overdo trips to the well. A weekend visitor to Harewood would have found yesterday's heroes relaxing together in a small paddock behind the yard. Neither was ridden again that season. They were gradually roughed off for the summer.

Silver Buck came up the following autumn apparently as well as ever but he was now 10 years old and younger pretenders were snapping at his heels. They did not come from rival stables, but from his own. His preparation for the King George went as smoothly as anyone could wish, culminating in a splendid victory over Burrough Hill Lad, receiving 21 lb., in what had come to be his race, the Edward Hamner at Haydock.

For the King George, however, he was joined by Wayward Lad for whom John Francome had been engaged. Stable opinion as to their two stars' merits, glowing for years now flared fiercely between the opposing parties.

Michael, Robert and Kevin remained faithful to Silver Buck. Head Lad 'Beano' Powell was 'always a Wayward fan' but ended up backing both.

He explained in America in the summer of 1988 with a little embarrassment under ribbing from Kevin, 'Well, I'd backed Wayward Lad ante-post, of course, much earlier. So I could have a free bet on "Bucket" and win whichever one did.' Even then he sounded reluctant to admit that business acumen had momentarily overcome singleminded loyalty.

After a thrilling race in which Wayward Lad, under a dream ride from John Francome, had just prevailed over Fifty Dollars More and Silver Buck, Powell generously maintained that had Francome ridden Silver Buck, he would have won. Michael disagreed. He felt sure that the older Silver Buck had not been quite at his best. In fact a throat infection was later diagnosed for which he was sent to Geoff Lane at Bristol for treatment. This proved successful and soon he was back

on the Gold Cup trail. It was the year of 'The Famous Five' and he was to be accompanied to Cheltenham not only by Wayward Lad (Jonjo O'Neill) and Bregawn (Graham Bradley) but also by Ashley House (Mr Dermot Browne) and Captain John (David Goulding). Media attention was unprecedented and the young trainer seemed likely to waste away from worry. The race was a triumph for Harewood, whose five contenders filled the first five places of the eleven runners. In instant recognition of this unique conquest, Captain Miles Gosling, Cheltenham's Chairman, waved all five into the railed-off winning enclosure instead of leaving out the fifth. This quick decision, honouring a feat which will, we are convinced, never be equalled, seemed to many whooping, ecstatic Dickinson fans that day to be typical of the best of steeplechasing.

Silver Buck, who was in touch at the top of the hill, gradually weakened as his stable companions swept ahead down the slope. He finished a distant fourth behind Bregawn who won by 5 lengths and 1½ lengths from Captain John and Wayward Lad.

Mrs Feather's horse's eclipse by his three stable-mates made no difference whatsoever to the generous, warmhearted and effervescent Christine. She tore into the winner's enclosure and kissed Michael warmly on both cheeks. Much touched by her impulsive sportingness Michael remarked wryly 'Couldn't imagine the Wildensteins doing that to Henry Cecil if one of theirs had been beaten by three stable companions!'

Michael watched the race on the television set in the weighing room with almost the same mounting disbelief as the crowd outside. 'My God! They're all Dickinsons!' we bellowed as the 'Famous Five' raced victoriously down the hill. Inside the weighing room, Michael shouted with increasing urgency a general's encouragement to his army: 'Come on, my lot!'

By 1983–84 Silver Buck's fires were burning a little lower but they were carefully maintained. Shrewdly placed, he won five of his eight races. He won his first two well enough, but defeat at Chepstow by Observe (on whom John Francome earned a £75 fine for over-zealous use of the whip) caused him to be re-routed away from the King George. This, it was felt, could be safely left to Wayward Lad. Silver Buck went instead for a handicap at Cheltenham, which he won impressively, but gloom descended when he ran very moderately behind Burrough Hill Lad in Sandown's Gainsborough Chase. It turned out that he was suffering from a virus. Evidently he still hadn't recovered when he turned in another disappointing performance at his favourite Haydock a month later. This defeat prompted Michael to abandon notions of Cheltenham and the Press to ask Mrs Feather if plans to retire her horse were imminent. She retorted roundly 'When it's time to retire Silver Buck, I'm sure he'll be the one to tell Michael.'

All clouds were gloriously swept away by a fine victory at Wetherby on St. George's Day. *Chaseform*'s comments 'looked well, jumped well, made all, quickened 13th, driven out flat,' say it all.

It was to be his epitaph. That spring Michael relinquished his jumping licence to prepare for his flat career and his mother took over. The following autumn Silver Buck went out for a normal morning's exercise ridden by Graham Bradley. It was drizzling and 'Brad' decided to ride back for a waterproof. As he was

jumping back on the horse who all his life had so feared and disliked mounting and dismounting, Silver Buck took off across the tarmac and galloped flat out across the yard. He was blindly hurtling straight at the high brick wall. He tried desperately to stop, slewed round on the concrete, crashing sideways into the wall with sickening force and fractured both his pelvis and several ribs. He was coaxed back into his box and shored up with bales of hay. But before the vet could reach him he died from an internal haemorrhage.

The Achilles heel in the make-up of the elegant little brown horse lay not in his physique but in his nerves. They had hindered early attempts to break him, sabotaged his first attempt on a racecourse and bedevilled his early days at Gisburn. Thanks to the devoted care and patience he received from the Dickinsons and their staff, particularly Robert Earnshaw, he managed to overcome them and to enjoy one of the most brilliant postwar chasing careers. But it was this one enduring weakness which so brutally killed Silver Buck that miserable wet September morning.

It seemed a dreadful portent for the start of Mrs Monica Dickinson's career as the third licence-holding trainer of this remarkable family.

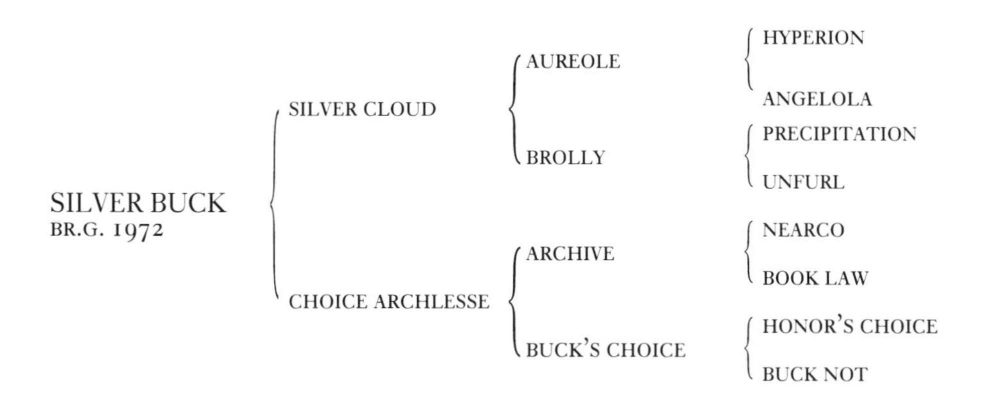

DATE	COURSE	RACE	DISTANCE	VALUE	WEIGHT	JOCKEY	PRICE	PLACE
Season 1977–78								
Nov 14	Carlisle	Ambleside Novices Hurdle (Div 1)	2m 330y	£306	11.3	M. Dickinson	12/1	unpl
Dec 21	Catterick	Brompton Amateur Riders Novices Hurdle (Div 2)	3m 300y	£463	11.9	Mr T. Tate	5/1	won
Dec 31	Worcester	Philip Cornes Novices Hurdle Qualifier	3m	£1194	11.5	M. Dickinson	6/1	won
Jan 9	Leicester	Nomad Novices Hurdle (Div 2)	3m	£600	11.12	M. Dickinson	7/4	won
Jan 21	Haydock Park	Bristol Novices H'cp Hurdle	2m 4f	£722	12.7	M. Dickinson	5/1	won
Jan 31	Chepstow	Persian War Novices Hurdle	2m 4f	£3226	11.10	M. Dickinson	9/4	4th
Mar 14	Cheltenham	Sun Alliance Novices Hurdle	2m 4f	£10317	11.8	M. Dickinson	14/1	4th
Mar 31	Liverpool	Maghull Novices Hurdle	2m 5f 110y	£1934	11.8	M. Dickinson	2/1j.f.	unpl
Season 1978–79								
Oct 31	Teesside Park	Greystoke Novices Chase	3m 31y	£567	11.3	T. Carmody	4/9f	won
Nov 16	Stratford	Adam Lindsay Gordon Novices Chase	2m 6f	£985	11.3	T. Carmody	30/100f	won
Nov 25	Wetherby	Embassy Premier Chase Qualifier	2m 4f 100y	£1449	11.7	T. Carmody	13/8f	won
Dec 18	Leicester	Christmas Tree Novices Chase (Div 1)	2m 4f	£979	12.3	T. Carmody	4/9f	won
Feb 21	Windsor	Fairlawne Chase	3m	£1865	11.8	T. Carmody	4/7f	bt dn
Mar 2	Haydock Park	Embassy Premier Chase Final	2m 4f	£10996	11.7	T. Carmody	5/2	won
Mar 13	Cheltenham	Sun Alliance Chase	3m	£12842	11.4	T. Carmody	13/8f	3rd

Season 1979–80								
Nov 1	Wincanton	Terry Biddlecombe Challenge Trophy Chase	2m 5f	£2071	11.8	T. Carmody	4/9f	won
Nov 6	Hereford	Dewchurch Chase	2m 4f	£1092	12.0	T. Carmody	2/11f	won
Nov 28	Haydock Park	Edward Hamner Memorial H'cp Chase	3m	£6082	11.6	T. Carmody	20/21f	won
Dec 10	Nottingham	Last Chance Chase	2m 6f	£2308	11.10	T. Carmody		wo
Dec 26	Kempton Park	King George VI Chase	3m	£17057	11.10	T. Carmody	3/1	won
Feb 9	Newbury	Compton Chase	3m	£3674	11.5	T. Carmody	8/13f	won
Mar 1	Hereford	Sean Graham Chase	3m 1f	£2022	12.7	T. Carmody	1/6f	won
Season 1980–81								
Nov 1	Worcester	ATV Today Chase	2m 4f	£1761	11.12	T. Carmody	4/7f	won
Nov 17	Folkestone	Whitelaw Gold Cup Chase	2m 4f	£2064	11.12	T. Carmody	2/7f	won
Nov 26	Haydock Park	Edward Hamner Memorial H'cp Chase	3m	£6467	12.0	T. Carmody	8/15f	won
Dec 13	Catterick	WL & Hector Christie Memorial Trophy H'cp Chase	3m 1f 80y	£2860	12.7	T. Carmody	2/5f	2nd
Dec 26	Kempton Park	King George VI Chase	3m	£18359	11.10	T. Carmody	9/4f	won
Feb 26	Wincanton	Jim Ford Challenge Cup Chase	3m 1f	£2601	11.11	T. Carmody	1/4f	won
Mar 19	Cheltenham	Tote Cheltenham Gold Cup Chase	3m 2f	£44259	12.0	T. Carmody	7/2f	3rd
Season 1981–82								
Oct 29	Wincanton	Terry Biddlecombe Challenge Trophy Chase	2m 5f	£2522	11.8	R. Earnshaw	1/6f	won
Nov 7	Chepstow	Rehearsal Chase	3m	£2716	11.8	R. Earnshaw	1/3f	fell
Nov 25	Haydock Park	Edward Hamner Memorial H'cp Chase	3m	£7166	11.12	J. Francome	5/2	won
Mar 6	Market Rasen	'Cox Moore' (Sweaters) H'cp Chase	3m	£2552	12.7	K. Whyte	5/6f	won

Mar 18	Cheltenham	Tote Cheltenham Gold Cup Chase	3m 2f	£48386	12.0	R. Earnshaw	8/1	won
Season 1982–83								
Oct 28	Wincanton	Terry Biddlecombe Challenge Trophy Chase	2m 5f	£3174	11.8	R. Earnshaw	1/6f	won
Nov 11	Stratford	Hawkes Bay Trophy Chase	2m 6f	£2706	11.12	R. Earnshaw	2/15f	won
Nov 24	Haydock Park	Edward Hamner Memorial H'cp Chase	3m	£7137	12.0	R. Earnshaw	8/11f	won
Dec 27	Kempton Park	King George VI Chase	3m	£24810	11.10	R. Earnshaw	evens f	3rd
Mar 5	Market Rasen	Budmo Shipping H'cp Chase	3m	£2107	12.7	K. Whyte	no s.p.	won
Mar 17	Cheltenham	Tote Cheltenham Gold Cup Chase	3m 2f	£45260	12.0	R. Earnshaw	5/1	4th
Season 1983–84								
Nov 14	Folkestone	Whitelaw Gold Cup Chase	2m 4f	£1192	11.12	R. Earnshaw	1/7f	won
Nov 26	Market Rasen	Limes H'cp Chase	3m	£2541	12.6	K. Whyte	no s.p.	won
Dec 3	Chepstow	Rehearsal Chase	3m	£3746	11.0	R. Earnshaw	4/7f	2nd
Jan 2	Cheltenham	Courage Cup H'cp Chase Qualifier	3m 1f	£4019	11.2	R. Earnshaw	2/5f	won
Jan 12	Wincanton	John Bull Chase	2m 5f	£2517	12.0	R. Earnshaw	4/11f	won
Feb 4	Sandown Park	Gainsborough H'cp Chase	3m 118y	£9438	11.5	R. Earnshaw	5/4f	unpl
Mar 3	Haydock Park	Greenall Whitley Breweries H'cp Chase	3m	£11343	10.12	R. Earnshaw	100/30	unpl
Apr 23	Wetherby	HS Commercial Spares H'cp Chase	3m 100y	£7647	11.8	R. Earnshaw	11/8f	won

Career Record
Ran – Hurdles 8; won 4, £2,979. Chases 40; won 30 (including 1 walk over), £174,200
Total – ran 48; won 34, £177,179

FIFTEEN

Wayward Lad

THATCHER WINS AGAIN. BJORN BORG RETIRES FROM TENNIS AND CECIL PARKINSON RESIGNS FROM CABINET OVER HIS LOVE CHILD. RUSSIA SHOOTS DOWN KOREAN 747. U.S. INVADES GRENADA. POLICE BATTLE WITH MINERS. IRA BOMB TORY CONFERENCE HOTEL AT BRIGHTON. MRS GANDHI ASSASSINATED. REAGAN WINS USA; GORBACHEV THE USSR.

The bald facts detailing lot 600 in Doncaster's white and red catalogue for Thursday 21 May were known to every keen follower of steeplechasing on both sides of the Atlantic. So too was the acrimony and strife which lay behind the announcement that Wayward Lad, one of the best British steeplechasers since Arkle, was being forcibly sold to dissolve a contentious partnership. Misunderstandings and conflicting ambitions had led to this dramatic curtain-down on the 12-year-old bay gelding's brilliant and, till then, little troubled career.

Great horses near well-earned retirement are simply not dispatched to the common market place, where their future will lie in the hands not of tested friends but of the highest bidder. But, in the end, there was no other way in which Wayward Lad's future could be decided but by a duel in the ring. The opposing parties owning this particularly handsome horse would have to return him to the same sales ring in which, in quite unpublicized circumstances, he had been sold as an unbroken three-year-old, nine busy and illustrious years before.

'Whatever his fate', declared *Timeform's 'Chasers and Hurdlers' 1985–86* a year before his final season, 'Wayward Lad has already earned an honourable place in steeplechasing's Hall of Fame'.

Wayward Lad had won 28 races from 55 starts in the hands of the training family Dickinson. His winnings of £218,732 had been exceeded in British steeplechasing history up till then only by those of Dawn Run. His intended swansong was a tremendous second victory in the Whitbread Gold Label Cup at Liverpool's Grand National meeting. Mrs Monica Dickinson, euphoric in triumph then announced that retirement plans had already been discussed for the great horse. 'At 12', she said roundly and soundly, 'he can only go downhill'. She understood that his owners would give him a happy retirement with her family who had cared for Wayward Lad all his working life. This much Monica Dickinson, much moved by her horse's final victory, announced to press and television in Liverpool's cavernous unsaddling enclosure which resembles a small Victorian railway station. A caring future seemed assured for the elderly star.

Then the storm broke. One of the horse's owners, Mr Les Abbott, pronounced himself most unhappy. He had not, he protested, been consulted. Wayward Lad, he declared, could very well run in point-to-points and hunter-'chases. Later, the Dickinsons heard that Mr Abbott, in conjunction with a former trainer based in Blackpool, planned to campaign the horse, who was rising 13, in further proper steeplechases, too.

Fruitless discussions ensued. Reports appeared with growing frequency in the press. The racing public in general and real horse-lovers in particular took Wayward Lad's welfare to their hearts. Having no financial interest in the horse's future earnings they all roundly declared the horse should, of course, be retired immediately. Then, as it became clear that the horse's fate depended on which of the partners might secure him at the Sales, an extraordinary number of people began to send money to the Dickinsons in the hope that their funds might help them to buy the horse safely back.

Mr Les Abbott had entered Wayward Lad's life in the following way. The horse's three original partners since his sale at Doncaster as a three-year-old had been Mrs Shirley Thewlis of 43, Lamb Hall Road, Longwood near Huddersfield, John Garner and David Ingham. The two gentlemen had subsequently sold out their shares, John Garner to Mrs Thewlis and David Ingham to Les Abbott who was a friend of Mr Garner's. This co-ownership had been handsomely rewarded by the thrills of Wayward Lad's record three victories in Kempton's King George VI Chase. The first two in 1982 and 1983 followed stable companion Silver Buck's double in 1979 and 1980, and the stable's domination of the race had been launched by Tony Dickinson's first King George triumph with Gay Spartan in 1978.

In sharing between them a quarter of a million pounds of prize money they had seen their scintillating jumper unplaced only five times in 55 races. The horse owed them nothing. They owed the great horse a lot and Shirley Thewlis fully understood this. But to buy a horse simply to retire him without hope of future winnings or capital profit on resale was the sort of philanthropic gesture very rare among hard-nosed racing folk.

Now this happy association was to be disbanded under fiercely critical public

scrutiny. The arguments which flickered into flame after Liverpool and flared up to Doncaster had all become wretchedly public, too.

A happy outcome of the sale now seemed precarious. Tony and Monica Dickinson and Shirley Thewlis grew increasingly agitated as the date rushed closer. They feared their beloved horse might fetch an impossible price, and that however much they wished to buy him his happy retirement, funds would probably not permit.

Point-to-pointing was enjoying a booming prosperity. Rich young city men seeking weekend diversion were paying hitherto undreamt-of sums for horses to race round temporary tracks on muddy Saturday afternoons for £100, a silver cup and a bottle of champagne. Top-class elderly chasers were high on their shopping list. For Wayward Lad a figure of 50–60,000 guineas was possible, a terrible price to pay.

Help for the Dickinson cause surged in from many quarters. Shirley Thewlis has always made it plain that she wished to give Wayward Lad to the Dickinsons as a present. She would waive her share of the proceeds – a grand gesture from one who was, as 'Mrs D' pointed out, by no means a wealthy woman.

Money and offers of it poured in from all over the country. One astonishingly generous donor who insisted on anonymity, put down £30,000 with full authority to use all or as much as was necessary. Mrs Miles Valentine, born in 1904 and resident in the centre of American foxhunting country, near Unionville, Pennyslvania, read the grim news of Wayward Lad's impending sale in *The Sporting Life*. This long-standing patron of Fred Winter, Burly Cox, Gillian O'Brien and others, whose colours of pink and cherry hearts had graced British, American and Irish steeplechasing for forty years, telephoned her grand-daughter, Joy Carrier, down the road. Joy's husband Rusty hailed from Middleburg, Virginia, another great horse centre. His grandmother-in-law felt at her age unable to buy the horse. 'You do it', she told Rusty. Moving rapidly he rang Michael Dickinson. 'We'll buy him and bring him over here and you can hunt him'. Dickinson was based close by, at the Fair Hill Training Center.

Rusty modestly remarked afterwards, 'I just regard myself as Chairman of Wayward Lad Inc.' He relayed his plans back to Harewood. He would provide money as necessary, a flight, a home at his lovely Unionville farm set among rolling downlands and woods of beech and oak. Here Wayward Lad would be properly looked after. He would not be treated as a spectacle but, as befitted so distinguished a horse, he could enjoy an occasional day's hunting with the local Cheshire Hounds.

So the stage was set. Wayward Lad had entered the packed sales ring to a burst of applause on the last day of the Doncaster Bloodstock Silver Jubilee May Sales.

The crowds were so dense that a way had to be cleared for him and the Dickinsons could find nowhere into which to squeeze. They had to stand in the ring itself. Beside them stood agent Jack Doyle who had been sportingly instructed by a group of clients to bid if – and only if – the Dickinsons dropped out. Knowing this, Doncaster's senior auctioneer, Harry Beeby had suggested that shrewd Jack Doyle, the old Irish Rugby International should stand close by their sides, lest there was any confusion in the battle's heat. Suave as the *maître d'hôtel* of

a very grand restaurant indeed, Harry Beeby, son of a top-class N.H. trainer, George, has always had more than a touch of the theatre about him. His shrewd mind and quick eyes miss few tricks. His command over his audience is one many an actor would envy. In all his year's selling he had never experienced anything approaching the drama engendered by the forced sale of this public hero.

Harry Beeby was not aware of the help the family had been promised or received. Knowing their desperation to retain the horse he was sorely afraid that Wayward Lad might fetch a price far beyond them. To general surprise then, Tony Dickinson boldly opened the bidding at 10,000 guineas.

The central figure now returned to this stage had been sired by the Irish St. Leger winner, Royal Highway. His dam, Loughanmore did not win, but was placed in a bumper. She came from a family long nurtured by the Lathams of Blackrath who hailed from Britain's North Country but who with Vulgan and Escart had established themselves as leading breeders of N.H. stock in the Republic of Ireland. Loughanmore was half-sister to two good winners and another unraced sister bred a couple of winners including Shirlath who won for the Dickinsons. Her dam Gallic Star won on the flat and over hurdles.

Wayward Lad was bred by Mrs A. M. D. Hutchinson and sold as a yearling for 2,500 guineas at the Ballsbridge November Sales to David Prentice of the Cottage Hill Stud in County Antrim. David Prentice stored him for 18 months and sent him across to Doncaster's May Sales as a three-year-old. There he failed to make his reserve but was bought privately for 5,250 guineas by Steve Norton acting for his original group of owners. But Norton was planning to concentrate on the flat and so he suggested that Wayward Lad should be transferred to Tony Dickinson. Meanwhile his head lad, the former jump jockey Jimmy Burke, had broken him in, 'very well indeed', according to Michael.

The Dickinsons never, as policy, ran their 'stores', all regarded as potential chasers, in three-year-old hurdle races against sharp and advanced horses off the flat. At their suggestion therefore, Wayward Lad spent the winter at Tom Corrie's Leighton Hall in Shropshire being hacked about. And again at this vital formative stage the young horse found himself in good hands which paid off throughout his career. 'Beano' Powell, the Dickinson's wise Head Lad, described him as 'a real gentleman', and Mrs D as 'an easy horse to train'.

In the spring of his four-year-old career the Dickinsons had first planned to give him a run 'to get over sore shins and that sort of thing', as Michael put it. But as he started serious work they decided against it, for a very good reason: 'we were sure he'd win first time out and so be out of novice events!'

Instead he went with a group of young horses to work 1½ miles over six flights of hurdles at Market Rasen. 'The only course apart from Kelso', Mrs D once darkly commented, 'where us poor Northerners can school our horses'. This expedition confirmed what everyone in the yard now guessed, that Wayward Lad was very useful indeed. He finished 20 lengths ahead of his companions with his head in his chest. Head Lad Brian Powell, who rode him in nearly all his work ('Though I let Robert ride him from time to time – like at Rasen'), was thrilled. 'He floated – he *oozed* class'.

Wayward Lad spent a peaceful summer on the hills near Huddersfield and

returned to Poplar House in the autumn to begin his first campaign as a racehorse proper.

Leicester on 19 November was the selected engagement. This may seem late but the Dickinsons rarely ran their horses before the end of October. Coming into steeplechasing via the hunting field and point-to-pointing, they stuck to the traditional system of resting their horses through the summer, conditioning them slowly and steadily through the autumn and running them from late October to the end of April. This patient policy produced a high proportion of horses who stayed sound and retained their form for several seasons.

The day started badly when their stable jockey Tommy Carmody was unshipped from the favourite Henlow Gamble in the seller, hurt himself, and was stood down by the doctor. Colin Tinkler came in for the fortunate spare ride. He found himself with little more than a steering job, as the always prominent Wayward Lad cruised into the lead at the last and strolled home by 6 extremely comfortable lengths. 'We all made a fortune', recalled 'Beano' Powell, chortling gleefully. 'We went in with fivers and tenners round all the small bookies in Harrogate and Leeds. We'd miss the big betting shops like Ladbrokes and Hills as they'd get wary and telephone London if they thought we'd got anything *"on"*.'

Wayward Lad was only beaten twice in seven more runs that season. In the second of these defeats he was ridden by 'Sooty' Whyte, who with his friend 'Beano' Powell, the Head Lad, followed Michael Dickinson into his American exile and were happily enjoying the American way of life plus some good winners in the summer of 1988. He and Powell were still arguing amicably about which of their two horses, Wayward Lad and Silver Buck, was really the best overall. In Wayward Lad's first season Irishman Whyte was still a claiming jockey but unable to claim his allowance because of the value of the race which was the final of the Philip Cornes Saddle of Gold novice hurdle series. Wayward Lad did not jump fluently, 'missed' the last and was beaten ¾ length, causing several newspapers to bemoan the absence of Carmody, who that day was scrambling home on a below-par Silver Buck at Hereford. The loyal Dickinsons firmly refuted these remarks and 'The Boss' to that effect dispatched a quick and indignant letter to *The Sporting Life.*

After Silver Buck's unhappy experience in 1978, the family were disinclined to submit Wayward Lad to the hurly-burly of Cheltenham's novice hurdles which, Mrs D believed, 'were too hard on a horse who'd be a chaser'. They went instead for a small race at Chepstow which provided little more than an exercise canter. The horse thus went fresh to Liverpool and wound up a highly satisfactory first season by winning the prestigious Maghull Novices Hurdle just as effortlessly. 'Led on bit flat, eased close home', reported *Chaseform*. Behind him in sixth place came another future star; the slightly backward Burrough Hill Lad.

Wayward Lad's first season's chasing ran less smoothly. Though on occasions he could jump spectacularly well, he often made overbold mistakes, unseating Tommy at Haydock and blundering his chance away both at Doncaster and in the 3 mile Novices Championship, the Sun Alliance Chase at the National Hunt Festival. These defeats prompted David Nicholson to inform Michael: 'your horse doesn't stay 3 miles'. 'The Duke's' view was quite often repeated, never

failing to infuriate Michael. Three years after he gave up training jumpers Dickinson still felt tetchy about 'The Duke's' bold opinions. He surmised that Nicholson might possibly have been jealous of his successes. 'You know', recalled Michael 'on my last day's jumping at Stratford, the Duke came up and said to me, "everyone else says they're sorry you're giving up jumping. Well *I'm* glad!" And from that moment', says Michael, 'we at last became friendly'.

In between Wayward Lad's disappointments he had scored a devastating victory at Ayr in the West of Scotland Pattern Novices Chase. The opposition was moderate, but he could not have won more impressively, jumping impeccably, cruising into the lead three out and quickening in the style of a really high-class horse. Michael watched on television from Doncaster racecourse. 'For the first time I realized we hadn't just got a useful horse – but a *great* one'.

The usually percipient *Timeform Annual* did not share the trainer's estimate. They opined in their lofty way that Wayward Lad had acquired 'a reputation higher than is warranted by the formbook' and considered him 'about a stone behind Silver Buck at the same stage'. At the time most of the Harewood staff, who would later become so partisan about their two famous stars, would probably have agreed with *Timeform.*

They may have been influenced by his lacklustre effort at Cheltenham. But Michael was firm in his belief that 'Wayward was a sick horse that day'. It was his first season as a trainer and he was bitterly disappointed when his high Cheltenham hopes yielded only one winner. Tommy kept reporting that the Dickinson horses were 'cutting out. One moment they're cruising; the next they're gone'. Such symptoms have proved wretchedly familiar to virus-stricken trainers in recent years.

That spring Tommy Carmody returned to Ireland and henceforth Wayward Lad like Silver Buck was for the most part ridden by Robert Earnshaw. In Michael's words 'he did a terrific job.' From then on Wayward Lad's mistakes dwindled and his combination of bold and accurate jumping became his most devastating weapon. Fred Winter, a trainer particularly admired by Michael, said he reckoned Wayward Lad to be the most spectacular jumper since his own Pendil. Michael, commenting on Robert's consummate horsemanship pointed out that Badsworth Boy, Wayward Lad, Bregawn and Captain John were 'all poor jumpers when Robert took them on. He made them all jump well.'

In 1981–82 Wayward Lad was beaten just once in seven outings. It was at Cheltenham's New Year meeting and after jumping sloppily he finished a dismal last of three behind David Elsworth's bold mare, Lesley-Ann. Afterwards he was found to be a sick horse with a low blood count. A happier day at Ascot, where he won the Lambert and Butler Premier Chase readily enough from Earthstopper and Captain John, was preceded by nail-biting drama.

Michael, going down to the stables for a routine check-up, was electrified to see Brian running out of Wayward's box – 'always a bad sign'. 'I think Wayward's broken a leg', he cried. It looked horribly like it. Wayward Lad apparently in a state of advanced shock was holding a hind foot up, and shaking it frantically as if he had broken his pastern. The panic turned out to be caused merely by some gravel in the foot but no-one yet knows why he reacted so wildly. Michael said afterwards,

'it was the worst moment of my life.' The afflicted foot was plunged in a bucket of ice and afterwards treated with pain-relieving spray. Wayward Lad was able to run – and win. But the incident probably explains why, after a brilliant display of jumping and a great surge of speed to take the lead, simply outclassing his opponents, he faltered after the last. Robert found himself desperately scrubbing away with little response on the run to the line.

The statistics of season 1982–83, five runs and only two victories, suggest a slight falling away of his fortunes. But the mere figures are, as so often, quite misleading. The season included his first 'King George' victory and two heroic defeats at Cheltenham. Michael continues to refute the theory that Cheltenham never suited him, but cannot deny that it wasn't his lucky track.

After an easy initial win at Worcester, Wayward Lad attempted both the Mackeson Gold Cup and the Kennedy Construction Cup at Cheltenham. Though he won neither, *Timeform* described his second performance, when failing by only ¾ length to give 17 lb. to Fred Winter's good chaser, Observe, as 'the best we have seen in a handicap all season'.

The perpetually self-critical Michael afterwards castigated himself for greed in attempting these rich handicaps which he describes as 'killers'. Henceforth his class horses were to be found more and more at unfashionable tracks. Folkestone, Market Rasen, Catterick and Sedgefield were gratified to find their gate receipts burgeoning as they hosted the Dickinson stars. Michael explains: 'once you know you've got a top-class horse, there are only two races in the whole season to go for – the King George VI and the Gold Cup. Otherwise, you must find condition

Wayward Lad (John Francome on the right) having been pushed along all the way, closes on stable companion, Silver Buck (Robert Earnshaw left, who was third) and Fifty Dollars More (Richard Linley, second) and goes on to win the 1982 King George. At this instant, most people's money would be on Fifty Dollars More.

races wherever you can.' This method of producing top-class chasers meant the stable approached their Christmastime targets with an *embarras des richesses.*

Wayward Lad accompanied Silver Buck to Kempton for the King George. With Robert remaining faithful to his Gold Cup winner, John Francome was engaged for Wayward Lad. In a fast run race spearheaded by Night Nurse and Little Owl, Francome reported, 'Wayward was off the bridle for most of the way'. Consequently he jumped without his usual fluency. However, turning into the straight, Wayward Lad was perceived to be moving sweetly behind Silver Buck. He quickened impressively on the run-in to pass his stable companion and the Winter-trained Fifty Dollars More. There was added piquancy in his victory. Francome always resented the fact that Richard Linley had been retained to ride all Sheikh Ali Abu Khamsin's horses, including those like Fifty Dollars More in the Winter stable, by which Francome was retained. So John, deprived of the ride on the Sheikh's Fifty Dollars More, had the final sweet satisfaction of beating him.

'Wayward was a great ride. He was a real athlete, a fabulous jumper,' he said, 'and he could quicken. He had everything.' He also paid a powerful compliment to the trainer. 'When you rode a horse for Michael,' (John rode four and they all won) 'he'd tell you how the horse would run, where he'd finish and where everyone else would finish – and, give or take a length or two, that's what would happen. I never rode for anyone else who had that knack and I can't think of anyone else who could, except maybe Jimmy FitzGerald or David Elsworth.'

The notable triumph was Wayward Lad's greatest till then. Even so, Michael was sure that he had not been at his best! He resolved to give him a good rest before the Gold Cup. Patience, however, was not this time rewarded. Wayward Lad had hardly resumed work, when a strained hock ground his preparation to a halt. He missed so much that his participation remained in doubt until the last minute. With five runners Michael had to call in outside jockeys and Jonjo O'Neill was engaged for Wayward Lad, as John Francome's Winter-retainer required him for Brown Chamberlin. A week before the big race Jonjo got up on Wayward Lad for a 2-mile spin over hurdles on Catterick racecourse. The horse blew like a grampus and Michael was far from happy. 'You wouldn't *believe* how unfit he was . . . I told the owners he couldn't possibly run.' Jonjo, however, thought he'd gone quite well and ought to be allowed to take his chance.

Possibly Michael over-reacted. No-one else has ever experienced the anxiety of simultaneously preparing five horses for the most important steeplechase in the world. The strain it imposed would be impossible, even for other trainers, to imagine. He admitted to losing a stone in weight and The Boss described his son as 'run up very light and walking his box!'

Indeed Jonjo was proved quite right: Wayward Lad ran a blinder. After an outstanding display of jumping, he looked a possible winner going to the last but here his interrupted preparation held him back. Not subjected to a hard race once his chance had gone, he finished an honourable third to his stable-companions Bregawn and Captain John, with Silver Buck fourth. Nor was he sent on any retrieving missions, but was immediately let down for a long summer's rest.

The season of 1983–84 was to be Michael's last as a National Hunt trainer. He

Michael Dickinson with his 'Famous Five' in the field behind the yard at Harewood. Bregawn, Captain John, Wayward Lad, Silver Buck and Ashley House filled the first five places in the 1983 Cheltenham Gold Cup.

announced that he would relinquish his licence at the end of it in order to set forth on a fact-finding tour of the world's leading flat trainers. He had finally accepted Robert Sangster's pressing offers to become his private trainer at his newly-purchased multi-million pound estate at Manton, west of Marlborough. Although Silver Buck was far from a spent force he was now approaching 12 and it seemed likely that the crown of Harewood would pass either to Wayward Lad or the able but enigmatic Bregawn. The latter's spare frame however seemed burnt out by his heroic achievements of the past two seasons: he never again blazed with his former fire.

Wayward Lad's early outings went smoothly enough, except for a close call at Huntingdon. Here Michael's policy of small and easy 'prep' races was nearly upset when the modest Peterborough Chase also attracted Fifty Dollars More – not at all the class of opponent wanted at that time of the season for that size of prize. Wayward Lad was flat out to win by a short head. This hard race however, so far from blunting his preparation, actually sharpened him for the forthcoming King George which would prove an epic.

One of the opposition was stable companion, The Mighty Mac, a newcomer to Harewood. This devastatingly bold-jumping front-runner was unbeaten in his previous five races. On fast ground round the sharp Kempton track he was by no means unfancied to beat his more distinguished stablemate. He set a ferocious pace, leading till two out. Then Wayward Lad quickened gloriously, to give a 5 length beating to the impressive Hennessy winner, Brown Chamberlin. He broke the course record by an astonishing 8.3 sec. In the 1987 race the French challenger Nupsala, with the pace set by the cut-throat tactics of Beau Ranger and Desert Orchid, took no less than 12.4 sec. longer.

That day when Wayward Lad won his second King George and broke the record, the opening novice hurdle was won by 15 lengths by a grey youngster called Desert Orchid and the mare Dawn Run staged one of her memorable last ditch rallies to snatch the Ladbroke Christmas Hurdle by a short head from Gaye Brief. It was a famous day's racing.

Gold Cup plans proceeded without a stumble. The ground was good and Wayward Lad was made 6–4 favourite. But there was to be no happy ending. He made a mistake at the seventh, blundered badly at the 19th and pulled up before two out. Robert reported 'he was never going well. He was gurgling at the top of the hill.' For Michael this race was the most devastating upset of his career. He had believed that his horse had never been better. Deeply shaken at the time, he still remains perplexed and troubled. He believes Wayward Lad might have been got at. As hot favourite in a strong antepost market for steeplechasing's classic he was the obvious target for racing's betting criminals. A stopped favourite makes a fortune for those in the know, taking the public's thousands. But dope tests proved negative. Beyond the obvious circumstances, nothing else could be discovered or proved. Yet the doubts linger on.

On Michael's retirement, 'Mrs D' became the third member of the family to hold the licence. She got off to a miserable start with a fire that burnt the haybarn to the ground followed by the tragic death of Silver Buck. Wayward Lad did his best to lift her spirits with a couple of handsome victories, including the important Edward Hamner Memorial Chase at Haydock. There he gave 15 lb. and a 2½-length beating to the Sun Alliance winner A Kinsman. Thereafter his fortunes declined. He was beaten comprehensively by Burrough Hill Lad at Wetherby and was even further behind and reportedly gurgling again when a distant third in the King George.

Mrs D, who knows what's what and doesn't hesitate to say so, was highly critical of Robert Earnshaw's tactics when the pair were beaten by Earl's Brig at Ayr. But no excuses were advanced when Wayward Lad had run a dull and gloomy race behind Forgive 'n Forget in the Gold Cup.

Theories of a low blood count and a possible oxygen deficiency were explored. They were treated, and an effervescent Wayward Lad reappeared at Liverpool to blow away the season's disappointments with a fine victory in the Whitbread Gold Label Chase over Earl's Brig and Half Free. John Francome had the ride, a change of jockey made at the request of the owners. Mrs D said it was not her own wish. After the race, an indomitable figure crowned by her familiar fur hat, she briskly rejected cheeky suggestions that Wayward Lad might have become too familiar with Robert's sympathetic horsemanship. Wayward Lad had not been himself before, she affirmed. Now he had come right. She was sure Robert would have won on him. Later she reflected. 'No-one could object to Francome riding our horse – he was quite simply the best. Robert was a beautiful horseman, but never a strong jockey.'

The following season found Robert moved away to the south and Graham Bradley was ensconced as first jockey at Harewood. After a satisfactory start winning the Charlie Hall Memorial at Wetherby, there was nearly a disaster in that favourite Dickinson race, the Edward Hamner Memorial at Haydock.

Wayward Lad collided with the running rail landing over the fifth fence when odds on. Bradley was inevitably unseated and Forgive 'n Forget went on to win at his leisure. It could not be said that his next two races, third to Burrough Hill Lad at Chepstow and second to Earl's Brig at Haydock, were disappointing. In each he ran a thoroughly sound, honest race, but they left little hope that Wayward Lad had a third King George in him. Indeed he drifted out of the market from 7–1 to 12–1, while his old rival Burrough Hill Lad hardened to 4–5 favourite. His starting price seemed exactly reflected when he lost his place half way down the back straight second time round. Then at the third last he suddenly rallied. He jumped past Burrough Hill Lad two fences from home and then gallantly withstood the sustained, vigorous challenge from Combs Ditch. He won by a neck. Earl's Brig was 12 lengths back in third place with Burrough Hill Lad a remote fourth and Half Free tailed off.

It was a tremendous victory heightened by its improbability during the previous two months. 'If there was a more courageous performance during the season, we didn't see it,' declared *Timeform*. No horse before had completed a hat-trick in the King George. Not only was it a great triumph for Mrs D in her second season but it provided an astonishing sixth victory for the stable in the last seven runnings of the race.

Monica Dickinson in her usual fur hat wins her first King George with Wayward Lad. This was his third King George, and the stables sixth . . . a remarkable record.

Timeform's badge of courage could have been awarded to Wayward Lad again in the ensuing Tote Gold Cup. This was the contest considered by most of those fortunate enough to be there to be the race of the century. Four horses rose in the air together at the last. Wayward Lad then seemed to be gradually asserting his authority. All the way up that grim and toiling hill he looked certain to prevail. Then 25 yards, a few weary, struggling strides from the post, he faltered and edged left. Suddenly Dawn Run, executing one of her extraordinary last moment rallies, swept through to get home by a length. The course record was broken by nearly 2 seconds.

When the great roars subsided, arguments began as to the fairness of the 5 lb. sex allowance for mares in steeplechasing's level weight classic. Previous female winners of the Gold Cup, Ballinode, Kerstin and Glencaraig Lady had after all enjoyed no such pull in beating the geldings. At level weights, the racing theory indicates that Wayward Lad must have finished a few lengths in front of her. Surely 5 lb. more at the end of the toughest 3¼-mile chase in Britain must have retarded even her brave spirit? No-one can ever prove such things, and in the bedlam surrounding Dawn Run's victory such matters were not considered. And Wayward Lad too was out of the spotlight of the rejoicing crowds.

Long afterwards 'Beano' Powell opined quietly that Wayward Lad never really did get 3¼ miles.

Asked if she still had nightmares about the race, Mrs D retorted crisply, 'certainly not'; pause, 'I don't think about it, I can't bear to'.

Her thoughts on his next and last race of the season at Liverpool were extremely coherent and forcibly expressed. She felt that Wayward Lad had been left with too much to do and she was not pleased. After the shocking first fence fall of Dawn Run, Beau Ranger was allowed matters his own way with Bradley riding a confident race in behind. Turning for home with apparently a lot of horse still under him, Bradley continued to bide his time. When finally he asked Wayward Lad to go and catch the leader there was a limited response. Beau Ranger, in receipt of 8 lb., kept going to win by 1½ lengths.

The consensus of racing opinion was that Mrs D was not being altogether fair, that Wayward Lad might well have been feeling the effects of his hard struggle in the Gold Cup after what cannot have been a perfect preparation: a frost which had gripped the country for a month had wiped out all racing between 5 February and 5 March.

Against the brilliance of his earlier triumphs, Wayward Lad's exploits in his final season were, though as gallant as ever, a little muted. The great horse was beginning to feel his age. He could no longer give 26 lb. and more to horses like the Grand Military winner Burnt Oak, and the Grand National third and Whitbread hero Lean Ar Aghaigh. He could never strike a blow in Desert Orchid's barnstorming King George VI Chase. By far his boldest show came in his bogey race, the Tote Gold Cup. After losing his place going up the hill, he launched a typically courageous rally at the bottom and went into the last with every chance. But the roar of his fans died on utterance. On snow-softened ground he could only plug on to finish a weary fifth to The Thinker. It seemed 'Beano' Powell's deductions were right. So, after these defeats signalling decline he came again to Liverpool. There was an ironic twist to the riding arrangements. Graham McCourt had lost his retainer to ride Terry Ramsden's horses and with it the ride on the favourite, Stearsby. Graham Bradley was offered it. Mrs D generously released him and promptly snapped up the rejected McCourt for Wayward Lad, little fancied at 7–1. Passing the toiling Stearsby, beaten three fences out, on his home run must have been a sweet salve to McCourt's bruised pride.

After the disappointments, the glory. And, in the minutes of glory, Mrs D's proud announcement of Wayward Lad's retirement. So then to the rumbles of discontent, to the open storm raging and the public show, and into the packed Sales Ring at Doncaster.

Glossy Harry Beeby on his rostrum. The Dickinsons in the ring. Jack Doyle close to them. The Bossman's opening bid is quickly capped. The tension crackles. Where was Les Abbott? How high would he go to buy out his old partner and send the old horse point-to-pointing? Battle is joined. Suddenly Les Abbott cracks, drops out. Victory? But at this stage the joker in the pack shows his hand. Pigtailed and stetson-hatted, Irish-based amateur Aidan O'Connell enters the fray.

He is a Disqualified Person under the Rules of Racing, forbidden to own, train or ride a racehorse or to set foot on a racecourse. Harry Beeby did not know this, having seen him at Ayr's Scottish National Meeting. In any case the premises of Doncaster Bloodstock Sales are not on a racecourse. The disqualification of the Jockey Club did not run that far. The eccentric O'Connell, pigtail nodding, began furiously to bid. The price of rescue soared. Tension grew unbearably. Finally at 42,000 guineas Aidan O'Connell was beaten off. 'And Wayward Lad goes back to

Wayward Lad celebrates his reprieve after being dramatically bought back by the Dickinsons at Doncaster Sales in May 1987. Monica Dickinson reported 'He went round all the horses doing this'. A reunion of old friends.

Mr and Mrs Dickinson at Harewood!' Harry Beeby sang out with happy pride.

Pandemonium broke loose. The crowd stamped and cheered and clapped. Amidst the roaring triumphant shouts of victory, Waywood Lad stood stock still in the middle of the ring looking as though he owned it. Mrs D went up to him, put her arms round his neck and wept.

So Wayward Lad's last battle was won. From his old stables he was flown, as Rusty Carrier had promised, across the Atlantic to the Carriers' pleasant farmhouse perched on a hillock with its stable barns behind. It stands close to Unionville, a small and pretty little town – and very olde-worlde in America – in Pennsylvania. It is a sort of Melton Mowbray of American foxhunting with a touch of Lambourn about it, too. It lies only 45 minutes' drive down very English winding lanes from the Fairhill Training Center in Maryland where Michael Dickinson was training with great success in 1988. The Carriers' land covers a swooping green valley thick with woods. The grassland is kept mown for the look of it, and for the pleasure of riding across it. The downland feels like southern Sussex set in the Chiltern Hills. 'We only keep horses here,' smile the Carriers in their comfortable living room, replaying video tapes of the latest Maryland Hunt Cup.

Here is Wayward Lad the brilliant hunter, so gentle that even Michael Dickinson's girlfriend Joan, an inexperienced rider, can hunt him easily with the local hounds. 'He just takes care of you. Stops when you want him to. Jumps at any speed. And never pulls.'

Wayward Lad hunting near Unionville, Pennsylvania in the fall of 1987 ridden by Joy Carrier who with her husband Rusty gave the horse his last happy home on their grassland farm. Even now, his pursuers seem defeated by Wayward Lad's famed precision jumping . . .

We look down from Rusty's Jeep to see his wife Joy cantering Wayward Lad quietly across the rolling grassland below. The old horse lobs contentedly up the hill, pops over a hunt jump into a strip of thick woodland and we can hear his hoofbeats on the fallen leaves. Then through dappled sunlight he pops out again onto grassland and stops beside us.

He stands, ears pricked, lustrous eyes staring across the valley at tiny cows grazing beyond the Carriers' home. He seems blessedly happy.

DATE	COURSE	RACE	DISTANCE	VALUE	WEIGHT	JOCKEY	PRICE	PLACE
Season 1979–80								
Nov 19	Leicester	Stoughton Novices Hurdle (Div 2)	2m	£791	10.10	C. Tinkler	85/40f	won
Nov 29	Haydock Park	Garswood Pattern Hurdle	2m	£2310	10.9	T. Carmody	1/2F	won
Dec 15	Nottingham	Philip Cornes Novices Hurdle Qualifier	2m 6f	£1797	11.0	K. Whyte	10/11f	won
Dec 29	Newbury	Panama Cigar Hurdle Qualifier	2m 100y	£2063	11.10	T. Carmody	Evens/f	2nd
Feb 21	Warwick	Lower Swell Novices Trial Hurdle	2m 5f	£2164	12.0	T. Carmody	7/4f	won
Mar 1	Newbury	Philip Cornes Saddle of Gold Novices Hurdle Final	3m 120y	£5758	11.3	K. Whyte	4/5f	2nd
Mar 14	Chepstow	Shamrock Novices Hurdle	2m 4f	£2113	12.0	T. Carmody	2/7f	won
Mar 28	Liverpool	Maghull Novices Hurdle	2m 5f 110y	£2771	11.11	T. Carmody	15/8f	won
Season 1980–81								
Nov 15	Newcastle	Lambert & Butler Premier Chase Qualifier	2m 4f	£1938	11.3	T. Carmody	7/4f	2nd
Dec 12	Sedgefield	Heighington Novices Chase (Div 2)	2m 4f	£668	10.10	T. Carmody	2/9f	won
Dec 19	Doncaster	Merryman II Novices Chase	3m 122y	£1424	10.12	T. Carmody	8/13f	2nd
Jan 23	Catterick	Stayers Novices Chase (Div 2)	3m 1f 80y	£990	11.10	T. Carmody	2/5f	won
Jan 31	Ayr	West of Scotland Pattern Novices Chase	2m 4f	£7119	11.0	T. Carmody	9/4	won
Mar 7	Haydock Park	Timeform Chase	2m 4f	£10782	11.7	T. Carmody	5/4	u.r.
Mar 18	Cheltenham	Sun Alliance Chase	3m	£19559	11.4	T. Carmody	5/2	unpl
Apr 21	Chepstow	Welsh Champion Chase	2m 4f	£10405	11.7	T. Carmody	30/100f	won

Season 1981–82								
Oct 31	Wetherby	Lambert & Butler Premier Chase Qualifier	2m 4f 100y	£2197	11.12	R. Earnshaw	2/5f	won
Nov 21	Ascot	Tote Silver Trophy Chase (H'cp)	2m 4f	£12866	11.10	R. Earnshaw	9/4f	won
Dec 1	Huntingdon	Peterborough Chase	2m 4f	£2351	11.12	R. Earnshaw	1/2f	won
Jan 30	Cheltenham	Tote Double Chase	3m 1f	£7660	11.12	R. Earnshaw	6/5f	3rd
Feb 24	Ascot	Lambert & Butler Premier Chase Final	2m 4f	£15281	11.7	R. Earnshaw	13/8f	won
Mar 6	Haydock Park	Timeform Chase	2m 4f	£12383	11.12	R. Earnshaw	2/5f	won
Apr 13	Chepstow	Welsh Champion Chase	2m 4f	£10883	11.12	R. Earnshaw	5/6f	won
Season 1982–83								
Oct 30	Worcester	Worcester Evening News Chase	2m 4f	£2528	11.12	R. Earnshaw	4/11f	won
Nov 13	Cheltenham	Mackeson Gold Cup H'cp Chase	2m 4f	£11319	11.13	R. Earnshaw	9/4f	3rd
Dec 11	Cheltenham	Kennedy Construction Gold Cup H'cp Chase	2m 4f	£12392	12.0	R. Earnshaw	5/2f	2nd
Dec 27	Kempton Park	King George VI Chase	3m	£24810	11.10	J. Francome	7/2	won
Mar 17	Cheltenham	Tote Cheltenham Gold Cup Chase	3m 2f	£45260	12.0	J. J. O'Neill	6/1	3rd
Season 1983–84								
Oct 29	Wetherby	Charlie Hall Memorial Wetherby Chase	3m 100y	£10590	11.10	R. Earnshaw	1/3f	won
Nov 29	Huntingdon	Peterborough Chase	2m 4f	£2898	11.12	R. Earnshaw	4/11f	won
Dec 26	Kempton Park	King George VI Chase	3m	£21768	11.10	R. Earnshaw	11/8f	won
Feb 11	Newbury	Compton Chase	3m	£5982	11.12	R. Earnshaw	5/4	2nd
Feb 25	Doncaster	Pennine Chase	3m 122y	£4334	12.0	R. Earnshaw	No s.p.	won
Mar 15	Cheltenham	Tote Cheltenham Gold Cup Chase	3m 2f	£47375	12.0	R. Earnshaw	6/4f	p.u.

DATE	COURSE	RACE	DISTANCE	VALUE	WEIGHT	JOCKEY	PRICE	PLACE
Season 1984–85								
Nov 1	Wincanton	Terry Biddlecombe Challenge Trophy Chase	2m 5f	£3502	11.8	R. Earnshaw	2/9f	won
Nov 21	Haydock Park	Edward Hamner Memorial H'cp Chase	3m	£7167	12.0	R. Earnshaw	8/15f	won
Dec 8	Wetherby	Charlie Hall Memorial Wetherby Pattern Chase	3m 100y	£9440	11.9	R. Earnshaw	10/11j.f.	2nd
Dec 26	Kempton Park	King George VI Chase	3m	£26467	11.10	R. Earnshaw	5/2	3rd
Feb 9	Ayr	Mercedes-Benz H'cp Chase	3m 110y	£5780	12.0	R. Earnshaw	9/4	2nd
Mar 14	Cheltenham	Tote Cheltenham Gold Cup Chase	3m 2f	£52560	12.0	R. Earnshaw	8/1	unpl
Mar 28	Liverpool	Whitbread Gold Label Cup Chase	3m 1f	£7180	11.5	J. Francome	6/1	won
Season 1985–86								
Nov 2	Wetherby	Charlie Hall Memorial Wetherby Pattern Chase	3m 100y	£10459	11.6	G. Bradley	evens f	won
Nov 20	Haydock Park	Edward Hanmer Memorial H'cp Chase	3m	£8908	12.0	G. Bradley	4/6f	u.r.
Nov 30	Chepstow	Rehearsal Chase	3m	£4409	11.8	G. Bradley	7/4	3rd
Dec 11	Haydock Park	Tommy Whittle Chase	3m	£5987	11.6	G. Bradley	5/1	2nd
Dec 26	Kempton Park	King George VI Chase	3m	£24836	11.10	G. Bradley	12/1	won
Mar 13	Cheltenham	Tote Cheltenham Gold Cup Chase	3m 2f	£54900	12.0	G. Bradley	8/1	2nd
Apr 3	Liverpool	Whitbread Gold Label Cup Chase	3m 1f	£9204	11.13	G. Bradley	13/8	2nd

Season 1986–87

Nov 1	Wetherby	Charlie Hall Memorial Wetherby Pattern Chase	3m 100y	£9428	11.10	G. Bradley	6/5f	3rd
Nov 29	Chepstow	Rehearsal Chase	3m	£4652	11.12	G. Bradley	11/8	3rd
Dec 13	Doncaster	Sheila's Cottage H'cp Chase	3m 2f	£5208	12.0	G. Bradley	6/4f	2nd
Dec 26	Kempton Park	King George VI Rank Chase	3m	£31696	11.10	G. Bradley	9/2	unpl
Feb 14	Ayr	Elk H'cp Chase	3m 110y	£3668	11.10	T. G. Dun	7/4f	4th
Mar 19	Cheltenham	Tote Cheltenham Gold Cup Chase	3m 2f	£55500	12.0	G. Bradley	11/1	unpl
Apr 2	Liverpool	Whitbread Gold Label Cup Chase	3m 1f	£10762	11.5	G. McCourt	7/1	won

Career Record

Ran – Hurdles 8; won 6, £11,946. Chases 47; won 22, £205,977

Total – ran 55; won 28, £217,923

SIXTEEN

Dawn Run

'CHUNNEL' AGREED. MARCOS FLEES PHILIPPINES. U.S. STRIKES LIBYA. DUCHESS OF WINDSOR DIES. CHERNOBYL DISASTER. MARADONA'S 'HAND OF GOD' GIVES ARGENTINE THE WORLD CUP. CARY GRANT AND HAROLD MACMILLAN RISE TO HEAVENLY STAGES. TERRY WAITE SEIZED IN BEIRUT. GUINNESS SCANDAL BREAKS. GORBACHEV LAUNCHES PERESTROIKA AND GLASNOST.

Ballsbridge Sales, Dublin, November 1981. The rangy, masculine filly stalked out of her box with that swing of the quarters which marks a real athlete and Mrs Hill knew that she wanted her very badly. She had deliberately left the Deep Run filly till last in her preliminary inspection of the dozen possibles that her search through the catalogue suggested she might hopefully acquire for the 6,000 guineas which was the very most she could afford to spend. One glance at the striking filly confirmed her fears. She was sure to be too expensive.

Had the youngster been a gelding, Mrs Hill would have had no chance. Not only was she by that phenomenally successful sire of jumpers, Deep Run, but her dam, Twilight Slave, was by the keenly desired sire of broodmares, Arctic Slave. She was a full sister to Frozen Dawn. She was a daughter of a decent winning point-to-point mare who was a half-sister to a top class chaser Brasher. Twilight Slave was already the dam of no fewer than five winners.

Paddy Mullins liked her too, though he is quick to say, and Mrs Hill even quicker, that he played no part in her purchase. He had been one of the judges in the pre-sale show and he had placed her second in the class for three-year-old fillies.

Paddy has an unusually high proportion of fillies in his yard and is very successful with them. He says this is not deliberate. He is just sent them. He did however profess deep affection for Deep Run mares, 'they are so very gutsy; there are sometimes a few kinks to start with but after that you can put the work into them and they thrive.' He does not – which may surprise many English trainers – treat them any differently to geldings.

Mrs Hill, having fallen for the bay filly, determined to risk all her eggs in this most desirable basket and resolutely refrained from bidding for any of the other possibles on her list. She laid her plans carefully. She listened keenly for the magic word 'sell' which would indicate that the filly had reached her reserve and was on the market. At 5,500 guineas it came and she jumped in with a quick, determined nod of 5,800. Such a bid, suggestive of confidence and unlimited funds, can often deter less single-minded buyers.

There was a pause. It continued. The hammer rose. The auctioneer pleaded for another bid. This was a handsome filly, beautifully bred and a great walker. Surely she was worth more? Mrs Hill held her breath. The hammer hovered – and fell. She had got her. She couldn't believe it. Right from the start she was convinced there was something special about the filly.

She named her Dawn Run and took the new purchase home to her forbidding, grey house on the outskirts of Waterford. The house is plain but the setting on a knoll above the estuary, is staggeringly beautiful. Meadows, dotted with fine old trees, run down to the water's edge. Though less than a mile from the port's centre, all that can be seen are grass, sea and sky.

It is called Belmont but, unlike Portia in the *Merchant of Venice*, its lady is not 'richly left'. Most of the work about the place is done by herself and it includes the horses. Warned that Dawn Run, though broken in, was flighty, her sexagenarian owner felt it might be prudent to wait until help was at hand before attempting to ride her. Meanwhile she 'spun her round on a rope. She seemed quiet enough'. Impatient for assistance, Mrs Hill boldly climbed aboard. Fortunately there was no trouble.

Apart from her own 30 acres, she had permission to ride over land belonging to the adjacent mental hospital. Otherwise she hacked round the narrow, congested back streets of Waterford. The filly seemed very placid. So much so that Mrs Hill wondered whether she had enough spark to be a racehorse. She popped her over the scruffy, homemade fence she'd built for her point-to-pointers. So calm was Dawn Run that she resolved to take her hunting. She meant only to go to the meet but, a keen and lifelong foxhuntress, she was unable to resist the temptation to follow. This proved a major error and Mrs Hill hastily returned home.

Charmian Hill is a tiny woman with an outsize spirit and courageous, very blue eyes. She is crippled now from a stroke but her mind is razor-sharp and her voice as incisive as ever. She had ridden since childhood and she and her doctor husband were loyal supporters of the local Hunt. A fiercely competitive spirit led her naturally to point-to-pointing, a move which provoked mixed reactions from

the local cavaliers. Her determination to win was legendary and her route the most direct, regardless of that charted by her opponents. 'Oh, they used to cuss her but you couldn't help but admire her,' chuckled Seamus Berry, vet and member of the famous Wexford racing and dealing family, who is a keen follower of point-to-pointing. Then, at an age when most women are preoccupied with the equestrian activities of their grandchildren, she progressed to running horses under Rules and riding some of them herself.

To start with she trained with Willie O'Grady but he died and, feeling that she would not be so happy with his son Eddie, she transferred to Paddy Mullins. Recognizing the qualities of a spirit gentler than her own, she says with affection, 'Paddy works so very hard and he really loves his horses.'

Her own riding successes made her fiercely critical of those employed to ride for her and her unsparing castigation of Tony Mullins was to have a major bearing on Dawn Run's career.

In the spring of 1982 Dawn Run was sent up to the Mullins' yard at Goresbridge, five miles down an almost impenetrably narrow road from Royal Oak, a former posting stage on the main road between Carlow and Kilkenny. The house, long, low and white-washed, fronts the lane and is surrounded by a pretty garden, bright with flowers. The yard has no pretensions to smartness but has an air of relaxed efficiency: of getting done what needs to be done with the minimum of fuss.

Inside the house there is a subtle difference. The long drawing room has good antique furniture, with books and flowers as well as racing trophies and old prints

Dawn Run, her owner up, returns to the Mullins yard at Goresbridge, after morning work. Mrs Hill talks things over with trainer's wife, Maureen.

as well as photographs on the walls. An air of great courtesy and slightly old-fashioned formality prevails.

All the family ride. Paddy, nearly 71 in 1989, was a fine amateur and won the prestigious La Touche Cup at Punchestown. His wife Maureen, a trim figure with blonde, curly hair and a striking face, rides out daily. All four sons are or have been actively involved in the yard. Willie rides most successfully as an amateur and was champion again in 1988. Both he and George assist. Tony, formerly National Hunt jockey to the stable, now has his own yard. Daughter Sandra is married but is still neatly booting home winners for her father.

Like most future chasers in Ireland, Dawn Run began her career in bumpers. Paddy thought her a grand stamp of filly but was not especially elated by her early homework. Moreover, noting her pronounced knee action, he was sure she'd need soft ground. Seeing her lay back her ears when the pace quickened in her first race at Clonmel, he wondered 'Is she a madam?' Mrs Hill retorted that it was jealousy. The mare was becoming competitive and resented having other horses round her.

Due possibly to this reasoning, she dropped Dawn Run right out at the back of the field for her second run at Thurles. 'What she was up to I wouldn't know,' reflected Paddy. Turning out of the back straight Mrs Hill realised she was a long way behind and gave the mare a slap. The result was electric. For the first time in her life Dawn Run gave a glimpse of her quality. She shot through the field and finished fourth. Her rapid late progress did not go unobserved by the stewards. One of them privately cautioned Paddy, 'only for Mrs Hill, we might have asked a question'.

In fact, time was running out rapidly for Mrs Hill's riding days. The day before the mare's intended third run at Tralee, her owner received a letter from the Stewards of the Irish Turf Club informing her that, owing to her age and previous injuries, her licence to ride would not be renewed. Goaded to fresh competitiveness by what she bitterly regarded as the outrageous male chauvinism of the Turf Club, Mrs Hill rode out to do battle determined that her last ride should be a winning one. The mare did not fail her, and won easily. Charmian Hill was 62 years old. Dawn Run continued her bumper career after her owner's last ride, running in two more races ridden by Tony Mullins and winning both. She also ran unplaced in the valuable Leopardstown November handicap.

The time had now come in any case for the mare to turn her attention to hurdling. Her rider would continue to be Paddy's son Tony, then not quite 21, who had turned professional after a brief but successful career as an amateur. The mare took well to jumping. Her attitude was bold and aggressive, but her trajectory was fast and flat. Jonjo O'Neill, her partner in the two great Cheltenham triumphs, reflected later 'she was never a natural jumper'. Moreover she increasingly disliked being dictated to. She liked to run her own race on a light rein, and preferably in front.

On her second outing she gamely won a fillies race at Navan, prompting her connections to aim higher and try for the important Findus Beefburger Hurdle at classy Leopardstown. Here she beat the highly regarded Buck House, who would go on to win the Waterford Crystal Supreme Novices Hurdle at Cheltenham's

National Hunt Festival. Buck House enjoyed a fine career, but whenever he met Dawn Run he always came off second best. The Leopardstown victory keenly whetted Mrs Hill's appetite. A second venture there was less successful but a third and very fluent victory at Punchestown set her course firmly for Cheltenham. Before crossing the water for the Festival Meeting she had one more run in a handicap at Fairyhouse. A mistake at the second last proved very expensive and she could only finish third. This defeat prompted Mrs Hill to look for another jockey to ride her in the Sun Alliance Novices Hurdle. Acutely aware that Dawn Run was easily the best horse she had owned, and now was ever likely to own, she wanted the very best for her. Twenty-one-year-old Tony was, she felt, too young and too inexperienced. She must substitute a top class jockey. It had to be an Irishman: 'I would never employ an English jockey'.

Her choice fell on Ron Barry, Penrith-based but Limerick-born and a dual Champion jockey in England. The mare ran a tremendous race to be second, beaten 3 lengths, to the Dickinson-trained, French four-year-old Sabin du Loir. Big Ron said afterwards 'If I'd known her better, I'd've won.'

Dawn Run was back in England three weeks later to carry top weight in the Page Three Handicap Hurdle at Liverpool's Grand National Meeting. She was reunited with young Tony. Undeterred by the weight and testing ground conditions the pair set out to gallop their opposition into the ground. They succeeded handsomely and, far from resting on their laurels, turned out the very next day to take on their seniors, including the Champion Hurdler Gaye Brief, in the £12,000 Sun Templegate Hurdle. It seemed likely that Dawn Run would be permitted to make the early running, but few calculated that, in receipt of only 6 lb., the novice mare would still be in contention between the last two flights. But she was very much so and she staged such a furious counter-attack against Gaye Brief's smoothly executed winning run that there was only a diminishing length between the pair at the post.

Dawn Run and her young rider crowned a triumphant season by running away with the BMW Champion Novices Hurdle at Punchestown. Her spirit undimmed by her arduous season of racing, and undisturbed by the return to 2 miles after three competitive and very close together races of 2½ miles or more, Dawn Run set off to race the only way she knew. Three flights from home her distinguished pursuers, who included Buck House, his Cheltenham runner-up Golden Friend and Sabin du Loir's Liverpool runner-up, Corrib Duke, were toiling and she won unchallenged by 10 lengths. She had run in no less than 16 races that season. *Timeform* rated her the best novice seen since Golden Cygnet. Mrs Hill knew she owned a champion, and thereupon set her heart upon a very distant dream: steeplechasing's greatest prize, the Cheltenham Gold Cup.

Her star was still only five years old. There were many tempting prizes for her over hurdles, not excluding the Champion. One advantage she would henceforth enjoy was the new 5 lb. sex allowance for mares which was introduced at the beginning of the 1983–84 season for all races in Britain, and for all but Championship races in Ireland.

After an initial run on the flat at the Curragh, Dawn Run won her first hurdle race up in Ulster at Down Royal without being extended. But at the last flight she

jinked left and then wandered slightly up the run-in. Tony, who always favoured a long-reined style, remarked afterwards that he could easily have prevented her, but saw no need, as he was fully 10 lengths clear. Mrs Hill felt differently. She had always wanted an absolutely top-class jockey for Dawn Run. A week later Jonjo O'Neill's Champion Hurdle mount, Ekbalco, was tragically killed when challenging to win the Fighting Fifth Hurdle at Newcastle. He might thus, she reasoned, be available to ride her mare for the rest of the season. She did not tell Jonjo this. He was engaged merely for the VAT Watkins Hurdle at Ascot.

The Mullins family accepted her decision and its accompanying media uproar with exemplary dignity. 'It's no disgrace to lose the ride to someone as good as Jonjo', said Tony courteously. Paddy and Maureen, while in no doubt as to Jonjo's skill and experience, were by no means convinced that his very different style would suit Dawn Run. The new partnership's first outing did nothing to dispel these worries. Starting 3–1 on, Dawn Run made heavy weather of an apparently simple task and only under the strongest possible driving from Jonjo did she get up to win by a short head.

That day the ground was firmer than she had ever encountered. Her trainer had always feared it might not suit her. Jonjo was adamant that it did not. 'She was like a cat on hot bricks.' He had been astonished by the size of her, for he'd often heard her referred to as 'the great little mare from Ireland'. Perched up on her massive, nearly 17 hands frame, he wondered 'what *little* mare is this?' He wasn't particularly impressed and told Mrs Hill firmly that this was no Champion Hurdle trial.

The excuse of the ground could not be advanced when she got beaten at Naas next time out. It was described as 'soft to yielding' which in Ireland means by English standards a bog. She made a bad mistake at the last and was beaten 3 lengths. Jonjo observed that though as genuine as they come if in the right frame of mind, she could be 'a right devil if she wasn't'.

Following this defeat, Gaye Brief was made odds-on favourite to beat her in Kempton's Ladbroke Christmas Hurdle, on the same terms on which she had run him so close at Liverpool the previous March. On good ground and a shorter, sharp track, Gaye Brief's superior speed was felt to be sure to conquer. No amount of speed however was of any avail against the mare's courage once her head was in front. Hard though Gaye Brief tried all the way up the straight, he could not pass her and she was still a neck up at the post. In two seasons only one other horse had beaten the reigning Champion, and Jonjo still rates the Kempton victory as one of her most remarkable performances.

For Mrs Hill it was a magically exciting day. She had cooked a family Christmas meal for 20 the night before and then got up at 5 a.m. to drive up to the Mullins and then on to catch the plane for Heathrow. She didn't reach home again until 10 p.m. in the evening. But, full of champagne and dreams, there was no room in her mind for dull fatigue.

Dawn Run then proceeded to accomplish the unique feat of winning the Irish, English and French Champion Hurdles. To this remarkable treble she added for good measure a valuable hurdle race at Liverpool, the Sandeman (formerly Sun Templegate) Hurdle and then a prep race in France.

The Wessel Cable Irish Champion Hurdle presented her with a stiff task, for the mares' allowance did not apply and she had incurred a penalty for her Christmas Hurdle win. So far from receiving any weight, she was conceding it all round. With Ra Nova in the field, the pace was a cracking one but Dawn Run galloped home an easy and impressive winner from Boreen Prince.

Despite his Kempton defeat, Gaye Brief was odds-on to retain his Champion's title at Cheltenham. He had not, disclosed the redoubtable Mrs Rimell, been at his best at Kempton. But he was not to get the chance to prove it. A week before the race torn ligaments in his back, a trouble which would return to plague him, enforced his withdrawal. The Mullins family were suddently presented with an unprecedented security problem. Many people held ante-post vouchers for the mare at long odds. Now she was hot favourite and, with a substandard English defence resting on the novice Desert Orchid, it was hard to see what might beat her. She was a frighteningly obvious target for the dopers. Villains know that the only true certainty in racing is to take money on a horse, and merrily to lay it, when it has been guaranteed not to win, or with a nice ante-post market, not even to run! The Mullins family and their staff kept a round-the-clock vigil on the mare and a professional firm of security guards was called in to assist them.

In retrospect, it may have been fortunate for the mare that Gaye Brief was not in the field. Desert Orchid, after disputing the lead till the third flight, dropped quickly away leaving what should have been a simple task for Dawn Run. Showing all her usual courage but not her zest and sparkle, she was all out to scramble home by ¾ length from Cima. Her legions of vociferous supporters cared not a jot as to

Mrs Charmian Hill and her jockey, Jonjo O'Neill in the Winners' Enclosure at Cheltenham after their tumultuous reception.

the manner of her victory. She was the first mare to win the Champion Hurdle since African Sister in the last pre-war Cheltenham Festival in 1939. She was mobbed. The diminutive Mrs Hill was lofted shoulder high and chaired in triumph into the enclosure. She had seen no reason to be awed by the occasion into wearing unaccustomed dressy clothes. Hatless as usual, she wore trousers for warmth and comfort. A badly broken hip and thigh, sustained in a fall, had left her slightly lame even before her stroke. She wore a practical, scarlet waterproof jacket which she had bought in a sale. Later she added a black belt, thus creating a replica of her racing colours and this became her lucky outfit.

By the time Liverpool came round Jonjo was injured. Would, Paddy enquired diffidently, Mrs Hill require him to engage another jockey? 'I'm not that bad I hope', was the reply, so Tony was back in the saddle to try and win the race in which he had so narrowly failed the previous year. The mare looked a picture in the paddock and was clearly eager to race. From the fifth flight she was clear and from then on the race became a procession. Even a shocking blunder at the last did not check her and at the post she had doubled her Cheltenham margin over Very Promising, her closest pursuer.

The decision to challenge for the French Champion Hurdle run in late June, was indeed a bold one for no English – or Irish – trained runner had won the race over its unusual obstacles and twisting track this century. Furthermore Dawn Run had had a long and arduous season.

The Mullins family laid their plans carefully. They chose a preliminary race, the Prix de la Barka, at the end of May and flew over 10 days before to give the mare and Tony plenty of opportunity to practise over the unfamiliar French hurdles, which are both larger and thicker than British and Irish ones. Though upright, which makes them harder to judge, they are deceptively soft and so the technique required to ping them fluently is quite different.

The French were amazed by the mighty mare, towering over their little flat-bred colts. *'Pas pur-sang'* they muttered with Gallic derision. They were soon to eat their words. Conceeding weight all round, Dawn Run, racing in front as she loved to, coped splendidly with the new hurdles and held off a former French Champion Hurdler, World Citizen, by 1½ lengths.

She came home gently by box and ferry and had a brief holiday in a paddock at Goresbridge before being prepared for the big one. Tony appeared to be re-established as jockey. The mare returned to France as a conqueror with a vast army of the Mullins family and their supporters in her train. She had already been voted National Hunt Horse of the Year.

This time the French did not make the mistake of underestimating her. No less than 20 of the 26 racing correspondents whose selections were published in *Paris-Turf* chose the mare and she started favourite at 6–5. Despite the distance of approximately 3 miles 1 furlong, half a mile further than she had ever travelled, Tony set out to ride his customary race. French television was relayed to Ireland for the great event but the commentator couldn't or wouldn't mention the runaway leader. The cameras focussed squarely on the vainly pursuing French pack. Michael O'Hehir cut in indignantly on the xenophobic commentary; 'There is another horse in the race, but she's so far ahead, you can't see her!' Dawn Run's

Mrs Hill 'parades' her Champion Hurdler at Punchestown at a brisk pace and by popular demand. Note the double-ringed snaffle fitted by Paddy Mullins for better braking.

gallop never relented and despite some sloppy jumps in the later stages and running a little wide into the final straight, she came home 6 lengths clear of her nearest pursuer. Her prize of £43,103 boosted her season's winnings to £149,957, then a record.

Everyone knew that Dawn Run would be switched to fences the following season and few débuts were more eagerly awaited than that of the bold mare who had so swiftly captured the hearts of the racing public. Tony too had much to look forward to. He had ridden a best-ever total of 55 winners to finish joint Champion N.H. Jockey of Ireland.

Dawn Run enjoyed a long holiday after her strenuous season and did not reappear until November at Navan. For this, her first attempt over fences, only Buck House and Dark Ivy took her on and they could act merely as respectful pages behind the runaway bride who led all the way and won by 10 lengths. Tragically, as it was to turn out, all three of these fine horses were to be cut down by accident and illness in their prime, a brutal reminder of the cruel dangers of the sport.

In Dawn Run's case, future plans after Navan were brought to an abrupt halt by injury. Unusually, the damage lay below and not in or above the fetlock joint. But any strain to the delicate tendons and ligaments of the forelegs lances dread into the hearts of trainers, and particularly those of steeplechasers, whose limbs bear most stress and strain.

Dawn Run's injury responded well to laser therapy. But she had lost the whole of the rest of that season. By February she was able to be roughed off with Mrs Hill

at Belmont. The water meadows there are not fenced apart from the cattlegrids on the drive and the mare ran out with Mrs Hill's homebred young stock. Among them was a colt not a year old. The masculine Dawn Run had never been noted in season when in training. Thus Mrs Hill was electrified when, looking out of her bedroom window one morning, she saw her precious mare all too obviously in season and the cheeky colt keenly interested. She rang her vet peremptorily. 'You'd better come over quick and do what you have to do'.

While Dawn Run was enjoying her enforced holiday, Mrs Hill opened a glossy racing magazine and noticed a swaggering stallion advertisement for Deep Run, featuring her own mare's achievements. She thought of her modest point-to-point brood-mare who had hitherto only enjoyed the attention of less glamorous stallions. She rang up Coolmore, the grandest stud in all Ireland which controlled Deep Run. 'How much do you charge for Deep Run?'

'£1,500' replied a superior secretary.

'Not for me it isn't, not with Dawn Run being used for advertising,' retorted Mrs Hill. 'I'll speak to the Magniers'.

She does not divulge what deal she achieved with the illustrious Irish family who part own and manage the Coolmore group of studs. Dark-visaged John Magnier is now a Senator. His father-in-law Vincent O'Brien holds an honorary Doctorate. The Magniers are the new Irish ascendancy, rich and powerful in a declining enonomy. And not to be trifled with.

Mrs Charmian Hill evidently spoke out with her usual directness. Two handsome Deep Run youngsters were in the summer of 1988 currently maturing in her lush water meadows above the Waterford estuary.

Dawn Run's injury was given a whole year to settle down and she did not reappear until December 1985. When she did it was with a roll of drums in the prestigious Durkan Bros International Chase at Punchestown. She took on a trio of experienced stars, including Royal Bond, the previous year's winner Bobsline and Rainbow Warrior. She treated them with contempt and won unchallenged by 8 lengths. A dreadful error at the last fence at Leopardstown, which she would have been lucky to survive at a stouter English obstacle, did not prevent her disposing of Buck House and Kilkilowen in a similarly disdainful fashion.

Mrs Hill had kept her heart set on that challenge for Cheltenham's Gold Cup. Cup. Such being the case, Paddy determined that a preliminary outing over its notoriously stiff fences and shifting gradients was essential. The Holsten Distributors Chase at the late January meeting was selected. The mare and Tony set forth in their usual flamboyant style but at the difficult open ditch at the top of the hill, she stood off recklessly, ploughed through it and unseated Tony. He caught her and nimbly vaulted back on to complete the course. But the blunder had sealed his fate in the eyes of Mrs Hill: she axed him.

'And that,' says Paddy Mullins with infinite sadness 'was the beginning of the end of the road for Dawnie'. He was also outraged at the intrusion into his close-knit family life of the cheaper sensation-seeking tabloids. Up till then he had done his best to co-operate with the racing press. Now he would no longer bother.

That was his point of view. Mrs Hill and her family were convinced that a more experienced, older head was needed for her insouciant mare if she was to realize

her dreams of Cheltenham glory. The obvious choice was Jonjo, a dual Champion who had won a Gold Cup on Alverton. He was recognized as one of the strongest, most experienced riders ever and was already acquainted with the mare. He was accordingly engaged for the Diners Club Chase at Punchestown. Afterwards, it was announced, a decision would be made as to who would ride the mare at Cheltenham.

But an unusually sharp frost for more temperate Ireland, caused the abandonment of this race, so Dawn Run had to complete her preparation with racecourse schools at nearby Gowran Park and at Punchestown. It was Jonjo's opinion that she wasn't a natural jumper and that she didn't like fences. Nevertheless, it was arranged that he would ride her at Cheltenham.

Television crews came to Goresbridge to record a preview for the big race. 'Would Dawn Run be returning to France this year?' they inquired. 'I don't think that would be a good idea,' replied Paddy.

The 1984 Gold Cup winner and ante-post favourite, Burrough Hill Lad, was a late withdrawal with leg trouble and, despite her inexperience, Dawn Run was made favourite. The opposition was formidable and included that year's King George first and second, Wayward Lad and Combs Ditch and the 1985 Gold Cup first and second, Forgive n' Forget and Righthand Man. With the ground riding unusually good and fast and the much improved Run and Skip sure to force the pace, the stage looked set for the most exciting Gold Cup ever staged.

Dawn Run and Run and Skip cut out the early running with the mare fencing more precisely than on her previous visit. She made a bad mistake at the water

Dawn Run early in her Gold Cup just ahead of Run and Skip. She jumps with real power and precision here.

Dawn Run and Jonjo O'Neill ride triumphantly into an ecstatic welcome after winning the Gold Cup and making steeplechasing history. Note the very mixed bag of her fervent fans.

however and seemed momentarily to lose interest. Another, worse mistake at the top of the hill five from home did nothing to help her cause and she was under strong pressure all the way down the hill. Jonjo conjured a magnificent leap out of her at the second last which regained her the lead but going to the last she appeared outpaced by Wayward Lad and Forgive n' Forget. Of the four contenders all in the air together at the last, she touched down third.

What happened next will glow for ever in the memories of those who saw it. Wayward Lad landed running and started up the hill with his race apparently won. Forgive n' Forget made a slight mistake and lost his momentum. Halfway up the run-in, riding with the strength of demons Jonjo incredibly coaxed fresh reserves of stamina and courage from the mare and within the shadow of the post she caught the tiring Wayward Lad and beat him a length. The course record was broken by 2 seconds.

The crowd went mad. There have never been such scenes at Cheltenham. The police and the executive pray there never will be again, for it still seems inconceivable that no one was hurt in the complete stampede. Within seconds, the great unsaddling enclosure filled like a giant's bowl with a running, heaving mass of delirious humanity. Cheering and whooping they rushed and shoved and cheered again. Raceglasses swung. Coats were half torn off by eager elbows. Hats got lost and were trampled regardless underfoot. The mare was mobbed.

The small figure of Mrs Hill, like a twig on a rising tide, was seized by her fans and flung aloft, floating above the heads of the triumphant crowd. Jonjo, bright-

eyed and pink, had the greatest difficulty in reaching the weighing room without losing parts of his saddlery. When he reappeared he was cheered again to the echo and then chaired around the shouting amphitheatre. Tony Mullins was not forgotten. With the generosity of spirit that has made him universally beloved, Jonjo hoisted his ousted colleague onto his shoulders so that he too might be involved in the celebrations.

After Queen Elizabeth made the presentations Mrs Hill was invited up to the Royal Box so that these two great lovers of steeplechasing could carry on an animated discussion of the sport and its heroes and heroines. Her Majesty had long been a keen admirer of Dawn Run. She had sent Mrs Hill a telegram of congratulation after the mare's great triumph at Auteuil. She was to send another just three months later – of commiseration. Mrs Hill, a fervent Irish patriot with limited enthusiasm for things British, was charmed. She also much appreciated the thoughtful gesture of the Cheltenham Steeplechase Company in sending her a handsome framed montage of photographs recording Dawn Run's unique Cheltenham Champion Hurdle and Gold Cup double. The picture now hangs in her sitting room. A bronze statue of the mare with Jonjo, fist raised in triumph, stands proudly at Cheltenham above the walkway back to the winner's enclosure freezing for all time that magical moment of victory.

'Follow that', say the film buffs. The fates who controlled Dawn Run's destiny could not. In three short months her fortunes plummeted to downfall, defeat and ultimate tragedy. Her challenge for the Whitbread Gold Label Chase at Liverpool was nasty, brutish and short. She completely failed to take off at the very first fence, giving Jonjo a horrible fall. He was never to ride her again. 'She would do that', reflected Mrs Hill philosophically. 'There wasn't anything you could do about it'.

Back in Ireland, Gowran Park had long been eager to attract their local heroine to race on the course where she had completed her Gold Cup preparation and in that hope had framed a conditions race over 2¼ miles worth £20,000 to the winner. Named the Coolmore and Purcell Exports N. H. Champion Chase, it was specifically designed to attract her and Buck House, who was owned by Mrs Purcell. As it was a last minute idea, the entry form was not included in the Racing Calendar but detailed on a separate sheet. This the Mullins family mislaid. 'I can't blame anybody', says Paddy remorsefully. 'The buck has to stop with me.' So Dawn Run failed to be entered and Mrs Hill was extremely displeased.

Help came unexpectedly in the shape of Vincent O'Brien. It was more than 30 years since the Tipperary maestro had ceased training jumpers but he had never lost interest in the sport in which he had made a matchless name. Feeling sorry for the Mullins and perceiving considerable appeal in such a contest, he proposed a match betwen Dawn Run and Buck House at the big April Punchestown meeting. Mrs Hill was agreeable, but declined to put up any money. Coolmore (where Deep Run stood) advanced £5,000 on the mare's behalf, a sum matched both by the racecourse and the connections of Buck House, who stipulated a distance of 2 miles. The Irish Racing Board put up £10,000.

With Jonjo injured, Tony took the ride. The match provoked sharp interest and attracted a huge crowd who were rewarded with a thrilling race. After the lead had

changed hands several times, both principals were in the air together at the last before Dawn Run drew away to win by 2½ lengths. It was a smashing performance to come back from 3 miles 2 furlongs to take on the Two Mile Champion chaser at his own distance and beat him. Mrs Hill, however, was critical that Tony had needlessly given away ground on the bends. It is interesting that when Tony saddled his first big winner as a trainer, the 1988 Galway Plate with Afford a King, he was asked afterwards whether he would advise his jockeys to make the running as he had so often chosen to do. 'I wouldn't be adamant about it', he responded, 'as you need a brave horse to do it. But one thing I am going to be strict about is not always going for the inside berth. I have won a lot of races by not sticking to the rails.'

Buck House went on to win the Gowran race but within two months of the match, both its principals were dead – Buck House of colic at home, Dawn Run in action in France.

The victory at Punchestown did not deflect Mrs Hill from her determination to mount a second challenge for Auteuil's Champion Hurdle. Since Jonjo had by now announced his retirement, it was agreed that Tony should ride. Dawn Run had not jumped a hurdle for two years so a preliminary race was clearly essential. As before, the Prix de la Barka was chosen, for which she escaped a penalty. This did not prove sufficient against the current French Champion Hurdler, Le Rhenosis and she was beaten 3 lengths. Again Tony was sacked. This time Paddy came close to despair. Long afterwards he wondered whether the upshot might not have been that Mrs Hill would move the mare to another stable, perhaps an English one. It seems very improbable, but that he should even think it, shows how unbearable he was finding the strain. 'Perhaps', he now suggested, ' a French jockey might be best.'

On the advice of Desmond Stoneham, for years *The Sporting Life*'s man in France and the representative there of the International Racing Bureau, 41-year-old Michel Chirol was engaged as the most experienced jockey available.

A truly international field lined up, comprising the current or former Champions of France, England, Ireland and the U.S.A. Le Rhenosis spearheaded the French defence, backed up by last year's leading four-year-old Gacko. Dawn Run flew the flag for Ireland, Gaye Brief for England, while the U.S.A was represented by Flatterer, trained by English-born Jonathan Sheppard at Unionville, and the winner of no less than three Colonial Cups and runner-up in the English Champion Hurdle.

It was a swelteringly hot day and the race was run at a cracking pace throughout. Approaching the fifth last, Dawn Run was in the leading group of three, about ½-length behind the first two. What actually happened was largely concealed by the high green hedges that form the wings. Was she half-lengthed or did she, as at Liverpool, fail to take off at all? It was academic. She broke her neck and instantly died.

Because of the heat Mrs Hill hadn't been wearing her lucky scarlet jacket. Afterwards she gave it to a charity auction in aid of handicapped children.

John Clarke had looked after the mare devotedly since both had arrived at Goresbridge together, she as a lanky four-year-old, he as a fresh-faced, curly-

haired school-leaver. Returning to his native Ireland from France, desolate and empty-handed, John just packed his bags and disappeared.

Paddy Mullins and Charmian Hill remain friends and he still trains for her. A month after the tragedy Paddy won the Galway Plate for her with Boro Quarter. Peter Kavanagh rode. She is unswerving in her admiration for her trainer – and still berating her jockeys. When Jonjo rode her mare, Icy Miss into third place in an invitation trainers' race at Dundalk in July 1988, she told Paddy crisply that it was the first time the mare had had a strong ride. It may have been a joke, but Paddy didn't think it funny. He pointed out that his sons Tony and Willie had won four times on her that season (and indeed the two sons ended the 1988–89 season as champion jockey and top amateur).

Though sadly incapacitated by her stroke, Charmian Hill is indomitable still. With help from her large, supportive family and from the Mullins, she gets about and goes racing. Her beadily acquired Deep Run youngsters graze the water meadows below the house and her sitting room is filled with photographs and trophies and memories. She looks back on the achievements of her mighty mare with tremendous pride. 'It was so sad she never bred a foal but that's racing, it's a risk you take every time a horse runs.'

Paddy Mullins' gentle brown eyes mist with unshed tears at the mention of his beloved mare. 'Only for Tony being jocked off, "Dawnie" would still be alive today.'

The Princess Royal unveils on 17 March 1987 the new statue to the great mare Dawn Run, only winner so far of the Champion Hurdle–Gold Cup double, and talks to Mrs Charmian Hill.

DAWN RUN B.M. 1978	DEEP RUN	PAMPERED KING	PRINCE CHEVALIER
			NETHERTON MAID
		TRIAL BY FIRE	COURT MARTIAL
			MITRAILLEUSE
	TWILIGHT SLAVE	ARCTIC SLAVE	ARCTIC STAR
			ROMAN GALLEY
		EARLY LIGHT	FORTINA
			BROKEN DAWN

DATE	COURSE	RACE	DISTANCE	VALUE	WEIGHT	JOCKEY	PRICE	PLACE
Season 1981–82								
May 29	Clonmel	Corinthian Fillies Flat Race (Div 2) (Amateurs) (F)	2m	£572	11.0	Mrs C. D. Hill	16/1	unpl
Jun 17	Thurles	Devils Bit Flat Race (4yo fillies (Amateurs) (F)	2m	£572	11.3	Mrs C. D. Hill	16/1	4th
Jun 22	Tralee	Castlemaine Flat Race (4–5yo) (Amateurs) (F)	2m	£572	11.0	Mrs C. D. Hill	5/1	won
Season 1982–83								
Jul 31	Galway	Tonroe Flat Race (Amateurs) (F)	2m	£1140	11.7	Mr T. Mullins	10/11f	won

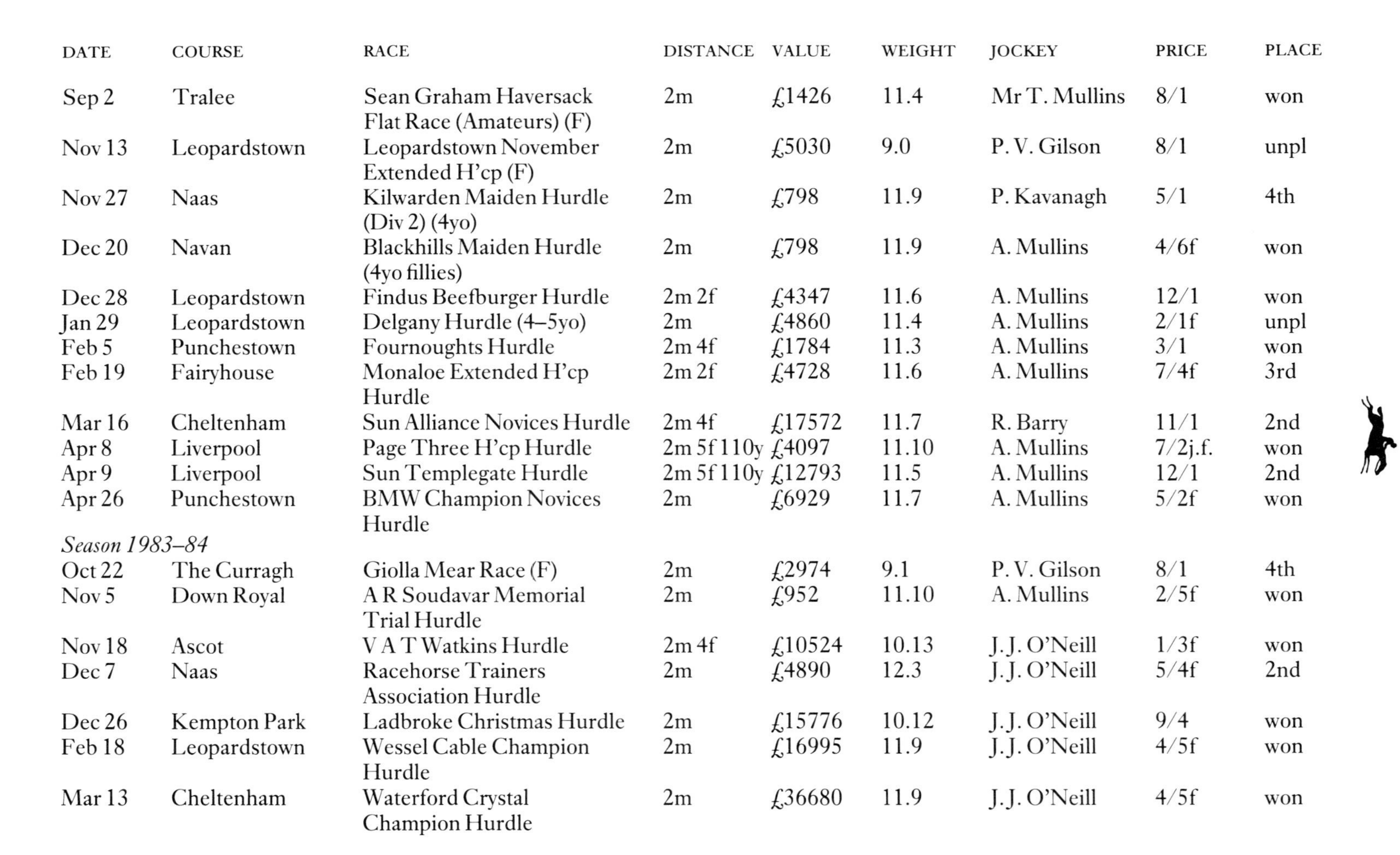

DATE	COURSE	RACE	DISTANCE	VALUE	WEIGHT	JOCKEY	PRICE	PLACE
Sep 2	Tralee	Sean Graham Haversack Flat Race (Amateurs) (F)	2m	£1426	11.4	Mr T. Mullins	8/1	won
Nov 13	Leopardstown	Leopardstown November Extended H'cp (F)	2m	£5030	9.0	P. V. Gilson	8/1	unpl
Nov 27	Naas	Kilwarden Maiden Hurdle (Div 2) (4yo)	2m	£798	11.9	P. Kavanagh	5/1	4th
Dec 20	Navan	Blackhills Maiden Hurdle (4yo fillies)	2m	£798	11.9	A. Mullins	4/6f	won
Dec 28	Leopardstown	Findus Beefburger Hurdle	2m 2f	£4347	11.6	A. Mullins	12/1	won
Jan 29	Leopardstown	Delgany Hurdle (4–5yo)	2m	£4860	11.4	A. Mullins	2/1f	unpl
Feb 5	Punchestown	Fournoughts Hurdle	2m 4f	£1784	11.3	A. Mullins	3/1	won
Feb 19	Fairyhouse	Monaloe Extended H'cp Hurdle	2m 2f	£4728	11.6	A. Mullins	7/4f	3rd
Mar 16	Cheltenham	Sun Alliance Novices Hurdle	2m 4f	£17572	11.7	R. Barry	11/1	2nd
Apr 8	Liverpool	Page Three H'cp Hurdle	2m 5f 110y	£4097	11.10	A. Mullins	7/2j.f.	won
Apr 9	Liverpool	Sun Templegate Hurdle	2m 5f 110y	£12793	11.5	A. Mullins	12/1	2nd
Apr 26	Punchestown	BMW Champion Novices Hurdle	2m	£6929	11.7	A. Mullins	5/2f	won
Season 1983–84								
Oct 22	The Curragh	Giolla Mear Race (F)	2m	£2974	9.1	P. V. Gilson	8/1	4th
Nov 5	Down Royal	A R Soudavar Memorial Trial Hurdle	2m	£952	11.10	A. Mullins	2/5f	won
Nov 18	Ascot	V A T Watkins Hurdle	2m 4f	£10524	10.13	J. J. O'Neill	1/3f	won
Dec 7	Naas	Racehorse Trainers Association Hurdle	2m	£4890	12.3	J. J. O'Neill	5/4f	2nd
Dec 26	Kempton Park	Ladbroke Christmas Hurdle	2m	£15776	10.12	J. J. O'Neill	9/4	won
Feb 18	Leopardstown	Wessel Cable Champion Hurdle	2m	£16995	11.9	J. J. O'Neill	4/5f	won
Mar 13	Cheltenham	Waterford Crystal Champion Hurdle	2m	£36680	11.9	J. J. O'Neill	4/5f	won

Mar 31	Liverpool	Sandeman Aintree Hurdle	2m 5f 110y	£13180	11.6	A. Mullins	4/6f	won
May 28	Auteuil	Prix la Barka (Hurdle)	2m 3f 110y	£12376	10.10	A. Mullins	no s.p.	won
Jun 22	Auteuil	Grande Course de Haies d'Auteuil (Hurdle)	3m 1f 110y	£41254	10.1	A. Mullins	no s.p.	won
Season 1984–85								
Nov 1	Navan	Nobber Chase	2m	£2695	10.13	A. Mullins	4/5f	won
Season 1985–86								
Dec 14	Punchestown	Durkan Bros Punchestown Chase	2m 4f	£8038	11.6	A. Mullins	5/4f	won
Dec 30	Leopardstown	Sean P Graham Chase	2m 2f	£3538	11.4	A. Mullins	4/9f	won
Jan 25	Cheltenham	Holsten Distributors Chase	3m 1f	£7059	11.1	A. Mullins	4/9f	u.r./ 4th
Mar 13	Cheltenham	Tote Cheltenham Gold Cup Chase	3m 2f	£54900	11.9	J.J. O'Neill	15/8f	won
Apr 3	Liverpool	Whitbread Gold Label Cup Chase	3m 1f	£9204	11.8	J.J. O'Neill	8/11f	fell
Apr 23	Punchestown	A Match (Chase)	2m	£21739	10.7	A. Mullins	4/6f	won
Jun 2	Auteuil	Prix la Barka (Hurdle)	2m 4f 110y	£16605	9.6	A. Mullins	no s.p.	2nd
Jun 27	Auteuil	Grand Course de Haies d'Auteuil (Hurdle)	3m 1f 110y	£46125	10.1	M. Chirol	no s.p.	fell

Career Record

Ran – Flat 7; won 3, £3,138. Hurdles 21; won 13, £165,692. Chases 7; won 5, £90,910
Total – ran 35; won 21, £259,740

NB: Prize money converted to sterling at official Jockey Club rate of exchange current at the time of the race. Races in France regarded as hurdle events.

S E V E N T E E N

Desert Orchid

S. AFRICA DECLARES STATE OF EMERGENCY BUT RUSSIA FREES SAKHAROV. 'HERALD OF FREE ENTERPRISE' CAPSIZES OFF ZEEBRUGGE. THE GREAT GALE. IRAN–IRAQ WAR FINALLY ENDS. REAGAN AND GORBACHEV SIGN MISSILE DEAL. LESTER PIGGOTT GOES TO JAIL. STOCK MARKET CRASHES. TERRORIST PAN AM BOMB KILLS 270 IN LOCKERBIE DISASTER. THE WORLD GROWS AWARE OF NATURE IN DANGER, MRS T GOES 'GREEN'. RUSSIA HOLDS ELECTIONS, AND A MILLION CHINESE STUDENTS PROTEST.

Listen to Richard Burridge and you begin to understand the compulsive grip that jump racing exerts on its fans. Disappointments, occasional heartbreaks, the continuing financial drain, count for naught for the faithful. Richard Burridge loves his horse with a passion. An eloquent man and a distinguished scriptwriter he stumbles with frustration over the impossibility of putting into words just what this horse means to him.

Desert Orchid's career is a fairytale that will inspire the vast and hopeful band of horse-lovers, who keep a mare or two at home, plan her matings, lovingly poring over dusty pedigrees and ancient formbooks through long winter evenings. They

will cherish the resulting offspring, handle them, rear them, break them in and finally dispatch them to trainers, and as fraught with anxiety that their fledgling will find favour as any parent sending their child away to school. And all to the end that one day they *might* breed a good horse.

Which is just what the Burridges did. Richard's father James bought Desert Orchid's grand-dam, Grey Orchid, for £170. He hunted her with the Belvoir and ran her in point-to-points. She won one – not with him riding – 'the only time I didn't', he recalled ruefully. Finally she developed leg trouble and he decided to breed from her. Sent to Brother, an H.I.S. stallion, chosen to inject some speed (he won over 5 and 6 furlongs but was wayward, wore a hood and needed top of the ground) she bred Flower Child who had plenty of speed but not – to start with – a lot of sense. 'She was an embarrassment out hunting', remembered 'Midge' Burridge, giggling. 'She ran away, she wouldn't queue, she behaved appallingly.' Feeling that her energies could be better channelled, they sent her to Charlie James, a son-in-law, like John Oaksey of the late Major Ginger Dennistoun. Charlie, who wears a battered hat and a jaunty air and who likes a little gamble, trains in the Berkshire village of East Garston where Colin Brown, the jockey, lives.

Flower Child was no world beater, but she did win a couple of modest novice chases on top of the ground, was placed several times and gave the Burridges a lot of fun. Desert Orchid was her first foal. James Burridge chose his sire, Grey Mirage, a class miler trained by curious coincidence at Whitsbury by Bill Marshall, whose son Tom is married to Colin Brown's sister. The world of racing is a close net. But once in it, you have friends around the world. Grey Mirage sired several good jumpers but was unfortunately exported to Saudi Arabia before they had proved themselves.

'Right from the start', insists Richard Burridge, 'Dessie was very special. He was a wonderful mover, and he had this charisma'. He was reared at Ab Kettleby, James and Midge Burridge's home in foxhunting Leicestershire, and broken there as a three-year-old. He wasn't difficult; the Burridges hacked him about themselves. 'In fact he was very lazy', recalls Midge. Richard took a half-share on condition he could choose a trainer. A family friend Simon Bullimore also took a quarter share. Richard had followed racing closely for years and had been a board-man for Ladbrokes in his flat-broke days. He chose David Elsworth, only in his fifth season, because he thought him capable of training big-race winners, but was not so large a trainer that he wouldn't take trouble with a horse who was neither expensive nor fashionably-bred. He admired the fact that David wasn't Establishment-born, but had prospered from the ranks of poorly-paid, struggling jump jockeys. He liked the privacy of Whitsbury, its beauty and tranquility and its glorious gallops. And he thought Colin Brown was especially good and sympathetic with young horses.

David Elsworth remembers meeting the Burridges quite clearly. 'They weren't normal, professional owners.' He sensed their tremendous optimism for their home-bred swan and felt the decision to choose him as trainer had not been lightly taken. Midge Burridge was a little apprehensive. Not all their friends shared their enthusiasm for Desert Orchid. One, a trainer, told them he was downright ugly and should be sent to Doncaster Sales forthwith. They were desperately hurt.

Meeting David Elsworth, James cleared his throat and murmured apologetically that Desert Orchid had an ugly head. David Elsworth's direct brown eyes twinkled engagingly, 'I rather like a plain head'.

So plans were made and Richard drove the horse down to Whitsbury, a beautiful estate laid out as a stud and training establishment by that mighty bookmaker, the late William Hill. Its training complex David Elsworth now leases from Hill's nephew, the bloodstock breeder, Chris Harper.

Richard was dying to know what David Elsworth would think of the horse. He was sure he could not fail to love the way the lanky grey moved, but what about his make, shape and outlook? The ramp was dropped and Desert Orchid poked his head out. But he would not descend. Pulling, coaxing, tempting were of no avail: he remained rooted. Eventually David Elsworth took over and backed him out. He was led into the Lower Yard, facing right onto David and Jane Elsworth's pretty, modern house, to a waiting box – and declined to enter. Again he planted himself and wouldn't budge. Again David took the rope and backed him in. Richard Burridge could bear it no longer. 'Well, what d'you think of him?' he burst out. David Elsworth hesitated, then smiled, 'I'd say he was a bit backward'.

To begin with Desert Orchid was not too much of a problem. He didn't know how to gallop but just lolloped along like a big, overgrown puppy. When he began to learn the way of the world, things grew more difficult. He took a ferocious hold and tried harder than was good for his gawky, unfurnished frame. Nevertheless he did have that vital commodity, a motor. Richard Burridge vividly recalls his elation when Whitsbury secretary, Chris Hill rang him up and said 'Your horse might be useful'. Vivaque and Buckbe were the juvenile stars of Whitsbury that year. Desert Orchid was said to have worked better than Vivaque. 'Is it true?' demanded Richard Burridge. 'Yes', replied David Elsworth, 'but I don't believe it.'

The first race at Kempton was a trauma that the Burridge family will never forget. There were 18 runners and Desert Orchid was easy to back at 50–1. The plan was to try to settle him and persuade him to relax. For the first mile things went to plan, but then the headstrong youngster launched himself from outside the wings and landed on the head of the fallen Robert Stronge. For the next two flights Colin couldn't concentrate. The sickening thought, 'Christ! I've killed Robert!', hammered into his brain like a power drill. Profiting from the situation, Desert Orchid hurtled to the front. He still led at the second last, but was tiring rapidly. Refusing to accept Colin's signals that he had done enough, he precipitated himself at the last. Exhausted, he plummeted horrifically, somersaulted and lay for dead. David and Richard rushed to the flight. Jane wouldn't let Midge go, so she remained in the stands numb with grief and shock and weeping unrestrainedly. After 15 agonizing minutes, the horse twitched, shook himself and got up. 'If he hadn't', said James Burridge, 'I think I'd've got out of racing.'

Desert Orchid had three more runs that season. His best effort was to be second, beaten a neck in the dying strides by Diamond Hunter, at the pucka Grand Military meeting at Sandown. *Timeform* criticised Colin Brown for giving Desert Orchid a lot to do in a slowly run race. David Elsworth thought this most unfair, '*Timeform* have never got him right. We all thought he had to be persuaded to settle, if he was ever going to be a racehorse.'

He wasn't settled at home either. Nor was he eating. Insatiably curious, he spent all day at his box door unable to tear himself away to go to his boring manger. Occasionally he would dive across to his manger at the back of the box, grab a mouthful and then charge back to the door, spilling most of it en route. 'An awful waste of good oats', was his trainer's terse summary. Now he has a box strategically placed opposite the entrance archway, enjoying a fine view of the whole yard. His manger is bolted to the door and he eats splendidly.

That summer and every succeeding one, Desert Orchid spent a full three months unwinding and recharging his well-spent batteries at the Burridges' Leicestershire home. At the beginning of August he comes in and spends four or five weeks walking round the roads. In the early days the Burridges did this themselves, but since he became so precious they have employed somebody to do it for them. David Elsworth doesn't believe in preliminary roadwork which would in any case hardly be feasible for upwards of 80 horses along the perilously narrow lanes round Whitsbury. His jumpers first trot round the all-weather track for a few days before beginning very slow hack-cantering. Their food is increased only gradually and thus, he reasons, they don't get too full of themselves and the chances of leg-injuries are lessened. The Burridges nevertheless stick to traditional methods, and Desert Orchid does his walking in Leicestershire.

Desert Orchid's second season at Whitsbury coincided with the arrival of a new head lad, Rodney Boult, a man who all the Burridges and David Elsworth insist

Desert Orchid with head lad Rodney Boult at Whitsbury.

has been a prime factor in the development of the headstrong grey. 'The art of training,' says David Elsworth, 'is training horses to be trained.' This the Whitsbury team were finding hard to do in the case of Desert Orchid. One morning he took off with his lass Melanie and ran clear off the all-weather gallop. After that Rodney of the battered, weathered face, rain-washed blue eyes and the hands of an angel, took charge. No nosebands, no fancy bit or other gadgets. 'I just talk to him.' Colin Brown, often seen with arms wrenched from their sockets and feet braced almost horizontally against the strain, never ceases to marvel at Rodney's light-fingered touch on the reins.

Rodney has known David Elsworth since the 1950s. He'd started, like Joe Mercer, with Major Sneyd. 'A rotten old bastard, but a great tutor', was David's caustic description. He rode a winner on the flat and nearly 30 over fences when with Doug Marks. Then he married and left racing for some years. But the drug was too strong, and he was drawn back. His great skill as a work rider was keenly sought. He'd been with Dick Hern and then John Dunlop who'd valued him so highly that he'd flown him to Ireland with Shirley Heights to do the dual Derby winner's final spin on The Curragh.

'He's far too good a work rider to be a head lad', says David, 'but', he shrugs, 'Rodney and I – we undertand each other'. Rodney, an old-fashioned stableman in highly polished boots and dapper chocolate jodhpurs, runs a smart outfit. He can't stand sloppiness or clock-watching, which is clearly to his Guv'nor's liking. The Elsworth horses glow with health, they look relaxed in their boxes, their manes and tails are neatly dressed and the yards are spick and span.

David Elsworth is concerned about his workforce. 'Good staff is the key', he emphasizes. 'We try. We've cottages here, a hostel, a nice canteen with two cooks, then there's the pub in the village and the stud over the road. I think they're happy. But there isn't enough money – once they're married and need a mortgage.'

Given the present levels of prize-money, he doesn't think that ordinary owners could stand much more in the way of fees. But with a Tote monopoly, he pondered, could senior staff be subsidized? Or perhaps a premium levied on horses costing more than a certain sum, could go to a central staff fund?

Colin Brown, who rode out twice a week, every week until his retirement in March 1988, comments that the Whitsbury staff seem in another world compared with those at Lambourn or Newmarket. 'They're like children, dedicated and so quiet; and if the Guv'nor tells them to take a horse out for a pick of grass for half-an-hour in pouring rain – they do it.'

Rodney was at first guarded in his optimism about Desert Orchid. 'He could gallop all right but would he settle? In his box as well as on the gallops – well, the one always follows the other.' If he didn't, he'd never make a racehorse.

These prognostications proved gloomy, for Desert Orchid bloomed exotically his second season. It was decided to abandon ideas of restraint and let him blaze away in front. In his first two races at Ascot, he never saw another horse, hurdled with dramatic extravagance and won by a total of 35 lengths. He was dappled grey like a rocking horse in those days and with his flying white mane and tail, his exuberance and his determination quickly caught the imagination of the jumping public. Defeat over 2¾ miles at Sandown, where he was beaten just ¾ length by

Desert Orchid ridden by his long-time partner, Colin Brown, goes on to win the Haig Whisky Novices Hurdle at Ascot in 1983. How dappled he was then . . .

Catch Phrase, was attributed by Richard Burridge not so much to the distance as to a loose plate which was clearly flapping with a whole circuit to go. He won with tremendous authority at Kempton on Boxing Day. Richard Linley rode, as Colin Brown went to Wincanton to ride a double on Buckbe and King's Bishop. Richard succeeded in settling him in front and Paddy Mullins, over with Dawn Run for the Christmas Hurdle, remembers being very impressed indeed.

So swift was Desert Orchid's progress that when he advanced from novice company to take on his seniors in the established Champion Hurdle trial, the Kingwell Pattern Hurdle at Wincanton, he was made favourite. His rivals included Very Promising, Schweppes Gold Trophy runner-up, Stan's Pride, Janus and Migrator, but he beat them all off, running on determinedly to beat Stan's Pride and Very Promising decisively.

Encouraged by this success and by the defection, through injury, of last year's winner Gaye Brief, it was decided to have a crack at the Champion Hurdle. He was made second favourite to odds-on Dawn Run, but he ran no sort of a race, weakening rapidly from the fifth and finishing out of the first nine. At this point the theory began to be mooted that he didn't like left-handed tracks. Until March 1989 he never won at Cheltenham, although he twice ran a marvellous race in the Queen Mother Two Mile Champion Chase. Until the spring of 1988, when he won at Liverpool, he had never won on any left-handed track. Nevertheless he ran too badly to be true in that Champion Hurdle. Significantly, he didn't reappear.

The season 1984–85 was that of the virus and although at times Desert Orchid appeared to have recovered and to show flashes of his old brilliance, his connections were never really happy about him.

He ran a good race first time out at Kempton in October, third to Ra Nova, but then he coughed and was off the course for two months. His defeat by See You Then on his reappearance could be attributed to lack of fitness and a fair second, splitting Browne's Gazette and See You Then, at Kempton on Boxing Day suggested he was on the way back. He wasn't. He hated travelling to Ireland for the Sweeps Hurdle, wouldn't eat, fretted and became dehydrated. Not surprisingly, he ran miserably. An easy win in Sandown's Otley Hurdle restored everyone's morale but he ran so wretchedly in the Champion Hurdle that Colin Brown pulled him up fully two flights from home.

Blinkers were tried for the Welsh Champion Hurdle, but they were clearly a disaster; he was again pulled up. Then at Ascot in April, the clouds seemed to roll away. Giving 24 lb. to five-time winner Comedy Star, he set off in his old flamboyant style, treating both hurdles and opposition with disdain. He was tiring but still holding a clear advantage when he crashed dramatically at the last. It was a rotten end to a rotten season.

As it had been decided that he should upgrade to fences the following season, he was given a school. 'He jumped those four fences in eight seconds flat,' recalled Colin, 'David shut his eyes after the first two; he was brilliant.'

By his first race in the autumn of 1985, he was, to quote David, 'dangerously well'. He stalked round the paddock, sweating slightly (always a good sign) and grinding his bit so ferociously that David feared he might break it in half. Appearances were not deceptive. Desert Orchid scorched off, hurdling with astonishing fluency and was still 15 lengths clear when he nosedived at the second last.

Undaunted he proceeded to reel off four high-class novice chases in a row. 'Unchallenged, easily, comfortably' are the precise adverbs employed by *Chaseform*. His jumping was another thing: it was hair-raising, breath-taking and to his rivals soul-destroying. There was no question but that Desert Orchid was intensely exciting to watch. He possessed abundantly the same charisma as Easter Hero of old. Like him he became a crowd-puller, and racecourse executives purred with pleasure when they had Desert Orchid on their cards.

He didn't win again that season after Christmas. He had a spectacular disagreement with Colin Brown at the downhill open ditch at Ascot. 'It was the bloody camera', explained Colin cheerfully from behind the Orchid Bar at his pub The Ibex in Chaddlesworth, 'I've always said it was dangerous. They drive along right beside the track and Dessie's looking at it and there's the ditch coming up and he picks up – puts down *on* the fence, banks off it and I'm still there – and he goes one way and I go the other and that's it.'

Desert Orchid was twice run out of it up the hill at Sandown on softish ground and ran a fine race to be third in Cheltenham's Arkle Chase behind Oregon Trail and Charcoal Wally. However, when he had met Charcoal Wally on any other track he had beaten him easily, so it seemed plain that, for whatever reason, Cheltenham simply did not bring out the best in him.

By the autumn of 1986 Desert Orchid was bleaching to a snowy white. He was also thickening, and had built up a massive top to his neck and a hefty rounding over his quarters, making him a far more imposing individual than he'd been in his

gawky, adolescent years. There were high hopes that autumn that the good ground and late sunshine would launch him on another successful season. So it was all the more disappointing when after an initial win at Sandown, he ran moderately in a 2½-mile chase at Ascot behind Church Warden and Berlin. Afterwards he was found to be slightly amiss and was off the course for a month. He reappeared at Ascot, this time over 2 miles. The presence of the fragile-legged but explosive Far Bridge meant that he could not have matters his own way but had to share the lead. For the first time in his life he came from behind, quickened nicely going to the last and won handsomely, this time putting 12 lengths between himself and his old rival Charcoal Wally.

At this juncture his connections became sharply divided. David Elsworth favoured a tilt at the King George and was backed up by Richard Burridge. Both reasoned that Desert Orchid had stayed 2 miles easily over hurdles, that Kempton usually provided goodish ground at Christmastime and was the sort of sharp track which usually suits front runners. Rose Park, basically a 2-miler, had won it thus in 1956. But James and Midge Burridge at home and Rodney Boult in the yard were adamant that Desert Orchid had no chance of staying 3 miles.

With Combs Ditch also engaged, Colin Brown was in a dilemma. He'd been second the last two years on the chunky, free-walking chestnut and had ridden many good winners for his skilled and incredibly lucky owner-breeders, the Torys of Dorset. They clearly expected him to ride their horse again. Combs Ditch however had cut a heel while out at grass during the summer. This had delayed his return to Whitsbury and it had not proved possible to give him a prep race. The Burridges relieved some of the pressure by saying squarely 'It's a difficult choice – whichever you choose, you'll ride Dessie next time'. Simon Sherwood who will burst so successfully into this story later, was engaged to ride whichever horse Colin declined.

David was unhappy at Rodney's robustly expressed opinion. 'It was the only time we've ever disagreed about anything. As he knows the horse so well, I was worried.'

The weather didn't help. It rained heavily the day before and then dried overnight. The result was dead, soggy ground officially described as 'soft'. 'I was very gloomy', Richard remembered.

Less than an hour before the race Colin made up his mind. He'd ride Combs Ditch. 'If there'd been no other consideration I think I'd've chosen Dessie, but there you go. I've deserted him twice and each time he's won.'

The understudy called at the eleventh hour to don the blue and grey Burridge colours was Simon Sherwood, public-school educated, elegantly lean, rich and sophisticated. He was bred for the game. His father 'Nat' had been Master of the Cambridge University Draghounds, had point-to-pointed robustly and was a well-known Essex sportsman with a look of Mr Punch. Simon had been a leading point-to-point rider, then Champion Amateur. On the surface a greater contrast to the barrel-chested, short-legged Colin who had left school at 14 and never been abroad until well into his 20s could scarcely be imagined. Colin's road to the top had been long and arduous, financed by dawn starts with a cloth stall in West Country markets and long evenings working pubs. Every winner had been dearly

earned. Yet at bottom there is little difference. No advantages of birth, wealth or education make a top jump jockey. Both men engaged in a dangerous game because they loved it. Both reached the top because they were very brave and very good.

Simon didn't mind which he rode and thought that on balance Colin would plump for Combs Ditch, the media selection. Worries about his mount's stamina were banished by David's brisk paddock briefing. 'Forget the trip. Let him run his own race.' Acting on this advice, Simon took him straight to the front and Desert Orchid proceeded to give a flawless exhibition of bold-jumping front-running, remarkable even by his standards. Nothing else could get in a blow. Wayward Lad and Forgive 'n' Forget were run off their feet and finished unplaced; no fewer than four horses, discarded like jetsam in his wake, abandoned the unequal struggle and pulled up. Simon increased the murderous pace down the back straight and dumbfounded the doubting Thomases by quickening again two out. Gamely though they tried, neither Door Latch nor Bolands Cross could mount any sort of challenge and Desert Orchid, ridden with hands and heels only, won by an astonishing 15 lengths.

'It was a fluke', said Simon. 'Like everything in racing it was the luck of being in the right place at the right time. But it's a memory that'll stay. When I'm old and grey and on sticks, I won't forget it.'

The Burridges went berserk. They couldn't believe it was true. Their gawky, ugly duckling, their crazy tearaway 2-miler had taken on the best staying chasers

Winning the 'King George' at Kempton on Boxing Day 1986.

in the land and beaten them hollow.

Queen Elizabeth, always appreciative of a good horse and said to be specially fond of Desert Orchid, joined the cheering, happy throng in the unsaddling enclosure. She wore an orchid pinned to the lapel of her turquoise blue coat.

Colin Brown had a foul meeting. Combs Ditch was never in the hunt and pulled up. Cavvies Clown gave him a nasty fall in the novice chase and the next day Floyd gave him an even worse one at the last flight of the Christmas Hurdle when looking likely to win. He kept smiling. He was pleased, he told reporters, for Desert Orchid, for the Elsworths and the Burridges. There was no gripe, no whinge of self-pity. 'You'll go a long way in racing before you'll find anyone to say an unkind word about Colin', says John Francome, 'he's quite simply the nicest man around.'

The King George was a triumphant vindication of David Elsworth's judgement. As early as 1984 he had predicted in a *Timeform* interview that Desert Orchid would make a chaser and a 3-mile chaser at that. Fifteen years as a not particularly successful jump jockey had left him with a lot of experience and many friends, but little else: certainly not much money, without which it is very hard indeed to get established as a trainer, unless backed by a rich patron. David gave up riding in 1972, and oddly enough the last winner he rode, Soixante-Neuf, provided Colin with his first at Newton Abbot. David had walked him round the tight West Country track.

David had always believed he could train. More importantly, he persuaded others to believe in him. In the early 1970s he had approached Lt. Col. 'Ricky' Vallance at Bishop's Canning and offered to work for nothing if he could bring a horse or two with him that he'd been asked to train. The arrangement prospered and the number of horses grew. Among them was Red Candle, who won the 1972 Mackeson Gold Cup and touched off Red Rum in a memorable Hennessy a year later. A portrait of him, with Jimmy Fox up, hangs over the fireplace in the Elsworth's sitting room. Then disaster struck. The stewards enquired into the improved form of Well Briefed when, heavily supported, he won at Devon and Exeter in May 1974. The matter was referred to Portman Square and Colonel Vallance's licence to train was withdrawn. The Jockey Club was perfectly well aware of the situation at Bishop's Canning and David's application for a licence of his own, previously lodged, was rejected. There followed four grim years. The Elsworths lived in a series of council houses. David did the markets in Salisbury, Devizes and Shaftesbury. Colin used to help. They rented a few boxes where they could. 'I did some liveries and backed a few wrong horses,' says David, lightly skimming over those grey times.

In 1978 the authorities relented and gave him a licence to train. He started with a handful of horses in a rented yard near Larkhill. His first four runners all won. He moved his rapidly expanding team in quick succession to Brigmerston, near Salisbury and then to Monty Stevens' estate at Lucknam Park near Colerne, not far from Bath. Here the problem was that there was nowhere to work the horses. In the sodden, rain-lashed March of 1981 matters became desperate. Finally David acquired permission to take his four National Hunt Festival hopes over to the isolation unit at Whitsbury, and to use the legendary gallops there. Colin

Brown went with him to help. The horses thrived and Lesley-Ann squelched home to win the Sun Alliance Chase at 25–1.

James Bethell, subsequently at Didcot, was rumoured to be leaving Whitsbury. The Elsworth team had grown to more than fifty. David was in urgent need of a big yard with good gallops. But could he afford to gamble on taking on such an establishment with nearly 90 boxes? Could he fill it and make it pay? It was a risk. But David felt he must take it.

He and Jane moved into Whitsbury on Friday 13 November. Jane couldn't at first think why the removal men were quite free that day. The date has certainly brought no ill-luck to the Elsworths. Their fortunes have prospered ever since.

Right from the start there were winners and not just jumping winners. Group winners, Royal Ascot winners, placings in the English, French and Irish Derbies, major handicaps winners like the Royal Hunt Cup and the Wokingham (a rare Royal Ascot double) all sallied forth from Whitsbury. Yet there is often a jumping link. The half-brother and sister Mighty Flutter (third in the Derby) and Mighty Fly (Lincoln and Royal Hunt Cup) were owned and bred by the Torys, hunting and point-to-point enthusiasts who also owned and bred Combs Ditch and Buckbe. The dam of the 'Mightys', Lettuce, was half-sister to the Grand National winner, Rubstic. Moreover there are many points about the Elsworth flat horses which one would find most attractive in a jumper: Indian Ridge (Jersey Stakes) was lengthy, had scope, and was a good walker; Naheez (Horris Hill, and placed in the Irish and French Derbies) was tall and long-striding; Governor-General is big, strong and good-bodied. Like so many of James Delahooke's shrewd and successful purchases for the flat, they have the stamp of being chosen by a man with his roots in jumping.

Desert Orchid's triumph in the 3-mile King George proved no flash in the pan. He was deeply impressive winning Sandown's Gainsborough Chase from Gold Cup hope Stearsby and the luckless Bolands Cross, giving weight to both. He then played a memorable part in what many felt to have been the race of the National Hunt Meeting, the Queen Mother Two Mile Champion Chase, which Pearlyman won by a neck and 3 lengths from Very Promising and Desert Orchid. When he'd finished 7 lengths in front of Very Promising at Sandown in November, he'd been receiving 25 lb. Now at level weights he was only 3 lengths behind, an improvement of more than a stone, and after coming back from 3 miles plus to 2 miles on a course which had never seemed to suit him.

His next triumph at Ascot in the Peregrine Handicap Chase was one that Colin Brown remembers with more pleasure and gratitude than any other victory. Inevitably Desert Orchid was set to carry top weight of 12 st. 4 lb., 29 lb. more than any of the other six runners. Moreover the ground was not as he would have preferred, but good to soft with sticky patches. Undaunted the pair set out to make the running in their customary style. By the time the field had turned the corner out of Swinley Bottom, however, Desert Orchid was perceived not to be going so strongly and a mistake at the last open ditch gave the lead to Gold Bearer ridden by the enterprising Guy Landau. Seeking to profit from his 36 lb. pull in the weights, Guy kicked boldly for home and Desert Orchid seemed beaten. Under vigorous driving, he rallied in the straight, regained the lead after the last and ran on

doggedly to win by 2 lengths. A dramatic picture of this pulsating finish hangs in the Orchid Bar of Colin's pub in the pretty downland village of Chaddlesworth.

By the season's end Desert Orchid had so entrenched himself in the public's heart that his appearance in the paddock for the Sandown's spectacular end of season climax, the Whitbread Gold Cup, was greeted by spontaneous applause. There was not, alas, a happy finale. Unknown to the outside world, the Whitsbury team had been battling for days against corns on both their champion's front feet. Equine corns are not like human ones. They are bruises made on the heel of the foot. In severe cases pus may be present. A jumper's feet are subjected to a great deal of wear and tear during the season, exacerbated by the constant change of working shoes for racing plates and back again. White hooves and the feet of grey horses lacking pigmentation are specially vulnerable. David Elsworth, his blacksmith and his vet thought they had the problem under control and crossed their fingers. But in vain. Desert Orchid was never galloping or jumping with his customary zest and was well in arrears when Colin pulled him up at the nineteenth. The race was won by another dashing front-runner, the National hero, Lean ar Aghaidh, known by his sporting owners and so by the racing public at large as 'Lean on the Aga'.

Despite this last set-back, Desert Orchid had ended the season garlanded with honours. Racing journalists voted him National Hunt Horse of the Year. *Timeform* rated him Champion Jumper with a rating of 177 and in the *Racing Calendar's* Handicap Ratings, he was allotted top figure of 101.

When Desert Orchid returned to Whitsbury in September David was faced with the delicate problem of allocating him to a new lad or lass. The fortunate selected would be the fourth to do the Burridge star. This unusually high turnover simply emphasizes David's continuing anxiety about keeping top-class staff on the level of wages even a good trainer can now afford to pay.

After Melanie, Desert Orchid had been entrusted to Gary Morgan, known at Whitsbury as 'Cooper man' because of his lanky, drawling resemblance to the matinée-idol film star. He had been succeeded by a lass, Jackie Parrish (now Young), a pretty girl who adored him, but wasn't able to ride him other than when he was walking out, or having the occasional steady canter soon after a race. She then married and left racing.

Allocating a horse as famous as Desert Orchid is, as David points out, a difficulty. 'You're sure to upset someone.' His choice fell upon Janice Coyle who was apprenticed to him. She is a beautiful horsewoman and has ridden several winners on the flat.

David thinks that, 'On the whole, girls are better at looking after horses. They don't ride as well as men, but if they can canter, it's O.K. A work-rider can do the fast work.' The basic work at Whitsbury is surprisingly on an all-weather track only 5 furlongs round. David doesn't hold with the theory that horses need variety or should do different things in different places every day. He thinks they appreciate routine. Desert Orchid canters every day. Afterwards he's offered a pick of grass and a roll, which he relishes, in one of the two sand-pits. He then returns to his box and relaxes. He will usually go to the grass gallops twice a week, depending on his programme and his well-being. 'The great thing about David',

enthuses Richard Burridge, 'is that he is always flexible. He doesn't make rules and he keeps an open mind about his horses' requirements.'

Richard Burridge thinks that Desert Orchid wasn't at his best for the first half of season 1987–88. He never ran a bad race and turned in some brave weight-carrying performances but he didn't seem to sparkle until March. His two preliminary outings were little more than exercise canters. He never saw another horse and won without coming off a tight rein. He then got beaten at Sandown but it was no disgrace to fail to concede 26 lb. to Long Engagement.

The King George however was another matter. This year the ground was good and he started favourite at even money. From the start, he was challenged by another headstrong front runner, Beau Ranger, and occasionally by Cybrandian. It appeared that the three cut each others' throats. Desert Orchid was the only one to finish in the frame and he had no answer when the sporting French crack, Nupsala, who had jumped magnificently throughout, ranged alongside at the second last and forged ahead to win comfortably by fifteen lengths. David said that the tactics were mistaken but that it wasn't Colin's fault. Richard Burridge was sure 'that was the only way to ride him.'

In fact the time was slow, nearly 12 sec. above Wayward Lad's record, so the pace cannot have been suicidal. In the light of his subsequent achievements it seems likely that Desert Orchid wasn't at his best.

His now legion fans were fractionally disappointed when on strength-sapping, heavy ground, he got beaten in Sandown's Gainsborough Chase. In hindsight, his attempt to give 17 lb. to the Gold Cup winner, Charter Party, and 21 lb. to his stable companion Rhyme 'n Reason, was heroic. Charter Party's trainer, David Nicholson said after the Gold Cup that he was very relieved Desert Orchid hadn't run.

Connections solved the dilemma of whether Desert Orchid should run in the Gold Cup by the simple expedient of not entering him. Richard Burridge fervently hoped then that he never would. Instead he went for the Queen Mother Two Mile Champion Chase which proved almost a re-run of the previous year's memorable contest. Again Pearlyman won it impressively, but Desert Orchid managed to beat Very Promising and ran so well that many thought he could break his left-handed bogey. It was obvious that the bends were his problem. By the end of the back straight he was clear and David thought 'we've got 'em', but up and down the hill is almost continuously on the bend and by the second last, he led only on sufferance. Once in the straight, he ran on again like a tiger, to pass Very Promising and to get within 5 lengths of Pearlyman. He had certainly jumped to the right coming down the hill, confirming in many observers' minds that this was an incurable bias. The duel between Desert Orchid and Pearlyman had so excited the public that the Kempton Park executive, never short of bright ideas or slow to maximize attendances, offered a November match between the two stars over 2 miles. Desert Orchid's camp was gamely keen; Pearlyman's had to decline: their horse was most unlikely to be ready to run before Christmas. There was talk that he might have injured himself when starting favourite but finishing only seventh in the 2-mile chase at Liverpool on Grand National Day.

After Desert Orchid's brave race at Cheltenham Colin took the opportunity to

announce his retirement. He had been licensee of The Ibex for a while now and decided he would like to get out at the top and in one piece. He'd never wanted to train and knew that David's offer of a job at Whitsbury would not yield him the sort of money he needed for his family. He still rides out. Mark Bradstock's horses occupy his boxes at East Garston and he follows Dessie's career with pride and affection – on foot or on television.

So Desert Orchid lost the cheerful, courageous partner who had steered him through the hazardous, rip-roaring days and made him the supreme professional he has become. Fortunately a ready-made replacement was waiting in the wings. Simon Sherwood, who had so splendidly seized the spare ride for the King George, was only too eager to return to the colours.

Thus began that unbroken partnership between horse and rider which became so vital a part of Desert Orchid's story. Without Simon Sherwood, would the horse have even been risked in the Tote Gold Cup of 1989, let alone have won it? It was going to be Simon who would show at Liverpool that the horse could indeed gallop round sharp left-handed bends, and that with a loose rein he could be persuaded not to fight, but to settle calmly.

The combination remained undefeated in an eight race sequence starting in April 1988 until the jockey's last ride on the horse at Liverpool exactly a year later. Then Desert Orchid bewildered the racing world and grieved his fans by crashing at the twelfth fence on the Mildmay Course in the Martell Cup. The 1987 Tote Gold Cup winner, Charter Party, fell at the same fence. And Dawn Run had fallen

Desert Orchid working on the famous Whitsbury gallops with his only work-rider Rodney Boult.

in the same race (but at the first fence) after her great Cheltenham victory.

Within eleven days of this débâcle in 1989 Simon Sherwood astonished his brother Oliver, who retained him, and shocked the Desert Orchid camp by abruptly announcing his retirement. He was always, as he said himself 'a quality, rather than a quantity, rider'. He disliked driving miles to ride poor horses at minor meetings. Who could blame him?

He was geared to start as a trainer the following year.

He was likened by experienced observers to have been the equal in big races of Bryan Marshall and John Francome. The latter had proved Sherwood's guiding star in many ways. Critics acclaimed Simon Sherwood as one of the best jockeys never to have been champion. His riding of the grey horse was a joy to behold.

But in April 1988 all that lay a full and glorious year ahead. His partnership with Desert Orchid, brought about by the retirement of bold Colin Brown, would resume at Aintree.

Their first target was the Martell Cup at Liverpool. Again, stable opinion was divided. Richard Burridge was sure the course would suit him, didn't worry about it being left-handed and didn't think, from a conversation he had had with Beau Ranger's owner, that the Pipe-trained chestnut would take Dessie on again as he had at Kempton.

David was not nearly so sanguine and was frankly relieved when Beau Ranger was withdrawn at the start due to a spread plate. So was Simon Sherwood. With no one to hustle him, he could now dictate the pace he chose and take a pull round the tight bend away from the winning post. From then on, though Kildimo, Weather the Storm and Contradeal furiously pursued him, they could never get to grips with the flying grey, and Desert Orchid won unchallenged by eight lengths. He had not jumped to the right anything like so markedly as he had before. Noting the very different styles of Simon Sherwood and Colin Brown, some experts considered that Sherwood's longer reins and quieter hands suited the horse better and that Desert Orchid now seemed less inconvenienced by a left-turning track like the Mildway Course at Liverpool. But David Elsworth and Richard Burridge both point out that, whereas Cheltenham is almost continuously turning, Liverpool enjoys two long straights.

The road to the Whitbread was again punctuated with corn-related problems. Desert Orchid completed his preparation barefoot and was boxed the short way to the gallops to avoid going on the road. Once on Whitsbury's famous turf he was scintillating. In a 6-furlong spin with a decent flat miler, Hymn of Harlech, despite the considerable weight advantage Janice enjoyed from Rodney, the five-year-old winner of two races in 1988 could never get to him. Rodney pulled up chortling, 'he's never been better'.

This time the Whitsbury staff were repaid for their devotion. Their star arrived at Sandown in magnificent fettle. The capacity crowd applauded his appearance in the paddock, grinding his teeth and sweating slightly. They clapped him again going down to the start. He did not, however, start favourite. Deterred by the twin problems of corns and distance (at 3 miles 5 furlongs and 118 yards, the Whitbread was ½ mile further than he had ever won over and Sandown's final hill offers no quarter to the spent), the market preferred Aquilifier, lightly weighted at

10 st. 3 lb. and the winner of no less than six races that season. Strands of Gold and Kildimo shared second favouritism with Desert Orchid at 6–1.

Simon Sherwood set an apparently steady pace but it was significant that two other proven front runners, Lean ar Aghaidh and Run and Skip, could never establish the lead until the last bend where Simon coolly gave Desert Orchid a breather and allowed Run and Skip to nose ahead. By the Pond Fence Desert Orchid's ears were tightly pricked again and he was back in command and, far from succumbing to the perfectly timed challenge of Kildimo, he dug deep into his reserves and found a little extra. Up the hill he strode unflinching and never looked in danger of losing the 2½-length lead he preserved to the line. Simon made the point that he never dictated to Dessie. 'I love a horse that front runs and I love one you can sit quiet on. It wouldn't be any use trying to hassle Dessie. His ears would twitch and you'd know he was not amused. It's like playing a fish. When Kildimo came to me I did start getting after him and he didn't like it. Then he heard the roar of the crowd and that was enough for him.'

They were still roaring when he returned to a tumultuous reception. British sporting crowds in the late 1980s had received with reason fierce criticism. But there are few more heartwarming sights or sounds than a jumping crowd welcoming a special hero. Languid Sloanes scamper, colonels quick march, ladies *d'un certain âge*, whose girths and lungs are no longer suited to such activity, holloa and run and elbow their way to the unsaddling enclosure. With them rush the young in stylishly torn old jeans and grubby trainers, and the pensioners in frayed-elbowed jackets and most old-fashioned ties. And even the despised yobs, not knowing quite why, join in the rush to celebrate a hero. In all the steam and sweat and jostle and noise there's scarcely a cross word. A polymorphic crowd, wildly diverse in wealth and styles and backgrounds, united in affection and admiration for a good, brave horse.

Desert Orchid is the first of our Winter Kings since Red Rum whose appeal reaches far beyond the jumping public. He is familiar to millions for whom steeplechasing is normally just something that happens on television on Saturday afternoons.

Two factors dominated Desert Orchid's 1988–89 campaign. The first was the cliff-hanging would he–wouldn't he challenge for the Cheltenham Gold Cup, hitherto firmly vetoed by the Burridge family. The second was his burgeoning popularity.

After holidaying as usual at Ab Kettleby under the watchful care of James and Midge Burridge, Desert Orchid went north to the remote and ruggedly beautiful moors of North Yorkshire. Richard Burridge had recently bought a house there. He could now realise a long-nurtured ambition to supervise Dessie's preliminary walking exercise. He would not, he hastily assured Dessie's myriad well-wishers, subject the horse to his own weight but he did accompany his star on a more robust horse. All of which made irresistably romantic copy for not just the racing pages but all the popular press.

Desert Orchid's reappearance in late October was heralded by a fanfare of trumpets and a vastly increased gate for Wincanton, whose Terry Biddlecombe Challenge Trophy often attracts good horses. Colin Brown went to watch his old

comrade-in-arms, taking his family with him. He stood paternally by the last fence where Desert Orchid, with a star's intuitive feel for the gallery, flung a particularly spectacular leap before racing up the run-in, white tail flaunting, to put fifteen lengths between himself and his useful pursuers, Bishop's Yarn and Golden Friend.

Hills and Ladbrokes instantly promoted him favourite at 10–1 for the Cheltenham Gold Cup five months ahead. Richard Burridge sounded a note of caution. He favoured a third crack at the Queen Mother Two Mile Champion Chase. After all, Very Promising had retired and Pearlyman was already rumoured to be side-lined with the leg-trouble which would later put him out for the season. Burridge added carefully what all horse lovers should say to hungry pressmen seeking plans, 'It'll be a wait-and-see situation'.

David Elsworth kept his cards close to his chest and would not commit himself beyond the King George.

Desert Orchid's next planned race was Kempton's Boxing Day Trial Chase, carefully framed by their lively executive as a King George 'prep'. It attracted but two runners. The cleverest racecourse cannot yet produce the going it wants. Changing world weather has given Britain summer in autumn. Everywhere the ground was fast. At Kempton it was firm. Wisely for him, most disappointingly for the public, many of whom had gone specially to see him, Dessie wasn't risked. Ninety minutes before the race he was withdrawn. As a welcome sop he jauntily paraded past the stands after the fifth race with lanky Richard Burridge pacing lovingly at his side.

Instead he went, as had always been the plan, for Sandown's two mile Tingle Creek Chase commemorating Tom Jones' electric chestnut whose course record, set in 1978, still stands. The plan raised eyebrows among racing's purists and their misgivings were mirrored by the bookmakers who clearly doubted his ability to give 22 lb. to the brilliant but cussed Vodkatini. The pair ended as 2–1 joint favourites but Vodkatini took no further part in the proceedings. He remained rooted and sulking as the tapes flew up and Desert Orchid flew off. The grey, never headed, won with devastating ease from Jim Thorpe and a below-par Panto Prince.

The racing world marvelled at his versatility, unequalled they claimed. Not so. Great chasers, including several of our 'Winter Kings' have demonstrated that the ability to sprint is built into every true champion. Manifesto, Easter Hero, Golden Miller and Dawn Run have all come back to win good races over two miles after victories, or very near misses, in the Gold Cup and, even more remarkably after the extended four miles of the Grand National.

On the same day that Desert Orchid was scorching round Sandown the sadder side of sport surfaced with the announcement that the National winner Corbière had had to be put down after a fortnight's sickness. The news reduced his outwardly tough trainer, Jenny Pitman, to tears.

It was precisely these grim risks which haunted the Burridge family and disinclined them to commit their beloved Dessie to a Gold Cup challenge. They had thought they had lost him the first time he ever ran. They had seen his promising younger brother Ragged Robin killed at Worcester. James' white, drawn face betrays agony every time the horse runs. Richard appears more composed, but his tension is palpable as he hovers round his horse during the long preliminaries.

They quite simply love him. To a chorus of rumours reporting offers of half a million, even a million pounds for their wonderful gelding, they have calmly stated, 'He is not for sale'.

As Christmas approached the racing world wondered whether Dessie could join the élite of dual King George winners. After his scintillating victory of 1986, he had been easily, disappointingly beaten by the Frenchman Nupsala in 1987. The threat of a repeat was dashed when it was announced, after Nupsala's arrival at Oliver Sherwood's Rhonehurst stables, that his entry had gone astray and he couldn't run. Cynical pragmatists wondered why Weatherbys couldn't suddenly have 'found' his entry after all. And everyone wondered why the Kempton executive, unlike keen Edward Gillespie at Cheltenham, hadn't rung round the trainers with runners in their 'classic' just to check.

Richard Burridge, on guard against persistent doping scares, spent a Christmas night vigil in the back of a car parked a few yards from Dessie's box.

Even without the spice of a French challenge, the King George, as always, produced a cracking race. Vodkatini, on his best behaviour, jumped off with the others. Kildimo's dubious back appeared to be in good working order and he ran and jumped more fluently than hitherto that season. All three had a chance at the last but Desert Orchid was brooking no challenge. He strode clear on the run-in to win convincingly by four lengths and to deafening applause.

Amid renewed urging for a commitment to the Gold Cup, David Elsworth coolly announced that his star would again revert to the minimum distance for Ascot's valuable Victor Chandler Handicap Chase. His task looked formidable indeed. Panto Prince, below par at Sandown, had since beaten the classy Saffron Lord and was set to receive 22 lb., while Vodkatini, only 9 lengths behind at levels in the King George, would receive 23 lb. In fact Vodkatini did not survive to mount a challenge. Attempting a Desert Orchid style leap at the tricky downhill fifth fence, he pitched and fell heavily, giving himself and poor Peter Hobbs a crunching fall.

Sickeningly this produced exultant cheers from the unacceptable section of Desert Orchid's fan club in the stands. Himself also overjumped and pitched at this fence, but nimbly recovered while Simon Sherwood sat tight. Meanwhile Panto Prince, under an inspired ride from Brendan Powell, was jumping with the speed and precision of a Cossack dancer and making the best of his way home. Turning into the straight it didn't look as though the grey would make it. Simon didn't think so either. But he remembered Colin Brown telling him, 'Never give up. He doesn't know when he's beat'.

Slowly but inexorably the gap closed. A slight mistake at the last did nothing to help their chance and Panto Prince was grimly determined not to relinquish his slender advantage. For the first time in their partnership Simon went for his whip – just once. It was scarcely necessary. Neither horse deserved to lose, but inch by inch Dessie wore his younger rival down and at the post it was that wise old grey head, for which James Burridge had once apologized, that was in front.

Jauntily off to the gallops with his habitual rider, head lad Rodney Boult . . .

. . . afterwards mutual affection between the two good companions.

Thousands in the stands and millions glued to their television screens found themselves hoarse and emotionally spent.

January tiptoed out as gently as a maiden aunt. Everyone talked darkly of dire weather but none came. Instead daffodils bloomed, confused birds nested and the grass grew green.

Desert Orchid was bound for Sandown for the Racecall Gainsborough Chase, a route he had taken for the last two years, successfully in 1987, unsuccessfully in 1988.

David and Jane Elsworth, urged by their owners, went to Australia for a month's holiday. It was their first since David started training eleven years before.

At Sandown the weather was kind to their horse too: sunshine and light winds producing good going, usually unheard of in mid-February. The handicapper was not. He required the concession of 15 lb. to Kildimo and 18 lb. to speedy and valiant Pegwell Bay, trained by Tim Forster and winner of both the Mackeson and A. F. Budge Gold Cups at Cheltenham that season. Desert Orchid also had to give 7 lb. to the Cheltenham Gold Cup winner, Charter Party. It looked an impossible task and once again he started at odds against.

There was a flurry of anxiety during the preliminaries when, swaggering along from saddling paddock to parade ring, he tore off one of his aluminium racing plates. Inevitably it was the foot bedevilled with corns.

He was replated, the race started 13 minutes late, and as soon as the tapes rose Desert Orchid jumped straight into the lead with Pegwell Bay, himself accustomed to front run, fencing boldly and accurately in pursuit. After a circuit the young pretender went on and gave a virtuoso exhibition down the railway fences. When the grey ranged back alongside at the second last, a roar shot up reverberating against the roofs of the packed stands.

Desert Orchid touched down fractionally in front at the last but Pegwell Bay skipped away from it quicker and gained half a length. Up the final hill it was nip and tuck with Kildimo, who had been making mistakes, finally getting into the fray. At the post Desert Orchid was three quarters of a length ahead with Kildimo 2½ lengths away third. Pegwell Bay's proud owner, Keith Barlow was as generous as trainer Tim Forster in defeat. Tim smiled, 'You don't mind so much, losing to a horse like him.'

The victors were applauded all the long way back up the rhododendron walk and down to the unsaddling enclosure. Once there they were uniquely given three cheers. All the jockeys came out of the changing room to clap him in. Champion Peter Scudamore summed up all their feelings. 'He has got to be the best since Arkle. He is just unbelievable.'

But still his connections would give no commitment to the Gold Cup. 'I think you could say we'd be inclined to have a go' said Richard. 'It's a hard race. If you think about the last six or seven winners – they're good horses. We wouldn't want to give him a hard race on a course he doesn't like, if everything wasn't in his favour. *He* doesn't know it's the Gold Cup. We just want him to go on enjoying himself.'

Soon after David returned from Australia he announced that Desert Orchid would have a break. He would go straight to Cheltenham, missing a possible

preliminary at Wincanton in the Jim Ford. But for which race?

On Monday 6 March under the banner headline across the front page columns of *The Sporting Life* announced, 'Break since Sandown has done him world of good says owner.' Richard Burridge declared 'he'll run in the Gold Cup come hell or high water.'

The weather at first favoured the brave decision. Ten days before the meeting Cheltenham's ground was still fast. Then on the first day, torrential rain flogged by winds howling straight into the weary heads of the finishers, soaked the ground.

Freak results, gratifying for bookmakers, ominous for connections of favourites, depressed the Desert Orchid camp and his million fans. Coquettishly the weather changed to smiles on Wednesday. A gold sun glowed from blue skies. Desert Orchid's supporters' spirits rose like larks.

At 4 next morning Colin Brown was roused by rain hideously lashing his bedroom windows. At 6 a.m. Simon Sherwood high in the Cotswolds, awoke with horror to see fully 2 inches of damnable snow. At 10 a.m. when Richard Burridge arrived on the course, firemen were striving to pump away sheets of water across the hurdles course. Racing was in jeopardy. Burridge said, nerves frayed, 'I just stood there laughing for 10 minutes.' Farce and disaster, like love and anger, come close coupled under stress.

The Cotswolds crouched white under a sullen ochre slit of sky beneath sleeting clouds. The BBC reported Richard as hoping racing would be abandoned. That would obviate any decision on his part to balance his wish for his horse's safety against the public's wish to see their horse run and win.

'Even so,' announced car radios as crowds converged, 'the favourite may not run.' Many of his most doting fans prayed he would not be risked. There was a noon stewards' inspection. They announced, 'Unless there is further deterioration, racing will take place.' But would Desert Orchid run? Canny old Ken Oliver from Scotland had already pulled out High Edge Grey, leaving an unlucky 13 possibles. As so often in the story, the Burridges resolved: 'We'll wait for David.'

As the rains fell, the spirits of the Irish rose. Their slashing young hope Carvill's Hill, trained by the son of Arkle's Tom Dreaper, wanted mud. Vincent O'Brien presenting his Gold Cup to him in Ireland had thought the world of Jim Dreaper's novice.

During lunch the downpour slackened. David Elsworth was coolly arguing the case for running. 'They had the best horse in the race, by next year Desert Orchid might have gone over the top, might have got a leg, and after all he'd won on the soft . . .' Of all the credit due to this remarkable trainer, little has been paid to his resolute, calm confidence, and his convincing powers of persuasion.

Within 20 minutes of declaration time there was still doubt. Then the Burridges resolved to stick to their guns. They soothed their unease with the decision to tell Simon Sherwood 'to pull up if the horse felt in any way unhappy.' Decision made, the favourite's connections took on a resigned, almost relaxed mien. As a friend reported, 'They simply felt the die was cast.'

In the saddling boxes Richard Burridge, habitually hatless, vigorously chewed gum. Father Jimmy, quite pink-faced, studied the sky. Basil Thwaites, reclusive owner of third favourite Ten Plus, 78-year-old Fulke Walwyn's last great hope of winning a fifth Gold Cup, left his handsome bay to chat for a moment to the owners of the smaller grey.

Scuttling under macks and maddeningly vast golf umbrellas the crowd squeezed round; oohing and aahing as the neat object of all their affections walked into the main parade ring to a spurt of clapping.

The weather had conspired to dash down all his fans' hopes. A total outsider, Ikdam, paying £143.70p for £1 on the Tote had just won the Triumph Hurdle. It could not be a day for favourites. Desert Orchid showed none of the qualms of his supporters. He was bright rather than jaunty, seeming in the pewter-coloured light even whiter by contrast. His huge eyes in that tough, unaristocratic head, glowed darkly. 'It's the wise head of a Snaffles' hunter,' someone remarked. 'Like in "The Finest View in Europe".'

Only when his rugs were slipped back could you see the stain of sweat behind the saddle. Like his connections, he had learned to mask his tension. Carvill's Hill and Ten Plus, two of the finest-looking 'chasers, stood out in the paddock to expert eyes. But the crowds had only eyes for their Dessie.

Off precisely on time, the grey lined up with only two outside him, and swiftly led, popping the second fence as nimbly as a show-jumper. He easily handled the long curving left-hand sweep with Simon's sensitive hands low in his lap and the reins slack. Thus settled, Simon set a sensible pace. But Desert Orchid was jumping out of the muddy ground as if off spring-boards, sometimes gaining a length on his pursuers.

On the last climb to the summit below snow-dappled Cleeve Hill, long-striding Ten Plus was sent up to join him. They jumped together. But on the hill top, Kevin Mooney sent on Walwyn's formerly clumsy jumper. Kicking for home he swiftly opened up a three-length lead. Desert Orchid suddenly seemed to be making heavy weather of it. Over the crowd an uneasy silence fell. Then mutterings of deep forebodings broke out. 'He's beat . . . The ground . . . He's had it . . .'

From the 14th fence down to the third last, Ten Plus boldly led, pursued by the hurrying grey. Then with a crack, the bay was gone, lurching left on landing, a hindleg shattered. Desert Orchid again showed in front. The 60,000 crowd began to roar him home as he came down the hill. But as they did so, something in yellow colours, galloped smoothly forward on the far rails to challenge, then pass him. It was Yahoo, a generally unconsidered 25 to 1 shot ridden by Tom Morgan.

To the crowd's horror, Yahoo strode on like a winner. Approaching the elbow Simon's stick rose and fell. Only once before had he ever hit him, and that only on the run-in in that hectic Ascot duel. Now it seemed again to everyone but the horse himself that Desert Orchid was beaten. A dreadful wail engulfed the stands, turning to roars of frantic encouragement as the grey under fierce driving approached the last fence. The mud-loving Yahoo galloped boldly at it. But Desert Orchid with the careful calculation of a wise survivor measured and shortened his last three strides, landed just after Yahoo, and slightly dwelt on landing.

Prestbury Park went demented as Simon sat down to drive the favourite up the hill. He had jumped a little right. He had drifted further right. He could afford to

lose no inch. Up shot Sherwood's stick. Six cracks he gave in perfect rhythm. And the horse, as uplifted by the crowd's colossal bellowing as any star is by his audience, dug deeper still into his last reserves. And quickened. And got to Yahoo, drifting left. Calmly Simon put down his whip. The resolution of the grey shone out. He would not be beat. Yahoo and Tom Morgan felt it. The heaving, shrieking stands knew it. In those last strides as Yahoo weakened, that tough old grey head forged past, drew clear, and won by 1½ lengths.

As Desert Orchid walked back in triumph, he passed below the stands the dreaded green screens flung up around a stricken racehorse. Just audible through the cheers for him, snapped the sharp crack of the humane killer, darkly dispatching the handsome Ten Plus.

But few of the tens of thousands knew of this black side of steeplechasing. The place was bedlam. Still shrieking, cheering, whooping and screaming, cuffing entire strangers with babbling words of praise, the crowds erupted. From every stand and rise, they poured like lava towards the amphitheatre round the winner's enclosure. Children and the elderly were carried along like flotsam on flood tides. Men wept. Youths blinked. Women happily cried.

Simon's eyes were damp as he rode in, steering Desert Orchid between the mob who only wanted to touch and praise. Three cheers were raised. And again. And one more time. And the Irish with no connections with the horse, but with their country's love of a good one, were as wild in their rejoicing as any Briton.

Tall Richard Burridge flung his arms round his horse's hot neck, then carefully slipped on his cooler and the Tote winner's sheet. Stout Colin Brown gripped tiny Janice Coyle, Dessie's slip of a loving lass and kissed her, twirling her around. David Elsworth set his square, furrowed face formally against further emotion. Jimmy Burridge had stars in his eyes. And as Desert Orchid – at racecourse manager Edward Gillespie's urgings – was led round and round and round to the booming adulation of thousands packed in tiers, David Nicholson, trainer of last year's winner and this year's third Charter Party, respectfully removed his hat. It was his courteous salutation to a good grey horse, who was now beyond all doubt a very great one.

Only when the next and unconsidered steeplechase race was well under way did the muddied unsaddling enclosure begin to empty. Desert Orchid had finally been allowed to leave his rapturous reception. His owners and trainer and jockey had received their trophies from Queen Elizabeth the Queen Mother. In different corners all were giving interviews to radio and television. The crowd's remnants, moist-eyed, still flushed with the thrill of it, babbled on in smaller groups.

By the enclosure's rails close to where the champion had stood in triumph sat a little old lady under a large umbrella. Her cheeks were still as red as berries. Her eyes were still bright with tears. 'I have been sitting here from before the first race to see him,' she said. 'And I saw him close. I saw him here. And it was wonderful.'

Such is the love the Winter Kings inspire.

Footnote: Desert Orchid's pedigree is on page 282.

DATE	COURSE	RACE	DISTANCE	VALUE	WEIGHT	JOCKEY	PRICE	PLACE
Season 1982–83								
Jan 21	Kempton Park	Walton Novices Hurdle	2m	£1638	11.0	C. Brown	50/1	fell
Feb 24	Wincanton	Mere Maiden Hurdle (Div 1)	2m	£645	10.10	C. Brown	9/1	unpl
Mar 11	Sandown Park	Lilac Novices Hurdle (Div 2)	2m	£1265	10.6	C. Brown	7/1	2nd
Mar 25	Newbury	March Novices Hurdle (Div 2)	2m 100y	£1501	11.0	C. Brown	5/2	unpl
Season 1983–84								
Oct 29	Ascot	Haig Whisky Novices Hurdle Qualifier	2m	£1932	10.10	C. Brown	11/8	won
Nov 18	Ascot	Bingley Novices Hurdle	2m	£2316	11.6	C. Brown	1/2f	won
Dec 2	Sandown Park	December Novices Hurdle	2m 5f 75y	£4885	11.3	C. Brown	5/6f	2nd
Dec 26	Kempton Park	Foodbrokers Armour Novices Hurdle	2m	£3548	11.10	R. Linley	7/4f	won
Jan 7	Sandown Park	Tolworth Hurdle	2m	£4482	11.11	C. Brown	5/6f	won
Feb 8	Ascot	Datchet Novices Hurdle	2m	£2977	11.11	C. Brown	11/10f	won
Feb 23	Wincanton	Kingwell Pattern Hurdle	2m	£6059	11.2	C. Brown	2/1f	won
Mar 13	Cheltenham	Waterford Crystal Champion Hurdle	2m	£36680	12.0	C. Brown	7/1	unpl
Season 1984–85								
Oct 20	Kempton Park	Captain Quist Hurdle	2m	£3915	11.10	M. Perrett	2/1f	3rd
Dec 15	Ascot	HSS Hire Shops Hurdle	2m	£4819	11.8	C. Brown	5/1	3rd
Dec 26	Kempton Park	Ladbroke Christmas Hurdle	2m	£15572	11.3	C. Brown	10/1	2nd
Jan 12	Leopardstown	Irish Sweeps H'cp Hurdle	2m	IR£24393	12.0	C. Brown	11/1	unpl
Feb 2	Sandown Park	Oteley Hurdle	2m	£4417	11.5	C. Brown	2/1f	won
Mar 12	Cheltenham	Waterford Crystal Champion Hurdle	2m	£38030	12.0	C. Brown	20/1	p.u.
Apr 8	Chepstow	Blue Circle Welsh Champion Hurdle	2m	£8480	11.9	C. Brown	20/1	p.u.
Apr 13	Ascot	Trillium H'cp Hurdle	2m	£3834	12.0	C. Brown	9/2	fell
May 1	Ascot	Mono Sagaro Stakes (F)	2m	£15171	8.8	B. Rouse	33/1	unpl

DATE	COURSE	RACE	DISTANCE	VALUE	WEIGHT	JOCKEY	PRICE	PLACE
Season 1985–86								
Oct 19	Kempton Park	Captain Quist Hurdle	2m	£3830	11.4	C. Brown	4/9f	fell
Nov 1	Devon & Exeter	Woolea Lambskin Products Novices Chase	2m 1f	£1608	11.0	C. Brown	4/5f	won
Nov 15	Ascot	Hurst Park Novices Chase	2m	£7987	11.4	C. Brown	4/9f	won
Nov 30	Sandown Park	Henry VIII Novices Chase	2m 18y	£3759	11.4	C. Brown	4/11f	won
Dec 14	Ascot	Killiney Novices Chase	2m 4f	£5638	11.11	C. Brown	5/4f	won
Jan 10	Ascot	Thunder & Lightning Novices Chase	2m	£7037	12.0	C. Brown	4/11f	u.r.
Feb 1	Sandown Park	Scilly Isles Novices Chase	2m 18y	£7680	11.10	C. Brown	10/11f	2nd
Mar 11	Cheltenham	Arkle Challenge Trophy Chase	2m	£21215	11.8	C. Brown	11/2	3rd
Mar 25	Sandown Park	British Aerospace Rapier Novices Chase	2m 4f 68y	£3993	11.8	C. Brown	10/11f	2nd
Apr 12	Ascot	Contiboard Novices H'cp Chase	2m 4f	£11107	11.7	C. Brown	5/1f	unpl
Season 1986–87								
Nov 1	Sandown Park	Holsten Export Lager H'Cap Chase	2m 4f 68y	£4950	10.3	C. Brown	7/4j.f.	won
Nov 15	Ascot	H & T Walker Goddess H'cp Chase	2m 4f	£18584	11.6	C. Brown	7/4f	4th
Dec 13	Ascot	Frogmore H'cp Chase	2m	£6801	11.5	C. Brown	7/2j.f.	won
Dec 26	Kempton Park	King George VI Rank Chase	3m	£31696	11.10	S. Sherwood	16/1	won
Feb 7	Sandown Park	FU's Jeans Gainsborough H'cp Chase	3m 118y	£15666	11.10	C. Brown	11/4	won
Feb 26	Wincanton	Jim Ford Challenge Cup Chase	3m 1f	£6323	11.11	C. Brown	1/2f	won
Mar 18	Cheltenham	Queen Mother Champion Chase	2m	£25775	12.0	C. Brown	9/4	3rd
Apr 8	Ascot	Peregrine H'cp Chase	2m 4f	£7142	12.4	C. Brown	7/4f	won
Apr 25	Sandown Park	Whitbread Gold Cup H'cp Chase	3m 5f 18y	£32250	12.0	C. Brown	7/2	p.u.

Season 1987–88

Date	Course	Race	Distance	Prize	Weight	Jockey	Odds	Result
Oct 29	Wincanton	Terry Biddlecombe Challenge Trophy Chase	2m 5f	£3842	11.8	C. Brown	1/7f	won
Nov 18	Kempton Park	Rank Boxing Day Trial Chase	2m 4f	£7502	11.10	C. Brown	1/5f	won
Dec 5	Sandown Park	Tingle Creek H'cp Chase	2m 18y	£8796	12.0	C. Brown	10/11f	2nd
Dec 26	Kempton Park	King George VI Rank Chase	3m	£31400	11.10	C. Brown	evens f	2nd
Feb 6	Sandown Park	Lee Cooper Gainsborough H'cp Chase	3m 118y	£20450	12.0	C. Brown	7/2	3rd
Feb 25	Wincanton	Jim Ford Challenge Cup Chase	3m 1f	£7572	11.11	C. Brown	1/2f	2nd
Mar 16	Cheltenham	Queen Mother Champion Chase	2m	£39836	12.0	C. Brown	9/1	2nd
Apr 7	Liverpool	Chivas Regal Cup Chase	3m 1f	£16040	11.5	S. Sherwood	3/1	won
Apr 23	Sandown Park	Whitbread Gold Cup H'cp Chase	3m 5f 18y	£45000	11.11	S. Sherwood	6/1	won

Season 1988–89

Date	Course	Race	Distance	Prize	Weight	Jockey	Odds	Result
Oct 27	Wincanton	Terry Biddlecombe Challenge Trophy Chase	2m 5f	£3694	11.8	S. Sherwood	2/7f	won
Dec 3	Sandown Park	Tingle Creek H'cp Chase	2m 18y	£8812	12.0	S. Sherwood	5/2	won
Dec 26	Kempton Park	King George VI Rank Chase	3m	£37280	11.10	S. Sherwood	1/2f	won
Jan 14	Ascot	Victor Chandler H'cp Chase	2m	£21949	12.0	S. Sherwood	6/4f	won
Feb 4	Sandown Park	Racecall Gainsborough H'cp Chase	3m 118y	£19340	12.0	S. Sherwood	6/5f	won
Mar 16	Cheltenham	Tote Cheltenham Gold Cup (Chase)	3m 2f	£67,871	12.0	S. Sherwood	5/2f	won

Career Record

Has Run – Flat 1; won 0. Hurdles 21; won 7, £25,731. Chases 33; won 20, £322,900
Total – has run 55; won 27, £348,631

<table>
<tr><td rowspan="8">DESERT ORCHID
G.G. 1979</td><td rowspan="4">GREY MIRAGE</td><td rowspan="2">DOUBLE-U-JAY</td><td>MAJOR PORTION</td></tr>
<tr><td>RENOUNCE</td></tr>
<tr><td rowspan="2">FAIR INEZ</td><td>PRINCE CHEVALIER</td></tr>
<tr><td>FLORIA TOSCA</td></tr>
<tr><td rowspan="4">FLOWER CHILD</td><td rowspan="2">BROTHER</td><td>NEARULA</td></tr>
<tr><td>AUNT AGNES</td></tr>
<tr><td rowspan="2">GREY ORCHID</td><td>NO ORCHIDS</td></tr>
<tr><td>HARBOUR LIGHTS</td></tr>
</table>

Index